D1765831

RV

Spices

Volume 2

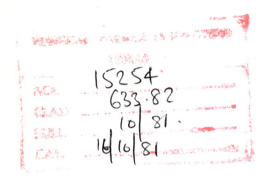
TROPICAL AGRICULTURE SERIES

The Tropical Agriculture Series, of which this volume forms part, is published under the editorship of D. Rhind, CMG, OBE, FLS, and G. Wrigley, AICTA

ALREADY PUBLISHED
Tobacco *B.C. Akehurst*
Tropical Pasture and Fodder Plants *A.V. Bogdan*
Sorghum *H. Doggett*
Tea *T. Eden*
Rice *D.H. Grist*
The Oil Palm *C.W.S. Hartley*
Cattle Production in the Tropics Volume 1
W.J.A. Payne
Spices *J.W. Purseglove, E.G. Brown, C.L. Green and S.R.J. Robbins*
Tropical Fruits *J.A. Samson*
Bananas *N.W. Simmonds*
Tropical Pulses *J.Smartt*
Agriculture in the Tropics *C.C. Webster and P.N. Wilson*
An Introduction to Animal Husbandry in the Tropics
G. Williamson and W.J.A. Payne
Cocoa *G.A.R. Wood*

Spices

Volume 2

J.W. Purseglove
E.G. Brown
C.L. Green
S.R.J. Robbins

Longman
London and New York

Longman Group Limited

Longman House, Burnt Mill, Harlow. Essex, Uk.

Published in the United States of America
by Longman Inc., New York

First published 1981

British Library Cataloguing in Publication Data

Spices, – (Tropical agriculture series).
  Vol. 2
  1. Spices
  I. Purseglove, John William   II. Series
  641. 3'38'3   TX406   80 – 40349

  ISBN 0 – 582 – 46342 – 4

Printed in Singapore by Huntsmen Offset Printing Pte Ltd

Contents

Volume 2

Chapter 8

Ginger

Ginger is derived from the rhizomes of *Zingiber officinale* Rosc., which is an herbaceous perennial, usually grown as an annual. It originated in South East Asia, but is nowhere known in a wild state. It is a plant of very ancient cultivation and the spice has long been used in Asia. It is one of the earliest oriental spices known to Europe and is still in large demand today. The dried rhizomes may be scraped or peeled before drying and are esteemed for their aroma, flavour and pungency. They may also be used in powdered form.

In Western countries ginger is widely used for culinary purposes in gingerbread, biscuits, cakes, puddings, soups and pickles. It is a frequent constituent of curry powder. It is one of the most widely used spices in Chinese cookery. It is used in the production of ginger beer, ginger ale and ginger wine. In the West it was formerly much favoured for spicing wines, possets and porter, the last being stirred with a red-hot poker.

Preserved ginger, which was produced mainly in Canton, is now chiefly exported from Hong Kong. It is also produced in Australia. It is prepared by boiling tender, freshly peeled rhizomes, after which they are bottled and sold in a sugar syrup. Crystallized ginger is produced in the same way, but the pieces are dried and dusted in sugar.

The rhizomes yield 1−3 per cent of a pale-yellow essential oil by steam distillation which lacks the pungent principle. It finds limited use as a flavouring essence and in perfumery, but in recent years has been increasingly used in men's toilet waters. An oleoresin is obtained by solvent extraction from ground ginger in which the full pungency of the spice is preserved; it is used for flavouring purposes, particularly for soft drinks and in medicine.

Ginger is used in medicine as a carminative and aromatic stimulant to the gastro-intestinal tract and externally as a rubefacient and counter-irritant. It had a reputation as an aphrodisiac. It is widely used in medicine in India and the Far East.

The largest ginger-producing country is India, which produces about 50 per cent of the world's total and is the largest exporter. Other important producers are China, Taiwan, Nigeria, Sierra Leone, Jamaica, Thailand and Australia. The countries importing the biggest amounts are the United Kingdom, United States and Saudi Arabia.

History

Ginger has been used as a spice and medicine in India and China since ancient times. It is not known in a wild state, nor is the country of origin known with certainty. It may have been India and it was certainly in China at an early date. The antiquity of its use in India is suggested by the fact that the living plant and dried rhizome are known by different names. Burkill (1966) considers that it did not originate in Malaysia. Rosengarten (1969) records that ginger was mentioned by the Chinese philosopher Confucius (551–479 B.C.) in his *Analects*.

Ginger was one of the first oriental spices known in Europe, having been obtained by the Greeks and Romans from Arab traders, who kept a secret of their origin of the spice in India. It was known to Dioscorides and Pliny in the first century A.D.; the former frequently refers to it in his *De Materia Medica* describing its warming effect on the stomach and as an aid to digestion and an antidote to poisons. The Sanskrit name *singabera* gave rise to the Greek *zingiberi* and the later Latin *zingiber*. Ginger is mentioned in the *Koran*. Reference to its alleged aphrodisiac properties is made in the *Thousand and One Nights*.

Rosengarten (1969) states that 'during the fifth century A.D. ginger plants were grown in pots and carried aboard oriental vessels on the long sea voyages between China and Southeast Asia to provide fresh food and prevent scurvy.'

The spice was known in Germany and France in the ninth century and in England in the tenth century, its medicinal uses being included in the Anglo-Saxon leech-books of the eleventh century. Ridley (1912) points out that in the thirteenth and fourteenth centuries, ginger in England 'was nearly as common in trade as pepper, costing no more at that time, when spices were expensive luxuries, than 1s. 7d. per lb, or about the price of a sheep.' Marco Polo during his travels, 1271–97, saw the plant in China, Sumatra and Malabar. The ginger plant was described by John of Montecorvino in 1292 and by the traveller Nicolas Conti.

Preserved ginger from China was imported into Europe as a sweet-meat as early as the Middle Ages. In the sixteenth century in England ginger was noted for its medicinal properties; Henry VIII appears to have valued highly its medicinal virtues and recommended it as a remedy against the plague. Later, fancy gingerbread became popular and was a favourite confection of Queen Elizabeth I and her court.

As the living rhizomes of ginger are very easy to transport, ginger was the first oriental spice to be widely introduced outside its original home. The Arabs took the plant from India to East Africa in the thirteenth century. The Portuguese took it to West Africa and other parts of the tropics in the sixteenth century. Within a short time Portugal was able to get its supply of ginger from São Tomé, thus cutting out Calicut, which had been the great mart for it until 1500. The Spaniard,

Francisco de Mendoza, introduced ginger into Mexico soon after the discovery of that country. The Spaniards also introduced the crop into Jamaica and according to Ridley (1912), quoting Renny's *History of Jamaica*, 1 100 tons of rhizomes are said to have been exported from Jamaica to Spain in 1547. Jamaica has continued exports of the crop up to the present day and is famous for the quality of its product.

Ginger has been introduced into most tropical countries, but exports are limited to a comparative few.

Botany

Systematics

Ginger, *Zingiber officinale* Rosc., is a monocotyledon, belonging to the family Zingiberaceae in the order Zingiberales. Other families in the order Zingiberales are Musaceae, to which the banana belongs; Strelitziaceae and Lowiaceae, in all of which the androecium is not petaloid; and the Marantaceae, which includes the arrowroot (*Maranta arundinacea* L.), and Cannaceae, both of which families are like the Zingiberaceae in having a petaloid androecium with a single solitary stamen.

Zingiberaceae has about 47 genera and 1 400 species of perennial tropical herbs, usually in the ground flora of lowland forests. It is divided into two subfamilies: Zingiberoideae, which are aromatic, with unbranched aerial stems, distichous leaves, open sheaths and hypogeal germination, mainly confined to the Old World tropics with the centre of distribution in Indo-Malaysia; and Costoideae, which are non-aromatic, with aerial stems often branched, spirally arranged leaves, entire tubular sheaths, the germination is epigeal, and is pantropical in distribution with the centre of distribution in Central America. The Costoideae are sometimes placed in a separate family, Costaceae; the principle genus is *Costus*.

The subfamily Zingiberoideae includes the important spice crops: ginger, *Zingiber officinale*; turmeric, *Curcuma domestica* (see Chapter 9); and cardamom, *Elettaria cardamomum* (see Chapter 10). It also includes a number of subsidiary spice plants belonging to the genera *Aframomum*, *Amomum*, *Kaempferia*, *Languas* (*Alpinia*) and *Phaeomeria* (*Nicolaia*), some of which will be briefly mentioned.

Key to the three principal Zingiberaceae spice crops
A   Herbs 0.3–1 m tall; cultivated for rhizomes
B   Internal colour of rhizome orange   *Curcuma domestica*
BB Internal colour of rhizome mainly pale yellow   *Zingiber officinale*
AA Herb 2.5 m tall; cultivated for fruits   *Elettaria cardamomum*

The genus *Zingiber* Boehm. has about 80−90 species of perennial rhizomatous herbs throughout South East Asia and extending to Queensland and Japan. Burkill (1966) mentions several species that are used in native medicine in South East Asia, of which the most important seem to be *Z. cassumunar* Roxb. and *Z. zerumbet* (L.) Sm.

Cytology

Zingiber officinale is a diploid with $x = 11$ and $2n = 22$.

Structure

Ginger is a slender perennial herb, usually grown as an annual, 30–100 cm tall, with a robust branched rhizome borne horizontally near the surface of the soil, bearing leafy shoots close together.

Roots, shoots and leaves

The fleshy sympodial rhizome is hard and thick, somewhat laterally compressed, often palmately branched, about 1.5–2.5 cm in diameter, and usually pale yellow within. It is covered with small distichous scales with an encircling insertion, and with fine fibrous roots in the top layers of the soil. The leafy shoots are annual, erect, about 50 cm (30–100 cm) tall and 5 mm in diameter. They are formed of the long leaf sheaths and are glabrous except for short hairs near the base of each leaf blade. The aerial pseudostems usually bear 8–12 distichous leaves. The lamina is thin, subsessile, linear-lanceolate, darkish-green above, paler beneath, usually 5–25 cm long and 1–3 cm wide, narrowed evenly to a slender tip, with an obtuse or rounded base. There is a broad, thin, glabrous ligule, about 5 mm long, and slightly bilobed.

Inflorescence

Holttum (1950) reports that flowers are seldom seen in Malaysia, but they are produced in some countries. The inflorescence arises direct from the rootstock and is spicate, 15–25 cm long. The scape is slender, 10–20 cm tall, with upper sheaths with or without short leafy tips. The spike is cylindrical, cone-like, 4–7 cm long and 1.5–2.5 cm in diameter. The bracts are appressed, ovate or elliptic, 2–3 cm long and 1.5–2.0 cm wide. They are green with a pale submarginal band and incurved translucent margins; the lower bracts have slender white tips. One flower is produced in the axil of each bract and is fragile and short-lived, each with bracteole as long as, and facing the bract. The calyx is thin, tubular, spathaceous, 1–1.2 cm long and is three-toothed. The corolla tube is 2–2.5 cm long with three yellowish lobes; the dorsal lobe, 1.5–2.5 cm long and 8 mm wide, is curved over the anther and narrowed to the tip. The labellum or lip, which probably corresponds to three stamens, is nearly circular, about 1.2 cm long and wide, is dull-purple with cream blotches at base, with side lobes about 6 mm long and 4 mm wide, ovate-oblong, free almost to the base, and coloured as the mid-lobe. The filament of the stamen is short and broad and the anther,

Fig. 8.1 *Zingiber officinale*: Ginger. A, plant with rhizome ($\times \frac{1}{10}$); B, leaf ($\times \frac{2}{5}$); C, inflorescence ($\times \frac{2}{5}$); D, flower ($\times 1\frac{1}{2}$); E, flower in longitudinal section ($\times 1\frac{1}{2}$).

about 9 mm long, is cream-coloured; the connective is prolonged into a slender beak-like appendage, 7 mm long, dark purple in colour and containing the upper part of the style. The stigma, protruding just below the apex of the appendage, has a circular apical aperture surrounded by stiff hairs. There are two slender free styloids. The inferior ovary is trilocular with several ovules per loculus. The fruit, which is very seldom produced, is a thin-walled, three-valved capsule, with small, black arillate seeds.

Cultivars

Ginger is always propagated vegetatively and the number of clones are limited. Each centre of production tends to produce a distinctive type, but this may be due to soil, climatic and cultural differences, as well as methods of preparation.

Several clones are recognized in India which differ in the size and the fibre and moisture content of the rhizomes and in yield. The cultivars tend to take their names from the area or region in which they are mostly cultivated. Paulose (1973) gives the names of some of the commonly grown cultivars and the areas in which they are popularly cultivated as listed in Table 8.1.

Table 8.1

Name of cultivar	Area of cultivation
Thingpui	Assam
Jorhat	
Nadia	
Thinladium	
Maran	
Burdwan	West Bengal
Wynad Local	Kerala
Wynad Manantody	
Ernad	
Thodupuzha	
Karakal	Karmataka (Mysore)
Narasapattam	Andhra Pradesh
China	Exotic cultivar from China
Rio-de-Janeiro	Exotic cultivar from Brazil

Paulose reports that 'Wynad Manantody' is the cultivar widely grown in Kerala, the state which produces the largest quantity of ginger in India, accounting for more than 50 per cent of the country's total production. 'Maran', an Assam cultivar which has been recently introduced into cultivation in Kerala, is becoming very popular because of its high yields and high percentage of dry ginger obtained. The cultivar 'Rio-de-Janeiro' from Brazil has been introduced into cultivation in Kerala and other ginger-growing areas in India. It has given much higher yields than the indigenous cultivars, but is not very suitable for conversion to dry ginger, on account of its high moisture content, and the dry ginger from it has a shrivelled appearance. It is becoming popular, however, where ginger is used in the green form or for the extraction of juice. The introduced 'China' cultivar is fairly high-yielding, but also has too high a moisture content.

Randhawa and Nandpuri (1970) record that at the Ambalavayal Research Station in Kerala 'Rio-de-Janeiro' gave the highest yield of 25 000–30 000 kg of green ginger per hectare with a fibre content of 5–19 per cent and the percentage recovery of dry ginger to green ginger of 16–18. 'China' gave the next highest yield of 18 000–20 000 kg per hectare with a fibre content of 3.43 per cent and a recovery of dry ginger to green ginger of only 13–15 per cent. Aiyadurai (1966) also records high yields of 'Rio-de-Janeiro' in trials in Kerala and a high moisture content.

Two types are known in Jamaica, as reported by Ridley (1912), Maistre (1964) and other writers. They are the white or yellow ginger, sometimes known as turmeric ginger, and blue or flint ginger, in which the interior of the rhizome has a bluish tinge, with harder, more fibrous rhizomes of poorer quality and poorer yield. It is impossible to distinguish the two types by their vegetative growth.

Canton ginger used for preserving has more succulent thicker rhizomes.

Three races are recognized in West Malaysia. These are given by Ridley (1912), Holttum (1950) and Burkill (1966) as *haliya bètal* or true ginger with pale-coloured rhizomes, *haliya bara* or *haliya padi*, and *haliya udang*. The last two have red rhizomes externally; they are very pungent and are only used in medicine.

Gollifer (1973) tested five types of ginger in the British Solomon Islands from Fiji, Australia and an indigenous type. All the samples, except the local one, were considered to be of the Indian (Cochin) type, as they had a higher citral content than Jamaican or Nigerian ginger. The local ginger was unsatisfactory as the rhizomes were small and shrivelled, and the volatile-oil content was low. Two of the other samples had a bluish tinge to the flesh and were therefore unacceptable. Of the remaining two samples, one had a satisfactory volatile-oil content and the clone is now being increased.

Ecology

Climate and soils

Ginger is mainly cultivated in the tropics from sea-level to 1 500 m, but it can be grown over more diverse conditions than most other spices.

In South East Asia, where ginger must have originated, it thrives in a hot, moist climate. In Kerala, the main ginger-producing state in India, the rainfall is fairly high, about 3 000 mm per annum on average, distributed over 8 to 10 months during the ginger-growing season. The day temperatures range from 28 to 35 °C (Paulose, 1973). In this state the spice is grown purely as a rain-fed crop, in areas from sea-level to 800 m or more.

Ginger is also grown successfully as an irrigated crop in areas of less rainfall in some of the northern states of India. In areas of higher elevation, 1 200 to 1 500 m, in Himachal Pradesh and the hill tracts of Assam and West Bengal the crop is grown under climatic conditions very different from those existing in the plains, with fairly low temperatures and rainfall.

The main ginger-producing areas of Jamaica are in the central mountains in the parishes of Clarendon and East Manchester at altitudes of 450–900 m, with a mean annual temperature of 21 °C and an average rainfall of 1 800 mm per annum (Prentice, 1959).

In the Buderim – Nambour region north of Brisbane in Queensland, Australia, where ginger is grown, Bendall and Daly (1966) give the annual rainfall of over 1 524 mm, with 80 per cent of the total being received in the summer wet season. The annual variability of the rainfall is fairly high, but irrigation is available in most areas. Midsummer mean temperatures are around 24–27 °C falling to 17–18 °C in the cooler months of the year. Temperatures in excess of 32 °C are commonly experienced for a few days each year and can cause sunburn. High relative humidities are general throughout the year. Low temperatures induce dormancy and the foliage and exposed rhizomes are destroyed by frost, which occurs infrequently· in the Queensland area, but the crop has usually been harvested by this time.

Cool winter conditions must also occur in Canton.

In the British Solomon Islands the climate is too humid to dry the rhizomes without artificial heat, which is provided by wood-burning Kukum copra driers.

Ginger thrives best on medium loams with a good supply of humus, particularly after cutting down forest or bush. It is very sensitive to waterlogging. Paulose (1973) and Yegna Narayan Aiyer (1944) report that ginger is grown in India on a wide variety of soils such as sandy loams, clayey loams, lateritic soils and black, rich clay soils. Paulose adds that virgin forest soils rich in humus have been found to be ideal.

Ginger is an exhaustive crop and, unless manures are readily available, the soil in which it is grown must be rich in plant food. When grown on slopes it is very subject to erosion unless adequate soil-conservation measures have been adopted.

In Jamaica the soils where ginger is grown are mainly clay loams on limestone or conglomerates and the slopes are often steep, which assists drainage, but often leads to erosion (Prentice, 1959).

Bendall and Daly (1966) say that ginger in Queensland grows well in heavier soils provided there is efficient drainage. Typical of a good soil would be a friable clay loam, neutral in reaction, 25 cm deep, overlying a compact but free-draining subsoil. As most of the soils in the Buderim − Nambour region are acid, lime is usually added to the soil before planting.

Cultivation

Propagation

Ginger is always propagated by portions of the rhizome known as seed pieces or setts. Carefully preserved seed rhizomes are cut into small pieces, 2.5 − 5 cm long and weighing 28 − 56 g, each having at least one good bud or growing point. The seed rate varies from region to region and with the methods of cultivation adopted. Paulose (1973) states that in Kerala and other southern states of India, 1 200 to 1 400 kg of seed rhizomes are used for planting 1 ha. In parts of northern India, especially at the higher altitudes in the Himalayan regions, a higher seed rate of 2 500 to 3 000 kg per hectare is adopted, using bigger seed bits.

Aiyadurai (1966) reports that at Thodupuzha in the Ernakulam district of India the planting of large-sized seed pieces, 3.7 to 6.2 cm long, gave significantly higher yields than the planting of small pieces, 1.2 to 2.5 cm long, and that the extra expenditure involved due to increasing the size of the seed material was quite commensurate with the profits obtained from the increased yields. Randhawa, Nandpuri and Bajwa (1972a) found that large piece of rhizome of 150 g with four to six buds gave higher yields than smaller ones of 60 g with two buds.

Bendall and Daly (1966) and Bureau of Agricultural Economics, Canberra (1971) give the normal weight of seed pieces or setts in Queensland as 28 − 56 g at the rate of 2.5 − 3.7 tonnes per hectare. The setts are prepared by breaking or cutting the rhizomes manually into pieces of the correct size, the rhizomes are inspected for the presence of disease or nematodes, and infected rhizomes are discarded. Before planting, the setts are dipped into a solution of ethoxyethyl mercuric chloride and dried, as a control measure against *Fusarium* root rot. Mechanical methods of seed cutting have been tried in Queensland, but have not proved satisfactory, owing mainly to unevenness and waste and the reduced scope for inspection for disease and nematodes.

At Wynad, Ambalavayal, in India, Aiyadurai (1966) reports that the practice of retaining a portion of the crop to be used as seed in the field itself without harvest under a thick mulch led to the recovery of a higher quality of seed material than leaving the crop in an unmulched condition. It was also found that storing seed rhizomes in pits under anaerobic conditions resulted in the maximum recovery of seed rhizomes and better development of sprouts than storage in pits under aerobic conditions. Treating the seed rhizomes with 0.1 per cent wettable Ceresan before storage resulted in the recovery of a higher proportion of healthy rhizomes. The setts and the soil at the time of planting can also be treated with wettable Ceresan or Cheshunt compound to control soft rot.

Planting and after care

Ginger is often the first crop taken on newly opened land. In Jamaica the crop is grown on smallholdings; even in Australia individually owned areas are small, varying from 0.2 to 4 ha. The land should be thoroughly cultivated and a fine tilth is required to produce good-shaped rhizomes. The crop may be grown in pure stand. In Jamaica it is often planted between rows of yams and in India it may be interplanted with pigeon peas or castor. Aiyadurai (1966) reports that in Assam, growing ginger completely exposed to the sun gave higher yields than under shade.

Bendall and Daly (1966) state that in Queensland a deep primary tillage is usually given in January or February, some six to nine months before planting in August to October. The land is fallowed until July when seedbed cultivation and drainage operations are carried out. Ginger requires a well-drained soil as waterlogging retards the growth and promotes the development of fungal diseases. The root-knot nematodes, *Meloidogyne javanica* (Treub) and *M. indica* R., are major pests in Queensland and the soil is often fumigated a month before planting with DD (dichloropane – dichloropene) mixture. Colbran (1972) found in five trials in Queensland that Nemacar gave the best control of *M. javanica* and *M. incognita* (Kolfoid & White) when applied after planting and increased yields by up to 15 per cent. Planting has now been mainly mechanized in Queensland.

A number of experiments have shown that planting early in the season is beneficial. Randhawa and Nandpuri (1970) and Randhawa Nandpuri and Bajwa (1972b) have shown in Himachal Pradesh in India, where it is the custom to plant in May and continue until the end of June, that the highest yields are obtained from ginger planted in the first and second week in May. Early planting ensures that the crop will make sufficient growth to withstand heavy rains and will grow rapidly with the receipt of heavy rains in July and August. Khan (1959) planted ginger a little before the onset of the monsoon in early May on the west coast of India and made plantings on 15 April, 1 May, 15 May and 1 June. The crop planted on the 15 April gave the highest yield, which was double that of the crop planted on 1 June. At Ambalavayal in Kerala, Aiyadurai (1966) showed that planting in the first week of April was best and gave 100 to 200 per cent more yield than the local practice of late planting in May and June.

In Jamaica planting takes place usually in May or June.

Generally close spacing in ginger gives the highest yields. Aiyadurai (1966) reports that spacings of 15 × 15 cm, 15 × 23 cm and 23 × 23 cm gave the maximum yields in India. Purseglove (1972) states that the normal spacing is 23−30 cm × 15−23 cm and the setts are planted 5−10 cm deep.

Paulose (1973) reports that, as a rain-fed crop, as grown in Kerala and adjoining areas of Mysore (now Karnataka) and Tamil Nadu, ginger is planted in raised beds. The land is dug or ploughed several times, with the onset of summer showers in April, to make a fine tilth. With the begining of the monsoon, the field is given a last ploughing and then made into raised beds, separated by channels. Usually the beds are 1 m wide, 15 cm high and of convenient length varying from 3 to 6 m. The width of the channels between the beds is about 30 cm. On hill slopes, the beds are made on the contour to reduce erosion. On level land, deep drains are provided to drain off excess water during the rainy season. The planting is done in shallow pits, 4−5 cm deep on the beds at a distance of about 20 cm in rows 25 cm apart. For an irrigated crop, the planting is done either on flat beds of convenient size for irrigation, or on ridges.

The crop is very conducive to weed growth except when mulched, and adequate weed control is essential during the early stages. Paulose (1973) says that in India two to three weedings are generally given to the crop, the first being done just before the second mulching and repeated at monthly intervals depending on the intensity of weed growth. Weeds can be controlled chemically or mechanically. Kasasian (1971) states that no firm recommendations have been made for the use of herbicides in this crop, but ginger appears to be highly tolerant of simazine applied as a pre-emergent. In India, 2,4-D pre-emergence has been reported to be promising. The Bureau of Agricultural Economics, Canberra (1971) reports that in Queensland diuron is usually applied immediately after planting at the rate of 4 lb per acre (4.5 kg/ha) and some growers make a second application at half this rate later in the crop. Some growers in Queensland use paraquat to control weeds in the growing crop, but it must be used as a spot spray, taking care to avoid contact with the ginger, which is very susceptible to it.

Most of the non-chemical control of weeds is carried out manually, as tractor-mounted cultivating implements cause damage to the crop. Manual weeding consists of either pulling the weeds, chipping with a hoe or cutting the roots with a knife. The last method is usually pre-ferred as, provided the weeds are not too large, cutting causes the least disturbance to the soil and reduces the possibility of bringing more weed seeds to the surface.

The first shoots appear above ground ten to fifteen days after planting and continue for a period of about four weeks.

In areas of low rainfall, irrigation is necessary. The Bureau of Agricultural Economics, Canberra (1971) record that most growers in Queensland use irrigation with the dual purpose of maintaining soil moisture and as a protective measure against sunburn damage in the young crop. The water requirement of ginger, irrigation and rainfall, has been estimated by the Queensland Irrigation and Water Supply Commission to be between 1 320 and 1 520 mm during the complete crop cycle. The growers use spray irrigation supplied by rotary sprinklers.

Paulose (1973) states that, for the irrigated crop in India, irrigation is given at fortnightly intervals, usually during the period from the middle of September to the middle of November.

A ratoon crop is sometimes taken, portions of the rhizome being left in the ground at harvesting. It is not usually of as good quality as the original plant crop and yields are less.

Manuring and mulching

Ginger is an exhausting crop and requires heavy manuring and mulching to obtain high yields. Paulose (1973) records that in India 25 to 30 tonnes per hectare of well-decomposed cattle manure or compost are applied at the time of planting. It may be put in each hole over the seed which is then covered with soil, or it may be broadcast over the entire area and mixed with the soil during the last ploughing. After planting, a mulch of green leaves at the rate of 10 000–12 000 kg per hectare is given, which may be repeated during the second and third months after planting, using about 5 000 kg of green leaves each time. The mulch helps to prevent drying of the soil and weed growth; it breaks the force of the monsoon rains and provides organic matter. While green leaves are more frequently used for mulching ginger in India, farmyard manure or compost is also used in some areas like Himachal Pradesh. Fertilizers to supply 60–100 kg per hectare each of P_2O_5 and K_2O may be applied as a basal dressing at the time of planting. Nitrogenous fertilizers to supply 60–100 kg per hectare of nitrogen may be applied in two split doses, the first about 40–60 days after planting and the second about 3 months after planting. A second dose of 60–100 kg per hectare of K_2O may be applied along with the first application of nitrogenous fertilizer. Paulose (*loc. cit.*) concludes that the common practice of applying fertilizers is to use 600–1 000 kg per hectare of a 8 : 8 : 16 mixture, popularly known as 'ginger mixture', in split doses, the first as a basal dressing at the time of preparing the land and the second two months after planting.

The above practices are similar to those recommended by de Geus

(1973), who, quoting Kannan and Nair (1965), says that in Kerala 25–30 tonnes per hectare of well-rotted cattle manure or compost should be applied at planting, and 36 kg N, 36 kg P_2O_5 and 72 kg K_2O per hectare at the second mulching. The mulch is applied in the form of easily decomposing green leaves at the rate of 10 000 kg per hectare. If not enough organic material is available, fertilizer dressings should be higher, e.g., 55–60 kg N, 55–60 kg P_2O_5 and 110–120 kg P_2O_5 per hectare. The fertilizer recommendation in Gujarat and Himachal Pradesh given by de Geus (1973) is 100 kg N, 40–50 kg P_2O_5 and 50–60 kg K_2O per hectare, with all the phosphorus and potassium given at planting and the nitrogen in two split applications within three months of planting.

Aiyadurai (1966) states that in Assam, mulching the crop twice or thrice with green leaves almost doubled the yield; non-mulching gave a yield of 7 700 lb of green ginger per acre (8 600 kg/ha), while mulching thrice gave 14 000 lb per acre (15 700 kg/ha).

The Bureau of Agricultural Economics, Canberra (1971) states that the soils of the Buderim – Nambour region of Queensland are predominantly acidic, and lime and dolerite are applied before planting. Filter mud from the sugar factory, which is rich in phosphate, may be applied at the rate of 110 tonnes per hectare. Some growers use poultry manure at the rate of 10 tonnes per hectare for 'clean' manure and 20 tonnes per hectare when it is mixed with sawdust. The fertilizer applied at planting recommended in Queensland is a N : P : K mixture of 12 : 14 : 10 at the rate of 750 kg per hectare and three subsequent side dressings of ammonium sulphate or mixed fertilizer at the rate of 125 kg per hectare per dressing. Mulching of the ginger crop is widely practised in Queensland using sawdust, which may be mixed with wood shavings, to a depth of 3.7–10 cm.

The method of growing ginger in the Canton District of China differs considerably from that practised in countries where dried ginger is the objective (Anon., 1962a). Low-lying ground is usually selected for the crop and the seed rhizomes are set at intervals of 15 cm in ridges about 30 cm high and 60 cm apart. Water is kept continuously between the ridges. After the shoots have reached a height of 15 cm to 30 cm the plants are heavily manured at frequent intervals with urine and night-soil mixed with water. This is said to favour the formation of succulent rhizomes characteristic of Chinese ginger.

Harvesting and yields

For the manufacture of preserved ginger the rhizomes are harvested before they are fully mature about 7 months after planting, after which they become more fibrous and more pungent and are better suited to the production of dried ginger. The early crop for the preparation of preserved ginger is pulled by hand in Queensland about March and is stored in brine until required for processing. For the production of dried ginger harvesting is done 8 to 10 months after planting when the leaves begin to turn yellow and the stems begin lodging. Aiyadurai (1966) states that in India results so far obtained have shown that the optimum time for harvesting ginger is 245–260 days after planting. If the rhizomes remain too long in the field they become more fibrous, which reduces their market value. In most countries, harvesting of the mature ginger is done by hand using a spade, hoe, or digging fork. In Queensland the late crop is now harvested by mechanical diggers. Care is required during harvesting to damage the rhizomes as little as possible. The soil, roots and tops are then removed and the rhizomes are washed.

As mentioned above, the stage of maturity of the rhizome has a significant influence on its quality characteristics and its suitability for processing into preserved ginger or dried ginger. Considerable attention has been given to investigating the optimum time of harvesting in India and Australia and this subject is discussed in detail in the 'Processing and manufacture' section, which also describes the variations in harvesting and processing practices in the major producing countries. The optimum conditions for the storage and shipping of fresh ginger intended for retail sales have been investigated by Akamine (1962) in Hawaii. He has recommended that the fresh rhizomes should be washed immediately after harvest and then air-dried in the shade for 1 or 2 days to partially heal cut surfaces. The rhizomes may then be safely stored for up to 6 months by maintaining the temperature at 55 °C and the relative humidity at 65 per cent. For shipping, condensation moisture should be allowed to evaporate after removal from the storage room and prior to packing. Fresh ginger exported from the Windward Islands is usually packed in 'bruce boxes' (wire-banded crates) to ensure maximum ventilation and is shipped under refrigeration at 13 °C.

Yields vary greatly. Prentice (1959) says that average yields in Jamaica are 1 400–1 800 lb per acre (1 570–2 000 kg/ha) of dry ginger. The Jamaica Agricultural Society (Anon., 1962b) states that 1 acre yields 1 000 to 1 500 lb of dry ginger (1 100 to 1 700 kg/ha) and in exceptional cases, 2 000 lb (2 250 kg/ha).

Maistre (1964) gives the yields on the south-western coast of India as 9 to 11 tonnes per hectare of green ginger, which gives 1.3 to 1.8 tonnes of dry ginger per hectare. In '*The Wealth of India*' (Anon., 1976) it is stated that the average yield of green rhizomes on an all-India basis varies between 7 and 10 tonnes per hectare, although yields up to a maximum of 40 tonnes per hectare have been reported from individual plots.

The same source collated yield values reported by Kannan and Nair (1965), Thomas (1966) and Paulose (1970) on 20 cultivars of Indian and foreign gingers, but these and other cultivars were cultivated under controlled, pilot conditions at the Central Horticultural Research Station, Ambalavayal, Kerala. Most of these cultivars gave yields considerably above the values mentioned above, as shown in Table 8.2. The average commercial yield per hectare of dry ginger is only about 1 tonne, with the lowest (940 kg) in Kerala and the highest (1350 kg) in Mysore (Kannan and Nair, 1965); Natarajan *et al.*, 1970; Nair and Varma, 1971; Muralidharan and Kamalam, 1973.

Table 8.2 *Yield, mean weight, fibre content and percentage* of dry ginger of cultivars cultivated at Ambalavayal, Kerala*

Type	Approx yield (tonnes/ha)	Mean wt of rhizome(g)	Crude fibre (per cent)	Percentage of dry to green ginger
Rio-de-Janeiro	36.5 (17−24)†	334.5	5.2	16.2
China	18.8 (13−18.5)†	257.9	3.4	15.0(17.1)†
Maran‡	17−23	—	—	21.1
Ernad (Chernnad)	17.8	136.1	4.4	24.4
Wynad Manatody	16.9 (17−18)†	141.7	4.5	17.8 (17.0)†
Narasapattam	16.8 (16−20)†	192.8	4.6	21.1
Burdwan	16.4	141.7	2.8−5.7	21.9
Mysore	15.9	161.6	7.6	19.4
Walluvvanad	15.0	85.0	4.9	21.9
Bajpai	14.6	119.1	6.9	18.7
Ernad Manjeri	14.2	107.7	2.4−4.3	21.2
Himachal Pradesh	13.4	189.9	15.9	23.1
Sierra Leone	12.5	124.7	5.9	23.1
Wynad Junnamangalam	12.2	153.1	3.3−5.0	20.0
South Kanara	11.4	121.9	6.2	23.1
Wynad Ambalavayal	11.2	113.4	6.4	17.7
Vengara	11.1	133.2	4.6	25.0
Uttar Pradesh	9.6	141.7	4.7	20.6
Karkal	8−10	—	1.8	23.0
Thodupuzha	7.6	68.0	6.1	18.7

* Thomas (1966)
† Paulose (1970)
‡ Kannan and Nair (1965)

Bendall and Daly (1966) state that normal yields in Queensland for the early harvest crop for preserved ginger may be about 10 000 kg of green ginger per hectare, while yields 50 per cent higher than that are commonly achieved for the late-harvest gingers. There seems to be ample scope for increasing average yields, as experimental yields of 37 000 kg per hectare of green ginger for the early harvest and 59 000 kg per hectare for the late crops have been reported.

Diseases

Soft rot is the most serious disease of ginger in India and in some other countries. It is caused by *Pythium spp.*, of which Randhawa and Nandpuri (1970) give *P. aphanidermatum* (*Edson*) Fitzp. as the principal species in India, although *P. butleri* Subr., *P. gracile* Schenk., *P. myriotylum* Drech., *P. nigriotilum* Drech., and *P. vexans* de Bary have also been recorded. The bases of the aerial shoots become soft, watery and they rot; the affected plants become pale; the tips of the leaves turn yellow, followed by complete yellowing and drying up of the leaves. The shoots fall and cease to produce rhizomes. The infection extends to the rhizomes, the inner tissues being reduced to a soft, black, putrefying mass. Losses can be high. The disease is favoured by high moisture content of the soil with insufficient drainage. It is thus important to select a well-drained site for planting, to practise a rotation to avoid repeated planting of ginger on the same land, and to select healthy rhizomes for seed purposes, which should be treated with wettable Ceresan or other fungicide. The use of Cheshunt compound helps to control the infection. Plant sanitation is important.

A rhizome rot in Queensland was found by Teakle (1965) to be caused by *Fusarium oxysporum* Schlecht. f. *zingiberi* Trujillo. It resulted in a severe rhizome rot and pseudostem collapse; a brown streaking of the vascular tissues of the rhizome and pseudostem was sometimes present. The disease spreads rapidly in the field during wet weather. It can be controlled by dipping the seed rhizomes in ethoxyethyl mercury cloride. The f. *zingiberi* is host-specific.

A bacterial wilt of ginger caused by *Pseudomonas solanacearum* E.F.Sm. was recorded from Queensland by Hayward *et al.* (1967) and has also been reported from Hawaii, Mauritius and Malaysia. The first symptoms of the disease are yellowing and wilting of the lower leaves which quickly spreads upwards. In advanced stages the base of the pseudostem becomes water-soaked, readily breaking away from the rhizome. The vascular tissues become dark brown or black. The cut pseudostem and rhizome give a white, milky exudate. Biotype 4 was found to produce the most severe symptoms.

In addition to rhizome rots caused by *Pythium* and *Fusarium*, Gupta and Verma (1966) report a leaf spot in Himachal Pradesh, India, caused by *Phyllosticta zingiberi* T.S. Ramakr. The same disease is given by Chattopadhyay (1967) in Andhra Pradesh, but is said not to be serious. Oval water-soaked spots occur on leaves, later becoming papery, and may coalesce, causing extensive discoloration and desiccation. Protection is provided by a 1 per cent Bordeaux mixture.

According to Chattopadhyay (1967) a leaf spot caused by *Colletotrichum zingiberis* (Sundar). Butler & Bisby is of common occurrence in different parts of India. The fungus attacks the leaves only, forming round to oval light-yellow spots which may coalesce to form large discoloured areas, often drying up in the centre to form a hole. The plants become stunted in growth and the development of the rhizomes is adversely affected. The disease can be controlled by removing and burning the affected parts and prophylactic spraying of 5–5–50 Bordeaux mixture.

Other diseases recorded include thread blight, *Pellicularia filamentosa* (Pat.) Rogers, by Chattopadhyay (1967) in India. Maistre (1964) mentions the following diseases from the Philippines: a root rot, *Nectriella zingiberi* Stev. & Ati.; a dry black rot, *Rosellinia zingiberi* Stev. & Ati., and leaf spot, *Coniothyrium zingiberi* Stev. & Ati.

Pests

A shoot-borer, *Dichocrocis punctiferalis* Guen. attacks the crop in India. The larvae bore into the shoots. According to Yegna Narayan Aiyer (1944) they can cause them to wilt and die. Paulose (1973) states that periodical spraying with 0.02 per cent endrin at intervals of one month, starting from the second month after planting, is found to control the pest effectively. He adds that it is the usual practice of ginger-growers in India to give one or two prophylactic sprayings as a precautionary measure against the incidence of the pest.

Fennah (1947) reports that a mealy-bug of the genus *Pseudococcus* and the scale insect *Aspidiella bartii* (Targ.) have been found on rhizomes in the Lesser Antilles; they do little damage, but may spoil the appearance of the sample; they may be killed by fumigating the rhizomes with carbon bisulphide, after which they can be removed in the process of cleaning. The same means may be used to combat a scolytid beetle, *Stephanoderes trinitatis* Hopk., the female of which burrows into the rhizomes to lay her eggs. A minute translucent mite of the genus *Rhizoglyphus* sometimes develops in large numbers in stored rhizomes in the Lesser Antilles, and while doing little damage may spoil the appearance of the produce; a light dusting with flowers of sulphur will kill the mites and prevent re-infestation.

Scale insects of the genus *Aspidiotus*, including *A. destructor* (Sign.), have been reported attacking ginger plants in several countries.

Stored ginger is attacked by the common stored-products pests. Paulose (1973) gives them in India as the common drug store beetle, *Sitodrepa panicea* (L.) and the tobacco borer beetle, *Lasioderma serricorne* (F.). Fumigation of the storehouses should be carried out regularly to control these pests.

Root-knot nematodes, *Meloidogyne javanica* (Treub) *M. indica R.* and *M. incognita* (Kolfoid & White), attack the crop in a number of countries. They can cause serious losses in Queensland unless controlled by nematocides such as DD or Nemacar.

Improvement

Apart from the introduction of a few cultivars from other countries and testing these out with the local cultivars, of which some information has been given under 'Cultivars' above, little work has been done on the improvement of the crop. Breeding is difficult as seed is seldom, if ever, produced.

Products and end-uses

There are three primary products of the ginger rhizome: fresh ('green') ginger, preserved ginger in syrup or brine, and the dried ginger spice. Preserved ginger is prepared from the immature rhizome, while the more pungent and aromatic spice is prepared from harvesting and drying the mature rhizome. Fresh ginger, consumed as a vegetable, is harvested both when immature and mature. The preserved and dried products are the major forms in which ginger is internationally traded. Fresh ginger is of lesser importance in international trade but this is the major form in which ginger is consumed in the producing areas. Dried ginger is used directly as a spice and also for the preparation of its extractives, ginger oleoresin and ginger oil.

Dried ginger has been traditionally traded internationally in the whole or split forms and is ground in the consuming centres. Export of the ground spice from the producing countries is on an extremely small scale. The major use of ground dried ginger on a world-wide basis is for domestic culinary purposes while in the industrialized Western countries it also finds extensive use in the flavouring of processed foods. Ground dried ginger is employed in a wide range of foodstuffs, especially in bakery products and desserts.

Ginger oleoresin is obtained by solvent extraction of dried ginger and is prepared both in certain industrialized Western countries and in some of the spice-producing countries, most notably in Australia. This product possesses the full organoleptic properties of the spice, i.e., aroma, flavour and pungency, and finds similar applications to the ground spice in the flavouring of processed foods. The oleoresin is also used in certain beverages and to a limited extent in pharmaceutical preparations.

Ginger oil is distilled from the dried spice mainly in the major spice-importing countries of Western Europe and North America, but oil is also prepared in some of the spice-producing countries. This product possesses the aroma and flavour of the spice but lacks the pungency. It finds its main application in the flavouring of beverages and it is also used in confectionery and perfumery.

Preserved ginger is prepared in certain of the ginger-growing countries, notably China, Hong Kong, Australia and India, but smaller quantities of fresh ginger are processed in some importing countries. It is used both for domestic culinary purposes and in the manufacture of processed foods such as jams, marmalades, cakes and confectionery.

The major types of dried ginger

The trade in dried ginger has been traditionally dominated by Jamaica, India, Nigeria and Sierra Leone, with minor supplies orginating from some other countries. During the mid-twentieth century, Australia and mainland China have emerged as important sources of the dried spice.

Dried ginger is normally marketed on a basis of geographical origin and the form of preparation. The chemical and physical characteristics of the spice differ from one producing area to another, and preferences as to the origin and the physical form are expressed by some users for certain applications.

The terms commonly used in commerce to describe the various physical forms of dried ginger are as follows:

'Hands' and 'fingers'

As dug up from the ground the stools of the plant are tangled clumps of interconnecting rhizomes, which have to be broken up into more convenient pieces for ease of subsequent processing. These pieces are laterally compressed and branched sympodially, and are known as 'races' or, owing to their palmate shape, 'hands', the branches being referred to as 'fingers'.

'Peeled', 'scraped' or 'uncoated'

Whole rhizomes from which the cork skin has been cleanly removed without damaging the underlying tissue.

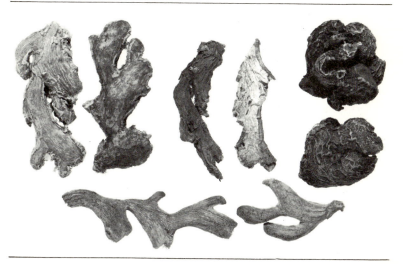

Fig. 8.2 Dried ginger (*Zingiber officinale Rosc.*). Top row, from left to right: Indian Cochin ginger (partially scraped); Nigerian split ginger (unpeeled); traditional Nepalese smoked ginger (coalesced, unpeeled rhizomes). Bottom row: Jamaican clean-peeled ginger. ($\times \frac{2}{5}$). (Crown copyright)

'Rough scraped'
Whole rhizomes from which the skin has been partially removed, usually only on the flat sides.

'Unpeeled' or 'coated'
Whole rhizomes which have been dried with the skin intact.

'Black' ginger
Whole rhizomes (live) which have been scalded for 10−15 minutes in boiling water before being scraped and dried. This kills the rhizome and makes scraping easier, but it tends to darken the colour of the resulting product.

'Bleached' or 'limed'
Clean-peeled, whole rhizomes which have been treated with lime or sulphurous acid to achieve a lighter colour.

'Splits'
Unpeeled rhizomes which have been split longitudinally to accelerate drying.

'Slices'
Unpeeled rhizomes which have been sliced to accelerate drying.

'Ratoons'
These are second-growth rhizomes from plants left in the ground for over one year. They are usually small in size, dark in colour and very fibrous.

Cleanly peeled dried ginger possesses the best appearance and it is the only type acceptable for sale in the whole form by the grocery trade in the UK market. The powdered spice is prepared in the UK from the lower grades of clean-peeled ginger while other European countries and the USA frequently use unpeeled gingers. Coated whole, split or sliced types are used for blending in the preparation of powdered 'mixed spice'. All types may be used for oil distillation and oleoresin extraction, but the coated types are the most extensively used for these purposes.

The characteristics of the major types of dried ginger entering the market are summarized below and further details on grading are provided under the appropriate country headings in the 'Processing and manufacture' section.

Jamaican dried ginger
This material is generally considered superior to other sources owing to its good appearance and to its delicate aroma and flavour. Jamaican dried ginger is marketed in the clean-peeled, whole form and is light buff in colour, 6−9 cm long and of irregular shape. The volatile oil

content is in the range of 1 to 1.3 per cent and the non-volatile ether extract is about 4.4 per cent.

The Jamaican spice is graded, according to its size and colour of the hands, into three qualities: No. 1 or 'bold', No. 2 or 'medium' and No. 3 or 'small'. Ratoon ginger is a fourth quality which is smaller in size than No. 3, more fibrous and lacks the fineness of flavour of the other three qualities. The top No. 1 grade is destined mainly for sale in the whole form in the grocery retail trade, but it is also used for distillation. The No. 2 and No. 3 grades are mainly used for grinding and distillation. Oil distilled from Jamaican dried ginger is extensively used in flavouring soft drinks.

Nigerian dried ginger

This resembles Jamaican ginger in aroma and flavour but it is of a lower quality, the aroma and flavour being coarser and possessing a pronounced camphoraceous note. It is marketed in the whole form and as splits, the latter being the major type exported in recent years. The whole form is peeled, but not as cleanly as the Jamaican spice, and is more fibrous. The splits, being coated and cut open, are, in terms of appearance, of an even lower quality and value.

Nigerian dried ginger is very pungent, possessing a non-volatile ether extract content of about 6.5 per cent. The volatile-oil content is in the range of 2–2.5 per cent. Nigerian ginger is in much demand for oil distillation and oleoresin extraction.

Sierra Leone dried ginger

This material is marketed as whole rhizomes which are either coated or only rough scraped. A large proportion of the crop is actually ratoon ginger. Sierra Leone dried ginger is smaller than the third grade of the Jamaican spice and is usually much darker than Jamaican ratoon ginger. Its aroma and flavour is rather harsh and has a slight camphoraceous note.

The coating of Sierra Leone dried ginger prevents its sale in the grocery trade but it is otherwise considered to be a good all-purpose ginger. It is very pungent with a non-volatile ether extract content of about 7 per cent and it has a good volatile-oil content of about 1.6 per cent. It is, for this reason, much in demand for distillation and for extraction of the oleoresin and for the flavouring of cattle feeds. Sierra Leone dried ginger bears more resemblance to the Indian spice than that from Jamaica.

Indian dried ginger

The two types of Indian spice entering the international market are Cochin and Calicut, named after the two major production areas on the Malabar coast of Kerala. The bulk of Indian exports are of rough-scraped, whole rhizomes. Sometimes coated dried ginger is exported. In addition, some bleached or 'limed' Calicut ginger is produced but this is mainly exported to Middle East countries as it is not favoured in European and North American markets.

Cochin dried ginger is about 12 cm long and has a light brown to yellowish-grey colour. Calicut dried ginger is orange to reddish-brown in colour and is generally considered to be inferior in quality to the Cochin spice. Both types are graded prior to export into three categories, according to the number of fingers on the rhizomes.

Cochin and Calicut gingers have volatile-oil contents in the range of 1.9–2.2 per cent. They are characterized by a lemon-like aroma and flavour, which is more pronounced with the Calicut spice. They are more starchy but are almost as pungent as Jamaican ginger. The non-volatile ether extract content is about 4.3 per cent. They are widely used for blending purposes and are the types preferred by ginger-beer manufacturers.

Australian dried ginger

This is grown in the Buderim region of Queensland and it has a pronounced lemon-like aroma and flavour. The bulk of production is of artificially dried slices of coated rhizomes. The quality of Australian dried ginger is generally considered to be intermediate between those of Jamaica and Sierra Leone. It is, however, offered free from mould, and has low microbiological counts in comparison with dried ginger from other sources.

Two harvests of the mature rhizomes are taken. Dried ginger from the 'mid-crop' possesses the greatest pungency and volatile-oil content (up to 4.4 per cent) and is used for oil distillation and oleoresin extraction. The 'late crop' is more fibrous and is sold for preparation of the ground spice.

Chinese dried ginger

This is marketed in the whole, peeled form and as coated slices. It is often bleached with sulphur dioxide which makes it unacceptable to a number of Western markets.

The major types of preserved ginger

Discounting green ginger preserved in brine, the two forms of processed, preserved ginger entering the market are:
1. Preserved ginger in sugar syrup.
2. Dry or crystallized ginger – this is ginger which has been impregnated with sugar syrup, dried and coated with crystalline sugar.

Chinese (Hong Kong) preserved ginger

In the absence of customers' specific requirements, preserved ginger in syrup and crystallized ginger have been traditionally prepared in four main grades: 'Young stem ginger' (the finest); 'Choice selected stem'; 'Fingers' or 'Third Quality'; and 'Cargo ginger'.

Australian preserved ginger

This is of a paler colour than Hong Kong preserved ginger and the grading system also differs in that it is usually produced to specific consumers' requirements. It is offered in diced, sliced, crushed or pulped form at various syruping ratios, the ginger-to-syrup ratio varying from 60:40 to 80:20. Both ginger in syrup and crystallized ginger are of a high uniform quality.

Differences also exist in the packaging practices undertaken in Hong Kong and Australia and this aspect is discussed in the 'Processing and manufacture' section, as is Indian preserved ginger, which is not exported.

Processing and manufacture

The suitability of ginger rhizomes for particular processing purposes

Two factors must be taken into consideration when selecting ginger rhizomes for processing, the stage of maturity at harvest and the intrinsic properties of the type grown.

Ginger rhizomes may be harvested from about 5 months after planting when intended for consumption in the natural fresh ('green') state as a vegetable. For processing into preserved ginger, the rhizomes must be harvested while they are still immature, tender, succulent, and mild in pungency; usually under 7 months in age. Dried ginger is prepared from mature rhizomes, which have developed a full aroma, flavour and pungency; and harvesting is usually carried out between 8 to 9 months after planting. Unduely delaying harvesting beyond this period results in a product with a high fibre content.

Gingers grown in different parts of the world can vary considerably in their intrinsic properties and their suitability for processing. This is perhaps more important with regard to preparing dried ginger than preserved ginger. The size is particularly relevant with the processing of dried ginger, and medium-sized rhizomes are generally the most suitable. Some areas grow types of ginger yielding very large rhizomes, which are marketed as fresh ginger, but are unsuitable for converting to the dried spice owing to their high moisture content. This causes difficulties in drying; frequently a heavily wrinkled product is obtained, and the volatile-oil content is often low and below standard requirements. Examples of the possible range in rhizome size and the conversion ratio to dried ginger are listed in the section on 'Harvesting and Yields' (p. 461).

It should be appreciated, however, that research has only been carried out in recent years, notably in Australia and India, to select gingers with desirable characteristics for particular processing purposes. In the West Indies and West Africa, the type of processing undertaken has been determined by the characteristics of the indigenous ginger and without the benefits of recent research.

Preserved ginger

Ginger preserved in syrup has a long history and was an article of trade in Europe as early as the thirteenth century. The standard for preserved ginger has traditionally been the Chinese or 'Canton' type, prepared from ginger grown chiefly in the Canton delta. Immature 'Canton' fresh ginger is regarded as less pungent and more succulent than other types, and has large, fleshy hands which are loose in texture, with widely separated fibres.

Originally, Chinese preserved ginger was processed only in Canton but ginger-processing factories were established in Hong Kong about the middle of the nineteenth century. Since then, most of the preserved ginger entering trade has been prepared in Hong Kong, except during recent years when an industry has been developed in Australia and exports from Canton have also increased.

Chinese (Hong Kong) preserved ginger

Supplies of immature ginger rhizomes, washed and the roots trimmed off by the growers, are imported into Hong Kong, chiefly from Canton, the traditional supplier, and Taiwan, whose exports now often exceed those coming from Canton, with smaller quantities coming from the Philippines, Thailand and a few other sources. In 1954, ginger was grown successfully on a commercial scale in Hong Kong (New Territories) and this source presumably augments the supply of raw material.

Although considerable quantities of ginger preserved in brine, or salted ginger, are imported into Hong Kong, additional supplies are obtained by salting part of the fresh ginger received. First, the rhizomes are cut up into appropriate sections, peeled, shaped and graded (see below). The ginger, in barrels or vats, is then mixed with salt in the proportion of 30 catties (about 18 kg) to 1 picul (100 catties or about 60 kg) of ginger, and it is covered with a weighted lid. After 24 hours, the liquid formed is drawn off, a fresh lot of salt (30 catties) and vinegar (30 catties) added, and the ginger is left to pickle for at least 7 days.

This is the form in which 'ginger preserved in brine' or 'salted ginger' is exported from Hong Kong, but most of the salted ginger is used domestically for preserving with sugar.

For the manufacture of preserved ginger, the salted ginger is removed from the acidified brine, washed and soaked in cold water for 2 days, several changes of water being made. It is then placed in cold water, which is heated and boiled for 10 minutes, after which the ginger is removed and pricked with a fork. The ginger is then boiled in syrup for 45 minutes (first boiling), the syrup being prepared by adding to each picul (60 kg) of ginger 80 catties (48 kg) of sugar and sufficient water to cover the ginger. It is left in the syrup to soak for 2 days or more, and then reboiled for 45 minutes (second boiling), after which it is packed in fresh syrup, the quantity of syrup used depending on the market for which the ginger is intended.

Dry (crystallized) ginger is prepared in the way described above until the second boiling is completed. After a further period of soaking, the ginger is reboiled (third boiling) to evaporate more water from the syrup, after which it is removed from the syrup, dried, mixed with crystallizing sugar and packed.

In the absence of customer's specific requirements, the following grades of preserved ginger, either in syrup or crystallized, are prepared in Hong Kong:

1. Young Stem Ginger: this is the finest quality and is obtained from the distal ends of the offshoots or 'fingers' of the rhizomes. For this grade, the fingers are cut into large oval pieces about the size of a pullet's egg.
2. Choice Selected Stem Ginger: this consists also of oval pieces of fingers, but they are smaller than those of the top grade.
3. Fingers or Third Quality: this consists of still smaller oblong pieces, too small for the second grade.
4. Cargo Ginger: this is prepared from the main stem of the rhizome and is offered in three sub-grades – bold, medium or small-medium.

In addition, a further grade, known as 'skins', 'shavings' or 'tops and tails' is prepared only in syrup, and comprises the waste material left over after the other grades have been sorted out.

Crystallized ginger is also supplied in 'cubes', the sides measuring about 21 mm, or 'slices', about 7 mm in thickness.

Ginger preserved in syrup is packed in 2 cwt (about 100 kg) casks, 1 cwt (about 50 kg) kegs and in smaller stoneware jars; of the bulk pack, the 2 cwt cask is most commonly used. For the United Kingdom trade, the cask contains 1 picul (60 kg) of ginger and 68 catties (about 40 kg) of syrup, the latter containing 30 catties (about 18 kg) of sugar. There is also what is known in the trade as the 'heavy pack'; this nominally contains $1\frac{1}{2}$ piculs (about 91 kg) of ginger and 18 catties (about 11 kg) of syrup containing 8 catties (about 5 kg) of sugar but, in practice, the 'heavy pack' may contain anything from 82 kg to 91 kg of ginger per 2 cwt cask. It is produced for the United States and Commonwealth markets. The jars, grey, green or 'fancy', are packed in cases, either of 6 jars each containing 5 lb (about 2.3 kg) of ginger, 12 jars each containing $2\frac{1}{2}$ lb (about 1.15 kg) of ginger or 24 jars each with 1 lb (454 g) of ginger.

Dry ginger (crystallized or partly crystallized) is nowadays mostly packed in casks, but it is also packed in cases of either 48 heavily soldered tins containing 1 lb (454 g) each or 96 tins containing $\frac{1}{2}$ lb (227 g) each of ginger.

Australian preserved ginger

Brief accounts of the industry in Australia have been given by Brown (1971) and Seely (1975). Although some ginger plants were imported into the country in the late nineteenth century, commercial production of ginger was not begun until 1941. This was done at Buderim, Queensland, about 104 km north of Brisbane, when an agricultural co-operative was formed to grow, process and market the ginger harvest. After initial success, production declined sharply after 1950, in the face of foreign imports; recovery was slow until 1964, when ginger production was given government protection, and thereafter output increased impressively.

From the mid-1940s, continuous research by the Buderim industry, in conjunction with the Queensland Department of Primary Industries and the Commonwealth Scientific and Industrial Research Organisation, has resulted in a steady improvement in the quality of the ginger products.

Horticultural experiments with ginger, such as aspects of plant growth, yield, seed piece size, plant density, fertilizer and agricultural chemical application, were begun by Groszman (1954) in the late 1940s, the work having been done at the Maroochy Horticultural Research Station at Nambour, near Buderim.

Technological investigations were commenced by Leverington (1969) in 1955, and continued by Brown (1969, 1972) and Brown and Lloyd (1972), the work including the correct time of harvesting, quality, grading, the techniques of ginger storing in brine and in sodium metabisulphite, softening and cooking methods, the method of preparation of the syrup, investigation of the vat system by which the ginger is processed, effects of syrup temperatures, flow rates and the sucrose – reducing sugar ratio on processing, the techniques of processing, and syrup concentration for obtaining the maximum drained weight of syruped ginger with the minimum shrinkage.

Three crops are harvested in a year (Seely, 1975). The main months for planting are September and October, and the early crop is harvested in a three-week period commencing late February or early March, when the ginger plants have not reached maturity and are, therefore, young, tender, mild and fibre-free, ideal for preserving. According to Whiley (1974) the stools are pulled up by hand, the tops are snapped off, surplus soil and roots removed and the rhizomes placed in bulk bins for transport to the factory. The mid and late crops are harvested later for conversion into dried ginger (see below).

The ginger from the early harvest, on arrival at the Buderim factory, is graded, washed and peeled, and stored in brine in large concrete vats.

Ginger grading is done manually, using a sharp knife, by means of which the operator can ensure the rejection of material that feels fibrous and, therefore, unsuitable for syruping. Manual grading is done for two purposes: payment to growers on an incentive basis, and quality grading for processing into confectionery products free from fibre. Intensive research has not so far resulted in a commercial method of grading superior to the manual operation. The preserving solution is usually brine (14 to 18 per cent of sodium chloride) (Ingleton, 1966), but it may be acidified or contain some other preservative, either as an additive or replacing the salt. Australian green ginger, stored in a solution of sodium metabisulphite, acidified with sulphuric acid, prior to processing in syrup, suffered rapid and relatively severe tip-tissue deterioration. With no information being available on storage techniques for green ginger, Brown (1972) and Brown and Lloyd (1972) have carried out exploratory investigations into the storage of ginger in acidified sodium metabisulphite solutions and in salt brine, with and without fermentation. The main conclusions were that the use of an acidified sodium metabisulphite solution led to excessive losses of sound ginger; however, the use of an equilibrium 16 per cent salt brine, with 1.0 per cent acid or 1.0 per cent acid and 0.5 per cent sulphur dioxide, resulted in an overall gain in drained weight of ginger after syruping. The inclusion of sulphur dioxide in the brine serves to prevent the development of a brown colour in the ginger on syruping (Maillard reaction), which is a normal feature in Chinese ginger. Ginger from these two salt brine treatments was preferred on the basis of its much higher recovery, crisp texture, and more desirable flavour.

After storage for 1 to 12 months, the ginger is subjected to a prolonged boiling in order to soften it, remove any sulphur dioxide and some of the pungency. It is then syruped over a period of about 12 days by a process of sugar impregnation at a temperature of 42−45 °C, by immersion in an acidified sucrose/invert sugar syrup, consisting of about 20 per cent of total soluble solids (TSS), 7 per cent of reducing sugars (RS) and pH not more than 4.0. Leverington (1969) found that the optimum content of reducing sugars was 25 to 35 per cent of the total sugars. The syrup is then concentrated, in stages, to about 72 to 75 per cent TSS by vacuum concentration or by the addition of sucrose, the ginger being contained in large stainless-steel vats arranged in series. If the ginger were to be treated with a high TSS syrup initially, it would lose water by osmosis to the syrup faster than it would absorb sugar, leading to shrinkage and loss of yield, and the ginger would become tougher and more fibrous.

The latest manufacturing techniques include vacuum concentration of the syrups, reducing the temperature of the boiling syrup process and thereby inhibiting the caramelization of the sugars and excessive losses of volatile oil. When the syruping operation is completed, the ginger is removed from the vats, drained and packed in fresh syrup.

Australian preserved ginger is paler in colour than Hong Kong ginger. Variations in the methods of processing, including the avoidance of the Maillard reaction and syruping at a low enough temperature to prevent caramelization, enables the Australian product to be marketed as 'Golden Buderim Syruped Ginger', of a high uniform quality.

Crystallized ginger is manufactured from the drained, syruped ginger, prepared as above, by immersing the ginger in an enrobing solution, cooling, coating with crystalline sucrose and drying in an air-draught dehydrator at 50 °C for 1 hour. The syrup used in the processing of the ginger should be so prepared that, at 75 per cent total soluble solids, the reducing sugar should be in the range 27 to 30 per cent. Syneresis ('weeping') occurs at over 30 per cent, and at less than 25 per cent, the sugar coating hardens on storage.

The commercial grading of Australian preserved ginger differs from the Hong Kong system in that relatively more Australian ginger is produced to customers' specifications. According to Seely (1975), the Buderim Ginger Factory is set up to produce on an all-year-round basis the range of preserved ginger in diced, sliced, crushed or pulped form, at various syruping ratios and at strictly controlled levels of internal sugar, soluble solids and acidity.

Indian preserved ginger

The production of preserved ginger or ginger *murabba* is a traditional industry in India, even though it has never achieved recognition in international trade. About 50 years ago, Kumara Das (1929) carried out a considerable amount of experimental work in developing a method for producing a palatable preserve from Cochin ginger. Compared with Canton ginger, the Indian form is hard, narrow and knotted, compact in texture and much more pungent. It soon became apparent that ordinary commercial supplies of Cochin ginger were quite unsuitable for the purpose, and it was found necessary to cultivate selected forms of the plant in fertile soils of light consistency, in order to obtain long, plump and well spread-out rhizomes. In spite of this, the ginger remained hard in texture and very pungent. Finally, it was found that heating in an autoclave for 30 minutes at about 2 atmospheres yielded a product which was satisfactorily softened throughout, and the pungency was slightly reduced.

Syruping was carried out by adding the cooked and drained ginger to a boiling syrup consisting of equal parts by weight of sugar and water, using 1.5 kg of sugar to 1 kg of raw ginger. Boiling was continued for 2 hours, water being added to replace that lost by evaporation. After cooling and standing for 3 days, the ginger was boiled as before for a second period of 2 hours; it was then transferred to containers, covered with the syrup, sterilized and sealed. This enabled the product to be kept for long periods of time, and subsequent tests showed that the penetration of the syrup throughout the rhizome took place very slowly – usually 3 to 4 months were required – while the mellowness (reduction of pungency) continued to improve up to 10 months or more.

Despite the relative success of this work, the preserved ginger industry in India remained undeveloped and, in 1966, Aiyadurai (1966) commented that 'though ginger is now being preserved in sugar syrup at certain centres on a small scale as a cottage industry, the quality of the ginger required for this purpose has not been determined by undertaking any scientific study.'

Aiyadurai's remarks were taken from his review of the progress of a scheme of ginger improvement in India. This study was initiated by the Government of Kerala in 1955–6, in collaboration with the Indian Council of Agricultural Research, at the Agricultural Research Station at Ambalavayal, Kerala. It involved the introduction of various types from all the important ginger-growing areas, and isolating the types which were most suitable to the edaphic and climatic conditions of Kerala. A few types were obtained from foreign countries – Sierra Leone, Brazil ('Rio-de-Janeiro') and China (Taiwan); after comprehensive trials at Ambalavayal, several types have emerged as the most favoured with respect to their end-uses. Gupta (1974) stated that, among the exotics, 'Ta-kuang' and 'Chu-chiang' are popular cultivars from Taiwan, known for their soft, almost fibreless ginger and are in large demand for the production of ginger preserve. Investigations on harvesting have shown that the green ginger crop is ready from the fifth month after sowing. It has been observed that the contents of crude fibre, total lipids and protein change at different stages of ripening and green ginger, for use as a fresh vegetable or for preserving, should be harvested within 195 days of planting out. After this stage, the crude fibre increases and the fat and protein contents decrease (Gupta, 1974; Paulose, 1970; Jogi *et al.* 1972). Gupta gave a very brief resumé of the process of ginger preservation in syrup, which showed clearly that the Indian industry has profited by the Australian researches. The Fruit Preservation and Canning Institute, Lucknow, has developed a process for preparing ginger to a specific tenderness, and the Central Food Technological Research Institute, Mysore, supplies a detailed method of processing.

There still may be technological problems facing the Indian industry, as indicated by Natarajan *et al.* (1970), and economic difficulties which are even harder to overcome, before Indian preserved ginger enters international trade.

Dried ginger

The process of preparing dried ginger after harvesting the fresh rhizome involves the following steps: washing and removing roots and overground parts of the plant; killing the rhizome; preparing the rhizome into the form required for drying; and finally drying.

Killing of the rhizome is achieved if it is peeled, rough-scraped or segmented into 'splits' or slices. When whole coated rhizomes are to be dried, killing may be accomplished by immersion in boiling water for about ten minutes.

Mechanization in the processing of dried ginger has been largely limited to the drying step. Mechanical grading and clean-peeling of rhizomes has generally been found to provide an inferior-quality product in comparision with manual handling. Mechanical washing and drying is practised by the Australian industry, but the other major producers of the spice continue to rely on traditional drying methods. In the Solomon Islands, where sun-drying is not possible due to high humidity and rainfall, Gollifer (1973) has reported experimenting with a wood-burning Kukum copra drier.

The following paragraphs describe the quality requirements for the spice, the factors influencing quality, and the differing processing methods practised in the major exporting countries.

Quality requirements

The appearance, the contents of volatile oil and fibre, the pungency level and a subjective assessment of the aroma and flavour are important in the quality evaluation of dried ginger. The relative importance of these quality aspects is dependent upon the end-use of the spice.

For whole dried ginger entering the grocery trade for domestic culinary consumption in the UK, the appearance of the spice is the primary quality determinant. The appearance is of less importance when the spice is intended for grinding.

When the spice is intended for industrial extraction purposes, i.e., distillation of the essential oil or preparation of the oleoresin, then the appearance is unimportant. In these cases, the aroma and flavour character, the content of volatile oil and the pungency level are the principal evaluation factors.

Factors influencing quality

A number of factors operative at both the pre-harvest and post-harvest stages can have a significant influence on the quality of the final product, and these are summarized below.
1. The dominant factor influencing the quality of dried ginger is usually the cultivar grown. This largely determines the content of volatile oil and fibre and the pungency of the freshly harvested rhizome, and also its suitability for drying.

    Quality improvements can be achieved by the planting of selected cultivars possessing the optimum combination of these quality-determinant factors together with a high crop yield.

However, it is only in Australia that these considerations have been implemented on a commercial scale. Considerable research has been undertaken on this subject in India but large-scale implementation apparently has not yet been achieved.

2. The stage of maturity of the rhizome at harvest is the second most important factor if the dried spice is to be sold on the basis of its volatile oil content and pungency for extraction purposes. At about 8 to 9 months after planting, the content of these components reaches a maximum and, thereafter, their relative abundance (on a dry weight basis) falls as the fibre content continues to increase. Again, it is only in Australia that this factor is taken into account in commercial production.

3. When harvesting the rhizomes, care must be taken to avoid injuring them as this can reduce their market value. It is also important to wash soil off the rhizomes immediately after they are lifted from the field, otherwise it is difficult to obtain a sufficiently pale colour in the dried product. The rhizomes should not be allowed to lie long in heaps as they are liable to ferment.

4. The extent of peeling the rhizome prior to drying has a considerable influence on the appearance of the dried product. The removal of the cork skin reduces the fibre content of the dried product but, if done without due care, it can reduce the volatile oil content by rupturing the oleoresin cells which are near the surface.

5. During the drying stage, ginger rhizomes lose about 60−70 per cent of their weight and achieve a moisture content of 7−12 per cent. Care must be taken to avoid mould growth during the drying operation.

   Ginger has been traditionally dried by exposure to the sun and in some areas a slow fire is employed as an alternative. Traditional drying methods can result in the loss of some volatile oil (up to 20 per cent) by evaporation and in the destruction of some of the heat-sensitive pungent constituents. Pungency reduction is usually less with split (or sliced) than with whole rhizomes, as the last takes longer to dry. The preparation of split ginger is often advantageous if the material is intended for extraction purposes and the appearance is not of great importance. Artificial drying, when carried out under carefully controlled conditions, minimizes the loss of volatile oil and pungency.

6. Dried ginger is susceptible to mould attack and it should be stored in a dry atmosphere. Even after bagging, it should be exposed periodically to the sun, while awaiting shipment. Prolonged storage of ginger can result in a deterioration of its aroma, flavour and pungency.

Jamaica

Ratoon ginger matures early and in Jamaica is harvested from March to

December, but 'plant' ginger is not ready for digging until December or January, the rhizomes being gathered as they mature from that time until March. They are twisted out of the ground with a fork or hoe, and are piled in heaps; the rhizomes are broken into manageable pieces or 'hands', the fibrous roots are broken off, and the soil and dirt removed immediately; and then the hands are usually thrown in water, to be ready for 'peeling' or 'scraping'. Ginger in Jamaica is a smallholder's crop and it is usually processed by the farmer's family, so that it is necessary to dig no more ginger than can be peeled in one day.

Peeling is done by means of a special knife, consisting merely of a narrow straight blade about 7.5 to 10 cm long, riveted to a wooden handle; the operation of peeling, if carried out in a proper manner, is a very delicate one, the object being to remove the skin without destroying the cells immediately below it, since these cells contain much of the oil upon which the aroma of the best qualities of ginger depends. Removal of the buds prevents the rhizomes growing out. According to Guenther (1959), a skilled person can peel up to 18 kg of fresh rhizomes per day; 100 kg of fresh rhizomes yield about 80 kg of peeled rhizomes.

As the rhizomes are peeled, they are thrown in water and washed in successive changes of clean water; the more carefully the washing is done the whiter will be the resulting product. As a rule, the peeled hands are allowed to remain in water overnight. Some planters add a small proportion of lime (fruit) juice to the wash-water at this stage, at the rate of about one-quarter of a litre to 25 or 30 litres of water (or about 1 per cent), in order to produce a whiter root. Over-washing should be avoided since, although an improved appearance results, the water-soluble extractive of the ginger may be low, to the detriment of the ultimate value of the spice.

The next morning, the ginger is again washed in clean water and transferred to cement barbecues or bamboo platforms or even corrugated-iron sheets, to dry in the sun. Drying should proceed for 5 to 8 days, with regular turning of the material, especially on the first day, when every hand should be turned over at least once. If, after drying, the ginger is not sufficiently white, it is bleached by a further washing in clean water and finally dried in the sun for another 3 or 4 days, when it is ready for bagging. If the weather is inclement, as it sometimes is in the Christiana Mountains, where much of the Jamaican ginger is produced, drying may be continued under cover over a slow fire. The quality of this fire-dried ginger is, however, inferior to that of the sun-dried spice.

The finished ginger is graded according to its size and colour of the hands into three qualities. Ratoon ginger is a fourth quality. No. 1 or 'bold' consists of attractively bold, firm, unwrinkled hands, uniform in size, pale cream in colour and free from blemishes and mildew, weighing on the average about 112 g. The No. 2 or 'medium' grade is less uniform in size, rather smaller, but has the same firmness, smoothness and freedom from blemishes and mildew as No. 1. The No. 3 or 'small' grade is small in size and may be slightly off colour. Ratoon ginger is smaller than No. 3 and is more fibrous. Jamaican ginger on fracture is short with projecting fibres, mealy or hard and resinous (Anon., 1962a, 1962b; Guenther, 1958, 1959; Rodriquez, 1971).

Sierra Leone

The cultivation of ginger in Sierra Leone was started shortly after the settlement there of liberated slaves at the end of the eighteenth century, and it is possible that the rhizomes were brought from Jamaica. Ginger is grown mainly in the Mano and Moyamba districts of the Southern Province, along the former railway line. This was used to facilitate transportation but this is now done by road.

The ginger is grown as a pure stand, either as a second-year crop on part of old rice farms or as separate ginger farms, formed by clearing young bush, 2 to 4 years old. The crop is thinned after the first year, completely harvested the next year, after which the bush is allowed to regenerate. In times of low ginger prices, the ginger remains in the ground, sometimes for several years, before being harvested. Much of the crop is, therefore, ratoon-type ginger.

The ginger is planted in May or June and harvested in January or February. The plants are carefully dug up with forks, topped and the roots removed, and the rhizomes washed clean. They are then scraped with spoons; this is done somewhat perfunctorily, the cork being partly removed from the flat side of the rhizomes or not at all. The rough-scraped or coated rhizomes are next set out to dry in the sun, without washing.

Sierra Leone ginger is smaller than Jamaican No. 3 and is usually much darker than Jamaican ratoon ginger. It bears more resemblance to the Indian gingers than that of Jamaica (Anon., 1951; Clarke, 1966; Guenther, 1952; Brown, 1958).

Nigeria

The ginger industry in Nigeria is comparatively young, having been started in the late 1920s as the result of pioneer work by the then Nigerian Department of Agriculture. The ginger is grown in the Province of Zaria, in northern Nigeria, in the neighbourhood of the market towns of Katchia and Zonkwa, the only two ginger markets in the entire country. The original plants came from Jamaica, and the method of preparing the ginger was modelled closely on that used in Jamaica. Nigerian ginger is grown extensively by farmers on small plots which, in most cases, do not exceed 0.4 ha in extent.

In the late 1940s, 'split' ginger was introduced to the market. This consists of the well-washed, coated rhizomes cut down the middle, parallel to the flat sides, and dried in the sun. This operation shortens considerably the time of drying, while it dispenses with the tedious process of peeling. This form of ginger, being coated and cut open, cannot compete in quality and value with Nigerian whole, peeled ginger, but split ginger rapidly became the major form exported.

India

Production of the dried ginger of commerce is confined exclusively to the State of Kerala and is of two types – one grown in central Kerala, mainly centred in the towns of Cochin and Alleppey, producing the Cochin type, and the other one grown in Malabar, giving rise to the Calicut type. Further information on the main producing centres may be obtained from the *Report of the Spices Enquiry Committee* (Anon., 1953) and from Vol. XI of *'The Wealth of India'* (Anon., 1976). According to Natarajan *et al.* (1970), there is no recognized commercial variety of dried ginger produced in any other state than Kerala. Kerala ginger is considered to be one of the best of the country, due to its lower fibre content, boldness and characteristic aroma and pungency. Gingers produced in other states have higher fibre contents, except in Assam, and are largely used for internal consumption in the form of green ginger.

Gupta (1974) stated that Kerala accounts for over 60 per cent of the total cropped area and about 90 per cent of India's ginger export trade. Nevertheless, the crop has its own importance in Himachal Pradesh, Madhya Pradesh, Orissa, Tripura and West Bengal, which largely meet the demand of the home market. The average crop yield in these states is low.

In contrast to Jamaican gingers, which are clean-peeled, Indian gingers are usually rough-peeled or scraped. The rhizomes are peeled or scraped only on the flat sides of the hands; much of the skin between the 'fingers' remains intact. Sometimes Indian gingers are exported unpeeled.

The plants mature about 7 months after planting, when harvesting for dry ginger begins. Aiyadurai (1966) stated that in India the optimum time for harvesting was 245 – 260 days after planting, when there was a minimum of crude fibre but a maximum of volatile oil, oleoresin and starch. Further delay in harvesting tends to decrease the oil content and increase the fibre content. In practice,the plants are harvested in stages, depending upon the demand, and the grower may not be able to comply fully with the recommendations. The plants are dug out with forks or spades, or even pulled by hand. The rhizomes reserved for seed purposes remain in the ground for about another 60 days.

On harvesting, the fibrous roots attached to the rhizomes are trimmed off and loose soil is removed by washing. Rhizomes which are to be rough-scraped are left to soak in water overnight and the following morning they are thoroughly cleaned by hand rubbing. The skin is scraped off with a sharpened piece of bamboo and the peeled rhizomes are again soaked in water and well cleaned. Steel knives are not used, because of the local belief that they stain the ginger. After this, they are dried in the sun for about a week, taking care to turn every rhizome frequently so as to dry the ginger uniformly. On drying, the rhizomes are again well rubbed by hand, in order to remove any outer skin. The dry ginger so produced is known as the rough or unbleached ginger of commerce, and the bulk of the dried ginger produced in central Kerala (Travancore – Cochin) consists of this quality only.

Bleached ginger is also prepared in Kerala, mainly in Malabar and South Kanara. For bleaching, green ginger is placed in large, shallow cisterns and water is added until the water level stands above the rhizomes by about 30 cm. The entire mass is trampled in order to clean the rhizomes of soil and roots and to peel off part of the skin. This process is repeated until the ginger is thoroughly clean and free of its outer skin. The peeled rhizomes are then repeatedly immersed in milk of lime and allowed to dry in the sun, until the ginger receives a uniform coating of lime (calcium hydroxide) and assumes a bright colour, the final drying taking about 10 days. Finally, the product is again well rubbed with gunny cloth to remove remnants of skin and to provide a smooth finish. This is known as bleached or 'limed' ginger.

Formerly, part of the ginger was bleached with sulphur. For this, ginger after liming but before the final drying, was treated with sulphur dioxide, produced by burning sulphur in specially constructed rooms, thus providing a white product. However, this practice has now been abandoned, due to the high cost of sulphur and to the prohibition by importing countries of sulphur dioxide residues in the spice. Bleached ginger is favoured in Middle East countries and also in India, whereas in European and American markets the unbleached spice is preferred (Anon., 1953; Sundaram, 1960).

Investigations of mechanizing the peeling operation have been reported by Natarajan *et al.* (1972) as a part of their studies of 26 cultivars of indigenous and exotic gingers grown at the Central Horticultural Research Institute, Ambalavayal, Kerala. The Hobart abrasive peeler, in which the hands of ginger are fed into a wire-mesh lined revolving drum, was found to be quick and effective in peeling ginger. Peeling for 60 seconds in this machine was conducive to the production of a high-grade ginger with satisfactory drying characteristics, and gave a product equal in volatile-oil content to the laboriously hand-peeled ginger. But hand-peeling was found to be superior to mechanical peeling in obtaining a dried product uniform in appearance, size and colour.

In Kerala, according to Natarajan *et al.* (1970), three cultivars of ginger are recognized: (*a*) 'Kuruppampadi'; (*b*) 'Thodupuzha'; and (*c*) 'Calicut' (Malabar) or 'Wynad Manantody' (Gupta, 1974). Furthermore, gingers from Malabar are divided into three quality groups: (*a*) 'Chernad'; (*b*) 'Ernad'; and (*c*) 'Wynad'. 'Kuruppampadi' ginger is well dried and has more 'fingers'; it is considered to be one of the best and is in very good demand for export. 'Thodupuzha' is considered to be inferior to the 'Kuruppampadi' type. The 'Chernad' quality is best and the rhizomes are bigger and less fibrous. 'Ernad' gingers vary in colour, are smaller in size and more fibrous. The 'Wynad' quality is considered to be inferior owing to its still greater fibre content.

For the foreign market, both Cochin and Calicut gingers are graded according to the number of 'fingers' in the rhizomes: B – three fingers; C – two fingers; D – pieces.

In addition to these two well-known types of Indian ginger, another type – Calcutta ginger – is occasionally seen on the market. This is possibly the same as Calicut ginger and it is greyish-blue in colour.

Australia

Three crops of ginger are harvested from each year's planting in Australia (see p. 472) and the mid- and late-crops are converted into dried ginger. The mid-crop is gathered in May or June, as then the volatile oil and oleoresin contents are at a maximum, and it is processed for sale to the aerated-water trade and the commercial extractors of the essential oil and oleoresin. The late crop is harvested from July to September, and is used exclusively to produce dried ginger for sale to spice grinders.

According to Whiley (1974), the methods of harvesting the ginger vary, but most growers in Queensland use adapted potato diggers to lift the rhizomes – three rows at a time. The rhizomes are then picked up by hand and, after surplus soil and roots are removed, they are bulk-handled to the factory. A small proportion of the late-harvest crop is retained for planting in the following season.

Artificial drying of the rhizomes is carried out by the Australian industry because, in the period March to June, heavy rain to light showers can occur in Queensland and sun-drying is impractical. Some peeled, whole ginger is produced but the main production is of coated, sliced ginger. At the factory, the rhizomes are first washed and are then prepared for artificial drying. Peeling of whole rhizomes is carried out by machine while rhizomes intended for the production of coated, sliced ginger are cut into slices $\frac{1}{8}$ inch (3.175 mm) thick. The optimum temperatures for artificial drying of high-quality sliced ginger has been studied by Richardson (1966), who used a cross-draught tray drier, with a single layer of slices on each tray, at temperatures of 48.5–81 °C. He found no significant difference between any of the samples in respect of their volatile-oil and oleoresin contents, but at 65 °C and above, the colour of the product was noticeably darker, and different from that of Jamaican ginger. He recommended that ginger for the spice market should be dried at under 57 °C but, for extraction purposes, 81 °C should be satisfactory.

For commercial purposes, the tray tunnel drier was found to be unsuitable, being very costly in terms of both labour and fuel. A batch rotary drier was designed and constructed by the Commonwealth Scientific and Industrial Research Organization and, though it was very satisfactory for drying whole, peeled ginger it was unsuitable for wet, sliced ginger which formed an impermeable mass though which air could not penetrate. Finally, a drier was constructed on the louvre drier principle, with air heated by direct gas firing, and the ginger fed into the drier by screw conveyors from small bins with sides at negative angles, giving a continuous flow of dried ginger at minimum fuel and labour costs. For the preparation of ground ginger, a high-speed microgrinder was added to the processing equipment. This was constructed to grind the dried, sliced ginger in vacuum conditions into up to 80 mesh (nominal aperture size: 190 μm) with less than 2 per cent retention.

The process is entirely mechanized, from the washing of the fresh ginger to the packaging of the dried product. The closely-controlled drying operation keeps the loss of volatile oil to a minimum and brings the final moisture content of the finished product, either in the whole, sliced form or the ground, powdered form, to a range of 6 to 10 per cent. Quality control is stringent, the ginger offered is free from mould, and has lower microbiological counts in comparison with ginger of other origins (Shrapnel, 1967).

The bulk density of ground, Australian dried ginger has been found to be three times that of the whole, sliced dried ginger, and studies have been made to compare packaging and storage properties. Richardson (1967) carried out controlled storage tests on whole sliced ginger and ground ginger, packed in several forms of multi-wall paper bags, the most likely package for commercial use. He determined the contents of volatile oil and oleoresin for all samples at the end of each month for five months. The results indicated that there was no significant change in oleoresin content in either the sliced or ground products. Packages of sliced ginger were found to have retained their full oleoresin and volatile oil contents, but the oil contents of all samples of ground ginger decreased by about 50 per cent.

Accordingly, Australian dried ginger is marketed in the whole, sliced form as, although the cost of packaging and storing ground ginger is lower, these benefits are offset by a deterioration in product quality.

China

In addition to the ginger grown around Canton, in the province of Kwantung, and in Taiwan, which is used for syruping, another form is grown at higher altitudes in various districts in central and southern China. The cultivation and harvesting procedures are broadly similar to those used or recommended in India and Australia, and the drying of the rhizomes is sometimes done in the sun but more generally above a smouldering fire. The dried ginger is produced mostly in the coated form (Anon., 1959) but Pomeranz (1977) reported that peeled, whole ginger and unpeeled slices are exported. It is reported that Chinese dried ginger is bleached with sulphur dioxide, which makes it unacceptable in the United Kingdom and some other markets.

Ginger oleoresin

The oleoresin from ginger is obtained conventionally by extraction of powdered, dried ginger with solvents, but notable differences in the yield and in aroma, flavour and pungency of the final product can be achieved by varying the geographical type of ginger employed, the age at which it is harvested, the choice of solvents and the method of extraction followed.

Raw materials

Jamaican, Sierra Leone, Nigerian, Indian and Australian gingers are all employed commercially, although manufacturers choose the ginger according to the use to which the oleoresin is intended, the flavour and pungency of the ginger and their prices. For example, Jamaican ginger oleoresin, with its pleasing topnotes, is preferred by many soft-drink manufacturers, but the meat industry favours the heavier-bodied, more pungent African oleoresin.

Australian mid-crop dried ginger is the only commercially available material which is selectively harvested for extractors at the stage of maturation when the volatile oil content and pungency are maximal. The age at which Jamaican, Sierra Leone, Nigerian and Indian gingers are harvested is relatively fixed by local tradition, i.e., at full maturity, at which stage the contents of volatile oil and oleoresin probably have declined from their peak values.

Solvents

The solvents used commercially are usually ethanol, acetone and trichloroethane, but others may be utilized. The oleoresins obtained by the use of these solvents may differ in varying degrees in their constituents and, therefore, in their odour and flavour. Moisture in the ginger may dilute water-miscible solvents, so that the ginger is actually extracted with a mixture of solvent and water. This may be detrimental, resulting in the extraction of non-flavour components, such as starch-like and sugar-like substances and water-soluble gums, causing difficulty in the removal of solvent and the final concentration of the oleoresin, which is frequently not homogeneous, and separation of sludge often occurs on storage. Poor solubility in fixed and essential oils sometimes results. Conversely, for the oleoresin required by manufacturers of soft drinks, a water-miscible solvent, usually ethanol, is desirable and actually necessary in order to obtain certain water-soluble flavouring extractives. The ethanol may be diluted by as much as 50 per cent of water, but the water content of the solvent should be controlled by the operator.

Preparation

Well-dried ginger is ground or pulverized to a coarse powder about 30 to 40 mesh (nominal aperture size: 500 to 400 μm), and is extracted with the selected solvent in plant as described in Chapter 2 for pepper. Goldman (1949) and Lewis *et al.* (1972) both describe the batch countercurrent method; in this, the ginger is extracted by cold percolation through beds of the ground material packed in stainless-steel columns. As compared with other spices, the percolation of solvents through beds of ground ginger is particularly slow. Fine grinding of ginger, although giving a slightly higher yield of oleoresin, leads to caking of the ground material in the extraction column, resulting in an abnormally slow rate of percolation. For quick and efficient extraction of ginger, optimum conditions have to be found for the size of particles, density of packing, bed height and area.

Fractions of extract, containing not less than 10 per cent of soluble solids, are drawn off and distilled under reduced pressure, to control foaming and, particularly, to reduce the damage caused by heat on the gingerols, the main pungent constituents of the oleoresin. Connell (1969) showed that excessive heating during the removal of solvent can cause the gingerols to be degraded to the less pungent shogaols, or to the weakly pungent zingerone and aliphatic aldehydes, with loss of pungency and the development of off-flavours (see section on 'Chemistry'). Oleoresin of good quality should have a high content of volatile oil, and losses of this component can be minimized by controlling the rate of distillation and by using tall fractionating columns.

Ginger oleoresin is a dark-brown viscous liquid, with a volatile oil content which can vary from 15 to 35 per cent. Ethanol gives a more viscous product than that extracted with acetone. The pungency of ginger oleoresin cannot be estimated at present, due to the absence of any reliable method for the determination of the pungent principles. These are readily soluble in ether, but a high proportion of the non-pungent substance are insoluble in this solvent; the proportion of ether-soluble substances, less the volatile oil, is a guide to the pungency (Connell, 1970; Lewis *et al.*, 1972).

Commercial ginger oleoresins usually have a volatile-oil content in the range of 25–30 per cent, and replacement strengths of 1 kg of oleoresin for 28 kg of good-quality ground spice have been claimed by some manufacturers. The commercial oleoresins are labelled according to the origin of the ginger used or as a blend, and they are offered in the liquid form or dispersed on sugar or salt.

Yields

Clevenger (1928) investigated gingers from different origins in the laboratory and found that the yield of ether-soluble extract (oleoresin) was 3.5–7.1 per cent, containing 34–42.2 per cent of volatile oil. Similarly, Elsdon and Mayne (1937), working on gingers from

Jamaica, Sierra Leone and India, found 3.8−7.8 per cent of oleoresin, containing 21.0−34.2 per cent of volatile oil.

Industrially, ethanol, acetone, trichloroethane and dichloroethane are the most widely used solvents. Yield values are generally confidential; those which are published are usually the results of bench or pilot-scale work, often in connection with industrial problems.

Elsdon and Mayne (1937), using ethanol, obtained 3.1−6.9 per cent of oleoresin, according to origin. Naves (1974) stated that hot ethanol extracts about double this quantity, by increasing the resin content.

Winterton and Richardson (1965) recorded that, with acetone, yields from Australian-grown ginger during a growing season have been found to vary from 5 to 11 per cent on a dried weight basis. On the same ginger, oleoresin yields of up to 20 per cent have been obtained using ethanol as the solvent. This is in contrast to the behaviour of Jamaican, African and Indian gingers tested by the authors, in which the yield of acetone-extracted oleoresin was only slightly lower than the yield extracted by ethanol. Naves (1974) quoted Winterton and Richardson as stating that the oleoresin content of the Jamaican, African and Indian gingers, with acetone, was 3.9−10.3 per cent, with less from Australian ginger. A general decline in oleoresin content, as measured on a dried-weight basis, was found throughout the Australian growing season. Connell and Jordan (1971) have reported the examination of oleoresins from the major ginger-growing areas (Jamaica, Nigeria, Sierra Leone, China, India (Cochin) and Australia), prepared by using a variety of conditions, and they found volatile oil contents varying between 7 and 28 per cent.

Lewis *et al.* (1972) recorded that a Darjeeling ginger has been found which also gives a high yield of ethanol extractive.

According to Naves (1974), the yield extracted by trichloroethane is, on average, 4−5 per cent: 2.6−4 per cent for Indian gingers and up to 7.2 per cent for African gingers. Lewis *et al.* (1972), in India, recommended the use of dichloroethane, and gave the results obtained in a typical extraction as follows:

Weight of material extracted, kg	209
Weight of solvent used, kg	336
Weight of oleoresin obtained, kg	12.4
Yield, per cent	5.9
Oil content in finished product, per cent v/w	34
Residual solvent, ppm	30

Ginger oil

Ginger oil is prepared commercially by steam distillation of dried ginger. Formerly, the oil was produced exclusively in the USA and Europe, but latterly commercial production has been undertaken by some of the spice-producing countries, notably in China, Australia,

India, Jamaica and Indonesia from their own forms of dried ginger. In the USA and the UK, dried ginger from Jamaica, India (Cochin), Sierra Leone and Nigeria are the most frequently used raw materials.

The most suitable material for oil distillation is coated African ginger, i.e., Nigerian splits, or Cochin ginger; but Jamaican ginger is frequently used, in spite of the fact that it is more expensive and gives a lower yield of oil than African ginger.

The dried ginger rhizomes are comminuted into a coarse powder, immediately before being charged into the still. The charge must be packed evenly, to avoid 'rat-holes', or channels through which the steam would pass without volatilizing the oil, resulting in a low yield. Guenther (1952) recommended that the comminuted ginger should be distributed evenly on several trays in the still. Distillation is carried out with direct (live) steam and, depending on the quantity of the charge in the still and the steam pressure applied, distillation of one charge may require up to 20 hours. The distillation waters may be cohobated. Finely ground ginger and steam which is too 'wet' should not be used as this can result in problems arising from 'caking' or swelling of the ginger starch. For similar reasons, hydro-distillation of ginger is not carried out by commercial producers.

The yield of oil varies from 1.5 to 3.0 per cent, averaging 2.0 per cent; yields above 3.0 per cent are exceptional. The oil obtained is a light-green or yellow, mobile liquid which becomes viscous on ageing. It has the characteristic aromatic, warm and spicy odour, but not the pungent taste of the spice.

Chinese ginger oil, of which a fair quantity is imported into the UK, is distilled from domestic dried, coated ginger (Anon., 1959; Pomeranz, 1977). In the first of these references, an account of the method used for the distillation of ginger oil (which is described as typical) in the province of Hunan, has been published. The *modus operandi* corresponds exactly with the procedure adopted by USA and European distillers. The yield generally ranges from 1.5 to 2.5 per cent, but this may be as high as 4 to 5 per cent from rhizomes produced in Hunan Province.

Chemistry

The chemistry of *Zingiber officinale* has been the subject of sporadic study since the early nineteenth century. In common with some other pungent spices, considerable advances were made in the early part of the twentieth century, but it has only been in recent years that a fairly clear understanding of the relationship of its chemical composition to its organoleptic properties has emerged.

Ginger, like pepper (*Piper nigrum*) and the fruits of *Capsicum* species, owes its characteristic organoleptic properties to two classes of constituents: the odour and much of the flavour of ginger is determined by the constituents of its steam-volatile oil, while the pungency is produced by non-steam-volatile components, known as the gingerols, which possess a 1-(4'-hydroxy-3'-methoxyphenyl)-5-hydroxyalkan-3-one structure.

General composition of the ginger rhizome and its oleoresin

The ginger rhizome contains a little steam-volatile oil, fixed (fatty) oil, pungent compounds, resin, proteins, cellulose, pentosans, starch and mineral elements. Of these, starch is the most abundant and comprises 40–60 per cent of the rhizome on a dry-weight basis. The relative abundance of certain other constituents can vary considerably between samples of ginger in both the fresh ('green') and the dried forms. The composition of the fresh rhizome is determined by the cultivar grown, the environmental conditions of growth and the stage of maturity at harvest. Further changes in the relative abundance of some constituents can also occur post-harvest during the preparation and subsequent storage of dried ginger.

The possible extent of composition differences arising from intrinsic factors in freshly harvested, whole ginger has been demonstrated by Natarajan *et al.* (1972) and Mathew *et al.* (1973) in a study of 26 cultivars grown in India. The ranges in the composition of commercial dried gingers are also fairly well documented in the literature (e.g. Clevenger, 1928; Winton and Winton, 1939; Gerhardt, 1969; Lewis *et al.*, 1972; Marsh *et al.*, 1977), and a brief summary of the characteristics of the major types of commercial dried gingers is provided in the 'Products and end-uses' section. The current standards for the spices are given in the 'Standard specifications' section.

The fibre and volatile-oil contents and the pungency level are the most important criteria in assessing the suitability of ginger rhizomes for particular processing purposes. The relative abundance of these three components in the fresh rhizome is governed by its state of maturity at harvest (Natarajan *et al.*, 1972; Seely, 1975). Young, tender rhizomes lifted at the beginning of the harvesting season, about 5 to 7 months after planting, are preferred for the manufacture of preserved ginger since the fibre content is negligible and the pungency is mild. As the season progresses, the relative abundance (on a dry-weight basis) of the volatile oil, the pungent constituents and the fibre increases. At about 9 months after planting, the volatile-oil and pungent-principle contents reach a maximum and thereafter their relative abundance falls as the fibre content continues to increase. The volatile-oil content of Australian ginger has been reported to increase from about 1.8 to 4.4 per cent (on a dry-weight basis) through the harvesting season, but remains fairly constant at about 0.4 per cent on a green-weight basis during this period (Winterton and Richardson, 1965). The mid-season crop is, therefore, preferred in Australia for the distillation of the essential oil or the extraction of oleoresin, while the late-season crop is used for the preparation of the dried spice. In India, the volatile-oil content of ginger has been reported to be at maximum between 215 and 260 days after planting (Gupta, 1974).

The drying of the ginger usually leads to the loss by evaporation of some of the volatile oil, and Mathew *et al.* (1975) have shown that this loss may be as high as 20 per cent during sun-drying. The extent of cleaning the rhizome prior to drying has a considerable influence on the volatile oil and fibre content of the end-product. Removal of the cork skin not only reduces the fibre content but also enhances the volatile-oil loss through rupture of the oil cells which are near the skin. For this reason, the cleanly peeled Jamaican product tends to have somewhat lower volatile-oil and fibre contents than other commercial dried gingers which are only partially peeled or unpeeled. Elsdon and Mayne (1937) have suggested that the extent of peeling might also influence the pungency level somewhat as their studies indicated that the pungent constituents, assessed as the non-volatile ether extract, are mainly located in the outer layers of the ginger rhizome.

The crude fibre content of unpeeled ginger may be as high as 10 per cent (on a dry-weight basis), but in commercial dried gingers it is usually in the range of 1.5–6 per cent. The volatile-oil content of commercial dried gingers has been reported to be 0.5–4.4 per cent but for the major types the range is usually 1–3 per cent. The abundance of the pungent constituents, the gingerols, in dried ginger is less certain owing to inadequacies in current analytical methods, but it is probably in the range of 1–2 per cent for freshly prepared commercial dried gingers.

Ginger oleoresins may be prepared from dried ginger by extraction with a number of organic solvents as has been described in the 'Processing and manufacture' section. The oleoresin contains the organoleptically important volatile oil and pungent principles together with fatty oil, palmitic and some other free fatty acids, resin and carbohydrates. The yield and the relative abundance of the components of the oleoresin are dependent, however, upon the raw material and the solvent used and on the extraction conditions. Commercial dried gingers have been reported to provide oleoresins in yields of 3.5–10 per cent and to contain 15–30 per cent of volatile oil (Winterton and Richardson, 1965; Connell, 1970; Lewis *et al.*, 1972; Naves, 1974). The pungent-principle content of the oleoresins is again less certain owing to shortcomings in analytical methods but it is believed to be in the range of 17–30 per cent for fresh extracts (Ananthakrishna and Govindarajan, 1974; Nambudri *et al.*, 1975). Extraction of some cultivars of ginger with alcohol gives an abnormally high yield (up to 20 per cent) of an oleoresin with a relatively low volatile-oil and pungent-principle content, owing to their dilution by other extractives. The flavour of alcohol extracts is considered by some workers to be inferior to that of acetone extracts.

The care taken during the preparation and subsequent storage of the dried spice and its oleoresin has an important influence on the organoleptic properties, and hence the quality, of these products. The major storage change with the dried spice, especially when in the ground state, is the evaporation of some volatile oil which results in a flat odour and flavour; while the oleoresin is particularly prone to loss of pungency during storage by degradation of the gingerols. Heat treatment of the spice and its oleoresin can lead to degradation of both the volatile oil and the pungent principles, and this factor is of importance when either material is used in the flavouring of processed foods. Thiessen (1970) has shown that changes in the organoleptic properties become noticeable in the spice and the oleoresin at 90 °C and the deterioration becomes more pronounced at higher temperatures.

Before proceeding to discuss the volatile oil and the pungent principles in greater detail, mention is appropriate at this juncture of two other aspects which have not been studied in such great depth. First, the fatty oil of ginger which is present at an abundance of 2 – 12 per cent in dried gingers. Salzer (1975b) has reported that the fatty oil in his sample contained saturated and unsaturated fatty acids in a ratio of 46 : 53; and the major component acids were found to be palmitic, oleic and linoleic acids, each having a relative abundance of about 23 per cent. By contrast, a qualitative analysis of fourteen Indian cultivars undertaken by Singh *et al.* (1975) revealed a predominance of saturated acids in the fatty oil, and linolenic acid as the major individual fatty acid. The second subject concerns the flavour of preserved ginger: Leverington (1969) has attributed the characteristic fermented flavour of Chinese ginger to yeast formation which proceeds either during the syruping stages or during the subsequent storage period.

The pungent principles

Composition

Thresh (1879) was the first to report the isolation of the pungent principles of ginger in a crude form. The non-volatile pungent oil obtained by solvent extraction of the spice was named gingerol. Little progress was made in characterizing gingerol in subsequent investigations carried out by Thresh (1881, 1884) or later by Garnett and Grier (1907, 1909). However, the latter suspected that gingerol was not homogeneous.

In 1917, important contributions to the subject were made by three groups of investigators. Nomura (1917) obtained a crystalline, optically inactive, pungent keto-phenol from the alkali-soluble fraction of an ethereal extract of ginger. This compound was named zingerone and its structure was proposed as 4-hydroxy-3-methoxy-phenylethyl methyl

Table 8.3: *The gingerols and some other compounds found in the pungent principle fraction of ginger*

(I) The gingerols:

$n = 1$; [3]-gingerol
$n = 2$; [4]-gingerol
$n = 3$; [5]-gingerol
$n = 4$; [6]-gingerol
$n = 6$; [8]-gingerol
$n = 8$; [10]-gingerol
$n = 10$; [12]-gingerol

retroaldol reaction

$+ Me - (CH_2)_n - CHO$

(II) Zingerone

dehydration

(III) The shogaols

(IV) where $R = Me$, $R' = H$;
[6]-gingeryl methyl ether

(V) where $R = R' = MeCO$;
[6]-gingeryl diacetate

(VI) where $R = R' = H$;
[6]-dihydrogingerol

(VII) where $R = Me$, $R' = H$;
[6]-methyl dihydrogingerol

(VIII): [6]-paradol

(IX) hexahydrocurcumin

ketone (See Table 8.3). Lapworth *et al.* (1917) simultaneously reported the isolation of gingerol as a viscous, dextro-rotatary phenolic oil by the alcohol extraction of African ginger (probably from Sierra Leone). This oil did not appear to be homogeneous, and upon treatment with hot alkali yielded zingerone and a mixture of straight-chain aldehydes of which *n*-heptanal was suspected to be the most abundant. Nomura's proposal for the structure of zingerone (Table 8.3) was confirmed by Lapworth and Wykes (1917). On the basis of a number other experiments, Lapworth concluded that gingerol was a mixture of at least two compounds in which zingerone was condensed with homologous straight-chain aldehydes. Two alternaive general structures were proposed for gingerol, structure I in Table 8.3 being preferred, and where $n = 5$ for the major constituent while $n = 4$ or 3 for the minor constituents. In the same year, Nelson (1917) also isolated gingerol from both ginger and grains of paradise (seeds of *Aframomum melegueta*) and carried out studies on its derivative, gingeryl methyl ether.

In a series of later investigations, Nomura (1918) and Nomura and Tsurami (1927) reported the isolation of another pungent compound from the alkali-soluble portion of an ethereal extract of ginger. This compound was named shogaol, from the Japanese name for ginger, and its structure was proposed as 1-(4'-hydroxy-3'-methoxyphenyl)-dec-4-en-3-one (III in Table 8.3, where $n = 4$). This structure corresponded to the dehydration product of Lapworth's proposal for the general structure for gingerol but differed from Lapworth's major constituent in possessing a shorter side-chain (i.e., $n = 4$, rather than 5). Subsequent investigations by Nomura and Iwamoto (1928) showed that the gingerol derivative, gingeryl methyl ether, yielded methyl zingerone and *n*-hexanal upon decomposition and no evidence for the formation of *n*-heptanal was obtained. This and other evidence led Normura to suggest the structure IV in Table 8.3 as the structure for gingeryl methyl ether.

No further investigations on the composition of the pungent principles of ginger were reported in the following 30 years although considerable effort was devoted to the synthesis of zingerone analogues. Summarizing, the pungency of ginger was attributed in the first half of the twentieth century to three pungent substances, gingerol (I in Table 8.3, where $n = 4$ or 5), shogaol (III, $n = 4$) and zingerone (II) whose relative abundance in ginger was uncertain. Interested readers are recommended to refer to the review by Connell (1970) for a more detailed discussion of these early chemical studies.

The composition and the relative status of the pungent principles of ginger was clarified only recently by the publication of two papers by Connell and Sutherland (1969) and Connell (1969). These workers isolated gingerol in a crystalline state from Australian (Buderim) ginger by a solvent extraction procedure and confirmed that it was composed of a series of homologous compounds consistent with Lapworth's general structure (I), that is, 1-(4'-hydroxy-3'-methoxyphenyl) -5-hydroxyalkan-3-ones. The major constituents were found to be condensation products of zingerone with saturated straight-chain aldehydes of chain length 6, 8 and 10, i.e., $n = 4, 6, 8$ in structure (I). These compounds were named [6]-,[8]- and [10]-gingerols according to the length of the aldehyde unit, and the relative abundance of these compounds in the sample was estimated as 53:17:30 respectively. The presence of [7]- gingerol (i.e. $n = 5$), claimed by Lapworth *et al.* as the major gingerol constituent, could not be detected. However, a little [6]-paradol (VIII in Table 8.3) was found in the sample, and the presence of traces of the [4]- and [12]- gingeryl methyl ethers (IV in Table 8.3) was suspected.

Little, if any, zingerone or the shogaols were found by Connell and Sutherland in carefully prepared, fresh ginger extracts, but these compounds appeared on storage, which suggested they were artefacts rather than naturally occurring compounds. This view has been supported by the investigations of Ananthakrishna and Govindarajan (1974), who found that carefully prepared, fresh oleoresins of Indian ginger contained about 22 per cent gingerol and 3 per cent shogaol.

Connell and Sutherland confirmed Nomura's proposal for the structure of [6]- shogaol as (III) in Table 8.3 (where $n = 4$) and demonstrated that the configuration of the double bond was *trans*. The gingerols and shogaols were also shown to possess an S-configuration at the asymmetric centre according to the Cahn-Ingold-Prelog convention.

The pungent principles of commercial Japanese ginger have been studied by two groups of workers who found [6]- gingerol to be the major constituent together with smaller quantities of [8]- and [10]-gingerols. Masada *et al.* (1973, 1974) also reported the presence of the [3]-, [4]- and [5]- (and possibly [12]-) gingerols in their samples together with some related compounds: dihydrogingerols, gingerol diacetates and their methyl ether derivatives. Yamagishi *et al.* (1972) also reported finding [6]- dihydrogingerol and hexahydrocurcumin, structures (VI) and (IX) respectively in Table 8.3, in their sample. The last-named compound is related in structure to the pigment, curcumin, of turmeric.

Reports of similar intensive scrutinies of the composition of the pungent principles of other important commercial types of ginger had not been published at the time of writing this review. However, the evidence obtained from the investigations of Australian and Japanese gingers suggests that [6]- gingerol is the most abundant principle of ginger and it is accompanied by several other gingerol homologues and analogues, the [8]- and [10]- gingerols being prominent. Knowledge of the relative pungency values of the individual compounds is at present rather limited, as is the case with the pungent principles of pepper

(*Piper nigrum*), but they are expected to differ somewhat according to the length of the side-chain. Kulka (1967) and Connell (1969) have indicated that gingerols have the greatest relative pungency values, followed by shogaols and then zingerone; and Arctander (1960) has stated that synthetic zingerone was not found to possess pungency at a concentration of 0.5 to 1 mg per cent. Yamagishi *et al.* (1972) found that [6]-dihydrogingerol tasted bitter rather than pungent while hexahydrocurcumin showed choleretic action in dogs.

Stability of the pungent principles

Connell (1969) has demonstrated that the gingerols are susceptible to chemical transformation to less pungent degradation products; and that these reactions can occur by poor handling during the preparation, storage and utilization of dried ginger and its oleoresin with consequent deterioration of quality.

The gingerols can undergo a retroaldol reaction at the β-hydroxy ketone group to yield zingerone and aliphatic aldehydes, such as hexanal (see Table 8.3). This reaction can occur by base catalysis or by the action of heat, and with oleoresins it proceeds rapidly at temperatures above 200 °C. The process is detrimental not only because of reducing the pungency level but also from the production of off-flavours by the liberated aldehydes.

The second, and more important, transformation to which the gingerols are prone is a dehydration at the β-hydroxy ketone group to form the corresponding, less pungent shogaols (see Table 8.3). This reaction is markedly influenced by pH and temperature. Under alkaline conditions, the dehydration occurs readily at room temperature, but higher temperatures are required under acid conditions. With oleoresins, the reaction proceeds at five times the rate under acid conditions than at pH 7.

The pH of ginger oleoresins is normally in the range of 3 to 5 and thus dehydration of the gingerols tends to proceed by the acid-catalysed mechanism during extraction and subsequent storage.

Shogaol formation can even occur during the drying of the ginger rhizome and it is more extensive with whole, dried ginger than with sliced, dried ginger. This is attributed to the longer drying time required for whole ginger.

The shogaols have also been found to be susceptible to acid pH and heat treatment and they probably transform to non-pungent polymers. Thus, the pungency of oleoresins decreases steadily on storage as the gingerols are first transformed to the shogaols, which are in turn degraded. Connell has estimated that over 50 per cent of pungency may be lost by poor handling during the preparation and storage of oleoresins, and this view has been confirmed by the investigations of Anathakrishna and Govindarajan (1974).

Pungency losses can also occur during the use of the spice or its oleoresin in food flavouring either by excessive heat treatment or, for example, by using potassium carbonate in ginger-flavoured baked goods.

Pungency assessment

The pungency of ginger has been traditionally estimated by a gravimetric method devised by Garnett and Grier (Parry, 1948). This is based on the differential extraction of the pungent principles with solvent, i.e., determining the non-volatile ether extract content of the spice. Since some non-pungent substances can be co-extracted, the method is inefficient and tends to overestimate the pungent-principle content. In addition, this method does not take into account any possible variations between samples in the relative abundance of the gingerols, shogaols and zingerone, which differ in their pungency values. This problem has parallels with those encountered in the traditional methods of estimating the pungency of pepper (*Piper nigrum*) and *Capsicum* products.

Recently, several workers have devoted attention to devising new techniques for assessing the pungency of ginger. Connell and McLachlan (1972) have reported a gas-chromatography procedure which is very effective in separating the individual pungent components and their artefacts. This method has a limitation, however, in that the gingerols undergo thermally catalysed degradation under the operation conditions and can only be estimated indirectly from derivatives. Thin-layer chromatography techniques have also been devised (Ananthakrishna and Govindrarajan, 1974; Nambudri et al., 1975) which can separate the gingerols and the shogaols from non-pungent constituents of extracts. This approach has demonstrated that the traditional gravimetric technique can overestimate the pungent-principle content by as much as 50 per cent. The thin-layer chromatography method is not without shortcomings, however, as it does not separate the individual gingerols from one another to permit an assessment of their relative abundance.

The development of a reliable, accurate method for the pungency assessment of ginger is yet awaited, and it is possible that this may be found to lie in the use of high-pressure liquid chromatography. The basic requirements for an accurate pungency assessment method are: first, the ability to separate the individual gingerols and shogaols from one another and to assess their relative abundance; and, second, knowledge of the relative pungency values of these compounds. Until such a method is devised, it will not be possible to make comparisons of any certainty between gingers (and oleoresins) of differing types and origins or to monitor accurately the variation in pungency of the rhizome in relation to its state of maturity and the processing and storage conditions.

The volatile oil

The aroma and flavour of ginger are determined by the composition of its steam-volatile oil which is comprised mainly of sesquiterpene hydrocarbons, monoterpene hydrocarbons and oxygenated monoterpenes. The monoterpene constituents are believed to be the most important contributors to the aroma of ginger, and they tend to be relatively more abundant in the natural oil of the fresh ('green') rhizome than in the essential oil distilled from dried ginger. Oxygenated sesquiterpenes are relatively minor constituents of the volatile oil but appear to be significant contributors to its flavour properties.

Investigations of the aroma and flavour of ginger have been carried out almost exclusively on the steam-distilled essential oil obtained from dried ginger. However, it should be appreciated that this oil not only differs somewhat in its composition and organoleptic properties from the natural volatile oil of fresh ginger, but can also differ from the volatile oil present in dried ginger prior to distillation through the formation of artefacts during the distillation process and subsequent storage.

Ginger oil prepared by steam distillation of dried ginger is obtained as a pale-yellow to light-amber mobile liquid whose viscosity increases on ageing or exposure to the air. Arctander (1960) has described the odour as warm, but fresh-woody and spicy. The initial fresh topnote has a peculiar resemblance to orange, lemongrass and coriander weed oil, while the sweet and heavy undertone is tenacious and rich. The organoleptic properties of ginger oils vary somewhat according to the geographical source of the dried ginger, as has been mentioned in the 'Products and end-uses' section. African ginger oil tends to be darker in colour and exhibits a more fatty sweetness, while the Jamaican oil is usually very pale in colour and has a pronounced odour freshness. The initial notes of freshly distilled Jamaican oil have a peculiar 'rubberlike' note, similar to that of nutmeg, which is hardly ever present in African oil. The citrus or lemon-like topnote is a characteristic of Indian ginger oil, and this is even more pronounced in Australian oil.

The steam-volatile oil content of some types of fresh ginger can be well over 4 per cent on a dry-weight basis. However, distillation of the more important dried gingers of commerce usually provides oil in the yields ranging from about 1 to 2.5 per cent. As has been mentioned previously, the oil distillation yield is influenced by a number of factors which include the ginger cultivar, the state of maturity at harvest, the method of preparation and drying the spice, its age, and to some extent upon the distillation method. The best oil yields are generally obtained from the partially scraped ginger from Nigeria. High yields (over 4 per cent) may also be obtained from distillation of fresh skin scrapings discarded during the preparation of dried ginger.

The physicochemical properties of ginger oils can also vary considerably between individual samples and these differences are influenced by those same factors listed above which effect the oil yield (Guenther, 1952; Gildemeister and Hoffmann, 1956). The optical-rotation value is a notable variable and this tends to be abnormally low in oils which have been distilled from old material or in oils which have been stored exposed to air and light.

Investigations of the composition of ginger oils were first reported towards the end of the nineteenth century, but relatively little progress was made at that time owing to the difficulties in isolating the individual components. The major sesquiterpene hydrocarbon constituent, (−)-α- zingiberene was first isolated by Soden and Rojahn (1900) and the elucidation of its structure was the subject of numerous studies during the subsequent 50 years. The currently accepted structure for this compound (X) was finally demonstrated by Eschenmoser and Schintz (1950) and the stereochemistry of the two asymmetric centres was determined by Mills (1952) and Arigoni and Jeger (1954).

(X):(−)-α-zingiberene.   (XI):(−)-B-sesquiphellandrene.   (XII):(+)-*ar*-curcumene.

Up until 1950, only limited progress was made in characterizing the other sesquiterpene constituents of ginger oil, although a number of the monoterpene constituents had been identified. With the introduction of improved analytical techniques in recent years, considerable advances have been made in identifying the whole range of constituents, including the low-boiling components (Kami *et al.*, 1972). Some 60 components had been reported at the time of writing and these are listed in Table 8.4.

The major sesquiterpenes in ginger oil are based on the bisabolane skeleton and the corresponding asymmetric centres have the same configuration in each compound. Among the sesquiterpene hydrocarbons, the structure of β-zingiberene is disputed; this has been proposed as an isomeric form of α-zingiberene (Herout *et al.*, 1953; Pliva *et al.*, 1960; Nigam *et al.*, 1964) but Connell and Sutherland (1966) have suggested that Pliva's compound may have been a mixture of α-zingiberene and β-sesquiphellandrene. The sesquiterpene alcohol, zingiberol, was

Table 8.4   *Constituents identified in ginger oils*

Sesquiterpene hydrocarbons
(−)-α-zingiberene[1,2,3,4,5,6]
β-zingiberene[7,8,9]
(+)-*ar*-curcumene[7,9,10,11]
(−)-β-bisabolene[4,7,9,10]
β-elemene[9]
β-farnesene[7,8,9]
γ-selinene[9]
(−)-β-sesquiphellandrene[10,11]
sesquithujene[12]

Oxygenated monoterpenes
d-borneol[9,13,20]
bornyl acetate[9]
1:8-cineole[9,16,17,20]
citrals *a* & *b*[9,11,13,20]
citronellyl acetate[22]
geraniol[9,13]
linalol[9,13,15,16]
α-terpineol[11]

Sesquiterpene alcohols
cis-β-eudesmol ⎫
trans-β-eudesmol ⎬ zingiberol[1,13,14]
nerolidol[11]   ⎭
cis-β-sesquiphellandrol[11]
trans-β-sesquiphellandrol[11]
cis-sabinene hydrate[12]
zingiberenol[12]

Monoterpene hydrocarbons
d-camphene[1,9,15,16,17]
△-3-carene[17]
p-cymene[9,18]
cumene[9]
d-limonene[9,16,17]
myrcene[9,17]
d-β-phellandrene[1,9,15,17,19]
α-pinene[9,17]
β-pinene[9,17]
sabinene[17]

Miscellaneous compounds
n-heptane[17]
n-octane[17]
n-nonane[17]
n-propanol[17]
2-heptanol[9]
n-nonanol[17]
2-nonanol[9]
acetaldehyde[17]
propionaldehyde[17]
n-butyraldehyde[17]
isovaleraldehyde[17]
n-nonanal[9,13]
n-decanal[1,9,21]
acetone[17]
methyl heptanone[9,13,16]
methyl acetate[15,17]
ethyl acetate[17]
methyl caprylate[15]
diethyl sulphide[17]
ethyl isopropyl sulphide[17]
methyl allyl sulphide[17]
chavicol(?)[13]

References: 1. Soden and Rojahn (1900); 2. Semmler and Becker (1913); 3. Schreiner and Kremers (1901); 4. Ruzicka and Van Veen (1929); 5. Soffer *et al.* (1944); 6. Eschenmoser and Schintz (1950); 7. Herout *et al.* (1953); 8. Pliva *et al.* (1960); 9. Nigam *et al.* (1964); 10. Connell and Sutherland (1966), Connell and Jordan (1971); 11. Bednarczyk and Kramer (1975); Bednarczyk *et al.* (1975); 12. Terhune *et al.* (1975); 13. Brooks (1916); 14. Varma *et al.* (1962); 15. Bertram and Walbaum (1894); 16. Jain *et al.* (1962); 17. Kami *et al.* (1972); 18. Thresh (1881); 19. West (1939); 20. Schimmel and Co. (1905); 21. Dodge (1912); 22. Salzer (1975a).

thought by Brooks (1916) to be related to zingiberene but Varma *et al.* (1962) have demonstrated that it is a 70:30 mixture of *cis*- and *trans*-β-eudesmol. Another sesquiterpene alcohol, zingiberenol, has been assigned the structure of 2-methyl-6-(*trans*-4′-hydroxycyclohex-2′-enyl)-hept-2-ene by Terhune *et al.* (1975). A number of dicyclic sesquiterpenes and sesquiterpene alcohols present in minor quantities in ginger oil have yet to be identified. Interested readers are recommended to refer to the review by Connell (1970) for a more detailed discussion of the identification and chemistry of these constituents of ginger oil.

The compounds listed in Table 8.4 were identified in ginger oils of diverse origins and the general occurrence of some of the constituents has yet to be confirmed. Quantitative data for the composition of ginger oils from the major spice areas is limited to the gas-chromatography studies of Nigam *et al.* (1964) and Connell and Jordan (1971), and in these investigations not all the components were fully resolved. However, the latter workers found that oils prepared by steam distillation of dried gingers from Australia, Jamaica, Nigeria, Sierra Leone, China and Cochin possessed similar composition patterns but some quantitative differences were apparent.

From these analyses, it would appear that the possible composition ranges for oils prepared from dried ginger are as follows: the sesquiterpene hydrocarbons are the most abundant component group (50–66 per cent), the oxygenated sesquiterpene content is modest (up to 17 per cent), while the remainder consists substantially of monoterpene hydrocarbons and oxygenated monoterpenes. Among the sesquiterpene hydrocarbons, (−)-α-zingiberene predominates (20–30 per cent) and is accompanied by lesser quantities of (−)-β-bisabolene (up to 12 per cent), (+)-*ar*-curcumene (up to 19 per cent) and farnesene (probably the β-isomer; up to 10 per cent). γ-selinene and β-elemene occur in relatively minor quantities. The quantitative balance in the oxygenated sesquiterpene group is less certain but the abundance of zingiberol has been reported to range from zero to 0.1 per cent (Varma *et al.*, 1962; Salzer, 1975a). With the significant exception of the citrals, the relative abundance of the low-boiling monoterpene constituents is generally low and of a similar order (up to about 2 per cent). The Australian oils examined by Connell and Jordan (1971) were notable in exhibiting high citral contents in the range of 8 to 27 per cent (averaging 19.3 per cent) compared with 0.5 to 4 per cent for oils from other sources. The ratio of citral *a* (geranial) to citral *b* (neral) in most samples was about 2:1. These authors have suggested that the pronounced 'citrus' or lemon-like note of Australian ginger oils is related to their high citral content.

The principal composition difference between the oils distilled from dried and from fresh, (green) ginger is that the latter usually contains a greater proportion of the lower-boiling components. Mathew *et al.* (1973) have noted that up to 20 per cent of the volatile oil can be lost during the sun-drying of Indian ginger, and that the lemon-like aroma becomes weaker in the process. The major oil loss to be expected during the drying of ginger is of the lower-boiling components, which include the citrals. Fresh (green) ginger of Australia, Cochin and Calicut are characterized by a pronounced fresh, lemon-like aroma; and it is possible that the retention of this characteristic in Australian ginger oils arises as much from more careful drying methods, in which volatile-oil losses are minimized (Richardson, 1966), as from intrinsic composition differences between the gingers of Australia and India.

Post-distillation changes in the properties of ginger oils can also occur, either during storage or utilization. Exposure of ginger oils to light and air results in an increase in viscosity, the formation of non-volatile (polymeric) residues and a decrease in the optical-rotation value. Connell and Jordan (1971) and Salzer (1975a) have shown that this change is associated with a decrease in the relative abundance of $(-)$-α-zingiberene and $(-)$-β-sesquiphellandrene and a concomitant increase in the relative abundance of $(+)$-*ar*-curcumene. Salzer has suggested that $(+)$-*ar*-curcumene is not in fact a true natural component of ginger oil but is an artefact which can be produced during the distillation stage by transformation of the other more labile sesquiterpenes. Thiessen (1970) has demonstrated that ginger oil is heat-sensitive and that detrimental changes in its composition and in its aroma and flavour can occur on heating above 90 °C.

Although several workers have monitored the changes in the volatile-oil content of fresh ginger as the rhizome matures, there have not been any reports of similar studies concerned with the possible changes in oil composition during maturation.

Studies of the relationship of the composition of ginger oils to their aroma and flavour properties have followed closely on the application of gas chromatography to oil analysis. As has been mentioned earlier, Connell and Jordan (1971) have suggested that the 'citrus' or lemon-like note of ginger oil is associated with the citral content but the significance of other low-boiling components was uncertain to these authors; and the major sesquiterpene hydrocarbons were not regarded as important contributors to the aroma. The relationship of the citrals to the lemon-note has also been proposed by Govindarajan and Raghuveer (1973); and Salzer (1975a) has implicated citronellyl acetate as important. The most sophisticated approach reported at the time of writing had been carried out by Bednarczyk and Kramer (1975) using a statistical analysis of a taste-panel appraisal of ginger-oil components. These workers attribute the lemon-note to the citrals together with α-terpineol, while β-sesquiphellandrene and *ar*-curcumene are regarded as partly responsible for the characteristic ginger flavour. Nerolidol was considered to contribute to the woody note; and *cis*- and *trans*- β-sesquiphellandrol were suspected to be significant contributors to the ginger flavour. In combination, these compounds accounted for 85 per cent of the taste panel's response.

Interested readers should refer to the articles by Connell (1970) and Salzer (1975a) for the gas-chromatography conditions recommended for ginger-oil analysis.

Standard specifications

The dried spice

United Kingdom standards

Ginger is one of the very few spices which is still recognized as a drug in the *British Pharmacopoeia*, 1973, although it is now regarded mainly as a flavouring agent. Until recently, the monograph on 'Ginger' was the only United Kingdom standard for this spice.

Ginger is defined as 'the rhizome of *Zingiber officinale* Roscoe, scraped to remove the dark, outer skin and dried in the sun. It is known in commerce as unbleached Jamaica ginger.' It is described as agreeable and aromatic in odour and agreeable and pungent in taste. After macro- and microscopical descriptions of the drug, the ginger should comply with the following tests:

Alcohol (90 per cent)-soluble extractive	Not less than 4.5 per cent
Ash	Not more than 6.0 per cent
Water-soluble ash	Not less than 1.7 per cent
Water-soluble extractive	Not less than 10.0 per cent

Powdered ginger is described as a light-yellow powder, with diagnostic structure as specified, and complies with the requirements of the tests as stated in the standard for 'Ginger'.

In 1970 the British Standards Institution published a more general standard for 'Ginger, whole, in pieces, and ground', BS 4593, based on the International Standards Organization Recommendation R. 1003, published in 1969. In this, the ginger, whole and in pieces, is described as 'the dried peeled or unpeeled rhizome of *Zingiber officinale* Roscoe, in pieces irregular in shape and not less than 20 mm in length or in small cut pieces, very pale buff to pale brown in colour, fibrous, either clean peeled, scraped or coated, washed and dried in the sun. The ginger may be garbled by removing pieces that are too light, and it may also be lime-bleached. The ginger, whole and in pieces, may be graded on the basis of its size, place of production, fibre and fibrous content and the method of treatment of the rhizomes.'

The odour and taste should be characteristic and wholesome and should not have a musty odour or a rancid or bitter taste. The ginger should be free from living insects and moulds and should be practically free from dead insects, insect fragments and rodent contamination visible to the naked eye. The proportion of extraneous matter in ginger, whole or in pieces, should be not more than 2.0 per cent, and ground ginger should be free from coarse particles.

The ginger should comply with the current UK statutory requirements concerning toxic substances in foods.

All forms of ginger should also comply with the requirements given in Table 8.5.

Table 8.5   *Requirements of BS 4593:1970 for ginger*

Characteristic	Requirement
Moisture, per cent (m/m), max	12.0
Total ash, per cent (m/m) on dry basis, max	
(a) unbleached	8.0
(b) bleached	12.0
Calcium (as CaO), per cent (m/m) on dry basis, max	
(a) unbleached	1.1
(b) bleached	2.5
Volatile oil, in ml per 100 g on dry basis, min	1.5

Ground ginger should also comply with the requirements given in Table 8.6.

Table 8.6   *Additional requirements of BS 4593:1970 for ground ginger*

Water-soluble ash, per cent (m/m) on dry basis, min.	1.9
Acid-insoluble ash, per cent (m/m) on dry basis, max.	2.3
Alcohol-soluble extract, per cent (m/m) on dry basis, min.	5.1
Cold water-soluble extract, per cent (m/m) on dry basis, min.	11.4

United States standards

The monograph on 'Ginger' has now been deleted from the *United States Pharmacopoeia*, XIX, [1975], with which the *US National Formulary* XIV has been amalgamated. In the *US Dispensatory*, 26th edn [1967], ginger is defined as 'the dried rhizome, the outer cortical layers of which may be partially or entirely removed, of *Zingiber officinale* Roscoe (fam. Zingiberaceae), known in commerce as Jamaica ginger, African ginger and Cochin ginger.'

A description of the external features of the three forms of ginger follows this definition. The standards for ginger have been given in the *US National Formulary*, XIII, as follows:

Water-soluble extractive   Not less than 12.0 per cent
Ether-soluble extractive   Not less than 4.5 per cent

The United States Government Standard defines ginger as being 'the washed and dried, or decorticated and dried, rhizome of *Zingiber officinale* Roscoe. The roots shall be irregular, varying from tan to a pale-brown colour, shall have an agreeable, aromatic, slightly pungent odour, and a pungent, biting taste.'

The standard stipulated that ginger should comply with the requirements listed in Table 8.7.

Table 8.7 *U.S. Government specifications for ginger*

Total ash, per cent, not more than	7.0
Acid-insoluble ash, per cent, not more than	1.0
Crude fibre, per cent, not more than	8.0
Volatile oil (expressed as ml per 100 g), not less than	1.5
Moisture, per cent, not more than	12.0
Starch, per cent, not less than	42.0
Sieve test (for powdered ginger only)	
US Standard sieve size	No.30
Percentage required to pass through, not less than	95

From: US Federal Specifications: *Spices, ground and whole and spice blends*, No. EE-S-631H, June 5, 1975.

For ginger, the limits of the various contaminants permitted under the Cleanliness Specifications of the American Spice Trade Association, are as shown in Table 8.8.

Table 8.8 *ASTA Cleanliness Specifications*

	Ginger	Ginger (split)
Rodent excreta, pellets per lb	2	2
Other excreta, mg per lb	3.0	10.0
Extraneous matter, per cent by weight	1.00	0.50
Whole dead insects, per lb	4	4
Insect defiled, per cent by weight	2.50	5.00
Mouldy ginger, per cent by weight	5.00	10.00

The Food and Drug Administration has specified that the defect action levels for ginger are: (*a*) an average of 3 per cent of mouldy and/or insect infested pieces by weight; and (*b*) an average of 3 mg of excreta per pound.

Canadian standards

The Canadian Food and Drug Regulations define ginger, whole or ground, as 'the washed and dried or decorticated and dried rhizome of

Table 8.9 *Canadian Government Specifications for ginger*

Moisture, per cent, not more than	10
Total ash, per cent, not more than	7.5
Ash insoluble in hydrochloric acid, per cent, not more than	2
Ash soluble in water, per cent on the dry basis, not less than	2
Cold water extractive as determined by the official method, per cent on the dry basis, not less than	13.3
Ginger starch, per cent on the dry basis, not less than	45
Crude fibre, per cent, not more than	9

From: Department of National Health and Welfare, Canada. Food and Drug Regulations, 1964.

the ginger plant'. The standard requires that the ginger should satisfy the requirements given in Table 8.9.

Indian standards

The Government of India has published 'Agmark' specifications for various grades of Cochin and Calicut dried gingers, both garbled and ungarbled, non-bleached and bleached, and ginger powder. However, the only two grades which comply with the United Kingdom Standards are the garbled, non-bleached Cochin and Calicut gingers. All the other Agmark grades fail to satisfy either or both the United Kingdom limits for content of extraneous matter and calcium (CaO).

Ginger oleoresin

There is no United Kingdom standard for ginger oleoresin, either pharmaceutical or commercial. There was an entry in the *British Pharmaceutical Codex*, 1968, but this referred only to its preparation – by percolation with acetone – and no information was included about its appearance or properties. Manufacturers have devised their own standards which, in most cases, satisfy the United States Standards.

The *US National Formulary*, XIII, included ginger oleoresin, prepared by percolation with acetone, in which the yield was specified as being 'not less than 18 ml and not more than 35 ml of volatile ginger oil from each 100 g of oleoresin'.

The Essential Oil Association of America has a specification for 'Oleoresin ginger', (EOA No. 243). The oleoresin is described as the product obtained by solvent extraction of the dried rhizomes of *Zingiber officinale* Roscoe, with the subsequent removal of the solvent, and has the following properties:

Appearance and odour:	A dark brown viscous to highly viscous liquid with the characteristic odour and flavour of ginger.
Volatile oil content:	18 to 35 ml per 100 g.
Refractive index of oil:	1.4880 to 1.4970.
Optical rotation of oil:	$-30°$ to $-60°$.
Residual solvent in oleoresin:	Meets with the Federal Food, Drug and Cosmetic Regulations.
Solubility:	Alcohol – soluble with sediment.
	Benzyl benzoate – soluble in all proportions.
	Fixed oils – slightly soluble in most fixed oils.
	Glycerin ⎫
	Mineral oil ⎬ insoluble.
	Propylene glycol ⎭

Ginger oil

No pharmaceutical or commercial standards for ginger oil had been published in the United Kingdom at the time of writing.

In the United States, the Essential Oil Association has a standard for 'Oil ginger', (EOA No. 13), which is described as the 'volatile oil with the aromatic, persistent odour of ginger but lacking the pungency usually associated with ginger. The African and Cochin gingers are the types most frequently used for distillation.' The standard specifies the following properties for the oil:

Colour and appearance:	Light yellow to yellow.
Specific gravity at 25 °/25 °C:	0.871 to 0.882
Optical rotation at 20 °C:	$-28°$ to $-45°$.
Refractive index at 20 °C:	1.4880 to 1.4940.
Saponification value:	Not more than 20.
Solubility:	Alcohol – soluble, usually with turbidity.

Benzyl benzoate
Diethyl phthalate } soluble in all proportions.

Fixed oils – soluble in most fixed oils.
Mineral oils – usually soluble in all proportions.

Glycerin
Propylene glycol } practically insoluble.

Production, trade and markets

Ginger has a number of similarities with chillies and capsicums in that the bulk of world production is consumed domestically within the producing countries, mainly in the fresh ('green') form. Also the number of countries producing ginger substantially exceeds the number trading in it internationally, and the volume of international trade in processed ginger, i.e., the dried spice and preserved ginger, is as great as that in fresh ginger. Strictly speaking only dried ginger, on account of its applications *vis-à-vis* those of the other forms, should be regarded as a spice, but it is scarcely practicable and certainly not desirable to disregard the fresh and preserved forms, and therefore the following discussion will cover all three types.

The cultivation of ginger for domestic consumption in the fresh form has been, and remains, widespread throughout South and East Asia for a considerable period. Since the era of colonization by Europeans, ginger has also been introduced into a number of areas in Oceania, Africa, the Caribbean and South America; but in many of these instances, production and exports, if any, have often been only on a very small scale, and frequently development never went beyond the stage of experimental trials. In the early years of the twentieth century, the most widely known producers and exporters of ginger were China, India, Jamaica and Sierra Leone. The first was renowned for its preserved ginger and the others for their dried gingers. In the intervening period a number of other countries have emerged as important ginger exporters, among which Nigeria and more recently Australia are the most notable as suppliers of dried ginger. Australia has also made a significant impact as an exporter of preserved ginger and as a competitor in international trade with the Chinese product. Singapore, Mauritius, Fiji, St Vincent and St Lucia are perhaps the best-known suppliers of fresh ginger to Western European markets, while Thailand, West Malaysia, Taiwan and the Philippines have attained importance in inter-regional trade of fresh ginger. Several other producing countries in South and East Asia occasionally export fresh or dried ginger, but some of these countries have often had to import ginger to supplement local production which was inadequate to satisfy domestic demand.

Production

India

Together with China, India is almost certainly one of the oldest producers of ginger and in most cases a large percentage of production is consumed domestically, mainly in the fresh form. During the last 25 years Indian production has generally been in the range of 12 000–25 000 tonnes (dried basis), with considerable annual variation. The 1949–50 season yielded 24 000 tonnes, whereas only 15 000 tonnes were produced during the following season. Relatively low figures were reported for the mid-1950s but during the 1960s there was a generally steady improvement. Production was 28 000 tonnes in the 1970–1 season and this level was exceeded in the late 1970s.

Cultivation of ginger is carried out in a number of states, but the most important is Kerala. This state also accounts for about 90 per cent of India's exports of ginger, providing the well-known Cochin and Calicut dried gingers (see 'Products and end-uses' and 'Processing and manufacture'). India now mainly exports dried ginger, while the domestic demand is predominantly for fresh ginger, but a small amount of preserved ginger is produced for the domestic market. Production and marketing are generally carried out under conditions of private enterprise although there exist some widely recognized quality-control procedures and the grading of dried ginger for export is to some extent influenced by the Agmark specifications which were drawn up in the 1960s to ensure marketing in batches of uniform quality and physical characteristics. The fairly steady level of local demand for ginger, combined with the considerable variation in annual harvests, bring about very substantial fluctuations in the quantities available each year for export.

China

All three forms of ginger have been produced and widely used in China for a very long time. However, statistics of Chinese production of ginger are not available. In international trade, China is best known as a supplier of preserved ginger but, as already mentioned in the 'Processing and manufacture' section, Hong Kong has been of greater significance for some time as a processor and exporter of this commodity than has the main ginger-growing area around Canton. Furthermore, ginger production has always been well established on the island of Taiwan and since the political separation from mainland China, which took place in 1948 – 50, China and Taiwan have been competitors, particularly as suppliers of green ginger to Hong Kong. Chinese dried ginger is produced mainly in South China. Chinese production of ginger is now probably organized on a co-operative or communal basis, whereas before 1950 private enterprise was the rule.

Other South and East Asian producers

In addition to India and China, most countries in this region produce ginger but mainly for domestic consumption. Thailand, West Malaysia and the Philippines are notable in regularly having a surplus production to permit inter-regional trade in fresh ginger. Thailand has a substantial internal market for fresh ginger but local production seems to have been sufficiently high for export to have been possible during the last 20 years. The quantities of fresh ginger available for export have not, however, been large and Thailand is significant more for its self-sufficiency than as a major international supplier. Production figures for West Malaysia are not available but export figures suggest substantial annual production, a considerable proportion of which is sent to Singapore either for re-export or for further processing before export. The Philippines sends fresh ginger to Hong Kong as well as supplying the needs of a fairly substantial local market.

Indonesia, Bangladesh and Nepal produce fresh ginger for the domestic market and small quantities for inter-regional trade and, on occasion, supply the international market with a little dried ginger.

Japan, Sri Lanka and Burma are ginger producers and have substantial local markets for ginger but they are not normally exporters.

Jamaica

Jamaica was a substantial producer and exporter in the sixteenth century, and there is no evidence to suggest that since then she has ever been other than a regular supplier. Unlike India and China, Jamaican production is oriented very strongly towards the export trade, to the extent that the export figures can be taken as a fairly accurate guide to production levels over a period of years. Jamaican dried ginger has generally been regarded as the yardstick by which dried gingers from other sources are judged in terms of quality, and although this is still true, the quantities available have diminished sharply in recent years. It would appear that agricultural work is unpopular in Jamaica and there has been a pronounced exodus of labourers to more remunerative work in the towns and in the tourist trade, and in any case smaller harvests have often yielded greater overall revenue than larger harvests. Production and marketing have generally been conducted on the basis of private enterprise, but there have been times, for example, during the Second World War and in the mid-1960s, when funds had to be made available to the Jamaican Agricultural Society in order that unsold dried ginger could be purchased at a price acceptable to the farmers. Purchases of this type would then be sold on the international market by the Government Marketing Department. These were exceptional circumstances at the time, but state involvement in the ginger industry has become more common in recent years.

Other Caribbean and South American producers

Besides Jamaica, several Caribbean islands grow ginger but in most cases production is fairly small and for domestic needs only. St Vincent and St Lucia, however, have been exporting fresh ginger to the UK for some years. Annual production of fresh ginger in St Vincent is around 1 000 tonnes. In 1975 ginger was declared a specified product under the terms laid down by the St Lucia Marketing Board, which is now the sole purchaser and exporter of the commodity, although licences can be issued to other parties who wish to handle it. The main objective of this measure seems to have been that of guaranteeing the growers a consistently fair price. Annual production of fresh ginger on St Lucia is around 200–300 tonnes.

Ginger is grown on a small scale by a few Latin American countries for domestic consumption, but Brazil and Nicaragua have developed a fresh ginger export trade.

Sierra Leone

Sierra Leone is similar to Jamaica in that ginger is produced almost solely for export, and again the export statistics, which are given in the next section, are a good guide to production levels although of course changes in the local level of stocks cause divergences between production and exports of dried ginger in the very short term. The crop is grown under private farming conditions rather than under state supervision, although, as in most of the other principal producing countries, there is some government surveillance and control over the quality of the dried ginger for export. Sierra Leone, like Jamaica, has in recent years somewhat declined in importance as a producer, and the focus on West African dried ginger has shifted towards Nigeria.

Nigeria

Nigeria was already an exporter of dried ginger before the Second World War, and although the quantities involved were then comparatively very small, local production of ginger was well established and, unlike the case of Sierra Leone, served a fairly extensive domestic market for fresh ginger, which is still the case today. Production seems to have been subject to some variation; for example, purchases by the Northern Nigerian Marketing Board of 3 800 tonnes, 2 800 tonnes and 1 650 tonnes in the 1963–4, 1964–5 and 1965–6 seasons respectively were followed by a purchase of less than 300 tonnes in 1966–7, although since then there has been considerable recovery.

Other African producers

Ginger is grown for domestic consumption in a number of countries in West, East and Central Africa but, Nigeria and Sierra Leone excepted, they have never been of great significance as exporters. East Africa as a whole is in fact an importer of ginger, although Uganda is recorded in trade statistics as an exporter to Western European markets for a period during the 1960s and early 1970s. Experimental trials have been carried out in Ghana in recent years, but it remains to be seen whether this country will develop into a regular producer and supplier.

Australia

The development of a successful ginger industry in Australia seems to have stemmed in part from discontent with former suppliers, problems having been experienced in terms of both quality and quantity. An extensive market-research survey was followed by the establishment in Queensland of a single large concern incorporating a growers' co-operative and a marketing board, with considerable investment in advanced capital equipment (see 'Processing and manufacture'). The result has been the arrival on the market of a preserved ginger of very good quality, serving both the local and overseas markets, and Australia is now a formidable rival to Hong Kong and China in the production of preserved ginger and its trade. Dried ginger is a less important but still considerable item in Australia's total production, but fresh ginger does not seem to have been marketed from this source. Trade statistics are provided in the next section but production figures were not available at the time of writing.

Mauritius

Mauritius is a producer of good-quality fresh ginger although it was scarcely of importance before the 1920s. In recent times there has been some production of dried ginger for the UK market but the drying process is not regarded as economic, except in times of high prices. For some time now there has existed a Ginger Marketing Society of which there were over 350 members in 1953. The society's function is mainly that of buying from the growers at agreed prices, rather than of overseas marketing, which still remains the preserve of the traditional exporters. In 1962 local annual production of fresh ginger was estimated as 700–800 tonnes, of which about 250 tonnes was consumed locally, up to 200 tonnes retained for planting and at least 350 tonnes exported, mainly to East and Southern Africa. These figures were considerable improvements on those recorded in the late 1940s and 1950s when the quantities marketed through the Ginger Marketing Society for local consumption and for export ranged erratically between 70 and 356 tonnes per annum, averaging 167 tonnes for the period 1949–57.

Fiji

Fiji is known to have exported ginger in 1890 but it was not until the 1950s that regular exports of fresh ginger started, and in the early years of the twentieth century the crop was mainly consumed by the Asian communities in the island, notably the Indians. Fiji's fresh ginger is produced and marketed under fairly typical conditions of private enterprise. The annual production of fresh ginger in recent years has been of the order of 1 000 tonnes. In recent years small quantities of both preserved and dried ginger have produced for the export market.

Other Pacific Ocean producers

Ginger is grown in Tonga, principally to meet domestic needs, but quantities of fresh ginger have been exported to New Zealand from time to time. Hawaii is also a ginger producer and shipped around 150 tonnes per annum of fresh ginger to the US mainland in the early 1960s.

In recent years, there have been experimental trials on the production of dried ginger in the Solomon Islands and in Papua New Guinea. However, it is as yet uncertain whether this work will be implemented to develop a significant export trade.

It may already have been appreciated that a statistical analysis of ginger production and trade is liable to be fraught with difficulty on account of the fact that it is by no means always clear whether quantities are expressed in terms of the rhizome's fresh weight or in terms of its dried weight, which is only about one-third of the fresh equivalent. This should be remembered particularly in the next section, which is concerned with international trade.

Trade

For the purpose of an analysis of the international ginger trade, it will be convenient to deal with each form of the spice separately, since the markets for each type are quite distinct. It should also be appreciated that ginger products from the various sources can differ considerably in their quality-determining chemical characteristics and physical form and that some users express definite preferences for particular applications. This is particularly important in the case of dried ginger. Readers are recommended to refer to the 'Products and end-uses' section for a summary of the characteristics and applications of the major types of ginger products entering the market.

Table 8.10 *Dried ginger: Exports from India, Jamaica, Sierra Leone and Nigeria, 1921–76, (tonnes)*

	India	Jamaica	Sierra Leone	Nigeria	Totals for the four countries
1921–25 (annual average)		810	1 500[1]	– [2]	
1926–30 (” ”)		1 160	1 840[3]	– [2]	
1931–35 (” ”)		960	1 630	160	
1936–40 (” ”)		1 390	2 210	290	
1941–45 (” ”)	3 710	1 190	1 510	70	
1946–50 (” ”)	2 120	1 380	1 500	170	
1051–55 (” ”)	2 830	1 230	1 930	460	
1956–60 (” ”)	5 920	850	850	930	
1961–65 (” ”)	5 440	660	630	2 130	
1966	5 300	840	470	2 750	9 360
1967	4 260	730	930	1 300	7 220
1968	2 230	460	1 560	1 960	6 210
1969	1 250	280	670	3 240	5 440
1970	2 240	305	440	3 780	6 765
1971	5 280	360	600	2 350	8 590
1972	7 010	350	500	2 090	9 950
1973	5 610	480	360	1 140	7 590
1974	4 770	335	210	630	5 945
1975	3 670	286	150	664	4 770
1976	4 786	...	...	...	...

Sources: Trade returns
Ministry of Agriculture
and Fisheries, Jamaica
USDA. Foreign Agriculture
Circulars

[1] Based on one year's export figures only.
[2] Not available, but probably negligible.
[3] Based on three years' export figures only.

... not available.

Dried ginger

Table 8.10 shows the export trade in dried ginger of the four most important suppliers from 1921 onwards, and it will at once be apparent that Nigeria has only relatively recently become an exporter of major importance. Jamaican peeled, whole dried ginger is regarded as the best in quality and is marketed in three grades, the top grade destined mainly for the grocery, retail trade. Nigerian ginger is supplied in the peeled, whole form or as coated 'splits' and has competed well against Jamaican ginger in certain areas of application, replacing to some degree the two lower Jamaican grades as the raw material used by grinders and blenders. The proportion of Nigerian ginger in the annual imports into the UK, USA and West Germany rose to over 50 percent by the early 1970s, but thereafter exports declined.

Sierra Leone's ginger, for many years referred to as 'African', is exported unpeeled and is therefore unsuitable for the grocery trade. It is, however, eminently suitable for essential oil and oleoresin extraction and for blending, and is in much demand for these purposes. The main destinations are the UK, USA and the Netherlands but ginger from Sierra Leone is no longer as important in terms of percentage of total imports into each country as it once was.

Of the two types of Indian dried ginger, Cochin and Calicut, the former is generally preferred and is the most commonly quoted on the European and North American markets. Indian dried ginger is well liked for grinding and blending and in the manufacture of beverages such as ginger beer. Nowadays a smaller proportion of Indian ginger exports are destined for Europe and North America than formerly, and very large quantities of Indian dried ginger are destined for markets in western Asia and the Middle East. For many years Aden was an entrepôt of major importance in these markets although it is now less so.

The recent impact of new entrants to the dried-ginger trade is best illustrated by the fact that whereas in the period 1960–2, 6.3 per cent of the UK's imports of dried ginger were from sources other than the four just discussed, in the period 1969–71 the equivalent figure was 22.0 per cent; for the USA the corresponding figures were 8.1 and 23.5 per cent. This diversification can be attributed to more than one factor, for example, supply problems on the part of the traditional exporters combined with an overall increase in market size and a readiness on the part of an increasingly sophisticated spice trade to consider new sources of production.

Australia did not turn to the export of dried ginger until its preserved-ginger industry was well established. Its quality is regarded as falling between that of the gingers of Jamaica and Sierra Leone. The dried ginger of China has gained in popularity in some European markets, notably France, but the Chinese practice of washing the ginger in a sulphur dioxide solution to give an almost white product and consequently a very pale ground powder makes this ginger unacceptable in some markets, such as the UK.

Table 8.11 gives a comparison of the quantities of dried ginger imported into a selection of countries.

Preserved ginger

As already mentioned in the previous section, the main development during the last 15 years has been the rise of the Australian preserved-ginger industry, which has enjoyed notable success in penetrating major markets such as the UK. There has been a corresponding decline in the share of Hong Kong and China, the traditional sources in the trade.

A problem encountered in interpreting the statistical information in relation to preserved ginger concerns the variation in the ratio of ginger to syrup in the various packs. One reason for the success of the Australian products is that the syrup content has been satisfactorily reduced, but a consequence of this is that the export of an equivalent

Table 8.11 Dried and fresh ginger: Imports by country, 1953–76 (tonnes)

	1953–5[1]	1960–2[1]	1963–5[1]	1966	1967	1968	1969	1970	1971	1972	1973	1974	1975	1976
UK	1 580	1 360	2 260	2 220	2 040	1 550	1 980	3 020	2 180	1 480	2 765	2 367	2 935	3 091
USA[2]	1 290	1 830	1 620	2 370	1 680	1 630	2 250	2 360	2 050	2 680	3 147	3 165	2 797	3 773[4]
Federal Republic of Germany	–	–	–	380	450	710	550	670	670	660	699	866	723	891
France	–	30	60	50	30	20	60	60	70	90	83	99	95	151
Canada	–	190	300	240	280	250	340	360	320	340	470	468	534	746
Japan	–	–	–	420	300	400	430	420	610	–	1 011	719	1 099	...[6]
Netherlands	–	–	–	160	160	210	250	240	270	290	320	339	365	371
Morocco	–	260	250	250	330	400	180	270	500	721	280	501	378	398
Iran	–	–	–	210	310	–	–	21	310	204	131	197	...	925[5]
Saudi Arabia[3]	474	705	664	1 235	1 225	666	473	818	2 271	1 306	1 301	1 511	1 966	...
South Yemen[3] (Aden)	1 558	2 012	1 756	2 241	1 834	757	361	727	742	1 184	757	263	588	...
Sri Lanka	–	150	110	150	80	60	70	–	–	–	...	–	–	...
New Zealand	–	60	80	80	80	120	60	90	60	–	...	...	...	...

– nil or negligible
... not available

Source: Trade returns

1 Annual average
2 After 1965 includes quantity of preserved ginger
3 Based on export statistics for India. Most imports into South Yemen (Aden) are re-exported to Middle East countries, in particular Saudi Arabia. Both sets of figures relate to the twelve months commencing 1 April. Up until the mid-1960s the import figures given under the Saudi Arabian heading were in fact often designated imports into 'Arabia' and therefore the quantities entering Saudi Arabia as such at that time may have been rather lower than these figures suggest.
4 Preliminary
5 Figure for 21 March 1976 to 20 March 1977.
6 Trade returns give a figure of 6 459 tonnes; but this seems to be unusually high in comparison with previous years.

weight of ginger which is preserved in syrup would be recorded as being a lower export volume in the case of Australia than for Hong Kong. Moreover, by no means all importing countries have a separate category for preserved-ginger products, and indeed the USA ceased to record this product separately after 1964. The only method of circumventing this problem is to examine the statistics of the exporting countries by destination.

Hong Kong processes green ginger imported from China, Taiwan, countries in South East Asia such as the Philippines and Thailand, and formerly from Japan. China and Australia rely on their domestic production of green ginger. The exports and re-exports of Hong Kong and the exports of Australia are shown in Tables 8.12, 8.13 and 8.14. In Table 8.15 are shown imports of preserved ginger from China into the UK, which is the major market for preserved gingers, the primary object of this table being to give an order of magnitude for Chinese exports.

Hong Kong's annual imports of green ginger for preservation rose from around 6 000 tonnes in the early 1950s to just over 8 000 tonnes in the early 1960s, but lately the annual import has been between 5 000 and 7 000 tonnes. Some of these imports, particularly from Taiwan, were in temporary preservative.

Chinese preserved ginger has been traditionally marketed in a number of qualities, which are described in the 'Products and end-uses' section. Although these traditional categories still apply to some extent, they have lost some of their significance with the advent of the Australian products, a larger proportion of preserved ginger in syrup now being made to specific user requirements. The Australian industry markets a variety of cuts depending on end-use, and these are known as sliced, diced and crystallized. The ratio of ginger to syrup varies, again according to end-use, from 60 : 40 to 80 : 20. Furthermore, the Australian product is sold in steel drums of 500–600 pounds (225–270 kg), whereas the Chinese and Hong Kong products have generally been exported in wooden casks or cases, which are nowadays liked less than the Australian drums.

In the 1950s some preserved ginger was exported from Japan, Macao and Cuba but, with the possible exception of Macao, it is unlikely that any has been exported from these sources since then. Japan would appear to be a net importer.

Fresh ginger

The importation of fresh and salted ginger into Hong Kong has been mentioned above and details of these imports are shown in Table 8.16. Some of this fresh material is re-exported unprocessed, the volume of this trade varying considerably in magnitude, but since 1966 never being more than 50 tonnes per annum. The main destinations for these products have been the UK, West Malaysia and Singapore.

Table 8.12 Preserved and dried ginger: Exports from Hong Kong by destination, 1953–76 (tonnes)

	1953–5[1]	1960–62[2]	1963	1964	1965	1966	1967	1968	1969	1970	1971	1972	1973	1974	1975	1976
Preserved ginger in syrup																
UK	2 170	2 380	1 090	1 600	2 290	1 815	1 390	1 000	1 345	705	445	970	1 216	560	295	172
Federal Republic of Germany	90	115	80	165	360	320	320	290	85	55	50	130	359	173	71	65
Netherlands	570	625	445	1 055	1 810	1 400	850	1 275	960	780	1 030	970	1 517	1 119	823	1 207
USA	65	40	10	30	60	40	45	50	40	50	40	55	55	34	31	25
Canada	50	100	90	90	105	70	65	30	30	45	45	15	30	11	9	8
Australia	330	240	170	100	50	25	40	45	30	40	35	30	50	87	62	56
South Africa	60	80	105	105	110	115	160	130	65	40	50	30	35	37	59	19
Others	110	90	50	75	75	70	70	80	65	60	60	60	82	62	55	62
Total	3 445[2]	3 670	2 050	3 220	4 860	3 855	2 940	2 900	2 620	1 775	1 755	2 260	3 344	2 083	1 405	1 614
Crystallized ginger[3]																
Total	–	12	6	11	18	17	34	35	45	40	38	45	51	45	40	53
Dried ginger																
UK	–	62	335	116	11	10	13	12	8	8	7	7	7	6	5	8
USA	–	39	49	19	14	11	13	9	10	9	2	4	7	14	25	35
Others	–	67	99	65	19	11	19	4	9	8	2	2	2	23	51	40[4]
Total	218[2]	168	483	200	44	32	45	25	27	25	11	13	16	43	81	83

1 Annual average
2 Includes re-exports
3 Not shown separately before 1959
4 Of which the Netherlands took 23 tonnes.
– nil or negligible

Source: Hong Kong Trade Statistics (Department of Commerce)

Table 8.13 *Preserved and dried ginger: Re-exports from Hong Kong, 1960–76 (tonnes)*

	1960–2[1]	1963	1964	1965	1966	1967	1968	1969	1970	1971	1972	1973	1974	1975	1976
Preserved ginger in syrup															
UK	180	430	370	–	5	20	1	740	160	105	50	–	19	–	2
Netherlands	435	355	290	–	40	–	–	240	405	210	40	–	193	137	175
Federal Republic of Germany	115	180	135	–	10	20	–	210	200	230	105	–	166	182	285
Other countries	40	45	30	8	10	25	7	25	25	20	20	17	17	15	29[2]
Total	775	1 010	825	8	65	65	8	1 215	790	565	215	17	395	334	491
Dried ginger															
Total	75	122	24	28	13	7	–	38	63	23	70	18	5	27	79

Source: Hong Kong Trade Statistics (Department of Commerce)
1   Annual average
2   Of which the USA took 20 tonnes
–   nil or negligible

Table 8.14 Fresh and preserved ginger: Australian exports* by destination, 1959–60 to 1975–6 (tonnes)

	1959–60 to 1961–2[1]	1962–3	1963–4	1964–5	1965–6	1966–7	1967–8	1968–9	1969–70	1970–1	1971–2	1972–3	1973–4	1974–5	1975–6[2]
USA	49	49	94	–	–	–	12	15	23	119	70	85	60	56	50
UK	–	–	–	68	62	62	184	313	355	451	567	887	685	818	501
New Zealand	36	30	–	46	59	70	66	31	118	120	103	90	64	–	–
Other countries	26	2	30	7	12	24	31	79	197[3]	215	139	271	260	238[4]	204[5]
Total	111	81	124	121	133	156	293	438	693	905	879	1 333	1 069	1 112	755

Source: Overseas Trade (Bureau of Census and Statistics)
* These figures include a very small quantity of re-exported material.
1 Annual average
2 Taken from exports into individual countries, from those listed in 1974–5.
3 Of which: Netherlands 68 tonnes
              South Africa 58 tonnes
              Canada 21 tonnes
4 Of which: Canada 69 tonnes
              South Africa 116 tonnes
              Netherlands 29 tonnes
5 Of which: Canada 32 tonnes
              South Africa 118 tonnes
              Netherlands 43 tonnes
– nil or negligible.

Table 8.15 *Preserved ginger: Imports into the UK, Netherlands, Australia and the Federal Republic of Germany, 1953–76 (tonnes)*

	1953–55[1]	1960–2[1]	1963	1964	1965	1966	1967	1968	1969	1970	1971	1972	1973	1974	1975	1976
(A) UK – Total	2 260	2 735	1 950	2 290	2 725	2 765	2 420	1 825	2 540	2 120	1 195	1 935	2 547	1 793	1 138	1 075
Sources of UK imports:																
China	–	85	15	160	345	795	905	560	235	410	275	320	554	372	305	345
Hong Kong	2 090	2 625	1 925	2 090	2 275	1 875	1 420	980	2 085	1 135	500	930	1 276	704	371	266
Australia	–	–	–	–	75	75	80	280	210	500	390	675	687	674	456	456
Other countries	170	25	10	40	30	20	15	5	10	75	30	10	30	43	6	8
(B) Netherlands	...	1 010	930	1 360	1 765	90[3]	85[3]	90[3]	1 778	1 742	1 916	1 852	2 156	2 209	1 907	1 964
(C) Australia[2]	280	380	410	380	200	120	130	100	90	75	40	40	45	93	8	12
(D) Fed. Rep. of Germany	...	...	...	...	...	...	...	...	500	400	410	400	363	389	363	706

Source: Trade returns

1 Annual average
2 For years 1959/60 to 1975/76
3 One category of preserved ginger not shown separately in these years
– nil or negligible
... not available

Table 8.16 *Fresh or salted ginger: Imports into Hong Kong, 1953–76 (tonnes)*

	1953–55¹	1960–62¹	1963	1964	1965	1966	1967	1968	1969	1970	1971	1972	1973	1974	1975	1976
Sources of imports																
China	4 125	1 165	800	3 860	4 570	3 795	805	795	2 475	1 370	2 000	1 340	2 442	1 738	1 000	691
Taiwan	750	5 060	5 610	3 120	1 980	2 180	3 010	1 575	3 720	5 220	3 765	4 680	3 962	5 557	6 041	2 924
Japan	960	720	30	120	15	10	–	–	–	–	–	–	–	–	–	–
Macao	205	25	–	–	–	–	–	–	–	–	–	–	10	–	–	7
Philippines	–	720	110	10	–	–	1 330	2 350	200	10	145	1 000	168	–	128	3 705
Thailand	–	365	45	–	–	–	10	90	5	–	–	100	79	73	2	–
South Vietnam	–	200	–	–	–	–	–	–	–	–	–	–	–	–	–	–
Fiji	–	–	–	–	–	–	–	25	370	285	–	–	–	30	–	61
Other countries	–	50	25	–	–	–	65	295	50	10	10	170	150	16	–	11
Total	6 040	8 305	6 620	7 110	6 565	5 985	5 220	5 130	6 820	6 895	5 920	7 290	6 811	7 414	7 171	7 399

Source: Hong Kong Trade Statistics (Department of Commerce and Industry)

¹ annual average
– nil or negligible

West Malaysia and Singapore are important sources of supply of fresh ginger and a large proportion of the trade they generate is in fact between the two countries, but the precise quantities are very difficult to assess since no differentiation exists in the records as between dried and fresh ginger. Singapore handles fresh ginger from several sources including China, Taiwan and Thailand and most of its exports are in fact re-exports, although some processing takes place within Singapore. A very substantial proportion of Singapore's ginger re-exports go to Pakistan, the Middle East, North and East Africa and, indeed, to West Malaysia, but again problems are encountered in distinguishing between the fresh and dried products. The volume of this trade varies considerably and was, for example, 590 tonnes in 1969 and 2 700 tonnes in 1972. As far as West Malaysia is concerned, it may be that as much as 90 per cent of its exports consist of fresh ginger destined for Singapore. Imports into West Malaysia varied between 1 500 and 2 500 tonnes per annum until 1966, but thereafter a decline set in and the present average is considerably less than 1 000 tonnes, with a low point in 1972 of 380 tonnes.

The market for fresh ginger in the industrialized West is far from small. Imports into the UK are of the order of 1 000 tonnes per annum. Apart from Singapore and occasionally West Africa, the suppliers to the UK market are Mauritius, Brazil, Fiji, St Vincent and St Lucia. Mauritius supplies East and Southern Africa with fresh ginger, while Fiji includes New Zealand among its buyers. Fiji's trade in fresh ginger was in the region of 500–1 000 tonnes per annum in the mid-1960s but increased slightly during the early 1970s, averaging about 950 tonnes for the period 1970–3.

The main market for fresh ginger is undoubtedly the South East Asian group of countries, where it is used extensively in cooking, and even in the UK a fair proportion of imports are destined for the Asian immigrant communities. In other outlets the market seems restricted, probably as much on account of the problem of deterioration during transit as of high transport costs attributable to the product's weight; in this respect the fresh ginger of Mauritius seems to have acquired a reputation for better keeping properties than other fresh gingers.

Market Structure

Dried ginger is traded in relatively large quantities by comparison with many other spices, and the number of firms and individuals actively participating in the trade is correspondingly large. The dealers in both exporting and importing countries are of prime importance and a large number of brokers act as intermediaries between dealer and user, or even dealer and dealer, on the usual commission basis although with an increasing number taking a larger commission from the seller and none from the buyer. Various shipping organizations and general-produce merchants also participate, and the dried spice tends to be subject to speculative activity.

The main entrepôts in the dried ginger trade are Singapore and Aden, the latter, however, having become less involved with the passage of time. With the gradual decline of the importance of Aden, a larger proportion of Indian exports is now destined direct for the West Asian and Middle Eastern markets, although how far this process will continue remains to be seen. London, New York, Hamburg and Rotterdam also conduct entrepôt trade in varying degrees, but the volume so traded is small in comparison with the two other ports just mentioned.

Hong Kong is the main entrepôt in the preserved-ginger trade although some other major ports import small quantities for re-export. In the case of fresh ginger, Singapore's entrepôt trade can be said to be the dominant feature of the structure of the market.

As one would expect, the number of links in the trading chain are far fewer in the case of preserved and fresh ginger than for dried ginger since, with the exception of the fresh-ginger market in South and East Asia, the markets are of lower volume. There is some evidence to suggest that the preserved-ginger market is becoming more specialized insofar as end-users are demanding preserved ginger of a fairly precise specification, and this development, already well advanced in the case of Australian preserved ginger, is bound to lead to more direct commercial links between producer and end-user. The number of dealers in fresh ginger in the industrialized West is few, mainly on account of the very limited nature of this market.

Fresh ginger also differs somewhat from dried ginger and, to a lesser extent, from preserved ginger in that it is marketed through the fruit-and-vegetable trade network as well as through the spice trade. This is, of course, due to the nature of demand, which in the West stems in large measure from immigrant communities of Asian origin, who buy fresh ginger together with various other vegetable products for the preparation of curry dishes.

Prices

Dried ginger

The price of dried ginger fluctuates over a wide range and there are quite large differences between dried gingers from different sources. These facts are illustrated in Table 8.17.

There has been some contention among suppliers and trade sources that over-production has sometimes occurred and depressed prices, for example in 1971. Whether or not this is true, any shortfall in either Indian or Nigerian ginger, which nowadays dominate the market, has a marked effect on general price levels. The high price commanded by

Table 8.17   *Dried ginger: Annual average prices (London c.i.f. spot), 1960–77*
(£ per tonne)

	Jamaica No. 3	Nigerian split	Cochin	Sierra Leone
1960	199	78	160	181
1961	200	105	129	178
1962	484	168	166	403
1963	617	144	238	293
1964	586	98	310	283
1965	394	89	283	235
1966	269	74	209	214
1967	249	99	183	171
1968	329	148	279	170
1969	650	334	403	135
1970	1 143	559	643	...
1971	1 008	264	331	...
1972	859	178	223	263
1973	879	364	313	451
1974	890	527	480	665
1975	766	450	517	640[2]
1976	945	522	871	669[3]
1977	1 475[1]	832[1]	1 187[1]	1 233[2]

Source: Public Ledger

[1]   Based on 2 qtrs only
[2]   Based on 1 qtr only, remainder unquoted
[3]   Based on 3 qtrs only
...   Not available

Jamaican No. 3, which it will be remembered is not the very best ginger from this source, can to a large extent be attributed to the high premium attached to it, but the relatively high price levels of the early 1960s were nonetheless a stimulus to the replacement of Jamaican ginger by less expensive gingers of slightly lower quality. Prices have on the whole remained high on account of supply problems and also of sustained high demand from the USA for Jamaican ginger.

No strong correlation seems to exist between the price of dried ginger and the volume of imports into particular countries, nor do high prices appear to bring about higher production levels in the producing countries. Annual fluctuations in price and volume of trade may be determined partly by the holding of stocks and by the inevitable speculative activity which can weaken the relationship between movements in price and in the volume of trade. The harvesting periods in Jamaica, India, Nigeria and Sierra Leone overlap to some extent, covering December to March, but the exporters exhibit a tendency to hold their stocks back in the hope of price increases. Thus the basic harvesting/ supply cycle is disturbed, and as a result the main importers do not normally experience much difficulty in obtaining their supplies at whatever time of the year it best suits them to do so. Undoubtedly there are periodic fluctuations in the stocks of both importers and exporters, but in general the number and geographical distribution of supplies combined with the speculative activities of intermediaries ensures that there are no months of the year in which a sudden spurt in demand could not normally be fully met.

The prices of dried ginger extractives, i.e., the essential oil and the oleoresin, are dealt with in the following section concerned with trends.

Preserved ginger

Prices for preserved ginger are published less widely than they used to be, particularly where the 'stem' and 'cargo-bold' qualities are concerned. For these qualities, recent prices have varied within the range £75–150 per tonne, c.i.f. Australian preserved ginger is rather more expensive and the average price for most grades has fluctuated around £150 per tonne, with the very best qualities fetching as much as £500 per tonne. Regrettably, continuous price series for preserved ginger are not nowadays available, but the movements in price during the 10 years up to 1963 are shown in Table 8.18.

Table 8.18 *Preserved ginger: Annual average prices (London c.i.f. spot, duty paid), 1953–63 (£ per tonne)*

	Stem	Medium[1]
1953	136	95
1954	247	176
1955	260	184
1956	176	128
1957	259	167
1958	165	117
1959	155	108
1960	161	125
1961	187	149
1962	147	106
1963	152	116

Source: Public Ledger

[1] The 'bold' grade was about 10 per cent more expensive and 'small medium' around 10 per cent less, during this period.

Fresh ginger

The price of fresh ginger is prone to wide seasonal fluctuations, certainly on the UK market. During the mid-1970s, the price fluctuated between £45 and £85 per tonne in the UK, depending upon the time of year and the source of supply, but it has reached as high as £150 per tonne. It has been known for fresh ginger to be air-freighted to its destinations to save time in transit, and it is then as much as three or four times as expensive as sea-freighted fresh ginger. Harvesting of fresh ginger commences in July in Fiji, May in Mauritius, November in St Vincent and February in St Lucia.

Trends in consumption and prospects

Dried ginger and its derivatives

The main uses of dried ginger are fairly similar to those of other spices. Most of it is ground in the importing countries before use, and in fact the grinding operation is certainly not unknown in the producing countries and entrepôt centres, although the quantities of ginger entering international trade in the ground state are not great. Some end-users prefer to grind their own ginger. It is likely that the proportion of total dried ginger consumption attributable to household culinary use is rather greater than for many other spices, so many and varied are its uses, although of course its uses are very widespread in other sectors. Ground ginger is used in home-made cakes and biscuits, puddings, and so on, the spice normally being retailed in cardboard drums of up to 100 g in weight. In the industrialized West there is probably still some room in the short and medium term for an increase in *per capita* consumption consequent on rising incomes, but in the longer term the rate of growth of this sector will be determined mainly by the rate of population growth.

The food industry is another very important user of the dried spice, although ginger oil and, particularly, ginger oleoresin have made considerable inroads into this area and have sharply retarded or even reversed the growth in its use. Bakery and confectionery products, meat preparations and sauces are typical of the wide range of products in which the spice is used, and now that the trend towards oleoresins has spent much of its force, the growth in demand for ginger in these applications should be roughly equivalent to the growth in demand for the food products themselves. Around 5 per cent of the dried ginger destined for industry is used in perfumery and pharmacy, for 'men's line' toiletries and in preparations for the combat of stomach disorders and throat infections, but it is probable that most of this consumption is in the form of essential oil or oleoresin rather than the dried spice.

Annual world consumption of ginger oleoresin is of the order of 150–300 tonnes at the present time. Its applications are similar to those of dried ginger and it is used dispersed on a base of either salt, rusk or dextrose, according to the intended application. Nowadays the majority of prepared Chinese dishes include some ginger oleoresins, and certain beverages based on the ginger flavour contain oleoresin as well as essential oil. Typical mid-1970s prices for dispersed oleoresin were in the range of £0.95–1.30 per kilogramme, the products prepared from the better grades of ginger naturally being the most expensive. Undispersed Nigerian ginger oleoresin, however, was quoted at £20 per kilogramme in the UK as a result of short supplies of dried ginger from both China and India. One effect of the increased consumption of ginger oleoresin has been an alteration in the chain of distribution to the food industry, flavour houses now occupying a more central position in the trade alongside the brokers and spice millers.

Initially, ginger oleoresin was produced mainly in the importing countries, but in the early 1970s production was started in some of the growing countries, in some cases under the control of Western-based flavour houses, but also increasingly by local entrepreneurs following independent investment. China is reported as having been a producer of a form of ginger oleoresin for many years, but this has not normally appeared on the world market.

The fourth major outlet for dried ginger is in the manufacture of ginger oil. Probably the greater part of world production of this spice oil originates in Western Europe and North America; but there are several sources among the ginger producers, mainly China, and the oil is also produced in Malaysia, Indonesia, Sri Lanka and the West Indies.

The major single use for ginger oil is as a flavouring material for various beverages, both alcoholic and non-alcoholic. Ginger wine and ginger ale are obvious examples. It is used in confectionery, and in modern spicy perfumes as well as in the traditional warm and sweet oriental fragrances. It is also occasionally added to the oleoresin to restore an ideal balance between aroma and pungency, a balance which is sometimes upset by the extraction process.

The long-term prospects for this oil seem to be steady and on a moderately upward trend. No steps seem to have been taken with a view to synthesizing the oil, although its price has sometimes fluctuated sharply. Annual world consumption is, however, only of the order of 10–20 tonnes, so the prospects for large-scale expansion of production are far from good. It is likely, however, that many end-users distil their own oil. Chinese oil has normally been marketed at between £10 and £33 per kilogramme, although in 1974 there was a pronounced peak of £38 per kilogramme. Indonesian oil, which in previous years was generally substantially more expensive than supplies from other ginger-growing countries, was quoted in 1977 at £24 per kilogramme, being much below the prices of Sri Lankan oil sold at £30 per kilogramme and the Chinese oil already mentioned above. Importer-distilled oils, however, are comparatively very expensive and 1977 prices ranged from £50 to £100 per kilogramme.

Generally speaking, the world market for dried ginger is stable. One or two consuming countries, notably those of the Middle East and Western Asia, seem to import fairly constant quantities without any significant long-term increase, while on the other hand there are countries, such as the UK and Canada, in which ginger consumption slumped sharply during the Second World War and has not yet recovered to its former levels. Trade opinions as to the future prospects for this market vary, but, it is possible that of the three basic forms of ginger, the dried product offers the greatest scope for aspiring new entrants in the longer term.

Preserved ginger

Although quantities of preserved ginger are retailed in jars or are converted into crystallized ginger, most of it is used by the preserve, sauce, pickle, confectionery and baking trades. None is used outside the food trade. The prospects for ginger in this form do not look encouraging. In the UK, which is the main market in Western Europe, there has been no significant upward movement since the 1950s, while growth in other markets, such as the Netherlands, has been only moderate. Australia's remarkable success in this market seems unlikely to be repeated by any prospective supplier.

Fresh ginger

The recent growth of Taiwan's export of fresh ginger to Hong Kong for use in the latter's preserving industry suggests that in this respect at least there may be some prospect for moderately increased international trade in fresh ginger. The raw product is, however, used mainly for culinary purposes, and in this respect increased usage would probably result mainly from population growth but will not generate much additional international trade, in view of the likelihood of increased production in the main consuming countries. The overall prospect is therefore not a very encouraging one for intending new producers of fresh ginger, for the international trade in fresh ginger which is destined for the preserving industry is not a very large proportion of the total trade in this item.

In conclusion, it may be stressed that the past fluctuations in the exports of existing producers render extremely hazardous any attempts to predict how much room there will be for new producers, although, provided the price is right and the quality consistent, users seem generally prepared to give full and due consideration to gingers on offer from unfamiliar sources.

References

Aiyadurai, S.G. (1966) *A Review of Research on Spices and Cashewnut in India.*, Ernakulam − 6; Indian Council of Agric. Res.

Akamine, E.K. (1962) *Storage of Fresh Ginger Rhizomes*, Univ. of Hawaii: Hawaii Agric. Expt. Stat., Bull. no. 130, July 1962.

Ananthakrishna, S.M. and Govindarajan, V.S. (1974) 'Evaluation of spices and oleoresins. IV. Estimation of pungent principles of ginger oleoresin', *Lebensm. Wiss. Tech.*, **7**, 220−2.

Anon. (1951) *Soil Conservation and Land Use in Sierra Leone*, Colony and Protectorate of Sierra Leone: Sessional Paper No. 1 of 1951.

Anon. (1953) *Report of the Spices Enquiry Committee*, New Delhi: Indian Counc. of Agric. Res.

Anon. (1959) 'Oil of ginger', *Essenoil News*, **2**(1), Feb., 1−8.

Anon. (1962a) *Memorandum on Ginger*, Trop. Prod. Instit. Report 13/62.

Anon. (1962b) *The Farmer's Guide*, Kingston: Jamaica Agric. Soc.

Anon. (1976) *The Wealth of India*, Vol. XI. New Delhi: Counc. of Sci. and Industrial Res.

Arctander, S. (1960) *Perfume and Flavour Materials of Natural Origin*, Elizabeth, N. J.: Published by the author.

Arigoni, D. and Jeger, O. (1954) 'Uber die absolute Konfiguration des Zingiberens', *Helv. Chim. Acta*, **37**, 881−3.

Bednarczyk, A.A. and Kramer, A. (1975) 'Identification and evaluation of the flavour significant components of ginger essential oil', *Chemical Senses and Flavour*, **1**, 377−86.

Bednarczyk, A.A., Galetto, W. G. and Kramer, A. (1975) '*Cis*- and *trans*-beta-sesqui-phellandrol. Two new sesquitrepenes from oil of ginger', *J. Agric. Food Chem.*, **23**, 499−501.

Bendall, R.L. and Daly, R.A. (1966) 'Ginger growing in the Nambour Area, Queensland', *Quarterly Rev. Agric Econ.*, **19**, 83−96.

Bertram, J. and Walbaum, H. (1894) 'Ginger oil', *J. Prakt. Chem.*, **49**, 15.

Brooks, B.T. (1916) 'Zingiberol', *J. Amer. Chem. Soc.*, **38**, 430−2.

Brown, B.I. (1969) 'Processing and preserving ginger by syruping under atmospheric conditions. (1) Preliminary investigation of vat systems; (2) Effects of syrup temperature, flow rate and sucrose/RS ratio on the processing of ginger in invert sugar; (3) Processing techniques and syrup concentration for maximum dried weight recovery of syruped ginger', *Food Tech. Australia*, **23**, 87−91, 93−100, 109−12,

Brown, B.I. (1971) 'Progressive trends in the Australian ginger industry', *Australian Food Manufac.*, **41** (3), Oct., 16, 19.

Brown, B.I. (1972) 'Ginger storage in acidified sodium metabisulphite solutions', *J. Food Technol.*, **7**, 153−62.

Brown, B.I. and Lloyd, A.C. (1972) 'Investigations of ginger storage in salt brine', *J. Food Technol.*, **7**, 309−21.

Brown, E. (1958) 'Discovery and production of spices', *The Times British Colonies Review*, 2nd quarter, 8−9.

Bureau of Agricultural Economics, Canberra (1971) *The Australian Ginger Growing Industry*, Canberra: Australian Govt. Publishing Service.

Burkill, I.H. (1966) *A Dictionary of the Economic Products of the Malay Peninsula*, Kuala Lumpur: Ministry of Agriculture and Co-operatives.

Chattopadhyay, S.B. (1967) *Diseases of Plants Yielding Drugs, Dyes and Spices*, New Delhi: Indian Council of Agric. Res.

Clarke, J.I. (1966) *Sierra Leone in Maps*, London: Univ. of London Press.

Clevenger, J.F. (1928) 'Analysis of ginger and its preparation', *J. Amer. Pharmaceut. Assoc.*, **17**, 630–4.

Colbran, R.C. (1972) 'Studies of root-knot nematode control in ginger with non-volatile nematocides applied at and after planting', *Queensland J. Agric. Anim. Sci.*, **29**, 275–80.

Connell, D.W. (1969) 'The pungent principles of ginger and their importance in certain ginger products', *Food Tech. Australia*, **21**, 570–1, 573, 575.

Connell, D.W. (1970) 'The chemistry of the essential oil and oleoresin of ginger', *Flav. Ind.*, **1**, 677–93.

Connell, D.W. and Jordan, R.A. (1971) 'Composition and distinctive volatile flavour characteristics of the essential oil from Australian-grown ginger', *J. Sci. Food Agric.*, **22**, 93–5.

Connell, D.W. and McLachlan, R. (1972) 'Natural pungent compounds. IV. Examination of the gingerols, shogaols, paradols and related compounds by thin-layer and gas-chromatography', *J. Chromatog.*, **67**, 29–35.

Connell, D.W. and Sutherland, M.D. (1966) 'Terpenoid chemistry.XI. (–)-beta-sesquiphellandrene', *Austral. J. Chem.*, **19**, 283–8.

Connell, D.W. and Sutherland, M.D. (1969) 'A re-examination of gingerol, shogaol and zingerone. The pungent principles of ginger', *Austral. J. Chem.*, **22**, 1033–43.

Dodge, F.D. (1912) 'Ginger oil', *Proc. of 8th Int. Congr. Appl. Chem.*, Washington, **6**, 77.

Elsdon, G.D. and Mayne, C. (1937) 'The examination of ginger', *Analyst*, **62**, 835–40.

Eschenmoser, A. and Schintz, H. (1950) 'Zur Kenntniss der Sesquiterpene und Azulene. 91: Zur Konstitution des Zingiberens', *Helv. Chim. Acta*, **33**, 171–7.

Fennah, R.G. (1947) *The Insect Pests of Food-Crops in the Lesser Antilles*, Depts of Agric. Windward and Leeward Islands.

Garnett, H. and Grier, J. (1907) 'The pungent principles of ginger – a preliminary note', *Pharm. J.*, **25**, 118–20.

Garnett, H. and Grier, J. (1909) 'Note on the determination of gingerol in ginger', *Yb. Pharm. Trans. Br. Pharm. Conf.*, 344–6.

Gerhardt, U. (1969) 'Routineuntersuchungen von Gewurzen auf aetherische Oelgehalte und andere Inhaltstoffe. IV', *Fleischwirtschaft*, **49**, 1356–8.

Geus, J.G. de (1973) *Fertilizer Guide for the Tropics and Subtropics*, 2nd edn, Zurich: Centre d'Étude de l'Azote.

Gildemeister, E. and Hoffmann, Fr. (1956) *Die Aetherischen Oele*, Vol. IV, Berlin: Akademie Verlag.

Goldman, A. (1949) 'How spice oleoresins are made', *Amer. Perfumer and Essential Oil Review*, **53**, 320–3.

Gollifer, D.E. (1973) 'The introduction of spice crops into the British Solomon Islands', *Proceedings of the Conference on Spices, 10–14 April 1972*, London: Tropical Products Institute.

Govindarajan, V.S. and Raghuveer, K.G. (1973) 'Evaluation of spice oils and oleoresins by thin-layer chromatography', *Lab. Practice*, **22** 414–16.

Groszmann, H.M. (1954) 'Ginger production', *Queensland Agric. J.*, **78**, 259–62.

Guenther, E. (1952) *The Essential Oils*, Vol V, New York: D. Van Nostrand Co.

Guenther, E. (1958) 'Ginger production in Jamaica', *Coffee and Tea Ind.*, **81**, 73–4.

Guenther, E. (1959) 'Ginger production in Jamaica', *Coffee and Tea Ind.*, **82**, 169–70.

Gupta, R. (1974) 'Process ginger for new products', *Indian Farming*, **23** (12), 7–9, 14.

Gupta, G.K. and Verma, B.R. (1966) 'Fungal foes that menace ginger crops', *Indian Farming*, **16**, 15.

Hayward, A.C., Moffett, M.L. and Pegg, K.G. (1967) 'Bacterial wilt of ginger in Queensland', *Queenland J. Agric. Anim. Sci.*, **24**, 1–5.

Herout, V., Benesova, V. and Pliva, J. (1953) 'On terpenes XLI. The sesquiterpenes of ginger oil', *Coll. Czech. Chem. Comm.*, **18**, 248–56.

Holttum, R.E. (1950) 'The Zingiberaceae of the Malay Peninsula', *Gardens' Bull.*, *Singapore*, **13**, 1–249.

Ingleton, J.F. (1966) 'Preserved and crystallised ginger', *Confectionery Prod.*, 32, 527-8.

Jain, T.C., Varma, K.R. and Bhattacharyya, S.C. (1962) 'Terpenoids'. XXVIII. GLC analysis of monoterpenes and its applications to essential oils', *Perfumery Essent. Oil Record*, 53, 678-84.

Jogi, B.S., Ishwar Pal Singh, Dua, H.S. and Sukhija, P.S. (1972) 'Changes in crude fibre, fat and protein content in ginger at different stages of ripening', *Indian J. Agric. Sci.*, 42, 1011. 42, 1011.

Kami, T., Nakayama, M. and Hayashi, S. (1972) 'Volatile constituents of *Zingiber officinale*', *Phytochem.*, 11, 3377-81.

Kannan, K. and Nair, K.P.V. (1965) '*Zingiber officinale* (ginger) in Kerala', *Madras Agric. J.*, 52, 163-76.

Kasasian, L. (1971) *Weed Control in the Tropics*, London: Leonard Hill.

Khan, K.F. (1959) 'Ensure two-fold ginger yield', *Indian Farming*, 9, 10-11.

Kulka, K. (1967) 'Aspects of functional groups and flavour', *J. Agric. Food Chem.*, 15, 48-57.

Kumara Das, C. (1929) 'Preservation of ginger in syrup', *Dept. of Industries, Travancore, Bull. no. 29.*

Lapworth, A., Pearson, L.K. and Royle, F.A. (1917) 'The pungent principles of ginger. Part I: The chemical characters and decomposition products of Thresh's "Gingerol" ', *J. Chem. Soc.*, 777-90.

Lapworth, A. and Wykes, F.H. (1917) 'The pungent principles of ginger. Part II: Synthetic preparations of zingerone, methyl zingerone and some related compounds', *J. Chem. Soc.*, 790-8.

Leverington, R.E. (1969) 'Ginger processing investigations. 3: Improving the quality of processed ginger', *Queensland J. Agric. Anim. Sci.*, 26, 264-70.

Lewis, Y.S., Mathew, A.G., Nambudri, E.S. and Krishnamurthy, N. (1972) 'Oleoresin ginger', *Flav. Ind.*, 3, 78-81.

Maistre, J. (1964) *Les Plantes à Épices*, Paris: Maisonneuve & Larose.

Marsh, A.C., Moss, M.K. and Murphy, E.W. (1977) *Composition of Foods, Spices and Herbs. Raw. Processed. Prepared.* Washington DC: USDA Agric. Res. Serv. Agric. Handbook, No. 8-2.

Masada, Y., Inoue, T., Hashimoto, K., Fujioka, M. and Shiraki, K. (1973) 'Studies of the pungent principles of ginger by GC-MS', *J. Pharm. Soc. Japan*, 93, 318-21.

Masada, Y., Inoue, T., Hashimoto, K., Fujioka, M. and Uchino, C. (1974) 'Studies of the constituents of ginger by GC-MS', *J. Pharm. Soc. Japan*, 94, 735-8.

Mathew, A.G., Krishnamurthy, N., Nambudri, E.S. and Lewis, Y.S. (1973) 'Oil of ginger', *Flav. Ind.*, 4, 226-8.

Mills, J.A. (1952) 'Correlations between monocyclic and polycyclic unsaturated compounds from molecular rotation differences', *J. Chem. Soc.*, 4976-85.

Muralidharan, A. and Kamalam, N. (1973) 'Improved ginger means more foreign exchange', *Indian Farming*, 22 (10), 37.

Nair, P.C.S. and Varma, A.S. (1971) 'Ginger in Kerala', *Indian Farming*, 20, 37.

Nambudri, E.S., Mathew, A.G., Krishnamurthy, N. and Lewis, Y. S. (1975) 'Quantitative determination of the pungent principles in ginger', *Flavours*, 6, 135, 137.

Natarajan, C.P., Kuppuswamy, S., Shankaracharya, N.B., Padma Bai, R., Raghavan, B., Krishnamurthy, M. N., Fazlulla Khan, Lewis, Y.S. and Govindarajan, V.S. (1970) 'Product development of ginger', *Indian Spices*, 7(4), 8-12, 24-8.

Natarajan, C. P., Padma Bai, R., Krishnamurthy, M.N., Raghavan, B., Shankaracharya, N.B., Kuppuswamy, S., Govindarajan, V.S. and Lewis, Y.S. (1972) 'Chemical composition of ginger varieties and dehydration studies on ginger', *J. Food Sci. Technol. (India)*, 9, 120-24.

Naves, Y.R. (1974) *Technologie et Chimie des Parfums Naturels*, Paris: Masson et Cie.

Nelson, E.K. (1917) 'Gingerol and paradol', *J. Amer. Chem. Soc.*, 39, 1466-9.

Nigam, M.C., Nigam, I.C., Levi, L. and Handa, K.L. (1964) 'Essential oils and their

Chem., **42**, 2610−15.

Nomura, H. (1918) 'The pungent principles of ginger', Part I: A new ketone, zingerone', *J. Chem. Soc.*, 769−76.

Nomura, H. (1918) 'The pungent principles of ginger'. *Sci. Rep. Tohaku Imp. Univ.*, **7**, 67.

Nomura, H. and Tsurami, S. (1927) 'The pungent principles of ginger. Part IV: Synthesis of shogaol', *Proc. Imp. Acad. Tokyo*, **3**, 159.

Nomura, H. and Iwamoto, K. (1928) 'The pungent principles of ginger', *Sci. Rep. Tohaku Imp. Univ.*, **17**, 973.

Parry, E. J. (1948) 'Resins', in *Allen's Commercial Organic Analysis*, Vol. 5, Philadelphia: The Blakiston Co.

Paulose, T.T. (1970) 'Development of ginger in India', *Indian Spices*, **7** (2), 2.

Paulose, T.T. (1973) 'Ginger cultivation in India', *Proceedings of the Conference on Spices, 10−14 April, 1972*, London: Tropical Products Institute.

Pliva, J., Horaka, M., Herout, V. and Sorm, I. (1960) *Sammlung der Spectren und Physikalischen Konstanten; Teil 1: Sesquiterpene*, Berlin: Akademie Verlag.

Pomeranz, Y. (1977) 'Food and food products in the People's Republic of China', *Food Technol.*, **31** (3), March, 32−41.

Prentice, A. (1959) 'Ginger in Jamaica', *World Crops*, **11**, 25−6.

Purseglove, J.W. (1972) *Tropical Crops: Monocotyledons*, London: Longman.

Randhawa, K.S. and Nandpuri, K.S. (1970) 'Ginger (*Zingiber officinale* Rosc.) in India − A review', *Punjab Hort. J.*, **10**, 111−22.

Randhawa, K.S., Nandpuri, K.S. and Bajwa, M.S. (1972a) 'Studies of the comparative efficacy of different sizes of seed and spacings on the yield of ginger (*Zingiber officinale* Rosc.)', *J. Resc., India*, **9** (2), 239−41.

Randhawa, K.S., Nandpuri, K.S. and Bajwa, M.S. (1972b) 'The growth and yield of ginger (*Zingiber officinale* Rosc.) as influenced by different dates of sowing', *J. Resc., India*, **9** (1), 32−4.

Redgrove, H.S. (1933) *Spices and Condiments*, London: Pitman.

Richardson, K.C. (1966) 'Effect of dehydration temperature on the quality of dried ginger', *Food Tech. Australia*, Feb., 93−5.

Richardson, K.C. (1967) 'Packaging and storage of dried ginger', *Food Tech. Assist.*, **19**, June, 165−6.

Ridley, H.N. (1912) *Spices*, London: Macmillan.

Rodriquez, D.W. (1971) *Ginger*, Kingston: Ministry of Agric. and Fisheries, Agric. Planning Unit, Jamaica.

Rosengarten, F., Jr. (1969) *The Book of Spices*, Wynnewood: Livingston Publishing Co.

Ruzicka, L. and Van Veen, A.G. (1929) 'Constitution of zingiberene', *Liebigs Ann.*, **468**, 143−62.

Salzer, U.-J. (1975a) 'Analytical evaluation of seasoning extracts (oleoresins) and essential oils from seasonings. II', *Flavours*, 206−10.

Salzer, U.-J. (1975b) 'Uber die Fettesaurezusammensetzung der Lipoide einiger Gewurze', *Fette, Seifen, Anstrichmittel*, **77**, 446−50.

Schimmel and Co. (1905) 'Ginger oil', *Ber. Schimmel*, Oct., 38.

Schreiner, O. and Kremers, E. (1901) 'Ginger oil', *Pharm. Arch.*, **4**, 141.

Seely, C. (1975) 'Australia produces ginger to order', *Baking Ind. J.*, **8**, 28, 30.

Semmler, F.W. and Becker, A. (1913) 'Ginger oil', *Chem. Ber.*, **46**, 1814.

Shrapnel, G.S. (1967) 'The technological development of the green ginger industry in Australia', *Food Tech. Australia*, **19** (13), 604−7.

Singh, I.P., Jogi, B.S., Dua, H.S. and Gupta, M.L. (1975) 'Tentative identification of various components and fatty acids in ginger lipids', *Indian J. Agric. Sci.*, **45** 545−9.

Soden, H.V. and Rojahn, W. (1900) 'Ginger oil', *Pharm. Ztg.*, **45**, 414.

Soffer, M.D., Steinhardt, C., Turner, G. and Stebbins, M.E. (1944) 'Structure of isozingiberene', *J. Amer. Chem. Soc.*, **66**, 1520−3.

Sundaram, M. (1960) 'Ginger earns good income for the West Coast', *Indian Farming*, **9** (4), 12.

Teakle, D.S. (1965) 'Fusarium rhizome rot of ginger in Queensland', *Queensland J. Agric. Anim. Sci.*, **22**, 263–72.

Terhune, S.J., Hogg, J.W., Bromstein, A.C. and Lawrence, B.M. (1975) 'Four new sesquiterpene analogues of common monoterpenes', *Canad. J. Chem.*, **53**, 3285–93.

Tewson, L. (1966) 'Australian ginger', *World Crops*, **18** (3), 62–5.

Thiessen, F. (1970) 'Behaviour of natural spices and essences when subjected to heat. II', *Fleischwirtschaft*, **50**, 813–15.

Thomas, K.M. (1966) ' "Rio-de-Janiero" will double your ginger yield', *Indian Farming*, **15** (10), 15.

Thresh, J.C. (1879) 'Proximate analysis of the rhizome of *Zingiber officinalis* and comparative examinations of typical specimens of commercial gingers', *Pharm. J.*, **10**, 171.

Thresh, J.C. (1881) 'The chemistry of *Zingiber officinalis*', *Pharm. J.*, **12**, 243.

Thresh, J.C. (1884) 'Further contributions to the chemistry of *Zingiber officinalis*', *Pharm. J.*, **15**, 208.

Varma, K.R.. Jain, T.C. and Bhattacharyya, S.C. (1962) 'Structure and stereo chemistry of zingiberol and juniper camphor', *Tetrahedron*, **18**, 979–84.

West, T.F. (1939) 'Addition of nitrosyl chloride to beta-phellandrene and the occurrence of the phellandrenes in some essential oils', *J. Soc. Chem. Ind.*, **58**, 122–5.

Whiley, A.W. (1974) 'Ginger growing in Queensland', *Queensland Agric. J.*, **100** (11), 551–7.

Winterton, D. and Richardson, K. (1965) 'An investigation of the chemical constituents of Queensland ginger', *Queensland J. Agric. Anim. Sci.*, **22**, 205–14.

Winton, A.L. and Winton, K.B. (1939) *The Structure and Composition of Foods*, Vol. IV, New York: John Wiley & Sons.

Yamagishi, T., Hayashi, K. and Mitsuhashi, M. (1972) 'Isolation of hexahydrocurcumin, dihydrogingerol and two additional pungent principles from ginger', *Chem. Pharm. Bull. (Japan)*, **20**, 2291–2.

Yegna Narayan Aiyer, A.K. (1944) *Field Crops of India*, Bangalore: Govt. Press.

Chapter 9

Turmeric

The rhizomes of *Curcuma domestica* Val.* (syn. *C. longa* Koenig *non* L.) are used as a spice and are best known in Europe and America for this purpose. Turmeric is an important spice among the rice-eating peoples of India, South East Asia and Indonesia and is indispensable in the preparation of curry powder. Its main use in the Western world is now for this purpose, and it gives the musky flavour and yellow colour to curries. Curry powder usually contains about 24 per cent of turmeric powder, and may only be exceeded in quantity by coriander seeds (*Coriandrum sativum* L.). Other ingredients usually included are: cumin seeds (*Cuminum cyminum* L.), cardamoms (*Elettaria cardamomum* Maton), fenugreek seeds (*Trigonella foenum-graecum* L.), chillies (*Capsicum annuum* L., *C. frutescens* L.), ginger (*Zingiber officinale* Rosc.), pepper (*Piper nigrum* L.) and dill seeds (*Anethum graveolens* L.). In India curry powders are specially prepared as required and the ingredients will depend on the sort of meat or other food being curried. Rosengarten (1969) states that curry powder may contain as few as 3 or as many as 30 species. On the average it contains 15 or 20. Other species may include: cinnamon (*Cinnamomum verum* Presl.), cloves (*Syzygium aromaticum* (L.) Merr. & Perry), nutmegs and mace (*Myristica fragrans* Houtt.), fennel seeds (*Foeniculum vulgare* Mill.), celery seeds (*Apium graveolens* L.), mustard seeds (*Brassica juncea* (L.) Czern. & Coss.), caraway seeds (*Carum carvi* L.), poppy seed (*Papaver somniferum* L.), sesame (*Sesamum indicum* L.), saffron (*Crocus sativus* L.) and leaves of the curry-leaf tree (*Murraya koenigii* (L.) Spreng.).

Turmeric is not known in a truly wild state and the country with far the greatest production is India, which is also the principal exporter of the crop. In addition to its use as a spice, it has other uses that are prominent in the life of the people of southern Asia, and has acquired magical properties in connection with birth, marriage, death and in agriculture. These uses spread widely in Oceania, but it is not used as a condiment in Melanesia and Polynesia.

---

* *Curcum domesticia* Val. is the correct botanical name for turmeric, but *C. longa* is sometimes used in the literature to describe the finger rhizomes and *C. rotunda* for the bulbous central rhizomes.

Turmeric is an important yellow dye in southern Asia; it was also used in Europe before the discovery of aniline dyes. Cultivars with harder, darker-coloured, less aromatic rhizomes are preferred for dyes. The rhizomes are boiled with a little water and made into a paste. With lime or other alkalis, it produces a red or reddish-brown colour. It can be used for dying cotton, silk or wool without a mordant, but the colour is fugitive.

Turmeric powder and water are used as cosmetics in India and elsewhere in South East Asia. Rice, coloured yellow with turmeric, is used on ceremonial occasions. Turmeric is used as a protective charm and in primitive medicine, both externally and internally, in southern Asia. It is used as a colouring matter in pharmacy, confectionery and food industries. Yellow turmeric paper can be used as a test for alkalinity, which turns it brown.

History

Sopher (1964) considers that 'the wild *Curcuma* from which *C. domestica* evolved may first have attracted attention as an incidental source of food, but the important property that became the object of conscious selection was the yellowish colour of the rhizome. As a quickly growing plant with a strikingly coloured rhizome, turmeric acquired magical properties, some apparently associated with the fertility of the earth . . . Attitudes and practices expressing these ideas would be disseminated together with human dispersal of the plant over a wide area.'

Turmeric was domesticated in southern or South East Asia. Raghavan and Venkatasubban (1943) believe that *C. domestica* is likely to have arisen by a process of triploidy, either from *C. aromatica* Salisb. or a form similar to it with 42 chromosomes. *C. aromatica* is a native of India from the eastern Himalayas to Sri Lanka, but it may be that some other diploid form, closely related morphologically to *C. domestica*, may be the true ancestral form. *C. domestica* is not now known in a wild state with certainty, but it seems to have arisen by continued selection and cultivation by vegetative propagation. It was earlier grown in India.

Sopher (1964) states that 'the distribution of uses of turmeric in domestic sites outside India, especially in Celebes, the Moluccas and Polynesia, indicates their antiquity, and suggests an early cultural connection between the people of these areas and the indigenous, pre-Aryan cultivators of India.' He suggests that 'the indigenous use of turmeric in magical rites intended to produce fertility then became an important part of the established Hindu ceremony, and as such was taken to the Hinduized kingdoms of South-east Asia.'

Turmeric seems to have reached China before the seventh century

A.D. Marco Polo records it as occurring at Koncha in China in 1280 and describes it, according to Ridley (1912), as 'a vegetable which has all the properties of true saffron, as well the smell as the colour, and yet it is not really saffron.'

The uses of turmeric by the Betsileo people of the Malagasy Republic suggest that the introduction was of Malayo – Polynesian origin. Burkill (1966), quoting Hammerstein, states that turmeric reached East Africa in the eighth century and West Africa in the thirteenth century; it is used in the latter area only as a dye. It was introduced into Jamaica by Edwards in 1783, where it has now become naturalized. The crop has now become widely distributed throughout the tropics, but its cultivation as a spice is largely confined to India, South East Asia and Indonesia.

Botany

Systematics

Curcuma longa of Linnaeus was based on a plant observed by Hermann in Ceylon (now Sri Lanka) and is not this species. *C. longa* of Koenig is probably the true turmeric, but as this name belongs to another species, Valeton proposed the new name of *C. domestica* in 1918.

Willis (1966) states that there are 5 species of *Curcuma*, which is obviously a mistake. Bailey (1949) says that there are 40–50 species, while Sastri (1950) says there are about 70. Shankaracharya and Natarajan (1973) state that, in India, nearly 30 species have been recognized by botanists. The centre of distribution is the Indo-Malesia region and they extend to Australia.

A brief account of some of the other species of *Curcuma* which are used and are occasionally cultivated is given at the end of the section on *C. domestica* (pp. 541 – 43).

Cytology

Darlington and Wylie (1955) give the basic chromosome number for the genus as $x = 16$ and 21. They give the somatic chromosome number of *C. domestica* as $2n = 32$ according to Sato (1948, quoted in Darlington and Wylie, 1955), 62 according to Raghavan and Venkatasubban (1943), and 64 according to Sugiura (1931, quoted in Darlington and Wylie, 1955). Sopher (1964) states that *C. domestica* is a sterile triploid, but Aiyadurai (1966) reports the presence of seeds, the germination of which is speeded up by treatment with concentrated sulphuric acid.

Structure

Turmeric is an erect perennial herb, but is grown as an annual.

Roots, stems and leaves

The primary tuber at the base of the aerial stem is ellipsoidal, about 5 cm by 2.5 cm, bearing many rhizomes, 5–8 cm long, 1.5 cm thick, straight or a little curved, with secondary branches in two rows, which may have tertiary branches, the whole forming a dense clump. The rhizomes have a distinctive taste and smell. They are brownish and scaly outside and inside are a bright orange colour. The young tips are white. The roots are fleshy, often ending in a swollen tuber to 4 cm by 2 cm.

The leafy shoots rarely exceed 1 m in height and are erect, bearing 6–10 leaves with the leaf sheaths forming a pseudostem. The thin petiole is rather abruptly broadened to the sheath. The ligule is a small lobe, about 1 mm long. The lamina is lanceolate, acuminate and thin, dark green above and pale green beneath with pellucid dots; it is usually up to 30 cm long and 7–8 cm wide, and is rarely over 50 cm long. The sheath near the ligule has ciliate margins.

Inflorescence

This is a cylindrical spike, 10–15 cm long and 5–7 cm wide, which is terminal on the leaf shoot with the scape partly enclosed by the leaf sheaths. The bracts are adnate for less than half their length and are elliptic-lanceolate and acute, 5–6 cm long and about 2.5 cm wide. The upper sterile bracts are white or white streaked with green, pink-tipped in some cultivars, grading to light-green bracts lower down. The bracteoles are thin, elliptic and up to 3.5 cm long. The flowers are borne in cincinni of two in the axils of the bracts, opening one at a time, and are thin-textured and fugacious, about 5 cm long. The calyx is short, unequally toothed and split nearly half-way down one side. The corolla is tubular at the base with the upper half cup-shaped with three unequal lobes inserted on the edge of the cup lip; it is whitish, thin and translucent with the dorsal lobe hooded. There are two lateral staminodes, elliptic-oblong, which are creamy white in colour, and with the inner edges folded under the hood of the dorsal petal. The lip or labellum is obovate, with a broad thickened yellow band down the centre and thinner creamy white side-lobes upcurved and overlapping the staminodes. The filament of the stamen is short and broad, united to a versatile anther about the middle of the parallel pollen sacs, and with a broad, curved large spur at the base. The cylindrical stylodes are about 4 mm long. The ovary is inferior and trilocular with a slender style passing between the anther lobes and held by them. Fruits are seldom, if ever produced.

Cultivars

A number of cultivars are distinguished in India by the names of the localities in which they are grown. Several appear in the trade, some of which may not be *C. domestica*. Two cultivars are grown in Bombay

Fig. 9.1 *Curcuma domestica*: Turmeric. A, plant ($\times \frac{1}{5}$); B, base of plant with rhizome ($\times \frac{2}{5}$); C, inflorescence ($\times \frac{2}{5}$); D, flower ($\times \frac{4}{5}$). C-D after Brown (1951).

(Maharastra), one with hard bright-coloured rhizomes which are commonly used in dyeing, and the other with larger, softer, more aromatic, lighter-coloured rhizomes which produce the best spice. Two cultivars grown in Assam and West Bengal are 'Deshi' and 'Patani', the latter having the better colour and flavour. 'Chinna nadan' and 'Perum nadan' are grown in Bhavani and Erode Taluks of Tamil Nadu, the former being more extensively cultivated because it grows more vigorously and its rhizome has a sweeter aroma (Sastri, 1950). Yegna Narayan Aiyer (1944) says that in some parts of Mysore three types of turmeric are distinguished: 'Mundaga', in which the clump of corms is larger and thick set with many fingers; 'Balaga', in which the corms are not so thick and so many in number; 'Yelachaga', with few small corms and numerous roots. He says that crops are generally mixtures, but when seed corms are selected the third kind is as far as possible picked out and removed. It is stated by Sastri (1950) that turmeric cultivated in the hills is reported to be of a better quality than that raised in the plains and that the same cultivar when grown in the plains and on the hills shows distinct differences in quality and yield. Madras turmeric is highly esteemed in the market. Rama Rao *et al.* (1975) state that about 100 types were collected from different districts of Andhra Pradesh, and from other turmeric-growing areas in India, for screening. Seven named types were assessed to be superior for multiplication in the turmeric-growing regions of the state. Krishnamurthy *et al.* (1975) obtained from the Research Stations in Andhra Pradesh, Maharashtra and Kerala, dried and cured turmeric of 25 local cultivars, collected from various cultivating centres in India, for examination of the curcumin content. Krishnamurthy *et al.* (1976) acquired, from the same sources, samples of 12 cultivars, in cured and dried form, for an investigation of the volatile oil and oleoresin of turmeric. A few were repeated in the three inquiries, but a total of 30 named cultivars were investigated, none of which are included in the foregoing remarks.

Ecology

Climate and soils

Turmeric can be cultivated in most areas of the tropics and subtropics provided that rainfall is adequate or facilities for irrigation are available. It requires a hot and moist climate. It is usually grown in regions with an annual rainfall of 1 000–2 000 mm; below 1 000 mm irrigation is required. Cultivation has been extended into wetter areas with over 2 000 mm of rain per annum. It can be grown up to an altitude of 1 220 m in the Himalayan foothills.

Turmeric thrives best on loamy or alluvial, loose, friable, fertile soils and cannot stand waterlogging. Gravelly, stony and heavy clay soils are unsuitable for the development of the rhizomes.

Turmeric can be rotated with crops such as finger millet (*Eleusine coracana*), rice and sugar cane. It is rarely cultivated in a pure stand, but is usually grown mixed with such crops as castor, maize, finger millet, onions, brinjal (aubergine) and tomato. Aiyadurai (1966) states that turmeric is not adversely affected by partial shade and that it can with advantage be mixed with sunnhemp without its yield being depressed.

Cultivation

Propagation

Turmeric is always propagated vegetatively by fingers or rhizomes with one or two buds. The literature gives variable advice on the form of rhizomes to plant. Aiyadurai (1966) states that in Orissa, mother rhizomes were found to be better than daughter rhizomes for use as seed material, that sprouts measuring 8 to 12 ins (20–30 cm) detached from sprouting rhizomes were found to be the best planting material and also recorded the highest yield. Studies on the effect of moist soil, moist sand, moist sawdust and moist paddy straw on the mother rhizomes for inducing early sprouting showed no difference among the treatments. In Andhra Pradesh the mother rhizomes when planted as whole or even as split halves gave rise to more vigorous sprouts than the fingers, but finger rhizomes were observed to keep better in storage, remained more tolerant to wet soil conditions and involved a lower seed rate. Hussain and Said (1965) found that large side-rhizomes, 4 cm long, gave a better germination and higher yields than primary mother tubers, whole or cut, and smaller-sized side-rhizomes. Yegna Narayan Aiyer (1944) says that 'for planting purposes only the fingers are used and not the rounds'.

It is necessary to store the seed rhizomes for 2 to 3 months from harvest to planting. This may be done by spreading them thinly under a covering of turmeric leaves or storing them in heaps under a layer of straw and soil.

Planting and after-care

The land should be thoroughly prepared either by digging or by several ploughings to provide a good tilth. The crop can be planted on flat beds or on ridges. Aiyadurai (1966) states that the former were found to be preferable in Orissa. In Andhra Pradesh the broad-ridge method of planting was found to be superior and more profitable than the ridge-and-furrow method, as the elevated beds provided better drainage. Sastri (1950) says that the crop is planted on ridges 22–25 cm high and 45–50 cm broad, the channels between being used for irrigation when necessary. He gives the planting distance as 30–37 cm at a depth of 7.5

cm, with a planting rate of 1 700–2 000 kg per hectare. In Orissa, Aiyadurai (1966) states that a spacing of 22.5 × 22.5 cm gave the best results, while in Andhra Pradesh using the ridge-and-furrow method of planting, the optimum spacing appeared to be between 45 and 60 cm between the rows and 22.5 cm between the hills. In Sri Lanka 15 cm × 15 cm gave significantly more rhizomes than a spacing of 30 cm × 30 cm or more. As stated earlier, turmeric is often grown in mixed cultivation with other crops.

The usual time for planting in India is May and June.

Weeds should be controlled manually or by herbicides. Early weeding may be avoided by the use of 2,4-D as a pre-emergent herbicide. Probably, like ginger, it may be highly tolerant of simazine applied pre-emergence.

Where irrigation is carried out, the frequency will depend upon the weather and the moisture-retentive capacity of the soil. A good soaking is needed at planting and thereafter each week until sprouting is completed, after which less frequent irrigation may be required. Weeding and hoeing are necessary at intervals. Earthing-up may be necessary some 8 weeks or so after planting. In furrow-planted turmeric the rows are earthed-up by splitting the ridges between the furrows.

Germination of the setts is completed in 2 to 4 weeks. Flowering occurs after about 5 months and the rhizomes are then beginning to form. Active rhizome development continues until the crop is ready for lifting at about 7 to 9 months, when the lower leaves turn yellow. *C. aromatica* (kasturi) is ready for harvesting in 7 months. There are two forms of *C. domestica* – 'kasari' which may be harvested in 8 months; and 'longa', which requires 9 months in the soil before it is lifted.

Manuring

The crop is usually liberally manured with farmyard and green manure. Sometimes tank silt is applied. Cattle or sheep may be penned on the field. Aiyadurai (1966) states that the application of ammonium sulphate at the rate of 100 kg per hectare was found to benefit the rainfed turmeric crop and that it gave nearly 100 per cent increased yield over the unmanured crop. De Geus (1973) gives the following recommendations per hectare: for Gujarat, 100 kg N, 35–40 kg P_2O_5, and 60 kg K_2O, with all the phosphorus and potassium at planting and the nitrogen in two split applications, 1 and 3 months after planting; for Maharashtra, a basal dressing of about 25 tonnes of farmyard manure or compost, supplemented with 100 kg N and 50 kg P_2O_5; for Tamil Nadu, a basal dressing of 25 tonnes of farmyard manure or compost supplemented with 50–55 kg N, 50–55 kg P_2O_5 and 50–55 kg K_2O, with all the phosphorus and potassium at planting and half the nitrogen at planting and half as a top-dressing.

A mulching of sal leaves, *Shorea robusta*, has been found to be beneficial in India, but may be replaced by sunnhemp.

Harvesting and yields

In harvesting the turmeric crop, care should be taken that the rhizomes are not cut or bruised and that the whole clump is lifted out with the dry plant, including the base of the stems, a process described by Rama Rao *et al.* (1975). The leafy tops are then cut off, the roots removed, all the adhering earth is shaken or rubbed off, and the rhizomes are then well washed with water. The fingers, sometimes called the daughter rhizomes, are separated from the rounds or mothers. Yields are very variable. Aiyadurai (1966) gives the yields of fresh raw turmeric as from 16 800 to 22 400 kg per hectare in the case of an irrigated crop, and 6 720 to 8 960 kg per hectare under rain-fed conditions.

A few rhizomes may be used fresh and, apart from those that are required for replanting, the remainder are subjected to a process of curing and polishing, which is described and discussed in the 'Processing and manufacture' section.

Diseases

A leaf spot, caused by *Taphrina maculans* Butl., is commonly present in India, wherever the crop is grown. Spots appear in great numbers; they are yellow in colour, about 1–2 mm in diameter, and coalesce freely. Chattopadhyay (1967) recommends spraying with Bordeaux mixture.

Another leaf spot, caused by *Colletotrichum* (*Vermicularia*) *capsici* (Syd.) Butl. & Bisby, is probably present throughout India, but occurs in serious form only in Tamil Nadu and Andhra Pradesh. It was first described as *Vermicularia curcumae* Syd., which was later found to be synonymous with *Colletotrichum capsici*. Elliptic to oblong spots, which may attain a size of 4–5 × 2–3 cm, appear on both surfaces of the leaf; they are greyish-white in the centre, with a brown margin and an ill-defined yellow halo. The spots may coalesce to form large necrotic patches. The disease is worse in times of high humidity. It can be controlled by spraying with 1 per cent Bordeaux mixture.

A rhizome and root rot, caused by *Pythium graminicolum* L.S. Subram., is reported in India in recent years according to Chattopadhyay (1967). A rhizome rot of turmeric caused by *P. aphanidermatum* (Edson) Fitz. has been recorded in Sri Lanka.

Pests

A shoot-boring caterpillar, *Dichocrocis punctiferalis* Guen., bores into and cuts the central shoot, as a result of which the plant dries up. Sastri (1950) states that removal of the affected shoots in the initial stages of attack and destruction of the larvae are the only practical control measures.

Other insects reported to damage turmeric include *Lema* spp., *Udaspes foleus* Cr. and thrips (*Panchaetothrips indicus*), while *Stegobium paniceum* attacks the stored product.

Improvement

A little sorting out of clones has been done in India. Aiyadurai (1966) reports that at Udayagiri in Orissa, although studies on the morphology and anthesis of the turmeric flower were undertaken, efforts to evolve a suitable technique for controlled pollination had not met with success. Sopher (1964) states that it is a sterile triploid, but Aiyadurai (1966) says that in Andhra Pradesh cultivars of the *longa* species flowered very rarely, but that viable seed could be collected from flowering types; the seedlings were found to be tardy in growth and development and the rhizome formation was poor.

A scheme for research on turmeric, with a view to evolving disease-free and high-yielding cultivars, was initiated in Andhra Pradesh in 1955. This has already been referred to under 'Cultivars'. Seven were selected as superior out of the 100 or so collected, and Rama Rao *et al.* (1975) have given a brief description of them and their properties – yield, percentage of cured product relative to the raw rhizome, curcumin content and their resistance to *Colletotrichum* leaf-spot disease and to leaf blotch caused by *Taphrina maculans*.

Bavappa (1974) considers that cultivars yielding lemon-yellow, orange or orange-yellow powders and having a curcumin content of 5 per cent or more are required in the international market. Indications from the preliminary work in progress were that polyploid breeding may be useful. Four high-yielding selections (C11, 325, 327 and Ca 73 of Andhra Pradesh) have been evolved from the germ-plasm collection available in India.

Other species

Other species of *Curcuma* which are used, and some of which are cultivated, include the following:

C. aeruginosa Roxb. is a native of Burma and Cambodia (Kampuchea) and is cultivated in Malesia, reaching the Moluccas. It is used medicinally.

C. amada Roxb., mango ginger, grows wild and is cultivated in India for its rhizomes, which have the odour of raw mangoes and are used in pickles.

C. angustifolia Roxb., Indian arrowroot or Travancore starch, is widely distributed as a wild plant in India and is occasionally cultivated. The starch from the rhizomes is extracted and is used in the same way as the true arrowroot, *Maranta arundinacea.*

C. aromatica Salisb., wild turmeric or yellow zedoary, occurs wild throughout India and is cultivated chiefly in Bengal and Travancore. The rhizome smells of camphor and is orange-red internally. It is used as a dye, cosmetic and drug, but is not used as a spice or condiment.

C. caesia Roxb., black zedoary, is a native of Bengal, where it is cultivated to a small extent. The aromatic rhizomes contain camphor and are used as a cosmetic and in local medicine.

C. mangga Val. & van Zyp is cultivated in Java, where it occurs wild, and in Malaysia. The rhizomes, which smell of mangoes, are used as seasoning for food.

C. purpurascens Bl. occurs in western and central Java, where it is also cultivated. The young shoots and the tips of the rhizomes are used for seasoning food.

C. xanthorrhiza Roxb., known as *temoe lawak* in Indonesia and in European trade, occurs wild in the teak forests of Java and is cultivated there and in Malaysia, where it is the largest species of *Curcuma*, often reaching a height of 2 m. The deep-yellow rhizomes have a pungent smell and bitter taste. They are extensively used in local medicine, and starch is extracted from them.

C. zedoaria (Berg.) Rosc., zedoary, is considered to be a native of north-eastern India and to have spread in cultivation throughout the Indian subcontinent and Malesia. The interior of the rhizome is yellow and when dried has an agreeable musky odour with a slight smell of camphor and a pungent bitter taste. The main tubers are ovoid, about 8 × 5 cm, with many short, thick branches and tuberous roots. The leafy shoots are up to 1 m tall with about five leaves. The lamina, of which the lowest are about 35 × 13 cm, but longer in the upper ones, have a purple band on either side of the midrib when young. Holttum (1950) states that the inflorescences, about 22 cm tall, are separate from the leaf shoots. The spikes are about 16 cm tall, with the lowest bracts green, the middle bracts tipped with purple and the uppermost bracts entirely purple. The flowers, about five to each bract, are pale yellow. The plant is propagated by portions of the rhizome and takes two years for full development. Zedoary rhizomes were an article of commerce to Europe by the sixth century, being taken by Arab traders from India. They attained their greatest popularity in medieval times, but the trade has now been discontinued. The rhizomes have stimulant and carminative properties. They are rich in starch, which is extracted in India to give *shoti* starch; this is valued as an article of diet, particularly for infants and invalids. Zedoary rhizomes are used in indigenous medicines in Asia and in perfumery in India. The leaves are used for flavouring fish and other foods in Java.

Plants belonging to related genera, of which the roots are used, include:

Languas galanga (L.) Stuntz (syn. *Alpinia galanga* (L.) Sw.), greater galangal, and *L. officinarum* (Hance) Farwell (syn. *Alpinia officinarum* Hance), lesser galangal, were both items of commerce between Asia and Europe in the Middle Ages. The smaller reddish-brown rhizomes of the lesser galangal from China are more aromatic and more pungent than the yellowish rhizomes of the greater galangal from India and Malesia, the latter being less highly regarded. *L. officinarum* is a herb often less than 1 m tall, with lanceolate leaves, 25–35 cm long and with a terminal inflorescence of smallish white flowers streaked with red. *L. galanga* is extensively cultivated in South East Asia and Indonesia; it is a robust herb, 2 m or more tall, with leaves about 50 × 9 cm and a terminal inflorescence with greenish-white flowers. The fresh rhizome is one of the most extensively used spices in Malaysia and Indonesia; it is also used medicinally. The fruits of *L. galanga* and other *Languas* spp. are also used as substitutes for cardamoms.

The tubers of *Kaempferia galanga* L., a native of India, and *K. rotunda* L., possibly native of Indochina, are used for flavouring food and also medicinally in South East Asia, where they are both widely cultivated.

Products and end-uses

The primary product of *C. domestica*, true turmeric, is the cured, dried rhizome. Turmeric is valued principally for its yellow-orange colouring power, but it possesses an appreciated aroma and flavour which necessitates classifying it as a spice. Turmeric is used directly as a spice or colouring agent in the ground form and also for the preparation of the solvent-extracted oleoresin. An essential oil may also be distilled from the turmeric rhizome but this is of little importance in international trade.

The major use of turmeric on a world-wide basis is for domestic culinary purposes and it is an important ingredient of curry powder. In the Western industrialized countries, ground turmeric is employed extensively in a wide range of processed foods and sauces. In many of these applications, the turmeric is used more for its colouring than for its flavouring properties; an example being mustard powder. Turmeric is also used as a dyestuff for textiles. The oleoresin finds similar applications to the ground spice in the colouring of processed foods and it is also used to a limited extent by the pharmaceutical industry.

Turmeric enters international trade mainly in the whole form, and grinding is carried out in the consuming centres. The oleoresin is manufactured from imported spice by the food industries of North America and Western Europe and also from domestically grown turmeric in India.

The major types of turmeric

The trade in turmeric is dominated by India. Other suppliers in Asia include Bangladesh, Taiwan and the People's Republic of China. Turmeric is also exported by several countries in the Caribbean, Central and South America, among which Jamaica, Haiti and Peru are the most important. The spice is marketed on the basis of geographical origin and its physical form. The chemical and physical characteristics of turmeric differ from one producing area to another, and preferences as to the origin and the physical form are expressed by some users for certain applications.

The terms commonly used in commerce to describe the various physical forms of turmeric are as follows:

Fingers

These are the lateral branches or secondary, 'daughter' rhizomes which are detached from the central rhizome before curing. Fingers usually range in size from about 2.5 to 7.5 cm in length and may be somewhat over 1 cm in diameter. Broken and very small fingers are combined and marketed separately from whole fingers.

Bulbs

These are the central 'mother' rhizomes which are ovate in shape and are of a shorter length but a greater diameter than fingers.

Splits

Bulbs which have been cut into halves or quarters before curing to facilitate subsequent drying.

Polished fingers possess the best appearance and are generally regarded as superior in quality to other forms of turmeric. All types are used for grinding and blending, and for oleoresin extraction.

The characteristics of the three major types of turmeric entering the international market are summarized below:

Alleppey turmeric

This is produced in Kerala State and marketed in Alleppey, but grown in the surrounding regions, particularly in the Thodupuzha and Muvattapuzha areas. Alleppey turmeric is deep yellow to orange-yellow in colour and has higher tinctorial powers (curcumin contents of up to 6.5

Fig. 9.2 Polished turmeric fingers (*Curcuma domestica* Val.) ($\times \frac{4}{5}$) (Crown copyright).

per cent) than other types of turmeric. Almost the entire production of Alleppey turmeric is exported, mainly to the US market and in the unpolished form, where it is used largely as a food colourant.

Madras turmeric

This type is produced in Tamil Nadu and marketed in Madras but grown from several regional cultivars. The rhizomes are mustard-yellow in colour and have a curcumin content of around 3.5 per cent. Madras turmeric is the most common type used in the United Kingdom, where it is regarded as superior in quality and flavour.

Further information on these two types of Indian turmeric is provided in the 'Processing and manufacture' and the 'Standard specifications' sections.

West Indian turmeric

This term embraces the spice exported from the Caribbean, Central and South American countries. The rhizomes are a dull yellowish-brown in colour, mostly small and of poor appearance. West Indian turmeric is regarded as inferior in quality to Indian turmeric.

Processing and manufacture

Quality requirements

The quality of cured turmeric is assessed on the basis of several factors which include the pigment (curcumin) content, the organoleptic character, the general appearance, size and physical form of the rhizome. The relative importance of these various quality attributes is dependent upon the intended end-use of the product.

In the United Kingdom and the United States, most consumers prefer turmeric in the form of polished fingers for spice applications. The chief factors of good quality in finger turmeric are a high content of pigment, giving a deep, yellow colour, and a low bitter-principle content. The rhizomes should also be rough, hard and brittle, with numerous encircling, ridge-like annulations. Length and thickness of the rhizomes and internal colour are also important characteristics in the differentiation of cultivars. When manually fractured, the break should be clean, not splintery or fibrous, and the broken surfaces waxy or horny and resinous in appearance. The endodermis, separating the cortex from the central cylinder (stele), should be clearly visible. When used as a spice or condiment, the aroma and flavour imparted by the volatile oil are important. The aroma should have a musky, pepper-like character and the flavour should be slightly aromatic and somewhat bitter.

When the turmeric is intended for use specifically as a colouring agent, either in the powdered form or as an oleoresin extract, the general appearance and physical form of the whole rhizome is less important. In this case, a very high curcumin content is essential and a low volatile-oil content is desirable. Bulbs, splits and old rhizomes are often suitable for this purpose.

The principal quality determinants of cured turmeric, i.e., the pigment, volatile oil and bitter principle contents, are mainly governed by the intrinsic characteristics of the cultivar grown and can be improved by appropriate selection of planting material. However, the quality is also influenced by the state of maturity of the rhizome at harvest and by the care taken in its handling, curing and grading.

Indian turmeric

The method of curing evolved in India consists of boiling or steaming the prepared fresh rhizomes in water, drying in the sun and finally peeling or 'polishing'. The object of boiling is to destroy the vitality of the fresh rhizomes and to obviate the raw odour, to reduce the drying time, to gelatinize the starch and give a more uniformly coloured product.

The boiling process

Precise details of this operation vary in different localities, but all processes involve the same principle. Where turmeric is grown in sugarcane districts, the shallow pans used for 'gur' boiling ('gur' is a highly concentrated sugar-cane juice containing 8 to 10 per cent of water) can be used for turmeric boiling also; in other places, deep earthenware pots fitted with lids are utilized. Metal tanks or vats are also used.

Formerly, the fresh rhizomes were heaped in the pans or filled into the pots and water was added; a thick layer of dried sugarcane or turmeric leaves was packed in to the remaining space and, in the pan method, the leaves were covered with cowdung; in the pot method, the lids were fastened with the same material or, in some places (certain areas of Tamil Nadu, producing Madras type turmeric), it was added directly to the water. The rhizomes were then boiled over a slow fire until they softened, when a thin pointed stick would penetrate them easily, the boiling taking 3 to 4 hours. The rhizomes were then cooled and spread out to dry in the sun.

It was believed that the cowdung served to protect the cured turmeric from insect damage and modified the colour of the core of the rhizome to a desired yellow-orange. It has long been realised that this practice was unhygienic and should be discouraged. Studies carried out by Agricultural Departments of some of the States and, more recently, by the Central Food Technological Research Institute on the processing of turmeric have resulted in a fresh understanding of the process. In place of the use of cowdung in the boiling operation (which may correspond with a dilute solution of ammonia), it was found that the boiling could be done by water alone; moreover, according to Krishnamurthy *et al.* (1975), boiling the rhizomes with very dilute solutions (0.05 to 0.1 per cent) of mild alkalies, such as lime water, sodium bicarbonate or sodium carbonate, influences in the same way the internal colour of the rhizomes by increasing the yellow-orange hue.

In the last 20 or 30 years, consuming countries have demanded increasingly higher standards of cleanliness in spices, as in other commodities, and producing countries have followed suit, availing themselves, in various degrees, of the benefit of scientific investigation of all aspects of the production of their saleable commodities. So in the case of Indian turmeric, production techniques have advanced, and the traditional method of processing has largely been abandoned.

The contemporary method of curing is as follows: after harvest, the leafy tops and fibrous roots are cut off the rhizomes which are then thoroughly washed in water. They are next heaped up, covered with turmeric leaves and left for some time to sweat, but Rama Rao *et al.* (1975) stated that the rhizomes have to be cured within 10 days after harvesting for securing maximum output. The purpose of 'sweating' does not seem to have been investigated. The fingers and bulbs (or mother rhizomes) are separated and are cured separately, since the latter take a little longer to cook; sometimes the bulbs are cut lengthwise in halves or quarters, known as 'splits', before boiling. The rhizomes are placed in large iron vats or other containers, water is added until the water level stands about 5 to 7.5 cm above the level of the rhizomes, and boiling is commenced above a direct fire, using whatever fuel is available locally.

The boiling lasts for 45 to 60 minutes, when the rhizomes are soft to finger pressure or, according to Rama Rao *et al.* (1975), until frothing occurs and white fumes appear emitting a characteristic turmeric odour. It is believed that the stage at which boiling is stopped largely influences the colour and aroma of the final product and, hence, skilled men are employed to supervise the boiling operation. Overcooking spoils the colour and increases the proportion of broken pieces obtained in the subsequent polishing.

Drying

After boiling, the vats should be emptied immediately, to avoid over-cooking and to effect rapid cooling. Shankaracharya and Natarajan (1973, 1975) stated that the boiled turmeric is spread out in a 2 in. (5 cm) layer on the drying floor exposed to the sun; a thinner layer is not desirable, as the colour of the dried product may then be adversely affected. Sun drying of sliced turmeric in particular gives a slight surface bleaching effect on the colour (Krishnamurthy *et al.*, 1975). During the night-time, the material should be heaped and covered over to protect it from dew. Shankaracharya and Natarajan said that it takes 10 to 15 days for the rhizomes to become thoroughly dry, when they become quite hard and brittle, and break (with the fingers) with a metallic sound. In a report published by the Indian Council of Agricultural Research (Anon., 1953) it was stated that after 5 to 7 days of drying the produce becomes fit enough for storage and sale, but more recently Shankaracharya and Natarajan (1975) expressed the opinion that the moisture content should be kept between 8 and 10 per cent, with only very limited tolerance, for better storage and, therefore, higher quality and value.

Polishing

The final operation in the processing of turmeric is 'polishing', in which the thoroughly dried product is cleaned of the outer skin, rootlets and remaining particles of soil, and transformed from the rough-coated, dirty-brown condition into relatively smooth, bright-yellow rhizomes ready for marketing.

This was done formerly by rubbing with the hands or feet, suitably protected by wrapping them in several folds of gunny cloth, or shaking the rhizomes, mixed with stones, in a long, narrow gunny bag or in a bamboo basket, or by rotating them in a polishing drum. This may be made from a wooden cask or barrel, closed at both ends. It is provided with a small door (15 cm by 23.5 cm) in the side and is perforated all round with holes about 7 mm in diameter and 10 cm to 15 cm apart. The barrel is fitted with a central axle, in the form of an iron rod long enough to project beyond both ends, enabling the barrel to be mounted horizontally on two wooden posts. A charge of 20 lb (9 kg) of cured turmeric can be polished in 1 hour by one man operating the drum (Anon., 1932).

An improved polishing drum, made by the Madras Agricultural Department (Charley, 1938), was formed of expanded metal fixed to solid, circular end-plates, and was provided with a handle at each end of the axle to permit operation by two men. It had a removable section in the side for charging and discharging. As small rhizomes or fingers might fall through the apertures of the expanded metal, the drum was covered with a tight wrapping of woven wire, the mesh of which was small enough to retain the turmeric but large enough to allow dust, dirt and rootlets to escape during the operation of the drum. A machine of this type is still used at the present time, and a drum 2 feet long and 3 feet in diameter (60 cm by 90 cm) will take a charge of about 70 lb (about 32 kg) of boiled and dried turmeric, which is cleaned and polished in 30 minutes at the normal working speed of 30 revolutions per minute. Its normal output is about 14 maunds (522 kg) of polished turmeric per day of 8 hours, with two men working on it (Shankaracharya and Natarajan, 1973).

In most of the assembling centres of turmeric, it is now polished in power-driven drums. In this method, turmeric receives a higher degree of polishing (smoothness). The capacity of the drum is about 16 maunds (598 kg) of cured turmeric and this weight requires about 1.5 to 1.75 hours for polishing. Usually 5 to 8 per cent of the weight of turmeric is the polishing wastage during full polishing, and 2 to 3 per cent during 'half polishing' (Shankaracharya and Natarajan, 1973).

The dried turmeric is coated with a slurry of turmeric powder in the course of polishing, to produce a better colour. The use of lead chromate, to achieve the same result, has now been abandoned in international trade, but Shankaracharya and Natarajan (1975) stated that in certain processing centres this practice was still being used.

Yield

The yield of polished turmeric from the raw material varies from 15 to 25 per cent. It is usually packed in bags of about 140 lbs net (64 kg).

Grading

Apart from separating the fingers from the bulbs, sometimes splitting the latter, the Indian growers do not grade the turmeric. From the many local forms available in the internal markets, the dealers prepare uniform mixtures of fingers or bulbs (or splits) for export, according to the purposes for which they are to be used, with due regard to the Indian standard specifications and those, if any, of the importing countries. These, known by various local trade names, are of different qualities, depending on botanical identity, appearance, maturity, hardness, weight, length and thickness, shade and intensity of internal colour, pungency and bitterness, odour and flavour, and other considerations. Most of the turmeric exported from India, as indicated, consists of mixtures of regional cultivars. Alleppey turmeric, which has the highest curcumin content (about 5.0–6.5 per cent), includes forms of the plant grown in the Thodupuzha and Muvattapuzha regions. Madras turmeric, which has a lower curcumin content, may be comprised of as many as nine cultivars, including 'Guntur', 'Salem', 'Rajamundry', 'Nizamabad' and 'Cuddappah'. 'Rajapore' (or 'Rajpuri'), which is a special grade of Madras turmeric, has thicker and stumpier fingers but about the same colour content as 'Guntur' (about 3.7 per cent). It is sold unmixed with other cultivars at a premium, and it is reputed to be popular because it is easier to hand-process in the household than other grades.

The Indian 'Agmark' standards include separate gradings for Alleppey, Rajapore and turmeric other than Alleppey (which includes Madras).

Storage

According to Rama Rao *et al.* (1975), the cured product is stored in suitable pits dug on a raised site. The bottom and sides of these pits are thickly lined with 'Rellu' grass twists (*Saccharum spontaneum*) and palmyrah mats. After filling up the pits with cured produce, they are covered with mats and grass and finally with earth. The produce can thus be stored for a year.

After the turmeric has been sold to the dealers and cleaned and graded, it is packed in new jute bags, in common with most of the Indian spices, or in sound, clean and dry, heat-sealed polythene bags. The jute bags may be treated with fumigants or insecticides to ward off moulds or insect infestations. The turmeric should be stored in a dry, cool warehouse, or in a godown, which should be provided with means of fumigation.

Improvement

Members of the Central Food Technological Research Institute at Mysore have studied the effect of varying the harvesting and processing conditions on the quality of cured turmeric. Most of this work was published in papers by Natarajan and Shankaracharya (1974), Shankaracharya and Natarajan (1975) and Krishnamurthy *et al.* (1975), using a number of named cultivars. A summary of the results achieved is given here.

Maturity: Preliminary studies indicated that the colour content increases during the first two months of the harvesting season

(November and December) and, subsequently, tends to decrease. As, however, variations were noticed in the different cultivars, it was considered necessary to study critically and fix the time of the harvest for each cultivar in the different regions of cultivation.

Washing: The use of water under pressure to wash the fresh rhizomes expedites the removal of soil and lessens the microbial load on the rhizomes.

Curing methods: Several procedures were investigated and compared. These included drying of abrasively peeled rhizomes and sliced rhizomes without the boiling treatment; boiling coated and peeled rhizomes in water or 0.1 per cent sodium bicarbonate solution for different times; and steaming the rhizomes. A Hobart abrasive peeler was found satisfactory for removing the outer skin of the rhizomes, but the time of the operation had to be closely controlled in order to avoid excessive losses. Slicing was undertaken by machine to prepare $\frac{1}{4}$ in. (7 mm) thick portions.

All of the procedures investigated provided cured turmeric after drying without any appreciable loss in the total pigment and volatile-oil contents. However, the optimum method proved to be boiling the rhizomes for 1 hour before drying. Boiling reduced the time of drying considerably, ensured an even distribution of colour in the rhizome and yielded a hard product by gelatinization of the starch.

Mechanically slicing the rhizomes after boiling was found to reduce significantly the drying time and gave a product which was somewhat easier to grind. The preparation of sliced 'fingers' is considered advantageous when the intended end-use is preparation of ground turmeric or the oleoresin and the appearance is not of paramount importance.

Drying methods: The conventional sun-drying operation carries with it the disadvantage of contamination with soil micro-organisms when drying is prolonged. If the sun-drying is carried out on raised platforms or on suitably designed racks, the contamination from the soil will be considerably reduced, and the drying rate will be better owing to the air-draught coming from under the rhizomes.

Artificial drying, using cross-flow hot air at a maximum temperature of 65 °C, was also investigated and found to provide a satisfactory product. In the case of sliced turmeric, artificial drying had clear advantages in giving a brighter-coloured product than sun-dried material which tended to suffer surface bleaching.

In reporting these results, the opinion was expressed that, in many cases, the facilities available to the growers are not sufficient to enable them to apply modern concepts of science and technology. In commercial practice, the growers adopt various modifications of the processing methods, without proper control over the curing process. The foregoing are some of the newer techniques which need application by the industry.

Processing in some other countries

Bangladesh, adjoining West Bengal in India, produces turmeric by methods similar to the conventional Indian procedures.

Pakistan

Formerly, the cultivation of the crop was confined to one small area around Haripur, in Hazara District, where it was prepared by the Indian methods, the rhizomes being boiled with water for 4 to 6 hours, dried in the sun and polished by rubbing on a leather-woven charpoy. In 1956, a research scheme was started to extend the cultivation to the Peshawar valley, involving agronomic, curing and processing techniques. Said and Hussain (1964) have reviewed this work and, among their recommendations, say that the rhizomes, covered by a film of mustard oil, are cured by roasting in hot sand for 8 to 12 minutes and dried in the sun. The drying of the roasted rhizomes is effected in less time than that required for the boiled rhizomes. The polishing is done in a perforated revolving drum. The ratio of the cured turmeric to the raw material is estimated at 18 to 20 per cent.

China

In mainland China, turmeric is cultivated in several provinces in the central and south-western parts of the country. The rhizomes are prepared for the market by being cleaned, freed from shoots and fibrous roots, heated in pots and dried in the sun. Externally, the rhizomes are yellow to light brown in colour, and internally their colour ranges from orange to saffron yellow (Anon., 1959). Chinese turmeric is highly regarded in the trade but it is not often seen on the United Kingdom market.

Jamaica

In the Caribbean area, as late as the 1950s, the agricultural information on the cultivation and preparation of turmeric was very elementary (Anon., 1954). Since then, Jamaica, as one of the largest producers of turmeric in the area and whose produce is imported mainly to the United States market, has modernized the preparation of the spice into a factory operation. From the washers, the turmeric is conveyed to an autoclave, for steaming and to soften the skin prior to drying. This operation is effected in a vertiflow-type grain drier, purchased from the United States, and the peel is removed in a revolving hexagonal drum.

Haiti, Peru and, recently, Argentina also supply this type of turmeric. The spice is usually imported into the United Kingdom market in the form of polished fingers, but Peru and Argentina have supplied the London market with 'splits' for curcumin extraction.

Turmeric oleoresin

Turmeric oleoresin, obtained by solvent extraction of the ground spice, contains colouring matter, volatile oil, fatty oil and bitter principles. According to Krishnamurthy *et al.* (1976), it is orange-red in colour and consists of an upper oily layer and a lower crystalline layer. The 'pure' oleoresin is viscous and relatively insoluble and is, accordingly, difficult to handle. For commercial use, it is usually mixed with a non-volatile edible solvent (often a known amount, in view of possible statutory maximum limits placed on the additive), such as a vegetable oil, propylene glycol or polyoxyethylene sorbitan fatty acid esters, in order to disperse the extracted material and to render it free-flowing and 'soluble' in aqueous media.

Manufacturers offer various turmeric oleoresins, differing in the amount of curcumin they contain. The American Spice Trade Association has standardized a spectrophotometric method by which the curcumin is determined, and this or similar methods are adopted in other countries.

A prominent manufacturer in the United Kingdom offers two turmeric oleoresins, one a mobile, homogeneous liquid with a curcumin content of 12.5 to 14.5 per cent, and the other a solid, with 38 to 42 per cent of curcumin. The dispersion rates recommended, based on sensory evaluation of the product against a good-quality freshly ground spice, are tentatively given as 5 per cent and 1.5 per cent respectively.

An equally well-known manufacturer in the United States offers a pourable turmeric oleoresin with a curcumin content of 8.5 per cent. It is claimed that 1 kg of this oleoresin will replace 5 to 8 kg of microground turmeric.

Preparation

Up until the late 1970s, turmeric oleoresin was prepared only in a few of the consuming countries, mainly the United States and the United Kingdom, and manufacturers did not disclose their methods of processing. India, however, has now embarked upon commercial production of turmeric oleoresin following the investigation of and the publication of information on processing techniques by the Central Food Technological Research Institute in Mysore.

Turmeric is closely related to ginger, and the methods by which ginger oleoresin is obtained may be applied to turmeric, the curcumin and the volatile oil being both extracted by the same volatile solvent. Krishnamurthy *et al.* (1976) have studied various aspects of turmeric oleoresin production from market samples available locally in India and from named cultivars. They collected data on the raw material, on the suitability of solvents, on processing steps, etc.

Extraction studies on market samples, ground to 40 mesh (nominal aperture size: 400 μm) using three different solvents, ethanol, acetone and ethylene dichloride, were performed in pilot-scale stainless-steel columns by cold percolation by the batch countercurrent technique: acetone was found to be superior to ethanol and ethylene dichloride in giving a slightly higher yield of oleoresin, with a high curcumin content.

Turmeric powder was extracted in a Soxhlet apparatus with acetone for different periods of time, from 3 to 24 hours; efficient extraction was possible in 4 to 5 hours, the time and cost involved in trying to extract the colour to near completion being considered to be unjustifiable.

Laboratory extraction of oleoresin from 12 named cultivars was carried out in small glass columns, in triplicate. The spices were ground to different mesh sizes – coarse, 30 mesh (nominal aperture size: 500 μm) and fine, 60 mesh (nominal aperture size: 250 μm), and extracted in the columns with solvent (ethanol, acetone or ethylene dichloride) by cold percolation; the solvent was then distilled off from the extract to obtain the oleoresin. The samples were also extracted by the Soxhlet method. The volatile-oil and curcumin contents of the samples were determined by standard methods.

The efficiencies of extraction by the Soxhlet and the cold percolation methods were compared using both fine and coarse powders, with acetone as the solvent.

1. In the case of the coarse powder, the Soxhlet method was more efficient in extracting curcumin than the cold percolation method, but the yield of extractives was lower.
2. In the case of the fine powder, both the Soxhlet and the cold percolation methods were more efficient in extracting curcumin than from the coarse powder.
3. However, cold-percolation extraction of the fine powder appeared to be superior to Soxhlet extraction with respect to extractives and curcumin content.
4. It was claimed that recovery of curcumin was near 100 per cent in most cases.

Yields

There appear to be no recorded values for yields of turmeric oleoresin, other than those found for 12 named cultivars by Krishnamurthy *et al.* (1976). Yields of extractives were from 7.9 to 10.4 per cent, containing 3.3 to 7.2 per cent of volatile oil and 2.2 to 5.4 per cent of curcumin for most of the cultivars, but one had yields of about half of these values.

Turmeric oil

Turmeric contains a volatile oil, which gives the spice its characteristic flavour but which is not sufficiently valuable or attractive to merit its commercial distillation. However, determination of the volatile oil is an essential part of the critical examination of turmeric samples. Burger

(1958) said that rasped turmeric yields 2 to 6 per cent of essential oil by distillation with superheated steam. More recently, Krishnamurthy *et al.* (1976) found that the volatile-oil contents of the 12 cultivars of cured turmeric, with which they worked, ranged from 2.5 to 7.2 per cent, although these distillations were done by means of atmospheric steam. Using a pilot-scale stainless-steel still, oil recovery from 15 to 20 kg of turmeric, amounting to about 3 per cent, was slow (4 hours) compared with pepper or cardamoms (30 minutes), owing to the fact that turmeric oil contains about 85 per cent of high-boiling sesquiterpenes.

Chemistry

The chemistry of true turmeric, *C. domestica* (syn. *C. longa* and *C. rotunda**), has been the subject of sporadic study since the early nineteenth century. However, some aspects of the chemistry of the spice, particularly pre- and post-harvest factors which may have a significant influence on the quality of the end-product, remain unclear.

The yellow-orange colour of the spice is due to the presence of non-steam-volatile diferuloyl methane derivatives, of which curcumin is the most important. The characteristic aroma and flavour of the spice is determined by the constituents of the steam-volatile oil.

General composition of the spice and the oleoresin

Cured turmeric rhizomes (*C. domestica*) contain volatile oil, pigments, fixed (fatty) oil, bitter principles, resin, protein, cellulose, pentosans, starch, mineral elements, etc. The major individual constituent is starch, which normally comprises 40 to 50 per cent of the dried rhizome. The relative abundance of some of the other constituents can vary somewhat between samples and this arises from differences in the cultivar grown and in some pre- and post-harvest factors. The possible ranges in the composition of turmeric entering international trade are fairly well documented in the literature, for example Winton and Winton (1939), Sastri (1950), Ferrara (1958), Luckner *et al.* (1967a), Shankaracharya and Natarajan (1973), Melchior and Kastner (1974), Marsh *et al.* (1977). The characteristics of some of the major commercial types of turmeric are summarized in the 'Products and end-uses' section and the current standards for turmeric are described in the 'Standard specifications' section.

Turmeric is valued principally for its yellow-orange colouring power, which is determined by the content of its curcuminoid pigments.

---

* In trade, *C. rotunda* is often used as a name for the bulbous central rhizomes while *C. longa* is used for the 'finger' rhizomes.

However, the presence of a significant quantity of volatile oil, which imparts a distinctive aroma and flavour, necessitates classifying turmeric as a spice rather than purely as a colouring agent (Wilhelm, 1958; Hengstenberg, 1958; Jellinek and Cremer, 1958). Contributions to the organoleptic characteristics of turmeric are also made by certain of the non-volatile components. The curcuminoid pigments impart a mild pungency and may also modify the flavour properties, while the bitter after-taste is considered to be due to some as yet uncharacterized bitter principles.

The two primary quality determinants for turmeric are, therefore, the content of the pigments and of the volatile oil. When turmeric is employed specifically for its yellow colouring power, e.g., as an ingredient in mustard powder, a high pigment content is required but the volatile-oil content should not be excessive since this results in an undesirably strong flavour. The content of the pigments (expressed as curcumin) and the volatile oil in the main commercial types of turmeric usually fall within the ranges of 0.5−6 per cent and 1.3−6 per cent respectively, but the possible range in the content of these constituents can be much wider (see Tables 9.2 and 9.5).

In comparison to, for example, ginger and the fruits of *Capsicum* species, little attention has been devoted to an assessment of the relative importance of pre- and post-harvest influences on the quality of dried turmeric. Recent studies in India have shown that the pigment and volatile-oil contents can differ considerably between cultivars of turmeric, but that a high pigment content is not always associated with a high volatile-oil content or vice versa (Rama Rao *et al.*, 1975; Krishnamurthy *et al.*, 1975, 1976; Mathai, 1976). In the case of the related species, *C. xanthorrhiza*, it has been known for many years that the volatile-oil and pigment contents are strongly influenced by the stage of maturity of the rhizome at harvest (Meijer and Koolhaas, 1939) but, surprisingly, study of the relationship of rhizome maturity at harvest to the quality of dried turmeric has been neglected until recently. Krishnamurthy *et al.* (1975) have found that the pigment content of turmeric increases to a peak and then declines during the maturation of the rhizome, and that the optimum time for harvesting can differ according to the particular cultivar and the location of cultivation. These authors have also reported that the various methods of curing the rhizome seem to have little effect on the content of the pigments or the volatile oil. The influence of harvest time and curing methods on the composition of the pigments and the volatile oil has not been investigated, however. Little information is available on the effects of the conditions and duration of storage on the quality of dried turmeric. Exposure of the spice to sunlight results in surface bleaching, but the extent of colour loss has not been thoroughly studied.

The limited information available suggests that the most important single influence on the quality of dried turmeric is the intrinsic characteristics of the cultivar grown, and that the second most important factor is probably the stage of maturity of the rhizome at harvest. Further research is required on all aspects of turmeric production in relation to improving quality, but the question of the optimum harvesting time would seem to demand a high priority.

Turmeric oleoresins prepared by extraction of the spice with organic solvents contain the pigments, the volatile oil and some other extractives (fatty oil, resin, etc.). The yield of the oleoresin and the relative abundance of its constituents are dependent, however, upon the raw material, the solvent and extraction technique used; by appropriate selection of solvents, an oleoresin with a high pigment content and a low bitter-principle content can be obtained. Oleoresins prepared with polar solvents (e.g. acetone) may possess pigment contents of up to 45 per cent, and volatile-oil contents as high as 25 per cent have been reported. The aroma and flavour of these turmeric oleoresins closely resemble those of the spice and are generally considered to be superior to those of the steam-distilled essential oil, which often possesses undesirable terpene-like notes. Oleoresins with a high pigment content and a low volatile-oil and bitter-principle content can be prepared by extracting turmeric with a polar solvent after an initial extraction with a hydrocarbon solvent.

Before proceeding to discuss the pigments and volatile oil in more detail, mention would be appropriate here of some other facets of turmeric chemistry. The fatty oil content of turmeric is about 5–10 per cent, but its composition, like that of the turmeric bitter principles, has not been studied. Turmeric has long been used in folk medicine in India (Shankaracharya and Natarajan, 1973) but only to a limited extent in European medicine and, then, not as extensively as *C. xanthorrhiza* (Luckner *et al.*, 1967b; Malingre, 1975). The curcuminoid pigments, which are present in both species, possess a cholagogic action* and have been used for gall and liver disorders. Antiseptic properties have been attributed to the volatile oil of turmeric.

The pigments

Reports of studies of the chemistry of the pigments of turmeric were first published in the early nineteenth century (Vogel and Pelletier, 1815) but the major pigment, curcumin, was not isolated in a crystalline form until much later (Daube, 1870; Iwanof-Gajewsky, 1870). Ciamician and Silber (1897) proposed a molecular formula of $C_{21}H_{20}O_6$ for curcumin, and its structure was finally elucidated by Milobedzka *et al.* (1910) as diferuloyl methane (see Table 9.1), which was later confirmed by synthesis (Lampe *et al.*, 1913, 1918).

---

* Cholagogues are compounds which increase the flow of bile by stimulating evacuation of the gall bladder.

Table 9.1   *The structures of the curcuminoid pigments*

R_1	R_2	
OMe	OMe	Curcumin: [1, 7-bis-(4-hydroxy-3-methoxy phenyl) hepta-1, 6-diene-3, 5-dione]
OMe	H	Desmethoxycurcumin: 4-hydroxy-cinnamoyl-(4-hydroxy-3-methoxy-cinnamoyl) methane
H	H	Bis-desmethoxycurcumin: bis-(4-hydroxy-cinnamoyl) methane

Further investigation of the pigments of turmeric was neglected for many years until Srinivasan (1953) demonstrated that the pigment extract was comprised of a mixture of analogues in which curcumin is the major component. Srinivasan proposed that the structures of the two main pigments accompanying curcumin were desmethoxycurcumin and bis-desmethoxycurcumin, and that all three compounds exist in the *trans-trans* keto-enol form, as shown in Table 9.1, rather than in the diketone form. A number of other pigments were observed to be present in minor quantities in the extract and Srinivasan suggested that they might possibly be the *cis-trans* or *cis-cis* forms of the three main pigments.

Later, Kuroyanagi and Natori (1970) isolated desmethoxycurcumin and bis-desmethoxycurcumin from *C. zedoaria* and confirmed their structures by physical methods. Roughley and Whiting (1973) provided additional confirmation of the structures of the two compounds by synthesis and supported the view that the three main pigments existed in nature in the *trans-trans* keto-enol forms. However, neither the Japanese nor the British workers could find evidence in *C. zedoaria* or *C. domestica* of the *cis*-forms of the compounds postulated by Srinivasan.

A few quantitative analyses of the relative abundance of the three main pigments present in *C. domestica* have been published and these are given in Tables 9.2 and 9.3.

While a little information is available on the changes in the total content of the pigments of *C. domestica* during maturation of the rhizome (Krishnamurthy *et al.*, 1975), it is uncertain whether their relative abundance alters during this phase. Similarly, information is lacking on their relative stability and the effect of the various methods

Table 9.2 *The occurrence of the curcuminoid pigments in certain* Curcuma *species*

	C.domestica	C.xanthorrhiza	C.aromatica	C.zedoaria
Reported range in total pigment content (per cent)	0.02–8.1 (refs: 1–10)	0.02–2 (refs: 1, 3, 4, 6, 7, 11)	0.02–1.6 (refs: 1, 3–5)	0–0.3 (refs: 3, 4)
Component pigments:				
Curcumin	+ [12]	+ [14]	+ [15]	+ [4,15]
Desmethoxycurcumin	+ [13]	+ [14]	+ [15]	+ [4,15]
Bis-desmethoxycurcumin	+ [13]	–	+ [15]	+ [4]

Table 9.3 *The relative abundance of the curcuminoid pigments in certain* Curcuma *species*

	Curcumin (per cent)	Desmethoxy-curcumin (per cent)	Bis-desmethoxycurcumin (per cent)	Ref.
C.domestica	61	24	15	(13)
C.domestica	54	20	26	(16)
C.domestica	49	29	22	(9)
C.domestica 'types'	36–58 (av. 47)	15–33 (av. 24)	23–39 (av. 29)	(3)
C.xanthorrhiza 'types'	58–71 (av. 62)	29–42 (av. 38)	0	(3)

References for Tables 9.2 and 9.3

(1) Luckner *et al.* (1967a, b)
(2) Khalique and Amin (1967)
(3) Jentzsch *et al.* (1970)
(4) Kuroyanagi and Natori (1970)
(5) Krishnamurthy *et al.* (1975)
(6) Karig (1975)
(7) Malingre (1975)
(8) Salzer (1975)
(9) Krishnamurthy *et al.* (1976)
(10) Mathai (1976)
(11) Lubis (1968)
(12) Milobedzka *et al.* (1910)
(13) Srinivasan (1953)
(14) Jentzsch *et al.* (1959)
(15) Jentzsch *et al.* (1968)
(16) Roughley and Whiting (1973)

practised for curing the fresh rhizome. In the fresh rhizome, the pigments are located together with the volatile oil in discrete oleoresin cells and the colour of the core is more intense than that of the rind. Boiling the fresh rhizomes results in a rupture of the oleoresin cells, and the pigments become more evenly distributed through the starch. The keto-enol structure of the pigments renders them sensitive to colour change by pH variation, turning yellow-red in acid media and red-brown in alkaline media, and this fact has traditionally been employed in the curing of turmeric to enhance the colour. For example, cowdung or sodium bicarbonate may be added during the boiling stage; and, in the past, it was not uncommon for the dried turmeric to be treated with lead salts to enhance the surface colour, but nowadays stringent measures are taken to eradicate this dangerous practice (Shankaracharya and Natarajan, 1975). The colour sensitivity to pH variation has been used also as a diagnostic test for turmeric starch.

It has been mentioned earlier that turmeric has been used as a drug, particularly in Asia. Jentzsch *et al.* (1959) have demonstrated that with rats, curcumin has a choleretic action*, whereas bis-desmethoxycurcumin decreases bile secretion.

A variety of methods have been published for the determination of the colour value of turmeric, and interested readers are recommended to refer to the articles by Luckner (1967a and b), Salzer (1975) and Malingre (1975). The pigment content (expressed as curcumin) is generally determined by a spectrophotometric method (American Spice Trade Association, 1968). Jentzsch *et al.* (1970) have described also a thin-layer chromatography/spectrophotometric method to estimate the relative abundance of the individual pigments.

The volatile oil

The aroma and flavour of turmeric are determined by the composition of its steam-volatile oil. Turmeric oil *per se* has never been of commercial importance and consequently relatively few studies have been made of the composition. The oil is comprised mainly of oxygenated sesquiterpenes which are accompanied by smaller quantities of sesquiterpene hydrocarbons, monoterpene hydrocarbons and oxygenated monoterpenes. The relative importance of individual constituents in contributing to the aroma and flavour of the oil is uncertain. The aroma of the steam-distilled essential oil differs in character from that of the spice and this is believed to arise from artefact formation during the extraction process.

The distilled oil

Steam distillation of the spice provides an essential oil possessing a yellow to orange-yellow colour, and which is occasionally slightly fluorescent. Arctander (1960) has described the aroma as spicy (peppery) and fresh, reminiscent of sweet orange, ginger and galanga, while the flavour is slightly pungent and bitter. The organoleptic properties of turmeric oils can differ somewhat according to the origin of spice and the age of the sample.

The yield of oil obtained on distillation and its physicochemical properties can also vary between individual samples (Gildemeister and Hoffmann, 1956; Khalique and Das, 1968; Krishnamurthy *et al.*,

---

* Choleretics stimulate an increase in bile secretion by acting on the liver.

1976). These differences can arise from a number of factors which include the origin and the method of curing the spice, its age, and the conditions of distillation. The stage of maturity of rhizome at harvest may also be of significance but this aspect has not been investigated. Turmeric oil is similar to ginger oil in that the optical-rotation value can be a notable variable. Oils distilled from good-quality spice have been reported to possess optical-rotation values in the range of $-25°$ to $-13°$, but on storage and exposure to air, the value steadily falls. Old samples of turmeric tend to yield oils with a positive optical rotation value which increases progressively on storage.

Studies of the composition of turmeric oil were first reported in the mid-nineteenth century, but little progress was made at that time. Jackson *et al.* (1882, 1883, 1896) were the first investigators to fractionate successfully from turmeric oil the major component, which was named 'turmerol' and was thought to be an alcohol with a molecular formula of $C_{13}H_{18}O$ or $C_{14}H_{20}O$. 'Turmerol' defied attempts at purifi-

Table 9.4 *Transformations of turmerone*

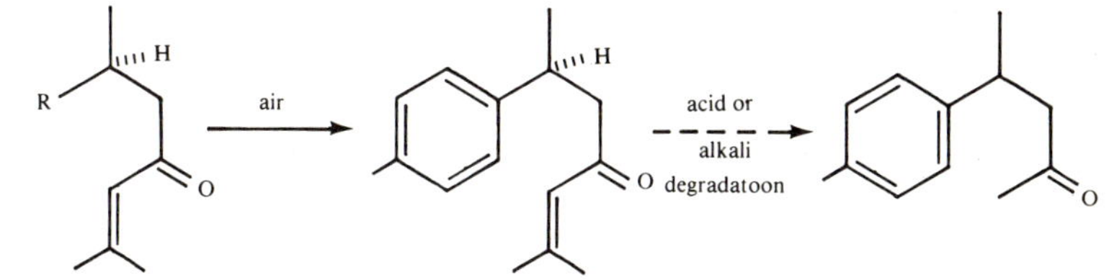

(1) Turmerone,

(2) ar-turmerone

(3) curcumone
+ $(CH_3)_2CO$

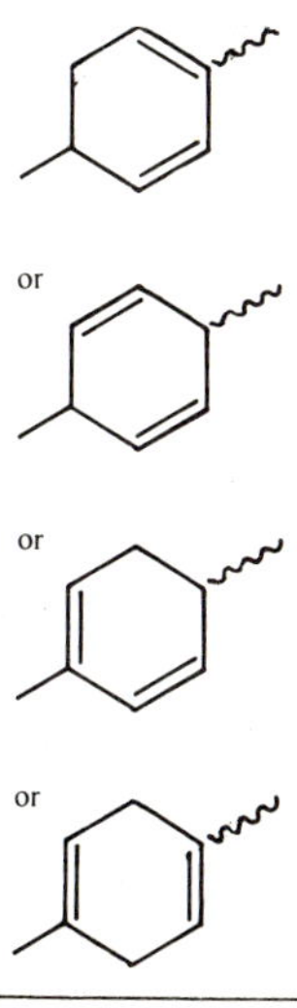

or

or

or

cation and further characterisation for some years, but Rupe *et al.* (1907, 1909, 1911) found that a ketonic artefact, curcumone, could be obtained by the action of hot alkali or acid. The structure of curcumone, shown in Table 9.4, was elucidated by Rupe and Wiederkehr in 1924. Further studies by St Pfau (1932) and Rupe *et al.* (1934, 1936) showed that 'turmerol' was, in fact, a mixture of a sesquiterpene ketone and its corresponding aromatic analogue, which were named turmerone and *ar*-turmerone (dehydroturmerone), possessing the structures shown in Table 9.4. Kelkar and Rao (1934) also reported discovering that 'turmerol' was a mixture of these two components. The S-configuration of (+)-*ar*-turmerone shown in Table 9.4 was deduced by Rao in 1965. At the time of writing, turmerone itself had resisted attempts to isolate it in a pure form and the position of the two double bonds in the cyclohexane ring is uncertain.

The detailed composition of turmeric oil remains poorly documented, and quantitative analysis data have only been reported by three groups of workers (Kelkar and Rao, 1934; Rupe *et al.*, 1934; Salzer, 1975). These analyses indicate that turmerone and *ar*-turmerone combined can comprise 50–80 per cent of the oil. The ratio of turmerone to *ar*-turmerone is variable and figures of 5 : 4 and 2 : 6 were found by Rupe *et al.* (1934) and Salzer (1975) respectively for oils distilled from oleoresin extracts. These two principal components are accompanied by other sesquiterpene hydrocarbons and oxygenated sesquiterpenes (6–25 per cent of the oil), among which Rupe *et al.* (1934) found small quantities of alpha- and gamma-atlantone, Kelkar and Rao (1934) found zingiberene (25 per cent of their oil) and Malingre (1975) identified beta-sesquiphellandrene. Kelkar and Rao (1934) also reported identifying several monoterpenes present as minor components (0.5–1 per cent each) in their oil. The constituents identified in turmeric oils are listed in Table 9.5.

The difficulties encountered in freeing turmerone from *ar*-turmerone, combined with the change in the optical rotation of the oil on storage, have led Khalique and Das (1968) to suggest that the latter may not be present as a natural product in the fresh rhizome, but that it is an artefact produced from the former compound. Salzer (1975) concurs with this hypothesis and has drawn an analogy between the general composition and properties of turmeric and ginger oils. The transformation probably commences during the curing of the freshly harvested rhizome, progresses slowly during storage of the dried spice, and is accelerated during isolation of the essential oil by distillation.

The relationship of the composition of turmeric oil to its organoleptic properties has received scant attention. However, the aroma of carefully prepared oleoresin extracts is generally considered to be closer to that of the dried spice than is the case with the distilled essential oils. This change in aroma properties must be related, at least in part, to artefact formation during distillation, but it is not known whether the

Table 9.5 *The essential oils of certain* Curcuma *species*

	C. domestica	C. xanthorrhiza	C. aromatica	C. zedoaria
Reported range in essential oil content (per cent)	1.2–7.2 (refs: 1–9)	3.5–11 (refs: 3, 7, 10)	1.2–10.6 (refs: 3, 9, 11–13)	1–1.5 (ref: 14)
Monoterpenes identified				
p-cymene	+ [7]	–	–	–
1:8-cineole	+ [15]	–	–	+ [14]
α-phellandrene	+ [15–18]	–	–	–
sabinene	+ [15]	–	–	–
borneol	+ [15]	–	+ [13]	+ [14]
camphor	–	+ [7,10,20]	+ [11,13]	+ [14]
myrcene	–	? [7,10]	–	–
α-pinene	–	–	+ [13]	+ [14]
β-pinene	–	–	+ [13]	–
camphene	–	–	+ [11,13]	+ [14]
α-terpineol	–	–	+ [13]	–
Sesquiterpenes identified				
turmerone	+ [7,15,19]	–	–	–
ar-turmerone	+ [7,15,19]	–	–	–
zingiberene	+ [15]	–	+ [13]	–
α-atlantone	+ [19]	–	–	–
γ-atlantone	+ [19]	–	–	–
β-sesquiphellandrene	+ [7]	–	–	–
xanthorrhizol	–	+ [21]	–	–
zingiberol	–	–	+ [13]	–
α-curcumene	–	–	+ [11]	–
β-curcumene	–	+ [7]	+ [11,13]	–
ar-curcumene	–	+ [7]	+ [13]	–
isofuranogermacreene	–	+ [7]	–	+ [22,29]
curcumadiol	–	–	–	+ [23]
curdione	–	–	–	+ [24]
curcumol	–	–	–	+ [25]
curcumenol	–	–	–	+ [26]
curculone	–	–	–	+ [27]
curzerone	–	–	–	+ [22]
epicurzerone	–	–	–	+ [22]
dehydrocurdione	–	–	–	+ [28]
furanodiene	–	–	–	+ [29]
isocurcumenol	–	–	–	+ [30]
procurcumenol	–	–	–	+ [31]
pyrocurcumenone	–	–	–	+ [32]
zederone	–	–	–	+ [33]
Misc. constituents				
azulene	–	–	+ [13]	–
p-tolylmethycarbinol	–	+ [10]	–	–
cuminyl alcohol	–	–	+ [13]	–
caprylic acid	–	–	+ [11]	–
p-methoxycinnamic acid	–	–	+ [11]	–

References for Table 9.5

(1)	Winton and Winton (1939)	(17)	Rupe & Wiederkehr (1924)
(2)	Parry, (1969)	(18)	Luksch (1906)
(3)	Luckner *et al*. (1967a,b)	(19)	Rupe *et al*. (1934)
(4)	Rosengarten (1969)	(20)	Meijer and Koolhaas (1939)
(5)	Guenther (1952)	(21)	Rimpler *et al*. (1970)
(6)	Rama Rao *et al*. (1975)	(22)	Hikino *et al*. (1968a)
(7)	Malingre (1975)	(23)	Hikino *et al*. (1971)
(8)	Krishnamurthy *et al*. (1976)	(24)	Hikino *et al*. (1967)
(9)	Mathai (1976)	(25)	Hikino *et al*. (1966)
(10)	Dieterle and Kaiser (1932)	(26)	Hikino *et al*. (1968c)
(11)	Rao *et al*. (1926)	(27)	Hikino *et al*. (1968d)
(12)	Krishnamurthy *et al*. (1975)	(28)	Hikino *et al*. (1972)
(13)	Tirumala Rao and Nigam (1974)	(29)	Hikino *et al*. (1970)
(14)	Rao *et al*. (1928)	(30)	Hikino *et al*. (1969)
(15)	Kelkar and Rao (1934)	(31)	Hikino *et al*. (1968f)
(16)	Schimmel & Co. (1890)	(32)	Hikino *et al*. (1968b)
		(33)	Hikino *et al*. (1968e)

ratio of turmerone to *ar*-turmerone is alone responsible or if the relative abundance of other oil constituents is also significant. It should be appreciated that the distillation of the oil from the spice proceeds fairly slowly owing to the very high sesquiterpene content, and complete recovery of the sesquiterpenes may not always be achieved. The balance of sesquiterpenes to monoterpenes in the distilled oil may, therefore, be different from that of the natural oil in the spice.

Readers interested in a more detailed discussion of the turmeric-oil sesquiterpenes are recommended to refer to the review by Alexander and Krishna Rao (1973). Conditions for the gas-chromatography analysis of turmeric oil have been recommended by Salzer (1975).

Related species and detection of adulteration

The curcuminoid pigments, whose content is the primary value determinant for true turmeric (*C. domestica*), appear to have a very restricted occurrence in nature and have been found in only a small number of the many species of *Curcuma* (Jentzsch *et al*., 1968; Lubis, 1968). There are three curcumin-containing species which are of real significance with regard to problems of adulteration: *C. xanthorrhiza* (Indonesian: *temoe lawak*); *C. aromatica* (wild turmeric or yellow zedoary; Hindi: *jangli haldi*); and *C. zedoaria* (zedoary; Hindi: *kachura*). In the producing countries of Asia, these three species are variously used as sources of starch, dyes and in folk medicine and are sometimes used as substitutes for true turmeric but not as a spice or condiment (Sastri, 1950). They all possess distinctive aromas with a camphoraceous note, and zedoary has been used to a limited extent in perfumery. In Europe, concern over possible adulteration relates mainly to the mixing of *C. domestica* and *C. xanthorrhiza*; the former finding its main application as a spice and colouring agent while the latter has been used as a cholagogic drug (Luckner *et al.*, 1967; Malingre, 1975).

Distinguishing between species by microscopy is often difficult with the ground material, particularly if the starch grains and oleoresin cells have been destroyed by boiling the rhizomes; and proof of identity by chemical methods has been sought. There are some broad differences between the four species in that the pigment content of commercial consignments of *C. domestica* is usually much higher than those of *C. xanthorrhiza* and *C. aromatica*, while the pigment content of *C. zedoaria* is often only at trace levels; and *C. xanthorrhiza* frequently has a high volatile-oil content of over 7 per cent. The pigment and volatile-oil contents cannot be used as reliable criteria for distinction, however, since these values can vary considerably between samples within a species and there is a degree of overlap in the possible ranges between species (see Tables 9.2 and 9.3). Attention has been directed mainly at devising distinguishing methods based on revealing differences by chromatographic techniques in the composition of the pigments and volatile oils.

Jentzsch *et al.* (1959, 1968, 1970) examined the pigment compositions of the four species and stated that classification could be made into two groups. *C. domestica* and *C. aromatica* are characterized by the presence of three pigments (curcumin, desmethoxycurcumin and bis-desmethoxycurcumin), while *C. xanthorrhiza* and *C. zedoaria* contain only the first two of these pigments. These workers devised a thin-layer chromatography/spectrophotometric method for estimating the relative abundance of the individual pigments and their results are summarized in Table 9.3. This approach has been adopted and advocated by Luckner *et al.* (1967a, b) for distinguishing between *C. domestica* and *C. xanthorrhiza*. Jentzsch *et al.* (1970) have acknowledged, however, that there are limitations with the method when applied to *C. zedoaria* since the pigment content is often extremely low; and the situation is further complicated, since Kuroyanagi and Natori (1970) have reported isolating and confirming the identity of all three pigments in *C. zedoaria* of Japanese origin.

The volatile oils of all four species are similar in as much as they are comprised principally of oxygenated sesquiterpenes (approximately two-thirds of the oils) but the limited information available indicates that they differ qualitatively in composition (see Table 9.5). Some of the older literature on the volatile oils should be viewed with some caution, however, since there are doubts over whether the authors gave the correct botanical classification to the samples which they examined. For example, the Indonesian '*C. domestica* Val.' of Dieterle and Kaiser (1932, 1933) has been regarded by more recent authors as *C. xanthorrhiza*.

Winkler and Lunau (1959) have proposed that the presence of *p*-tolylmethylcarbinol in *C. xanthorrhiza* essential oil, first reported by

Dieterle and Kaiser (1932), is a criterion for identifying this species. However, this compound is now regarded as an artefact, produced during distillation, which is not always present in the oil (Luckner *et al.*, 1967b; Malingre, 1975), and it is not a reliable criterion for identity. The apparently unique occurrence of the sesquiterpene, xanthorrhizol, in *C. xanthorrhiza* essential oil, discovered by Rimpler *et al.* (1970), has been proposed by Sirait *et al.* (1971) as a more reliable criterion for distinguishing this species from *C. domestica*. Karig (1975) has drawn on the information available on the qualitative differences between both the essential-oil and pigment compositions of these two species and has devised a thin-layer chromatography method for proof of identity and to check on adulteration. The presence of *C. xanthorrihiza* in *C. domestica* is detected by the presence of xanthorrhizol in the essential oil, and the converse case is detected by the presence of bis-desmethoxycurcumin in the pigments.

Sen *et al.* (1974) have proposed that the adulteration of *C. domestica* by *C. aromatica* or *C. zedoaria* can be detected by the presence of camphor and camphene, which occur as minor components in the essential oil of the last two named species but are absent in the first.

Herisset (1972) has recommended the use of spectroscopic techniques in preference to chromatographic methods for identifying the unadulterated essential oils.

Standard specifications

The spice

United Kingdom Standards

There are no United Kingdom Standards for turmeric, although an ISO International Standard is in course of preparation; it is expected that a British Standard Specification will be based on the International Standard.

United States Standards

The United States Government Standard defines 'turmeric (whole) as being the clean, sound, dried rhizome or bulbous root of *Curcuma longa* L. [*sic*].

    A.   Alleppey turmeric shall have the characteristics of the type grown in Alleppey regions.

    B.   Jamaican turmeric shall have the characteristics of the type grown in the Jamaican regions.'

The turmeric shall be in accordance with the requirements listed in Table 9.6.

Table 9.6   *Requirements of the US Government Standard*

Total ash, not more than	7.0 per cent
Acid-insoluble ash, not more than	0.5 per cent
Crude fibre, not more than	9.5 per cent
Volatile oil (expressed as ml per 100 g), not less than	3.5
Moisture, not more than	9.0 per cent
Colour power (expressed as per cent curcumin)	5.0 to 6.6
Sieve test	
US Standard sieve size	No. 40
Weight required to pass through, not less than	95 per cent

From: US Federal Specification: *Spices, ground and whole, and spice blends.* No. EE-S-631H, June 5, 1975.

The limits of the various contaminants in turmeric, permitted under the Cleanliness Specifications of the American Spice Trade Association, are shown in Table 9.7.

Table 9.7   *ASTA Cleanliness specifications for turmeric*

Extraneous matter, per cent by weight	0.50
Excreta, rodent, pellets per lb	2
Excreta, other, mg per lb	5.0
Whole insects, dead, per lb	3
Insect defiled, per cent by weight	2.50
Mould, per cent by weight	3.00

The Food and Drug Administration have not set any defect action levels for turmeric in the Fifth Revision of their list, dated 1 March 1974.

When used solely as a colouring material, turmeric is subject to the FDA Colour Additives Regulations. The spice is specifically defined in Section 73.600 and, when used in the form of turmeric oleoresin, in Section 73.615 of volume 4 of the *Federal Register* (1977).

Canadian Standards

Turmeric, whole or ground, is merely defined as being the dried rhizome of *Curcuma longa* L. [*sic*], in the Canadian Food and Drug Regulations, 3 September 1964.

Indian Standards

Turmeric is included in the list of spices which must have an 'Agmark' grading before they can be exported from India (Anon., 1971). Three grades of finger turmeric, two of bulb turmeric and one grade of powdered turmeric are specified, as follows:

Finger turmeric, other than Alleppey variety, sub-graded into 'Special', 'Good' and 'Fair'.

Alleppey finger turmeric, sub-graded into 'Good' and 'Fair'.

Rajapore finger turmeric, sub-graded into 'Special', 'Good' and 'Fair'. Maximum percentage limits are specified for extraneous matter, pieces (fingers, whole or broken, of 15 mm or less in length), immature fingers or bulbs and defective bulbs, (sound) bulbs and, in the case of Rajapore, on the admixture of other varieties of turmeric.

Turmeric bulbs ⎫ Both sub-graded into 'Special', 'Good'
Rajapore turmeric bulbs ⎭ and 'Fair'.

Maximum percentage limits are enumerated for extraneous matter and immature and defective bulbs.

Turmeric powder: In this case, the characteristics are more exacting. Maximum percentage limits are specified for moisture, total ash, acid-insoluble ash and starch; maximum limits for lead (2.5 ppm) and a test for chromate, which should be negative.

The maximum limit for extraneous matter in the prime sub-grades of the above five grades of whole turmeric is 1.0 per cent; in the case of Alleppey finger turmeric exported to the United States, the content of extraneous matter is usually less than 0.5 per cent, according to information from the American Spice Trade Association.

More detailed information on these grades is available by reference to the Agmark standard (Anon., 1971).

Turmeric oleoresin

United States Standards

The Essential Oil Association of America has issued a standard for Oleoresin Turmeric (EOA No. 271), which is described as the product 'obtained by solvent extraction of the dried rhizomes of *Curcuma longa* L. [*sic*] (fam. Zingiberaceae) with the subsequent removal of the solvent. Since the oleoresin thus obtained is not homogeneous and is difficult to handle, most of the oleoresin turmeric in commerce contains a suitable vehicle or vehicles (e.g. propylene glycol, Polysorbate 80, etc.). Oleoresin turmeric is evaluated strictly on colour.'

Physical and chemical constants:

Appearance and odour: A deep red or orange-red, somewhat viscid liquid, with a characteristic odour. Some types are not homogeneous and may contain a crystalline lower layer.

Colour value: As labelled (measured by spectrophotometric assay, using a Beckman Model DU or DK2 or equivalent).

Residual solvent in the oleoresin: Meets with Federal Food, Drug and Cosmetic Act Regulations.

Solubility: Due to the varying types of oleoresin turmeric available, no definite solubility information can be given.

Turmeric oleoresin is not listed in the United States Federal Specification: *Spice flavourings, soluble*, No. EE-S-645b, June 20, 1966.

United Kingdom Standards

There are no United Kingdom Standards for turmeric oleoresin. Manufacturers have had to devise their own standards, as with most of the oleoresins from other spices.

Production, trade and markets

In addition to the true turmeric of commerce (*C. domestica*; syn. *C. longa*), several other *Curcuma* species are exploited for various purposes in Asia (see 'Other species' and 'Chemistry'). However, true turmeric is the only species which is used as a spice and which enters international trade in a significant volume. For example, the imports of *C. xanthorrhiza* (Indonesian: *temoe lawak*) into Western Europe for pharmaceutical purposes are negligible in comparison to imports of turmeric spice.

True turmeric can differ considerably in its characteristics according to its geographical source (see 'Products and end-uses') and the main types recognized in international trade are the Indian 'Madras' and 'Alleppey' turmerics and 'West Indian' or 'Haiti' turmeric. Madras turmeric is the mostly highly valued as a spice in most Western markets, while Alleppey turmeric is preferred when a very high colouring power is required. The West Indian type of turmeric is regarded as of a lower quality and value in comparison with the two Indian types.

It should not be concluded, however, that all internationally traded turmeric is invariably or readily classifiable into one or other of the above categories. Consignments from minor producers may differ from all three on account of the particular growing conditions and of the cultivars used. For a few users, and in one or two applications, the source and colour of the turmeric is not of over-riding importance and precise grading is of little consequence, but for the majority of users and uses the differences between the various geographical types are of some relevance.

Production

India is the largest producer of turmeric, followed by Bangladesh. Other known producers include Jamaica, Sri Lanka, Taiwan, the People's Republic of China, Burma, Indonesia, Peru and Haiti, although it is certain that the spice is grown in many other countries in Southern and South East Asia; it is a popular ingredient in Asian cooking recipes and is widely used as a condiment and dye throughout the region. As demand for the spice is concentrated mainly in the Asian sub-continent, all the producers in that region are heavy consumers of their own produce and some are net importers; only non-Asian producers such as Haiti, Jamaica and Peru export the greater part of their annual production. Jamaican production declined in the 1970s.

India has generally exported in the region of 10 per cent of her annual production of turmeric, although accurate production statistics are difficult to obtain, and there is an additional difficulty in as much as prior to 1947 India and Pakistan were a single entity, and further, in 1971 East Pakistan became the independent state of Bangladesh. Pakistan (formerly West Pakistan) also produces turmeric. However, at the commencement of the 1950s Indian production was of the order of 125 000 tonnes of turmeric per annum which is in excess of known average annual production of pre-independence 'India' during the 1920s and 1930s, when recorded totals of maybe one-half this figure were the rule. Recent production figures have revealed some variation from year to year, but normally the annual outturn has been in the range of 100 000–150 000 tonnes, the figures for the 1968–9 season being at the lower limit of this range and those for the 1970–1 season near the upper limit.

Bangladesh also exports a small proportion of its production, although this proportion tends to vary rather more than in the case of India. Annual production is considerably lower than that of India, averaging 20 000 tonnes with considerable annual variation. Sri Lanka is another major producer in the region whose importance, already considerable, is increasing each year, although heavy local consumption still necessitates substantial imports to supplement the local crop.

Of the other producers, only the annual production of Jamaica can be estimated and then only from the export returns. Neither production nor complete export statistics relating to turmeric are available in respect of any other country.

In India turmeric is produced mainly by private farmers although there is some State participation in the marketing and distribution processes. State involvement is also increasingly evident in Sri Lanka and Jamaica, while in China production is, as expected, organized on cooperative or communal lines. In general, there is little difference between turmeric and other spices in terms of the conditions under which it is produced.

Trade

International trade in turmeric is conducted mainly under conditions of private enterprise, and as with most other spices, a proportion of the total quantity exported from the producing countries is routed through Singapore. Table 9.8 shows the quantities exported from India from the early 1920s, and from some other producers from 1961. India, Bangladesh, Taiwan and Jamaica were the main exporters, the minor

Table 9.8 *Exports of turmeric from India, Pakistan[1], Taiwan and Jamaica (tonnes)*

	India[2]	Pakistan[1,3]	Taiwan	Jamaica
1921−25 (annual average)	2 700			
1926−30 (,, ,,)	3 800			
1931−35 (,, ,,)	3 800			
1936−40 (,, ,,)	4 550			
1941−45 (,, ,,)	5 500[4]			
1946−50 (,, ,,)	9 500[4]			
1951−55 (,, ,,)	9 850			
1956−60 (,, ,,)	7 650			
1961	3 450	680	604	143
1962	2 950	...	311	55
1963	3 150	1 490	775	45
1964	9 548	2 818	1 016	135
1965	10 403	1 698	688	262
1966	9 490	602	392	256
1967	5 976	1 218	341	−
1968	6 351	1 575	291	484
1969	7 026	390	523	587
1970	11 109	216	473	1
1971	14 173	230	378	...
1972	6 731	69	136	7
1973	7 921	917	309	...
1974	9 227	...	218	...
1975	6 800	...	...	...
1976	11 755	...	176	...

Sources: *Review of the Trade of India* (Dept of Commercial Intelligence and Statistics); Annual Trade Statistics.

[1] Refers to both halves of Pakistan until the political separation; thereafter Bangladesh only.
[2] Statistics relate to the 12 months April – March.
[3] Statistics relate to the 12-month period commencing in the July of the year shown.
[4] Estimates
− nil or negligible
... not available

suppliers included Haiti, Peru, Burma and mainland China. Morocco and Pakistan have also exported the spice, although it is possible that the former may merely have re-exported previous imports.

The leading importer is, and has for a long time been, Iran. Second in importance used to be Sri Lanka, but the local agricultural development and diversification programmes which have been in progress there for some years have given rise to a sharp decrease in imports, corresponding to the increase in local production, and Sri Lanka's status as an importer is now far lower than that of both the USA and Japan. Most of the Arab countries of the Middle East and North Africa import substantial quantities of turmeric, notably Iraq, Libya and Morocco, although there are many others. A higher proportion of Bangladesh's exports are shipped to Middle Eastern destinations, such as Muscat and Oman, than is the case with India, whose exports are destined for a much wider range of importers. Taiwan's exports are destined principally for Japan, and indeed between 1956 and 1960 about 96 per cent of exports were so routed, although since then the proportion has generally been lower, with Hong Kong, the USA and Iran taking a larger percentage. Jamaican turmeric was exported mainly to the North American market but substantial consignments were shipped to the United Kingdom and continental Europe.

In some instances, recorded imports of turmeric from India substantially exceed recorded exports from India to the countries concerned. These discrepancies are likely to occur as a result of one or a combination of the following reasons: firstly, a significant re-export trade by importers of Indian turmeric where third-country importers record their imports as being of Indian origin; and secondly, inaccurate recording of exports from India or of imports by consumer countries, or both.

International trade in ground turmeric is very small. In the ground form it is shipped mainly to certain African countries, notably Zambia, and to some of the more important Middle Eastern buyers. Trade in ground turmeric used to be of greater importance than it is nowadays.

At one time most of Iran's imports came from India, but as already indicated the former eastern part of Pakistan, now Bangladesh, is a supplier of equal importance. In recent times China has also supplied turmeric to this market. Some supplies to Iran have been channelled through Dubai. Sri Lanka's imports have almost always been of Indian origin, but during the mid-1970s turmeric virtually disappeared from the import statistics. Whether this exceptional decline is due to unusual factors or whether it is because Sri Lanka has already succeeded in attaining self-sufficiency remains to be seen, but it is clear that India is losing one of her major turmeric markets, and it could even be that before long she will have to contend with Sri Lanka in the export trade. The USA imports turmeric mainly from India but also takes substantial quantities from Jamaica, Haiti and Taiwan, and sometimes from Peru. Japan is an important outlet for turmeric of mainland Chinese as well as Indian and Taiwanese origin. North American and Japanese imports have increased fairly steadily since the mid-1960s, whereas Moroccan and Iraqi imports have exhibited no such growth and, in fact, have tended to decline.

Iran currently accounts for around 30 per cent of the international market, while other Arab countries account for a further 30 per cent. The USA's share is around 10–15 per cent. Table 9.9 shows recent movements in the level of imports for selected countries.

Movements in the price of turmeric, which is dealt with in more detail in a subsequent section, indicate that supplies fell short of demand in some recent years. Bangladesh's exports have been lower

Table 9.9 Imports of turmeric into selected countries, 1961–76 (tonnes)

	1961	1962	1963	1964	1965	1966	1967	1968	1969	1970	1971	1972	1973	1974	1975	1976
Iran[1]	1 407	2 076	2 541	3 320	2 905	2 467	1 624	1 930	2 228	3 327	4 836	2 728	2 979	3 245	...	4 404
USA	1 181	1 410	1 212	1 621	1 474	1 723	874	1 535	1 418	1 606	1 423	1 672[2]	1 067[2]	1 255[2]	1 169	1 597*
Japan	1 268	694	1 336	1 166	1 862	1 602	1 419	1 556	2 052	2 126	3 066	1 312	2 066	2 454	1 615	2 132
Sri Lanka	1 198	1 393	1 153	1 399	1 325	1 436	846	810	737	970	955	–	...	2	17	...
Iraq	267	292	250	376	447	340	87	–	332	–	–	105	139	464	199	...
Morocco	555	489	532	857	825	203	324	301	379	520	402	79	–	290	289	360

Sources: Annual Trade Statistics of the above countries. *Plantation Crops*.
1 Figures relate to 12 months commencing 21 March.
2 Imports from India only.
– nil or negligible
... not available
* preliminary

than they were in the 1960s, although there was some recovery in 1973, while Taiwan's exports also have been lower on average than they were in the late 1960s. Jamaica's exports have also been depressed and for some recent years information has not been readily available. Increases in exports from other sources did not counterbalance these falls, and although India's export trade has generally held up well, supply shortages have occurred.

Market structure

Turmeric is, as already indicated, traded mainly under free competitive conditions with the usual participation by shippers, merchants, dealers and, of course, the brokers who take their customary commission for bringing about sales and purchases. The spice grinders and processors and one or two of the flavour houses in the EEC and the USA sometimes buy direct from source, with or without the services of a broker. Turmeric is not one of the most important spices but it is nonetheless traded in substantial quantities and the number of individual persons and organizations active in the trade is correspondingly fairly large.

Singapore has already been mentioned in terms of its entrepôt trade although its importance in this respect seems to be largely limited to Asia and the Middle East. South Yemen (formerly Aden) at one time conducted some entrepôt trade but turmeric was seldom listed separately and it does not appear as if it was ever as important an entrepôt item as some other spices. There is a little re-export trade from some of the main West European buyers, but this is of little practical significance.

Prices

The price of turmeric is largely determined by the geographical type and by the grade. Turmeric 'fingers' are considered superior in quality to 'bulbs' or 'splits' and fetch a higher price. Table 9.10 illustrates the movements in the price of 'Madras finger' turmeric, the most important type on the market, during the last 20 years. It would appear that the fluctuations in price have tended to be exaggerated by the reactions of the producers to price changes, low prices causing undue cutbacks and high prices the reverse. The prices during the 1973—4 commodity boom were considered exceptionally high and were followed by a slight decline in their levels during 1975. This decline, however, was soon reversed in 1976, and in 1977 prices rose much faster resulting from a sharp fall in supplies to the world market. These supply shortages were caused by widespread cyclonic damage to crops in the main turmeric-growing areas of south India, as a result of which Indian exports of turmeric were banned for a period. The price of 'Madras fingers' reached £950 per tonne during March 1978.

Table 9.10 *Turmeric (Madras finger): Annual average prices, c.i.f. United Kingdom,*
   1961–77 (£ per tonne)

1961	101
1962	136
1963	136
1964	136
1965	114
1966	92
1967	118
1968	174
1969	300
1970	210
1971	131
1972	163
1973	267
1974	285
1975	233
1976	296
1977[1]	417

Source: *Public Ledger*
[1] first two quarters only

Trends in consumption and prospects

Turmeric differs from all other high-volume spices, save paprika, insofar that the colouring properties are usually more important than its flavour attributes. Thus although its flavour renders it popular as a condiment in cooking, it is widely used as a colouring agent in the food, confectionery, textile and pharmaceutical industries, and as an ingredient in some Indian cosmetic preparations. In the UK turmeric is generally regarded as a satisfactory, even if a little inferior, colouring substitute for the very much more expensive saffron, although it cannot be denied that there are one or two applications in which the latter is still preferred in spite of its great cost. The use of turmeric in the textile industry has declined sharply in some countries, and it is probable that this will be a general trend, but in food applications there is no reason to suppose that synthetic colours will supplant turmeric. It is possible that the increasingly more stringent controls on the use of certain synthetic colours in food preparations in the United States could result in a somewhat greater demand for turmeric in this field of application.

In the preparation of pickles and sauces there is a rather greater difference in emphasis between practice in the UK and continental Europe on the one hand, and in the USA on the other, than in the case of some other spices. This difference relates mainly to oleoresin usage. In the EEC countries, turmeric has generally continued to be used in its natural form while other spices have increasingly been used in the form of dispersed oleoresins. Evidently, tastes in pickles in Western Europe have required that for reason of texture and colour, turmeric should be used in its ground state and that there is little or no advantage to be derived from the extraction process. In the USA, however, where pickles of a rather higher texture are preferred and the food and drug regulations are more stringent, turmeric oleoresin is used in substantial quantities. It is not possible to estimate the actual amount produced and used in the USA but it may well be considerably less in proportion to usage of the raw spice, in comparison with other spices.

An essential oil can be distilled from turmeric and this is sometimes called 'turmerol' or 'oil of curcuma'. It seems to be distilled mainly in India rather than in the West. The principal applications are in some confectionery products and certain aerated waters. By comparison with other spice oils its importance is far from great.

By and large, turmeric users seem to remain faithful to established sources with which they are familiar, and therefore new producers can expect to gain ground only gradually. British users mainly prefer Madras turmeric, although the Alleppey and Jamaican types are also imported. In the USA it is Alleppey turmeric which dominates, and excess demand for this type has at times pushed its price above that of Madras turmeric, which as already noted is normally regarded as setting the standard by which other types are judged. The demand for Alleppey turmeric, which has a very high colouring power, is almost certainly related to the level of turmeric-oleoresin production in the USA. The present pattern of consumption is likely to be maintained and the prospects for the turmeric trade generally seem to be favourable, especially as the demand for curry powder is buoyant, the main need being adequacy of supplies in order to keep the long-term price level acceptably low. It is possible that beyond the short term this is a market which would support the gradual entry of new exporters. At the same time, turmeric is not a cheap spice to produce and the effects of unduly low prices have already been mentioned.

References

Aiyadurai, S.G. (1966) *A Review of Research on Spices and Cashewnut in India*, Ernakulam-6: Indian Council of Agric. Res.

Alexander, J. and Krishna Rao, G.S. (1973) 'The chemistry of ar-turmerone, atlantone and related monocyclic sesquiterpenoid ketones', *Flav. Ind.*, 390–3.

American Spice Trade Association (1968) *Official Analytical Methods*, 2nd edn, New York: American Spice Trade Association.

Anon. (1932) *Preparation of Turmeric for the Market*, Bombay: Dept. of Agric. Leaflet No. 7 of 1932.

Anon. (1953) *Report of the Spices Enquiry Committee*, New Delhi: Indian Council of Agric. Research.

Anon. (1954) 'Cultivation and preparation of turmeric', *Farm J. (Br. Guiana)*, **17** (1), 18.

Anon. (1959) 'Oil of Curcuma', *Essenoil News*, **2** (1), 13–14.

Anon. (1971) *Instructions for Grading and Marking of Whole Spices under Agmark*, Marketing Series No. 173, Faridabad: The Agricultural Marketing Advisor to the Government of India.

Arctander, S. (1960) *Perfume and Flavour Materials of Natural Origin*, Elizabeth, N.J.: Published by the author.

Bailey, L.H. (1949) *Manual of Cultivated Plants*, rev. edn, New York: Macmillan.

Bavappa, K.V.A. (1974) 'Development and prospects of spice industry', *Proceedings of a Symposium held at the Central Food Technological Research Institute, Mysore, 28 February – 2 March 1974*, 13, Mysore: C.F.T.R.I.

Burger, A. (1958) 'Curcuma root and its essential oil', *Perfumery Essent. Oil Record*, **49** (12), 801–2.

Burkill, I.H. (1966) *A Dictionary of the Economic Products of the Malay Peninsula*, Kuala Lumpur: Ministry of Agriculture and Co-operatives.

Charley, N.G. (1938) 'Preparation of turmeric for the market'. *Agric. and Livestock in India*, **8** (6), 695–7.

Chattopadhyay, S.B. (1967) *Diseases of Plants Yielding Drugs, Dyes and Spices*, New Delhi: Indian Council of Agric. Res.

Ciamician, G. and Silber, P. (1897) 'Zur Kenntniss des Curcumins', *Chem. Ber.*, **30**, 192–5.

Darlington, C.D. and Wylie, A.P. (1955) *Chromosome Atlas of Flowering Plants*, London: George Allen and Unwin.

Daube, F.W. (1870) 'Ueber Curcumin, den Farbstoffe der Curcumawurzel', *Chem. Ber.*, **3**, 609–13.

Dieterle, H. and Kaiser, Ph. (1932) 'Uber die Inhaltstoffe des Rhizoms *Curcuma domestica* (Temoe lawak)', *Arch. Pharm.*, **270**, 413–18.

Dieterle, H. and Kaiser, Ph. (1933) 'Uber die Inhaltstoffe des Rhizoms *Curcuma domestica* (Temoe lawak). II. Mitteilung', *Arch. Pharm.*, **271**, 337–42.

Ferrara, A. (1958) '*Curcuma longa* and *C. rotunda*', *Riv. Agric. Subtrop. & Trop.*, **52**, 67–70.

Geus, J.G. de (1973). *Fertilizer Guide for the Tropics and Subtropics*, 2nd edn, Zurich: Centre d'Étude de l'Azote.

Gildemeister, E. and Hoffmann, Fr. (1956) *Die Aetherischen Oele*, Vol. IV, Berlin: Akademie Verlag.

Guenther, E. (1952) *The Essential Oils*, Vol. V, New York: D. Van Nostrand Co.

Hengstenberg, K. (1958) 'Curcuma als wurzender Bestandteil von Speisesenf', *Deut: Lebensm. – Rundshau*, **54**, 14–16.

Herisset, A. (1972) 'Distinguishing similar essential oils. VII. Essential oils of *Curcuma* (*C. xanthorrhiza* and *C. longa*)', *Plant – Med. Phytoether*, **6**, 281–91.

Hikino, H., Meguro, K., Sakurai, Y. and Takemoto, T. (1966) 'Sesquiterpenoids. V. Structure of curcumol', *Chem. Pharm. Bull. (Tokyo)*, **14**, 1241–9.

Hikino, H., Sakurai, Y., Takahashi, H. and Takemoto, T. (1967) 'Structure of curdione', *Chem. Pharm. Bull. (Tokyo)*, **15**, 1390–4.

Hikino, H., Agatsuma, K. and Takemoto, T. (1968a) 'Structure of curzerone, epicurzerone and isofuranogermacreene', *Tetrahedron Letters*, **24**, 2855–8.

Hikino, H., Agatsuma, K., Konno, C. and Takemoto, T. (1968b) 'Thermal rearrangements of curzerenones', *Tetrahedron Letters*, **24**, 4417–19.

Hikino, H., Sakurai, Y., Seiichiro, N. and Takemoto, T. (1968c) 'Structure of curcumenol', *Chem. Pharm. Bull. (Tokyo)*, **16**, 39–42.

Hikino, H., Sakurai, Y. and Takemoto, T. (1968d) 'Sesquiterpenoids. XX. Structure of zederone', *Chem. Pharm. Bull. (Tokyo)*, **16**, 827–31.

578 *Turmeric*

Hikino, H., Takahashi, S., Sakurai, Y., Takemoto, T. and Bhacca, N.S. (1968e) 'Sesquiterpenoids. XXII. Structure of zederone', *Chem. Pharm. Bull. (Tokyo)*, **16**, 1081−7.

Hikino, H., Sakurai, Y. and Takemoto, T. (1968f) 'Sesquiterpenoids. XXVI. Structure
of procurcumenol', *Chem. Pharm. Bull. (Tokyo)*, **16**, 1605−7.

Hikino, H., Agatsuma, K. and Takemoto, T. (1969) 'Sesquiterpenoids. XXXII.
Structure of isocurcumenol', *Chem. Pharm. Bull. (Tokyo)*, **17**, 959−60.

Hikino, H., Agatsuma, K., Konno, C. and Takemoto, T. (1970) 'Sesquiterpenoids.
XXXV. Structure of furanodiene and isofuranogermacreene', *Chem. Pharm. Bull.
(Tokyo)*, **18**, 752−5.

Hikino, H., Konno, C. and Takemoto, T. (1971) 'Sesquiterpenoids. XXXIX. Structure
of curcumadiol, a sesquiterpenoid of *Curcuma zedoaria*', *Chem. Pharm. Bull.
(Tokyo)*, **19**, 93−6.

Hikino, H., Konno, C. and Takemoto, T. (1972) 'Sesquiterpenoids. XLIII. Structure of
dehydrocurdione, a sesquiterpenoid of *Curcuma zedoaria*', *Chem. Pharm. Bull.
(Tokyo)*, **20**, 987−9.

Holttum, R.E. (1950) 'The Zingiberaceae of the Malay Peninsula', *Gardens' Bull.
Singapore*, **13**, 1−249.

Hussain, A. and Said, M. (1965) 'Effect of size of seed on yield of turmeric (*Curcuma
longa*)', *W. Pakistan J. Agric. Resc.*, **3**, 122−3.

Iwanof-Gajewsky, Y. (1870) 'From a report given by V.V. Richer of a meeting of the
Petersburg Chemical Society', *Chem. Ber.*, **3**, 624−6.

Jackson, C.L. and Menke, A.E. (1882) 'XXVIII-Turmeric oil – Turmerol', *Amer.
Chem. J.*, **4**, 368−74.

Jackson, C.L. and Menke, A.E. (1883) 'Turmeric oil – Turmerol', *Pharm. J.*, II, **13**, 839.

Jackson, C.L. and Warren, W.H. (1896) 'LXXXIX – Turmerol', *Amer. Chem. J.*, **18**,
111−17.

Jellinek, G. and Cremer. H.D. (1958) 'Curcuma: Gewurz oder Farbstoff?', *Deut.
Lebensm. – Rundschau*, **54**, 280−1.

Jentzsch, K., Gonda, Th. and Holler, H. (1959) 'Papierchromatographische und
pharmakoligische Untersuchungen von Curcuma – Farbstoffe. I. Papierchromatographische Unterscheidung von *Curcuma domestica* Val. und *Curcuma xanthorrhiza*
Roxb.', *Pharm. Acta Helv.*, **34**, 181−8.

Jentzsch, K., Spiegel, P. and Kamitz, R. (1968) 'Qualitative und quantitative
Untersuchungen uber Curcuma Farbstoffe in verscheidenen Zingiberaceendrogen. I
Teil: Qualitative Untersuchungen', *Sci. Pharm.*, **36**, 257−64.

Jentzsch, K., Spiegel, P. and Kamitz, R. (1970) 'Qualitative und quantitative
Untersuchungen uber Curcuma Farbstoffe in verscheidenen Zingiberaceendrogen. II
Teil: Quantitative Untersuchungen', *Sci. Pharm.*, **38**, 50−8.

Karig, F. (1975) 'Schnelle Kennzeichnung von Curcuma – Rhizomen mit dem
TAS – Verfahren', *Deut Apoth. Ztg.*, **115**, 325−8.

Kelkar, N.C. and Rao, B.S. (1934) 'Essential oil from the rhizomes of *Curcuma longa*
L.', *J. Indian Inst. Sci.*, **17A**, 7−24.

Khalique, A. and Amin, M.N. (1967) 'Examination of *Curcuma longa* L. Part I: Constituents of the rhizome', *Sci. Res.* (Dacca), **4**, 193−97.

Khalique, A. and Das, N.R. (1968) 'Examination of *Curcuma longa* L. Part II: Constituents of the essential oil', *Sci. Res.* (Dacca), **5**, 44−9.

Krishnamurthy, M.N., Padma Bai, R., Natarajan, C.P. and Kuppuswamy, S. (1975)
'Colour content of turmeric varieties and studies of its processing', *J. Food Sci.
Technol.* (India), **12**, 12−14.

Krishnamurthy, N., Mathew, A.G., Nambudri, E.S., Shivashankar, S., Lewis, Y.S. and
Natarajan, C.P. (1976) 'Oil and oleoresin of turmeric', *Trop. Sci.*, **18**, 37−45.

Kuroyanagi, M. and Natori, S. (1970) 'Some observations on curcuminoids from *Zingiberaceae* plants', *Yakugaku Zasshi*, **90**, 1467−70.

Lampe, V. and Milobedzka, J. (1913) 'Studien uber Curcumin', *Chem. Ber.*, **46**,
2235−40.

Lampe, V. (1918) 'Synthese von Curcumin', *Chem. Ber.*, **52**, 1347−55.

Lampe, V. and Godlewska, M. (1918) 'Synthese von p,p'-Dioxy- und p-Oxy-dicinnamoylmethan', *Chem. Ber.*, **51**, 1355–60.
Lubis, I. (1968) 'The phenolic compounds of *Curcuma*', *Ann. Bogoriensis*, **4**, 219–25.
Luckner, M., Bessler, O. and Luckner, R. (1967a) 'Vorschlage fur den Drogenteil des DAB 7. 30 Mitteilung: Rhizoma *Curcumae longae*', *Pharmazie*, **22**, 371–5.
Luckner, M., Bessler, O. and Luckner, R. (1967b) 'Vorschlage fur den Drogenteil des DAB 7. 31 Mitteilung: Rhizoma *Curcumae zanthorrhizae*', *Pharmazie*, **22**, 376–8.
Luksch, E. (1906) 'Uber Curcumoel' (inaugural dissertation), Basel: Univ. Basel.
Malingre, Th. M. (1975) '*Curcuma xanthorrhiza* Roxb., temoe lawak, als plant met galdrijvende werking', *Pharm. Weekblad*, **110**, 601–10.
Marsh, A.C., Moss, M.K. and Murphy, E.W. (1977) *Composition of Foods Spices and Herbs. Raw, Processed, Prepared*, Washington DC: USDA Agric. Res. Serv., Agricultural Handbook No. 8–2.
Mathai, C.K. (1976) 'Variability in turmeric (*Curcuma* species) germplasm for essential oil and curcumin', *Qual. Plant – Pl. Fds. Hum. Nutr.*, **25**, 227–30.
Meijer, Th. and Koolhaas, D.C. (1939) 'Variations in constituents from the rhizome of *Curcuma xanthorrhiza* Roxb. (Temoe lawak) during different seasons', *Arch. Pharm.*, **277**, 91–100.
Melchior, H. and Kastner, H. (1974) *Gewurze (Botanische und chemische Untersuchung)*, Berlin: Paul Parey.
Milobedzka, J., Kostanecki, St. V. and Lampe, V. (1910) 'Zur Kenntniss des Curcumins', *Chem. Ber.*, **43**, 2163–70.
Natarajan, C.P. and Shankaracharya, N.B. (1974) 'Development and prospects of spice industry', *Proceedings of a Symposium held at the Central Food Technological Research Inst., Mysore, 28 February – 2 March 1974*, 8, Mysore: C.F.T.R.I.
Parry, J.W. (1969) *Spices*, Vol II, New York: Chemical Publishing Co.
Raghavan, T.S. and Venkatasubban, K.R. (1943) 'Cytological studies in the Family Zingiberaceae with special reference to chromosome number and cytotaxonomy', *Proc. Indian Acad. Sci.*, **17**, 118–32.
Rama Rao, M., Rama Chenna Reddy, K. and Subbarayadu, M. (1975) 'Promising turmeric types of Andhra Pradesh', *Indian Spices*, **12**, 2–5.
Rao, B.S., Shintre, V.P. and Simonsen, J.L. (1926) 'Constituents of some Indian essential oils. XX. Essential oil from the rhizomes of *Curcuma aromatica* Salisb.', *J. Indian Inst. Sci.*, **9A**, 140–4.
Rao, B.S., Shintre, V.P. and Simonsen, J.L. (1928) 'Constituents of Indian Essential oils. XXIV. Essential oil from rhizomes of *Curcuma zedoaria* Roscoe', *J. Soc. Chem. Ind.*, **47**, 171–2T.
Rao, A.S. (1965) 'Absolute configuration of (+)-ar-turmerone from *C. longa*' *Indian J. Chem.*, **3**, 47–8.
Ridley, H.N. (1912) *Spices*, London: Macmillan.
Rimpler, H., Hansel, R. and Kochendoerfer, L. (1970) 'Xanthorrhizol, ein neues Sesquiterpen aus *Curcuma xanthorrhiza*', *Z. Naturforsch*, **256**, 995–8.
Rosengarten, F., Jr. (1969) *The Book of Spices*, Wynnewood: Livingston Publishing Co.
Roughley, P.J. and Whiting, D.A. (1973) 'Experiments in the biosynthesis of curcumin', *J. Chem. Soc.*, (Perkin I), 2379–88.
Rupe, H. (1907) 'Uber Curcumaoel', *Chem. Ber.*, **40**, 4909–10.
Rupe, H., Luksch, E. and Steinbach, A. (1909) 'Uber Curcumaoel', *Chem. Ber.*, **42**, 2515–20.
Rupe, H. and Steinbach, A. (1911) 'Uber Curcumaoel. III. Synthese der γ-p-Tolyl-γ-methyl-n-buttersaure', *Chem. Ber.*, **44**, 584, 1218.
Rupe, H. and Wiederkehr, Fr. (1924) 'The constitution of curcumone from curcuma oil', *Helv. Chim. Acta.*, **7**, 654–69.
Rupe, H., Clar, G., St. Pfau, A. and Plattner, Pl. (1934) 'Uber Turmeron, den Riechstoff des Curcumaoels', *Helv. Chim. Acta*, **17**, 372–89.
Rupe, H. and Gassmann, A. (1936) 'Zur Kenntnis des ar-Turmerons aus dem Curcuma-Ol', *Helv. Chim. Acta.*, **19**, 569–81.

580   *Turmeric*

Said, M. and Hussain, Ch. A. (1964) 'Curing and processing of turmeric', *West. Pak. J. Agric. Res.*, **2** (3), 22–5.
St Pfau, A. (1932) 'Sesquiterpene ketones', *Helv. Chim. Acta.*, **15**, 1481–3.
Salzer, U.-J. (1975) 'Analytical evaluation of seasoning extracts (oleoresins) and essential oils from seasonings. II', *Flavours*, 206–10, 253–8.
Sastri, B.N. (ed.) (1950) *The Wealth of India: Raw Materials*, Vol. 2, New Delhi: Council for Scientific and Industrial Research, 402–5.
Schimmel and Co. (1890) 'Curcumaoel', *Ber. Schimmel*, October, 17.
Sen, A.R., Sen Gupta, P. and Ghose Dastidar, N. (1974) 'Detection of *Curcuma zedoaria* and *C. aromatica* in *C. longa* (turmeric) by thin layer chromatography', *Analyst*, **99**, 153–5.
Shankaracharya, N.B. and Natarajan, C.P. (1973) 'Turmeric – chemistry, technology and uses', *Indian Spices*, **10** (3), 7–11; **10** (4), 8–10.
Shankaracharya, N.B. and Natarajan, C.P. (1975) 'Technology of spices', *Arecanut and Spices Bull.*, **7** (2), 27–43.
Sirait, M., Langhammer, L. and Rimpler, H. (1971) 'Notiz zur Analytik von "Temu Lawak und Kunjir" ', *Deut. Apoth. Ztg.*, **111**, 1526–8.
Sopher, D.E. (1964) 'Indigenous uses of turmeric (*Curcuma domestica*) in Asia and Oceania', *Anthropos*, **59**, 93–127.
Srinivasan, K.R. (1953) 'A chromatographic study of the curcuminoids in *Curcuma longa* L.', *J. Pharm. Pharmacol.*, **5**, 448–57.
Tirumala Rao, J. and Nigam, S.S. (1974) 'Essential oil of the rhizomes of *Curcuma aromatica* Salisb.', *Flav. Ind.*, 234–6.
Vogel, J. and Pelletier, R. (1815) 'Curcumin', *J. Pharm.*, **2**, 50.
Wilhelm, C. (1958) 'Curcuma, Gewurz oder Farbstoff?', *Deut. Lebensm. – Rundschau*, **54**, 12–13.
Willis, J.C. (1966) *A Dictionary of the Flowering Plants and Ferns*, 7th edn (rev. by H.K. Airey Shaw), Cambridge Univ. Press.
Winkler, W. and Lunau, E. (1959) 'The differentiation of essential oils of *Curcuma xanthorrhiza* and *C. longa* by thin layer chromatography', *Pharm. Ztg.*, **104**, 1407–8.
Winton, A.L. and Winton, K.B. (1939) *The Structure and Composition of Foods*, Vol IV, New York: John Wiley & Sons.
Yegna Narayan Aiyer, A.K. (1944) *Field Crops of India*, Bangalore: Govt. Press.

Chapter 10

Cardamom

Cardamoms are the dried fruits of a perennial herb, *Elettaria cardamomum* Maton, belonging to the ginger family, Zingiberaceae. The fruits are picked when they are almost, but not quite ripe. Cardamom is an expensive spice, the price being only exceeded among spices by saffron and vanilla. The plant is indigenous to southern India and Sri Lanka, where it grows in evergreen rain forests at altitudes between 760 m and 1 500 m. It is also cultivated in this region and in Guatemala.

The seeds have a pleasant aroma and a characteristic warm, slightly pungent taste. The spice is used for flavouring curries, cakes and bread and for other culinary purposes. In India cardamoms are used as a masticatory and may be included in the betel quid with areca nuts, *Areca catechu* L., and the leaves of betel pepper, *Piper betle* L. Substantial quantities are imported into the Middle East and are used in Arab countries for flavouring coffee. Another important market is Sweden and Finland, where they are widely used in confectionery. They are thought to have aphrodisiac properties. Cardamoms are official in the British and US pharmacopoeias and are used as an aromatic stimulant, carminative and flavouring agent. An essential oil is obtained from the seeds by steam distillation. It is used for flavouring of processed foods, in perfumery and for flavouring liqueurs and other beverages.

Cardamom substitutes, which sometimes appear in trade and are given the name cardamom, are obtained from *Aframomum* spp. in Africa and *Amomum* spp. in Asia. They are dealt with briefly in this chapter.

History

Cardamoms occur wild in the evergreen monsoon forests of the Western Ghats in southern India and Sri Lanka. Up to 1800 the world's supply came from these forests, with the only cultivation being the partial clearing of the forest around the wild plants. Later purposeful planting was done.

Rosengarten (1969) states that 'cardamom was an article of Greek trade during the fourth century B.C. The inferior grades were known as *amōmon*; the superior, more aromatic, as *kardamōmon*. By the first century A.D. Rome was importing substantial quantities of cardamom from India . . . It was one of the most popular Oriental spices in the Roman cuisine. Cardamom was listed among the Indian spices liable to duty in Alexandria in A.D. 176.'

Ridley (1912) affirms that 'there was a spice known to the Greeks and Romans as *cardamomum* and *amomum*, but it appears to be certain that these spice plants, whatever they were, were not the cardamoms of the present day, although the name of this spice, as we know it, is evidently taken from these words.'

Burkill (1966) also doubts whether the Greeks and Romans had the true cardamoms from *Elettaria*. He reports that Theophrastus in the fourth century B.C. mentions the inferior *amōmon* and superior *kardamōmon*, as transported through Media, but did not describe them. Five centuries later Dioscorides 'wrote that to him *Kardamomon* was the best of the aromata which came to the Levant by Commagene, Armenia, and the Bosphorus, the best of the group of spices called collectively *amōmon*, pungent and rather bitter. At roughly the same period Pliny, in Italy, used the word cardamomom to cover four spices. . . . Galen lived a century after Dioscorides; and he, too, called *Kardamōmon* bitter. . . . As it is not bitter, it has been suggested that the true cardamom of Dioscorides was not derived from *Elettaria* as is the true cardamom of today. This may or may not be the case. It is impossible to demonstrate anything satisfactorily'.

Whatever the Greeks and Romans had, Europe has now ceased to ask for any cardamom other than that of *Elettaria*, and the word 'cardamom' has passed into all the languages of Europe.

There are no early records from India, although, as Burkill (1966) says, it can be assumed that cardamoms have long been an article of trade there; certainly from the time of Ibn Sena (A.D. 980–1037). Ridley (1912) records that the writer Edrisi describes the spice as a product of Sri Lanka in A.D. 1154. Marco Polo does not mention it in his travels. The present-day trade with the Malabar coast was described by the Portuguese traveller Barbosa in 1514. Garcia da Orta in 1563 differentiated between the smaller, non-aromatic form (var. *cardamomum*) from India and the larger-fruited form (var. *major*) from Sri Lanka.

Cardamom cultivation in India is concentrated mainly in those regions which form the natural habitat of the species, except for a small area in North Kanara in Maharashtra, where it is grown as a subsidiary crop in the areca nut gardens. Approximately 40 500 ha are scattered throughout the hill forest zone of the Western Ghats. Some 50 per cent of the area lies in the Cardamom Hills in Travancore – Cochin, some 23 per cent in the Shimoga, Hassan and Kadur districts in Karnataka, 13 per cent in Coorg and 13 per cent in Tamil Nadu in the southern foothills of the Nilgiris and Anamalai, Nelliampathy and Kodaikanal hills. In Sri Lanka there are about 4 050 ha in the hill ranges and hill slopes of the districts of Kanda Matale and Nuwara Eliya, with nearly 60 per cent in the district of Kandy.

India is still the world's largest producer and provides about 80 per cent of the world's exports. Sri Lanka was the second largest exporter until overtaken by Guatemala, where seeds were introduced about 1920 to the department of Alta Verapaz. Subsequent plantations in Guatemala have been developed in the south-western departments of Suchitepéquez, Sololá and Quezaltenango.

Cardamoms have been introduced into other parts of the tropics, but do not seem to have been very successful, although there have been small exports from Tanzania, and they are growing in Papua New Guinea. Exports from Thailand are *Amomum*.

Botany

Systematics

According to Willis (1966) the genus *Elettaria* has seven species in Indo-Malesia. Holttum (1950) describes one species from Malaysia and says that the genus occurs in Ceylon (Sri Lanka) and southern India, Malaysia, Sumatra and Borneo. The wild and cultivated cardamom is *Elettaria cardamomum* Maton. The botanical source of cardamoms early imported into Europe is not known.

Some confusion exists in regard to the systematics, local races, types and grades of *E. cardamomum*. The varieties and races are interfertile, which may add further to the confusion.

Two botanical varieties have been recognized based on the size of the fruit:

var. *major* Thwaites

This is the wild cardamom of Sri Lanka, occurring in the wet forests; it is also occasionally cultivated. It is a robust plant, about 3 m tall, with pinkish pseudostems, broad leaves and erect panicles. The ovary and calyx are subtomentose. The fruit, which is larger than that of the succeeding variety, is elongated, 2.5–5.0 cm long, slightly arched, yellowish-green when ripe and darkish-brown when dry, with more numerous, larger and less aromatic seeds. It is known in the trade as 'long wild native cardamom' and was at one time more common in the cardamom trade than at present.

var. *cardamomum* (syn. var. *minor* Watt; var. *minuscula* Burkill)

This includes most of the cultivated races. The stature varies from 2.5–5 m tall. The panicle is longer with more numerous flowers and may be procumbent, arching or erect. The ovary and calyx are glabrous. The fruits, about 1–2 cm long, are smaller than the first variety above and with fewer, smaller, more aromatic seeds. The fruits are yellowish when dried.

Several races are recognized, of which the most important are:

Malabar cardamom

The plants rarely exceed 2.7 m in height with short leafy shoots. The leaves are 30–45 cm long and hairy on the lower surface; the panicles are 60–90 cm long and prostrate; the fruits are small, globose, rounded or ovoid, and lightly ribbed. This race is very susceptible to katte or mosaic virus. The wild cardamom of South India, with one doubtful exception, is the Malabar cardamom and it is cultivated chiefly in the districts of Mysore and Coorg and to a limited extent in Travancore. The Malai and Manjarabad cardamoms, distinguished by the size of the capsules, belong to this race.

Mysore cardamom

The plants are of robust growth, with leafy stems up to 5 m high and large coarse leaves which are glabrous beneath. The panicles are erect or arching and the fruits are longer, fusiform, three-angled and ribbed. This race shows resistance to katte or mosaic disease. It is considered to be more suitable for higher elevations than the Malabar cardamom. It thrives well over a wide range of conditions and is hardier and not very exacting in its water requirements. It is suitable for extensive planting and is cultivated in the larger holdings of Travancore, Anamalai and Nelliampathy hills.

Cytology

Darlington and Wylie (1955) give the basic chromosome number of *Elettaria* as $x = 12$ and the somatic number of *E. cardamomum* as $2n = 48$, quoting Gregory (1936), and as 52 according to Chakravorti (1952).

Structure

Cardamom is a tall herbaceous perennial with branched subterranean rhizomes from which arise several erect leafy shoots and erect or decumbent panicles. There is a stout, rather woody horizontal rhizome with numerous fibrous roots in the surface layer. The leafy shoots, 10–20 in number and 2–5.5 m tall, are composed of leaf sheaths, and are borne in thick clumps. The leaves are distichous with lanceolate acuminate lamina, 25–90 cm long and 5–15 cm wide, dark green and glabrous above, and paler beneath. The lower surface may be either glabrous or pubescent depending on the variety and race.

The inflorescences arise from the rootstock at the base of the leafy shoots and are 60–120 cm long. They are erect, recumbent or decumbent, slender panicles. There are fairly large alternate bracts with axillary cincinni, usually two- to three-flowered. The flowers are hermaphrodite, zygomorphic and about 4 cm long and 1.7 cm across. The bracteole is tubular, as is the calyx, which is green, shortly three-toothed and persistent. The corolla tube is about the same length as the calyx with three narrow, strap-shaped, spreading, pale-green lobes about 1 cm long. The most conspicuous part of the flower is the obovate labellum composed of three modified stamens, about 1.8 cm long with an undulating edge; it is white with violet streaks radiating from the centre. There are two further rudimentary staminodes and one functional stamen. The latter has a short, broad filament, with a longer anther, and a connective with a short crest at the apex. The inferior ovary consists of three united carpels with numerous ovules in axile placentation and a slender style with a small capitate stigma.

The fruit is a trilocular capsule, fusiform globose, pale green to yellow in colour, varying in size according to the variety (see 'Systematics' above). It contains 15–20 seeds, which are dark brown, angled, rugose, aromatic, about 3 mm long, and with a thin mucilaginous aril. They contain some white perisperm and a small embryo.

Pollination

The flowers are said to be self-sterile, so it is necessary to plant a mixture of clones. They are visited by bees which bring about cross-pollination. The flowers open from the base of the panicle upwards over a long period. Parameswar (1973), studying the floral biology of cardamom at Mudigere in Mysore, observed flowering throughout the year on panicles of the current year as well as those of the previous year. The buds required about 31 days from initiation to full bloom and the capsule development took about a further 110 days. The maximum number of flowers opened during the early hours of the day and anthesis took place in 65 per cent of the flowers between 6 and 8 a.m., when the pollen was shed. Although apparently 85 per cent of the pollen appeared fertile, germination tests on an artificial medium containing 20 per cent sucrose and 1 per cent agar solution, which was found to be the best, showed a maximum of 70 per cent germination. Studies on the viability of the pollen grains showed a reduction to 6.5 per cent after 2 hours' storage, and after 8 hours' storage the viability was nil. The stigma was found to be most receptive between 8 and 10 a.m. on the day the flower opened, giving about 72 per cent fruit set. Thereafter the receptivity decreased gradually, giving a fruit set of 24 per cent at 4 p.m. and nil at 6 p.m. hours.

After the panicles have flowered, fruited and died, the vegetative shoots bearing them also die off.

Ecology

Climate and soils

In the Western Ghats in India, cardamoms are grown at altitudes between 760 m and 1 400 m in areas with an annual rainfall of 1 500−7 000 mm and a temperature range of 10−35 °C. The heaviest rainfall occurs during the period of the south-western monsoon in June to September, which is followed by the north-eastern monsoon, which may continue up to December. The length of the dry season is the main factor in determining the natural range of the species and does not extend for more than three months in the south, but can be of 5 months' duration in the north, although the total annual rainfall is higher in the latter. In the Cardamom Hills of central and northern Travancore, latitude 10−11°N, rainfall seldom exceeds 3 000 mm, whereas in Coorg, some 400 km to the north, wild cardamoms are restricted to the heaviest forest near the westerly edge of the hills with an annual rainfall of at least 5 000 mm.

Cardamoms are very susceptible to wind, and in selecting a site for cultivation, an eastern or south-eastern aspect is preferred.

With the exception of cardamoms planted with areca nuts or coffee, almost all successful cardamom plantations have been established on evergreen forest land, which supplies the most favourable soils for the crop. Such soils usually owe more to the climate and their vegetative cover than to their mineral content. Thus cardamoms can be cultivated on chocolate-coloured forest loam extending to a considerable depth below the humus layer, to white quartz gravel with only a shallow zone of humus accumulation. Under ravine cultivation they may make good growth in pockets of soil among boulders. The crop does best in soils which have received minimum of disturbance with good mulch and adequate water supplies. Cardamoms require good drainage and cannot tolerate waterlogging (Mayne, 1942; Sastri, 1952). The crop thrives best under moderate natural shade.

Cultivation

Propagation

Cardamoms can be propagated vegetatively by division of the rhizomes, or from seedlings usually raised in nurseries. The method used will depend upon the region and the area to be planted.

For vegetative propagation, rhizomes from large clumps of growing plants are taken out, separated into small clumps, each consisting of at least one old and one young shoot, and planted in prepared pits. The method is simple and reliable and permits the use of selected clonal material. It is less costly and gives an earlier yield than is obtained from seedlings. It is difficult, however, to obtain sufficient planting material for planting up large areas and it is very dangerous when diseases and pests are present, particularly the katte or mosaic virus and thrips. There is also the danger of incompatibility within clones.

The most primitive method of establishment is the clearing of small areas of jungle where cardamoms were known to be present, when seedlings, which come up spontaneously, may be thinned or trans-planted into nurseries for use elsewhere, as can seedlings from old cardamom plantings.

For large-scale production it is usual to sow selected seed in specially prepared nursery beds; the seedlings are later transplanted into further nursery beds, and finally into the field. The nursery should be established on deep rich soil in a sheltered position and near a reliable water supply. The seed beds are usually 0.9–1.2 m wide and are prepared on raised ground, divided by 0.6 m paths. Overhead shade is provided.

One kilogramme of seeds contains about 44 000 seeds, but germina-tion is often erratic, delayed or poor. The seed is broadcast on the surface of the beds and covered with soft earth. Sastri (1952) states that the sowing time is usually August to October in Coorg, Mysore and North Kanara, and February and March in Madras. Pattanshetti and Prasad (1973a) sowed freshly extracted seeds during the five months from September to January in Mysore. September gave the highest germination with 72 per cent, compared with only 7 per cent in January. The seedlings from September sowing developed better, withstood leaf spot and leaf rot better and had attained a suitable size of about 45 cm for transplanting in August, whereas other seedlings took more than $1\frac{1}{2}$ years to attain the required size.

Seed for sowing should be collected from ripe capsules of vigorous, high-yielding, disease-free plants of the desired type, preferably more than 5 years old. They should be washed in water and sown imme-diately, or they may be mixed with ash and dried for 2 to 9 days before sowing. Storage affects viability. Yegna Narayan Aiyer (1944) states that about 1 lb of good seed will furnish enough plants for one acre in the field (1.1 kg per hectare). The seeds germinate 5 to 7 weeks after sowing, but germination is irregular and sprouting may continue even up to one year. Seedlings are transplanted when 3 to 4 months old and about 15 cm high at a spacing of 15–45 cm apart into nursery beds, prepared in the same way as the seedbeds. The seedlings need careful attention. They may be sprayed occasionally with Bordeaux mixture to prevent fungal attack.

Aiyadurai (1966) states that in Madras, cardamom seeds are best sown immediately after harvest and that the best season for sowing was December to March when fresh seeds are available. It is recommended that equal quantities of well-rotted cattle manure and wood ash should be spread over jungle soil to a depth of 6 mm and that the seeds should be sown shallow at a seed rate of 90 seeds per 1 000 cm^2. They should be covered with a layer of fine sand and dried leaves or grass. The beds should be kept moist, but not too wet, and given fortnightly sprayings of 1 per cent Bordeaux mixture.

Seedlings are usually transplanted into further nursery beds at a spacing of 15–30 cm apart when they have grown a couple of leaves and are large enough to handle. This is usually when they are 4 to 6 months old, but they may sometimes be left for a year before transplanting. The young plants, after hardening off, are usually planted out into the fields when they are about 2 years old. They may occasionally be younger. Pattanshetti and Prasad (1973b) showed that when seedlings 8–9 months old raised in plastic containers were planted into a rain-fed plantation, 9 per cent were lost in the following dry season. There was no mortality when older seedlings were used which had remained in the nursery for two seasons of 20–21 months or longer. Three years after planting the cumulative yield was greater for the older material. Seedlings maintained in the nursery for more than 2 years became too unwieldy for transplanting.

Planting and after-care

Although cardamoms have been an article of commerce for a very long time, it is only in comparatively recent times that purposeful plantations have been made. Previously the procedure consisted of harvesting a forest product. The next step was the encouragement of the growth of the cardamoms where they were known to occur, by felling a few large trees, after which the volunteer seedlings were thinned and others planted in bare patches, together with an occasional weeding. Little more is done in the Coorg *malai* or male system of cultivation, in which small plots of forest, about 0.1 ha in area, longer than broad, with the long axis running north and south, are cleared of forest and planted up with cardamoms using self-sown or nursery seedlings. Lateral shade is provided by the surrounding forest trees. The area is weeded periodically. Harvesting commences about the third year and continues for some 8 to 10 years, after which the plot is allowed to revert to jungle and new plots are opened up.

In the North Kanara system, cardamoms are grown as a secondary crop in the areca nut and pepper gardens. The seedlings are raised in nurseries and planted 1.5–1.8 m apart.

The plantation system, sometimes known as the southern system, is the most important for commercial production and accounts for about 90 per cent of the total cardamom crop of India. It is the system adopted in Travancore – Cochin and Madras. It consists of clearing selected areas of forest or jungle of all undergrowth and thinning out the overhead shade, usually only leaving trees of the topmost tier. Planting material is obtained by splitting up established clumps, but more usually, and particularly in large holdings, by planting seedlings grown in nurseries (see 'Propagation' above). The size of the holding varies widely, but the greater part are of 2–20 ha, although there are a few estates of 200–400 ha in area.

In Mysore, cardamoms are often planted in coffee plantations on the margins of ravines, while the main area of the hill-slopes are devoted to coffee. In the majority of the areas of India south of the Nilgiris, the principal type grown is Mysore·cardamom, whereas the type grown in Mysore and Coorg is the Malabar cardamom.

In Guatemala cardamoms are interplanted in coffee.

The maintenance of the correct amount of shade is an important feature of cardamom cultivation. It thrives best under moderate shade, but can tolerate a loftier canopy and a heavier shade than coffee. Regulation of the shade includes thinning of the tree canopy if the shade is heavy and the planting of new shade-trees or encouraging self-sown tree seedlings if the shade is insufficient. In Travancore – Cochin and Madras, *Macaranga peltata* Muell. Arg., which appears spontaneously in secondary forest growth in open patches, is encouraged for providing temporary shade. In cleared areas where sufficient shade is not available, and under coffee, temporary shade trees such as *Erythrina subumbrans* (Hassk.) Merr. (syn. *E. lithospermum* Miq.) may be planted. In the areca-nut plantations shade is provided by the areca palms.

Malabar cardamom is less sensitive to sunlight than Mysore cardamom, provided abundant soil moisture is available, but is liable to suffer more damage than Mysore cardamom at lower light intensities if soil moisture content is not so favourable. Pits are dug in cleared land for planting cardamom seedlings or divisions, and are usually 0.6 m wide and 0.45 m deep. The spacing between the pits varies from 1.5 to 3.0 m depending on the type of cardamom grown, the soil fertility and the period for which the plantings are expected to last. The spacing for Mysore cardamom is usually about 3 m each way, while for Malabar cardamom the spacing is usually about 1.8 m. The care given to the preparation of the pits is very variable and ranges from a small hole scooped out at planting time to carefully prepared pits filled with surface soil or a mixture of soil and compost or well-rotted cattle manure. Cardamom plants are shallow-rooted, and deep planting should be avoided. Two seedlings are sometimes planted in each pit, one of which can be used later for filling in gaps in the plantation.

The after-care of cardamoms consists of weeding, removal of old and dying stems, mulching, regulating the shade, manuring and the filling up of vacancies. Cardamoms come into bearing three years after planting, which may be the fourth or fifth year after sowing. Frequent weeding in the first year or so is essential to keep down the regenerating undergrowth. The plants themselves receive comparatively little attention, although the periodic removal may be made of old leafy shoots which have completed their cropping life and are showing signs of dying off.

In view of the need for high soil organic matter, heavy applications of organic matter are recommended, supplemented by inorganic fertilizers. Yegna Narayan Aiyer (1944) recommends the following mixture on the larger estates: 5 cwt per acre (600 kg per hectare) of a mixture of 3 cwt (152 kg) of castor-oil cake, 1 cwt (51 kg) of steamed bone meal and 1 cwt (51 kg) of potassium chloride, in addition to cattle manure when possible. De Geus (1973) gives the following recommendations for fertilizers per hectare: for Kerala 45 kg N, 45 kg P_2O_5 and 45 kg of K_2O; for Mysore 67 kg N (half in organic form), 34 kg P_2O_5 and 100 kg of K_2O; for Tamil Nadu 45 kg N, 34 kg P_2O_5 and 45 kg of K_2O.

Cardamoms planted in areca-nut gardens receive the benefit of the cultivation given to the palms and are often mulched with the leaves of *Emblica officinalis* Gaertn. (syn. *Phyllanthus emblica* L.), together with an application of cattle manure.

Where growth conditions are favourable and the plants are free from mosaic and other diseases and pests, Sastri (1952) gives the economic life of a plantation as 10−15 years for Mysore cardamoms and 7−10 years for Malabar cardamoms.

Harvesting and yields

The first crop, which is usually obtained in the third year after planting, is small; higher and sustained yields are obtained in subsequent years up to the tenth or fifteenth year, depending on the type cultivated, after which the plants become exhausted (Sastri, 1952). Cardamom fruits ripen over an extended period and are usually gathered at intervals of 30−40 days.

In India flowering commences in April and May and continues until July and August, although some flowers may be seen almost throughout the year. The climatic conditions and race differences influence the time and duration of the harvest. Development and ripening of the fruits take about 3 months in the case of the Malabar cardamom and 4 months for the Mysore cardamom. In the Malabar cardamom, fruits begin to ripen in August and harvesting is completed in December or January; ripening of the Mysore cardamom starts in September and harvesting may be prolonged until April.

Fruits are picked just before they are fully ripe. Fully ripe fruits tend to split on drying and do not give such a good colour when dry. Small immature fruits produce an uneven, shrivelled, badly coloured sample. Consequently it is desirable that fruits should be harvested individually at the correct stage of ripeness. This is indicated in the Malabar cardamom by a paling of the fruit; in the Mysore cardamom there is no such indication and considerable experience is necessary to judge the correct time. The fruits are picked with their pedicels and each clump is visited periodically to gather the fruits. A few smallholders cut off the fruiting shoots and strip the capsules; this is to be deplored as it produces a poor sample.

The procedures employed for the preparation of the various forms of the dried spice and the factors influencing their quality are discussed in the 'Processing and manufacture' section.

Sastri (1952) gives the average yield of dry capsules from a well main-tained cardamom estate as 100–150 lb per acre (112–168 kg per hectare). Mayne (1954) states that yields vary greatly, being much affected by climate, more particularly by the rains between December and March. He says that crops of 100 lb per acre (112 kg per hectare) are considered very good, but that they are usually lower than this and that 40–70 lb per acre (45–78 kg per hectare) would represent the more usual level.

Diseases

Mosaic, marble or katte disease is a virus disease of cardamoms. It is transmitted by the banana aphid, *Pentalonia nigronervosa* Coq. Siddappaji and Reddy (1972) give the form on cardamom and *Colocasia* as *caladii* Vanda Goot, as distinct from the form *typica* which occurs on bananas. Mosaic, known as katte in North Kanara and marble in the Anamalais, is the most serious disease of cardamoms in South India. Planting of diseased rhizomes is a serious source of infection and where the disease is serious it is better to propagate the crop by seedlings. The plants may be attacked at any stage of growth. Chattopadhyay (1967) gives the following symptoms. The disease is noted first in the young leaves which show a general chlorosis of the entire leaf with slender, interrupted parallel streaks of pale-green tissue running along the course of the veins from the midrib to the margins. Later the streaks become evenly distributed giving the characteristic mosaic pattern, and diseased plants can be recognized even from a distance by their pale appearance. The affected clumps deteriorate rapidly. Newly formed shoots arising from them dwindle in size, and yield is reduced. Within a year or so of the first appearance of the disease, the clumps usually become useless. The rhizomes gradually shrivel up and the entire clump eventually dies. If young plants are attacked, they generally die before flowering begins. The only control measures appear to be the careful roguing of affected plants and the planting of non-affected seedlings.

A nursery leaf rot, caused by *Coniothyrium* sp. or *Phyllosticta* sp., results in spotting and eventual rotting of the leaves in the nursery. Small water-soaked spots first appear, which gradually extend into large areas and the affected tissues become flaccid and dead and shrink up to the midrib. A large number of dark-coloured pycnidia appear on the dead tissues. The disease is worst in the wet season. Mayne (1942) reports that the disease may be controlled by timely application of Bordeaux mixture.

A rhizome or root rot causes a gradual decline in vigour of the plants. The disease is often confused with mosaic, but the infected plants can be distinguished by yellowing of the leaves without the mosaic pattern. Chattopadhyay (1967) states that older leaves die prematurely and new shoots are weak and unhealthy. Later decay and rotting of the rhizomes at the stem bases occur; shoots become very brittle in that region, collapse and can be pulled out easily. Rhizomes are often found to be rotted and covered with fungal mycelium. Fungi isolated from such rhizomes include *Cephalosporium* sp., *Pythium aphanidermatum* (Edson) Fitzp., and *P. vexans* de Bary. Affected plants may contain the rhizome borer, *Prodioctes haematicus*. Control measures for the disease have not been properly investigated.

Other diseases of cardamoms recorded by Chattopadhyay (1967) but of little economic importance are: a leaf rust, *Uredo elettariae* Thirum.; a leaf spot, *Chlamydomyces palmarum* (Cooke) Mason; and two leaf diseases the pathogens of which are not known.

Pests

Thrips, *Taeniothrips cardamomi* Remak., was first reported in the Anamalai Hills in Madras Province in 1934 and by 1940 had affected almost all cardamom growing districts (Mayne, 1942). They live in the sheathing leaf bases and the floral bracts. In extreme cases the flowers fail to set and this may cause a very severe loss of crop. When injury is less extreme the flowers may set, but injuries caused by thrips result in rough corky scabs on the fruits, varying from slight injury along the angle to extensive scabbed areas which may check fruit development and lead to malformations. The thrips are small greyish-brown or yellowish insects, about 1–1.5 mm in length, with their wings fringed with hairs. The eggs are laid in the softer tissues and the nymphs hatch out in about a week. They moult thrice in 3 weeks and then pupate for 10 to 15 days. Warm, dry weather favours breeding and a rapid build-up of the pest population. Mayne (1942) says that types with prostrate panicles suffer less than types with erect panicles. Aiyadurai (1966) states that the pest is best controlled by Gammexane dust containing the active principle B.H.C. He also gives the following plants which have been observed to be alternate hosts of the thrips: *Hedychium flavescens*, *Amomum cannaecarpum*, *Ramasatia vivipara*, *Colocasia* sp., *Alocasia* sp., and *Musa* sp.

The hairy caterpillar, *Eupterote mollifera* Wlk. (syn. *E. canaraica* Moore), can appear in enormous swarms, attacking the leaves and defoliating whole clumps. It is a forest pest which attacks cardamoms incidentally, but a serious outbreak can do a great deal of damage. The large moth, with a wing span of nearly 10 cm, lays its eggs in large clusters on the undersurface of leaves such as those of the shade trees. After the second moult the caterpillars descend from the trees by threads and attack the cardamoms. They feed by night. The caterpillars, which finally become 7.5 – 10 cm long and greyish-black with tufts of stinging hairs, pupate in the debris of soil, leaves and excreta. Collecting and destruction of the pupae assists in control, as does spraying the caterpillars with insecticide.

Cardamoms are attacked by a number of borers. The weevil, *Prodioctes haematicus* Chevr., bores into the rhizomes and can cause damage both in Sri Lanka and in India. The female oviposits at night in the upper part of the rhizome and the larval stage, which lasts about 3 months, makes tunnels in the stem and rhizome. These provide points of entry for the root-rot fungus. Pupation takes place within the plant and lasts from 4 to 6 weeks. The adult weevil is brown in colour, with three dark lines on the pronotum and six dark spots on the wings. It feeds on the leaves and at this stage is open to attack by insecticides.

The shoot and capsule borer, *Dichocrocis punctiferalis* Guen., is one of the commonest stem borers in the tropics, and, in addition to being a pest of cardamoms, it also infests castor, ginger and turmeric. It is rarely more than a minor pest. The symptoms of attack are the drying up of the shoot tip and bore holes about 3 mm in diameter on the stem, through which the grub pushes out its frass.

The pod borer, *Lampides elpis* Godart, is a minor pest. The butterfly lays its eggs on the flowers and buds. The larvae enter the tissues and pupate in the young fruits.

A tingid bug, *Stephanitis typicus* Dist., may breed in numbers on cardamom leaves.

Two unidentified root borers have been recorded and there are records of attacks by a number of polyphagous coccids and lepidopterous larvae.

Sastri (1952) states that damage is frequently caused by rats, monkeys, porcupines, wild pigs and birds – 'a type of damage almost inseparable from the ecological environment in which the crop is grown.'

Improvement

Being cross-pollinated, considerable variability occurs in the crop. As cardamoms are easily propagated vegetatively, high-yielding clones can be selected. Care is required, however, because of the transmission in vegetative material of mosaic or katte virus and of self-incompatibility within clones. What is required is selection or hybridization for resistance to mosaic or katte virus and thrips, followed by clonal propagation.

Aiyadurai (1966) reports that 120 single plant selections were made from the indigenous cardamoms of the Singampatti Hills in Madras. As a result of subjecting these selections to careful screening, two outstanding selections, Nos '71' and '81', were found which were capable of giving two to five times the yield of the cultivated bulk cardamoms.

Other species

Cardamom substitutes which sometimes appear in trade and which may be confused with true cardamom, *Elettaria cardamomum*, are species belonging to the genera *Aframomum* K. Schum. and *Amomum* L. in the family Zingiberaceae. *Aframomum melegueta* (Rosc.) K. Schum. (syn. *Amomum melegueta* Rosc.) is the melegueta pepper, also known as grains of paradise or Guinea grains. It is a West African plant, which grows wild and is sometimes cultivated in Ghana, Guinea, Ivory Coast, Sierra Leone, Dahomey and other West African countries. At one time it was planted on a small scale in Surinam and Guyana in South America. It was formerly of more importance in Europe than it is today. The earliest record, according to Ridley (1912) was at a festival held at Treviso in 1214. There are records, according to Harten (1970), that physicians as far apart as Nicosia, Rome, Lyons and Wales included it in their prescriptions. In those early days the spice was carried by Mandingo traders from West Africa across the Sahara to the port of Mundibarca on the coast of Tripoli. Later it was brought by the Portuguese by sea from the Guinea coast, which was also known as the Grain coast.

Melegueta pepper was in demand as a spice and a stimulating carminative. Queen Elizabeth I of England is said to have been very partial to it. It was used for spicing wines and for strengthening beer. The custom was prohibited by law in the reign of George III and heavy fines were prescribed; an Act of Parliament was passed that no brewer or beer-dealer should have any grains of paradise in their possession, or use it in making beer, under a penalty of a fine of £200, and any druggist selling it to a brewer was fined £500.

During the eighteenth and nineteenth centuries interest in the spice in Western countries gradually decreased, but Harten (1970) states that even in 1940, 19 857 pounds (9 015 kg) were imported into the United States. Exports from Ghana were 191 011 pounds (86 719 kg) in 1871, of which 85 502 pounds (38 818 kg) went to the United Kingdom, 620 191 pounds (281 567 kg) valued at £10 303 in 1872, and 151 783 pounds (68 909 kg) valued at £912 in 1875. Although the use in the West has declined, the fruit pulp of this and other species of *Aframomum* are chewed as a refreshing stimulant and the seeds are used for seasoning foods and in local medicine in West Africa.

A. melegueta is a perennial reed-like herb up to 1.8 m high with short

rhizomes from which arise distinct leafy shoots and short inflorescences. The narrow lanceolate leaves are 18−22 cm long and 1.8−2.5
cm broad, mostly glabrous, glossy green, with an acuminate apex. The
inflorescences are borne at the base of the leafy shoots on very short
peduncles with reddish bracts. The delicate trumpet-shape flower has
one erect lanceolate lobe, two linear lobes which are white and pale
violet, and a large, spreading fan-shaped lip or labellum, which is a
petaloid staminode, white tinted with pink and with a red or yellow
blotch at the base. There is a single fertile stamen. The fruits are ovoid
or pear-shaped, 5−10 cm long, red or orange in colour. They contain a
sweet, white, edible pulp in which are embedded 60−100 brownish
seeds, 3−4 mm long, which are aromatic and pungent.

Aframomum granum-paradisi (L.) K. Schum., which also grows in
West Africa, is a distinct species and is not now regarded as the true
grains of paradise. Substitutes for them and for cardamoms are: *A.
daniellii* K. Schum. (syn. *A. hanburyi* K. Schum.), Camerouns
cardamom, from West Africa; *A. korarima* Pereira, Korarima
cardamom, from Ethiopia; and *A. angustifolium* (Sonn.) K. Schum.,
Madagascar cardamom, from Madagascar.

Amomum subulatum Roxb. is the greater Indian or Nepal
cardamom, sometimes called the large cardamom. It is a native of the
eastern Himalayan region. Mukherji (1973) gives the area cultivated in
Darjeeling District as 1 620 ha at altitudes between 830 and 1 830 m. It
is also cultivated in neighbouring Nepal, Bhutan and Sikkim. It is
usually grown by the sides of springs or streams under light forest shade
in areas with a maximum temperature of 14−33 °C, a minimum
temperature of 6−22 °C, and an annual rainfall of 2 000−2 500 mm.

The plant, which is perennial, grows to a height of 2 m, with oblong
to lanceolate glabrous leaves. The inflorescence is a dense short spike
borne near the ground. The flowers have a large, white, central, strap-
shaped lip, and open from the base of the spike upwards. The fruit,
about 2.5 cm long, is ovoid and triangular, deep red when ripe, and
ribbed. It contains 40−50 hard, dark brown, round, aromatic seeds,
embedded in a soft, slimy pulp which is sweet to taste.

Mukherji (1973) states that it is a highly cross-pollinated crop, 'the
pollinating agents being insects like bees, ants, etc, wind and water.'
Despite this there is little variability in the plants of an area as the crop is
largely propagated vegetatively by pieces of rhizome. A plantation
thrives for well over 25 years and it is said not to be uncommon to find
plantations as old as 100 years or more. The planting distance is usually
2 m between plants. Yields continue to increase for a period of 6 to 10
years, thereafter remaining steady. In Darjeeling, emergence of the
inflorescences begins in June and July and harvesting starts from the
end of September and continues until January. Ripe capsules are
harvested once per month. They are dried in the sun or on platforms
under shade with artificial heat. Dried capsules are black or dark brown

and contain not more than 15–20 per cent moisture. Mukherji (1973) gives the yields per hectare as 2–6 quintal (200–600 kg) of ripe fruit and 1–4 quintal (100–400 kg) of dry spice.

The most serious disease is the foorki virus transmitted by the banana aphid, *Pentalonia nigronervosa* Coq., which can cause serious havoc. The disease is quite distinct from the mosaic or katte virus of the true cardamom, *Elettaria cardamomum*. The tips of the leaves dry up and the flowering spikes are leaf-like and bear no fruit. The whole plantation may assume the look of a burnt-out field. Chattopadhyay (1967) states that plants affected by the disease produce at the base a large number of vegetative shoots, which do not grow beyond a few centimeters. The only effective control is to uproot the plants, burn them and replant with healthy disease-free seedlings raised from the true seed. The plants may first be killed by using a herbicide such as Agroxone-4. Aiyadurai (1966) reports that the Sikkim cultivar 'Kopringay' exhibits a fair amount of resistance to foorki disease. He also states that germination studies revealed that large cardamom seeds have a long resting period which is influenced by temperature, low temperature delaying germination. He adds that the maximum number of seeds germinated in June and seeds sown in November gave the best results. A cardamom development scheme was started in 1962 at Kalimpong in Darjeeling District with the object of raising disease-free seedlings, seedlings of improved cultivars and their distribution to bona fide growers at a nominal subsidized rate. By 1972 Mukherji (1973) reported that so far, more than 0.15 million such seedlings had been distributed.

Another virus disease known as chirkay, in which the leaves show mosaic symptoms and the plants get stunted and no fruit is formed, is found occasionally, but does not appear to cause large-scale damage. A third virus disease known as leaf streak is also reported. A leaf blight, caused by *Alternaria* sp., and a clump rot caused by *Pythium* sp., are found in small patches in very damp places. Thrips and hairy caterpillars can damage the young crop.

Mukherji (1973) states that *A. subulatum* seeds are primarily used as a flavouring agent for sweet dishes, cakes and pastries, as a masticatory and for medicinal purposes. For local consumption in Darjeeling it is highly valued for chewing and as an accessory with the betel *pan*.

Cardamom substitutes belonging to the genus *Amomum* which are used in some areas include: *A. aromaticum* Roxb., the Bengal cardamom; *A. kepulaga* Sprague and Burkill (syn. *A. cardamomum* L.), the round cardamom from Java; *A. dealbatum* Roxb. (syn. *A. maximum* Roxb.), also from Java; and *A. krervanh* Pierre, Cambodian cardamom.

The following species are also used and an account of them is given on folios 616–19: *Amomum globosum* Lour.; large round Chinese cardamom, from Southern China; *Amomum xanthioides* Wallich, bastard cardamom, from Thailand; *Aframomum mala* K. Schum. from East Africa.

Products and end-uses

The cardamom spice of international commerce is obtained by drying the fully developed fruit capsules of *Elettaria cardamomum* var. *cardamomum*. In trade the spice is frequently known as 'true cardamom' to distinguish it from the spices obtained by drying the fruit capsules of various *Amomum* and *Aframomum* species and from wild *Elettaria* varieties. While some of these related spices, particularly certain of the *Amomum* species of Asia, are produced in substantial quantities, they are regarded as much inferior in aroma and flavour quality in the major international markets for 'true cardamom', where they are sometimes collectively known as 'false cardamoms'. For simplicity and convenience, the terms 'true cardamom' and 'false cardamoms' will be employed where appropriate in the following sections of this chapter to emphasize the acceptability distinctions.

True cardamom is used directly as a flavouring material in three forms: whole, decorticated seeds, and ground. The spice is also processed on an industrial scale to prepare the distilled essential oil and the solvent-extracted oleoresin. True cardamom is traded internationally predominantly in the whole form, while trade in decorticated seeds is smaller and that in the ground spice is negligible. Grinding is carried out in the consuming centres and the manufacture of the essential oil and the oleoresin is undertaken mainly, but not exclusively, in certain of the main Western importing countries.

The major use of true cardamoms on a world-wide basis is for domestic culinary purposes in the whole or ground form. In Asia, the spice plays an important role in a variety of spiced rice, vegetable and meat dishes. International trade in true cardamoms is dependent, however, on the demand created by specialized applications which have evolved in two distinct markets, namely the Arab countries of the Middle East and in Scandinavia. In the former, the spice has been traditionally used for flavouring of coffee, and in the latter, for flavouring a range of baked goods, including cakes, buns, pastries and bread. In other European countries and in North America, the spice is used mainly in the ground form by the food industries as an ingredient in curry powder, some sausage products, soups, canned fish and to a small extent in the flavouring of tobacco.

Cardamom oil is produced in small quantities in certain Western spice-importing countries and also in India, Guatemala and Sri Lanka. The essential oil finds its main application in the flavouring of processed foods, but it is used also in certain liquid products such as cordials, bitters and liqueurs, and occasionally in perfumery.

Cardamom oleoresin, which is produced in certain of the Western spice-importing countries and in India, has similar applications to the essential oil in the flavouring of processed foods but is less extensively used. Both the oil and oleoresin tend to develop 'off-flavours' when exposed to the air for prolonged periods and their usage is generally confined to meat products of intended short shelf-life, such as sausages.

The major types of true cardamom

True cardamoms are normally marketed on a basis of geographical origin and on their physical form. Some users express strong preferences for particular types in certain applications and this is reflected in price differentials. The four forms in which the spice is supplied to the market and in the usual order of decreasing value are:

1. Whole green cardamoms: these are mature fruits picked while still green, their colour having been preserved by special treatment.
2. Whole bleached cardamoms: mature fruits picked after the green colour has faded and which have been bleached with sulphur dioxide to produce a uniform white appearance.
3. Whole, straw coloured cardamoms: mature fruits which have been simply dried in the sun.
4. Decorticated seeds: this tends to be a product of expediency where due to poor processing the capsules have been blemished or split.

Whole cardamoms are further distinguished into two main categories, Malabar and Mysore types, on the basis of their appearance and chemical characteristics.

Malabar type

This race has the most pleasant and mellow aroma and flavour character. It is, however, not so well suited for the preparation of green cardamom, for when the seeds have developed their full flavour character the capsule has begun to turn pale yellow. The green colour cannot be regained during curing. The cured fruits are generally rounded in shape (this is its most useful distinguishing feature) and are about 18.5 mm in length.

Mysore type

This race has a somewhat harsher aroma and flavour character. However, it is the type most widely grown since the seeds reach flavour maturation when the capsules are still green, which facilitates preparation of the green spice, although judgement of the harvesting time is more difficult. The cured fruits are three cornered and ribbed and tend to be slightly longer than the Malabar type, being about 21 mm in length. (The fruit shape rather than its length is the most useful distinguishing feature for these two races.)

Malabar and Mysore cardamoms, as the names imply, are indige-

Fig. 10.1 Alleppey green cardamom (*Eletteria cardamomum* var. *cardamomum*) ($\times 1\frac{1}{4}$). (Crown copyright).

nous to India but both types have been introduced into other countries.

The world's major source of true cardamoms is India, followed by Guatemala and with Sri Lanka and Tanzania in the third rank. Latterly, Papua New Guinea has also marketed small quantities of true cardamoms. The characteristics of the spice supplied to the market by these countries are summarized below:

Indian cardamoms

Indian exports are comprised mainly of Mysore-type green cardamoms with a smaller proportion of bleached cardamoms (Malabar type) and relatively little decorticated seed.

Mysore-type cardamoms are grown mainly in Kerala and consist of a number of cultivars taking their names from the areas where they are grown or the port of export. The most well known is the Alleppey green which sets the standard by which other types of green cardamom are compared.

Malabar-type cardamoms are mainly grown in Karnataka and similarly consist of a mixture of local cultivars, most of which are bleached for export. Some green cardamoms are produced, however, and Coorg greens are the best known of this type.

Indian green and bleached cardamoms and decorticated seeds are graded into a number of categories prior to export, and the grading system is described in the 'Standard specifications' section.

Guatemalan cardamoms

These consist of green cardamoms and decorticated seed. Guatemalan green cardamoms have achieved a good reputation for quality which is considered comparable to that of the Indian product. They appear to be predominantly of the Mysore type.

Sri Lankan cardamoms

These consist mainly of green cardamoms with a good colour but they are of variable size, Mysore and Malabar types being grown together, and this is considered to detract from their quality by buyers in the Middle East market.

Tanzanian cardamoms

The main export is of sun-dried fruits with a pale-straw colour.

Papua New Guinea cardamoms

Exports are mainly green cardamoms but they are not consistent in colour, reflecting the local difficulties in harvesting and processing, together with the fact that the Malabar type thrives best in the areas where the spice is grown.

'False cardamoms' as 'True cardamom' substitutes

Thailand has been the traditional major supplier for many years of several Indo-Chinese *Amomum* species, classified as 'bastard' or 'best' cardamom, but this source does not appear to have made any real incursions into the traditional market areas for 'true cardamoms'. By

Fig. 10.2   Left − Nepal or large cardamom (*Amomum subulatum*). Right − Ethiopian or Korarima cardamom (*Aframomum korarima*) ($\times \frac{2}{3}$). (Crown copyright)

contrast, quantities of the Ethiopian or Korarima cardamom (*Aframomum korarima*) and the Nepal or large cardamom (*Amomum subulatum*) were sold in Scandinavia in the early 1970s as cheap substitutes for true cardamoms when the prices for the last were very high. The characteristics of these two spices are summarized below:

The Ethiopian or Korarima cardamom

This is produced in the south-western provinces of Gemu Gofa and Keffa. The spice is dark brown in colour, measures between about 3–5.6 cm in length and about 1.5–2.6 cm in diameter, and frequently has a hole in the shell owing to the practice of drying on a string. The volatile-oil content is low (a maximum of about 4.5 per cent) and the aroma and flavour is harsh and camphoraceous.

The Nepal or large cardamom

This is produced in Eastern Nepal, Sikkim, Bhutan, Assam and West Bengal. The freshly harvested capsules are deep red in colour but after drying by the traditional smoking method the spices acquires a dark brown colour. The size is variable but the length averages about 2.3 cm and the diameter about 1.5 cm. The volatile-oil content rarely exceeds 3.5 per cent, usually averaging much lower. The aroma and flavour are coarse and camphoraceous with a smoky note.

Processing and manufacture

Preparation of the spice

Quality requirements

The quality of true cardamoms is assessed on the basis of their appearance and the aroma/flavour character and strength (i.e. content) of the volatile oil. The appearance of the spice and its organoleptic quality are regarded as closely related by many consumers, particularly in the major market of the Middle East; and a premium is paid for small olive-green capsules of intense and uniform colour without surface blemishes of any kind.

This association of the capsule colour with the organoleptic quality of the volatile oil contained within the seeds has arisen from the fact that fading of the green colour closely parallels the deterioration in flavour strength by volatile-oil evaporation losses. The age of green cardamoms is, therefore, more readily discernible than in the case of bleached cardamoms.

Decorticated cardamom seed generally commands a disproportionately lower price than whole cardamoms due to the fairly rapid loss of volatile oil during storage and transportation. Seeds are also classified by weight into 'prime' and 'light' seed, the former fetching a better price.

Factors influencing quality

The content and organoleptic character of the volatile oil, and the colour of the fruit at harvest and hence its suitability for conversion to the bold dried, green form, are primarily dependent upon the cultivar grown. The Malabar type of true cardamom is probably superior in regard to the flavour quality while the Mysore type facilitates the production of the bold green grades.

The stage of maturity of the fruits at harvest is the second most important influence on the quality of the final product. Harvesting should be undertaken when the fruits are fully developed but still green in order to produce the dried, green form of the spice. Over-ripe fruits acquire a yellow colour and also tend to split during drying, while under-ripe green fruits have a low volatile-oil content and shrivel during drying. With both Malabar and Mysore types of cardamom, careful judgement is necessary in deciding the optimum stage for harvesting, and it is normally marked by the fruits breaking away cleanly when bent back from the stem shoots.

Drying of the fruits must be done efficiently to avoid mould formation, which results in skin blemishes that detract from the appearance. At harvest, the fruits have a moisture content of about 75 per cent, which must be reduced to less than 13 per cent for safe storage. In the preparation of green cardamom, described below, the fruits should not be unduly exposed to light during the drying or subsequent storage period, and elevated temperatures during the drying stage must be avoided to prevent volatile-oil loss.

Green cardamoms

The green curing procedure used in India, Guatemala and Sri Lanka is basically similar but with some local modifications. In the usual procedure, the freshly picked green cardamoms are first washed to free them from adhering dirt, then the stalks are clipped off with scissors. Undertaking the clipping after washing rather than before has generally been found to reduce splitting. Some processors favour removal of the stalks after the curing process as they are then detached easily by rubbing with rough canvas.

The curing of the fruits is generally accomplished using a flue heating system in a special shed or barn about 4.5 m square constructed from brick, wood or any suitable local material. A grate furnace is constructed outside the shed from which a flue pipe is run in a U-shape round the inside of the shed at just above floor level, exiting as a stack outside. Wood or any waste material to hand is burnt to provide the source of heat. The walls of the shed are lined with detachable shelves and these are changed periodically during the curing operation from top to bottom to facilitate even drying.

A direct-firing method is also carried out in similar sheds but over an open charcoal fire. This method, although rather more simple to construct, has the disadvantage of being difficult to maintain temperature control, and risks the contamination of the cardamom by smoke. According to McConnell and Upawansa (1972) the method is falling into disuse in Sri Lanka due mainly to the difficulties of preparing suitable charcoal.

After spreading the washed, clipped fruits evenly on the trays, the curing room is completely sealed and the temperature is allowed to rise rapidly to about 54 °C and it is maintained at this level for 3 hours. This treatment arrests further vegetative development in the fruit and fixes the colour of the chloroplasts.

Ventilators are then opened to allow moisture to escape and to reduce the temperature to around 43 °C, at which it is maintained for about 30 hours. Final drying is accomplished by raising the temperature to about 54 °C for a further 3 hours. The total curing time is therefore about 36 hours.

Natarajan *et al.* (1967) have suggested that moisture removal during the second phase of the drying would be facilitated by fitting fans just below ceiling level together with some air inlets above ground level. However, this presumes the availability of electricity, to which many processors do not have access.

The cardamoms are removed from the trays while still hot, and stalk and calyces are removed by rubbing over a wire gauze. They are finally winnowed and graded by hand and stored in rat- and light-proof bins or boxes until required for packing.

A relatively new innovation to the curing procedure described above involves soaking the fruits in 2 per cent washing soda (Natarajan *et al.*, 1968) for 10 minutes prior to drying. This alkali treatment has been claimed to inhibit colour loss during the drying operation and to extend colour retention during subsequent storage from the conventional 3 month period to 10 months (Natarajan *et al.*, 1967, 1968; see also the 'Chemistry' section).

Sun-drying and bleaching

In cases when the cultivar yields fruits which turn yellow before they are ready for picking or where facilites for green-curing are not available, sun-drying of the fruits is practised. The freshly picked cardamoms are laid out in the sun on sacks or rush matting. The process takes 3 to 5 days, during which time the cardamoms are frequently turned to allow even drying. They are also taken indoors overnight to avoid the nocturnal dew and possible theft. This procedure is longer than artificial drying and so can result in surface blemishes if care is not taken to avoid mould formation.

In India, a proportion of the crop is bleached after sun-drying by exposing the spice to fumes from burning sulphur. These bleached cardamoms are particularly favoured in Iran.

Grading

Grading is by bulk density, colour and size. Major exporting countries have an elaborate system of grading and these are described in the 'Standard specifications' section.

Packaging and storage

The factors determining the preservation of the quality of cardamom during storage are the moisture content together with the avoidance of physical damage and excessive heat (Shankaracharya and Natarajan 1971). In the particular case of green cardamoms, light must also be excluded. Green cardamoms should be packed in wooden boxes or tins lined with heavy-gauge black polythene, metal foil or waterproof paper. New jute bags with a waterproof lining are also used where the presentation is less significant as in the packaging of lower grades.

   Cardamom seeds lose their volatile flavour components at a greater rate than whole cardamom; they are therefore not stored in bulk for prolonged periods and should be packed in airtight tins for export.

The essential oil

Cardamom oil is produced commercially by steam distillation of crushed fruits. The yield and organoleptic properties of the essential oil so obtained are dependent upon the type of spice used. In general, spice from a recent harvest, which has not suffered excessive volatile-oil loss, should be employed in order to obtain a good yield. The best oil yields are obtained with Alleppey greens, but the manufacturer's choice of the type of material takes into account the economics of oil recovery.

   Very little has been published on the technique of cardamom oil distillation, except that Baruah *et al.* (1973) have pointed out the necessity of complete distillation to obtain the full flavour character of the oil. They have shown that at least 4 hours' distillation is required to produce the full ester content of the oil.

The oleoresin

Cardamom oleoresin is produced on a relatively small scale and little information has been published on the methods of extraction employed by manufacturers. Solvent extraction yields are of the order of 10 per cent and the content of volatile oil in the oleoresin is dependent upon the raw material and solvent used. Commercial cardamom oleoresins have been offered on the market with volatile-oil contents ranging between 52 and 58 per cent. Cardamom oleoresin used for food flavouring is normally dispersed on salt, flour, rusk or dextrose.

   Replacement strengths quoted by manufacturers suggest that 1 kg of oleoresin cardamom will replace 20 kg of the ground spice.

Chemistry

Study of the chemistry of cardamoms has largely been concerned with that of the true cardamom, *E. cardamom* var. *cardamomum*, and even with this very important commercial species, activity was sporadic up until the 1950s. In more recent years, there has been a resurgence of interest in the subject which has been aimed at improving crop production and product quality.

The characteristic odour and flavour of true cardamom is determined by the composition of its aromatic steam-volatile oil. Recent studies have led to a clearer understanding of the formation of the volatile oil in the fruit and the factors influencing its behaviour during processing, handling and utilization of the dried spice. Similarly, this work has shown the relationship between the composition of the volatile oil to the organoleptic distinctions made between Malabar and Mysore cardamoms.

True cardamom (*Elettaria cardamomum* var. *cardamomum*; syn. var. *minor* Watt; var. *miniscula* Burkill)

The dried fruit of the true cardamom plant contains a steam-volatile oil, fixed (fatty) oil, pigments, proteins, cellulose, pentosans, sugars, starch, silica, calcium oxalate and minerals. The major constituent of the seeds is starch (up to 50 per cent) while in the capsule (husk) it is crude fibre (up to 31 per cent). The relative abundance of some of the constituents of the spice can vary somewhat between individual sample lots owing to intrinsic differences between cultivars, variations in the environmental conditions of growth, in harvesting and drying procedures and the subsequent duration of storage. The possible extent of variation in the general composition of the spice entering international trade has been reported in the literature by Winton and Winton (1939), Pritzer and Jungkunz (1944), Gerhardt (1968), Shankaracharya and Natarajan (1971, 1975), Siebert (1976) and Marsh *et al.* (1977). In addition, Krishnamurthy *et al.* (1967) have given analytical data for a number of cultivars grown in India. The characteristics of the main types of the spice entering trade are summarized in the 'Products and end-uses' section and the current standards in the 'Standard specifications' section.

The principal quality determinant for cardamoms is the content and composition of the volatile oil, which governs the odour and flavour of the spice. For some consumers, however, the colour of the capsule is also regarded as important and a premium is paid for cardamom fruits possessing a good green colour. The initial colour of the dried fruit, whether green or bleached, has no intrinsic value in organoleptic terms, but the extent of colour fading in green cardamoms is a pragmatic indicator of the age of the spice and of the probable deterioration in the organoleptic properties through evaporation losses of the volatile oil.

The volatile-oil content of the spice is dependent upon a number of factors which include the cultivar grown, the stage of maturity at harvest, whether in the form of the whole fruit or as decorticated seeds, and the conditions and duration of storage. Whole cardamoms imported by the major consuming countries usually have volatile-oil contents in the range of 3.5−7 per cent. The content of volatile oil is normally highest in Alleppey greens, a Mysore type of cardamom grown in Kerala, which are generally regarded as the best source of oil.

The volatile oil is located predominantly in the seeds, which comprise 59−79 per cent of the whole dried fruit weight (averaging 65−70 per cent in Indian cardamoms). For cardamoms from a recent harvest, the volatile-oil content of seeds can range up to almost 11 per cent, while that of the husks rarely exceeds 1 per cent (Moudgill, 1924; Fischer *et al.*, 1945; Guenther, 1952; Wellendorf, 1966; Lewis *et al.*, 1966, 1967; Krishnamurthy *et al.*, 1967).

Clevenger (1934) noted that on average the seeds from green cardamoms yield appreciably more volatile oil than those from bleached cardamoms. At that time, it was not known whether the oil content differences were influenced by the variations in the harvesting and/or the processing practices employed in the production of the two spice forms. A recent study by Lewis *et al.* (1967) has indicated, however, that the oil-content differences are probably mainly determined by the intrinsic characteristics of the cultivar grown rather than by any processing effects. It is common for a single cultivar to be grown within a specific production area and the cultivar largely determines whether it is more suitable for drying in the green form or for processing to the bleached product (see the sub-section below dealing with pigments). Lewis *et al.* (1967) confirmed that Alleppey greens (Mysore type), which comprise the bulk of Indian exports of green cardamoms, are outstanding in their high content of volatile oil in the seeds (10.8 per cent). However, examination of Coorg greens and Saklespur bleached cardamoms, Malabar types which are produced in neighbouring areas in Karnataka, revealed only slight differences in their volatile oil contents (9 and 8 per cent respectively).

The relationship of the stage of fruit maturity to the volatile-oil content has been studied by Natarajan *et al.* (1968). As the fruit advances in maturity on the plant, the colour of the seeds within the green pod changes from white, through brown to black. This colour change in the seeds is accompanied by an increase in the volatile-oil content. A significant increase in volatile-oil content occurs on the transformation of the seed colour from white to brown. Black seeds, however, contain only slightly more volatile oil than brown seeds, and there is no marked difference between black seeds in green or fully-ripe, yellow-coloured fruits.

During storage, the volatile-oil content of the spice progressively decreases owing to evaporation losses and there is a concomitant deterioration in the organoleptic quality. The rate of oil loss with various physical forms of the spice during prolonged exposure to the atmosphere has been studied by several workers. Clevenger (1934) reported oil losses over a period of 8 months of 10 per cent in whole cardamoms and 30 per cent in decorticated seeds. Ogzewalla and Willms (1962) found losses over 14 months of 40 per cent in whole cardamoms and 90 per cent with decorticated seeds, while ground seed retained only traces of oil after 13 weeks. Gerhardt (1972) found that decorticated seeds contained only a little oil after 4 months and none after 8 months. The seriousness of the problem with the ground spice has been demonstrated by Strauss (1977), who examined numerous samples sold on the German market over a period of 10 years and found that 25 per cent of the sample lots contained less than 0.9 per cent volatile oil. The influence of storage conditions on the rate of oil loss from decorticated seeds and ground cardamom has been studied by Griebel and Hess (1940), Gerhardt (1972) and Koller (1976). The last-named author concluded that the temperature of storage has a greater influence on the rate of oil loss than does the type of container or the duration of storage.

The organoleptic character of Malabar and Mysore cardamoms are quite distinct and this is due to differences in the composition of the volatile oil which is discussed in the following sub-section. Some other constituents of the spice, however, do have an influence on the flavour perception. The seeds of Mysore cardamoms initially taste sweet owing to the presence of sugar (about 8 per cent) in the mucilage surrounding the seeds, whereas Malabar seeds taste more pungent due to the absence of free sugars.

The fatty (fixed) oil present in the fruits may also have some modifying influence on the flavour perception. The abundance of this component has been reported to range from 1 to 10 per cent and it is predominantly located in the seeds. Some ten fatty acids have been identified in the fatty oil. The major constituent fatty acids have been reported by Miyazawa and Kameoka (1975), Salzer (1975a) and Marsh *et al.* (1977) to be palmitic (28 – 38 per cent), oleic (43 – 44 per cent) and linoleic (2 – 16 per cent). Somewhat different analytical results have been reported by Khrishnan (1951) and Kasturi and Iyer (1955) for seeds of two Indian cultivars in which high stearic acid contents (18 – 38 per cent) were quoted. Kasturi and Iyer have suggested that the relative abundance of the fatty acids may differ according to the cultivar grown.

Cardamom oleoresin is prepared by extraction of the spice with organic solvents, as has been outlined in the 'Processing and manufacture' section. The yield, composition and organoleptic properties of the oleoresin are dependent upon the raw material used, the solvent and the method of preparation. The volatile-oil content of oleoresins usually ranges between 54 and 67 per cent (Salzer, 1975b), whereas the fixed-oil content varies according to the extraction solvent. Hydro-carbon solvents provide oleoresins with a fixed-oil content of 10 to 20 per cent while polar solvents, such as alcohol, give a virtually fat-free product (Naves, 1974).

The volatile oil

The aroma and flavour of cardamom is determined by the composition of its steam-volatile oil. This is comprised mainly of 1,8-cineole and alpha-terpinyl acetate together with smaller amounts of other oxygen-ated monoterpenes, monoterpene hydrocarbons and sesquiterpenes. The differing relative abundance of these constituents accounts for the organoleptic distinctions made between the Malabar and Mysore types of cardamom.

Investigation of the relationship of the oil composition to its aroma and flavour character has mainly been carried out on the steam-distilled essential oil. However, it should be appreciated that the distilled essential oil may contain some artefacts and can differ somewhat in its composition and organoleptic properties from that of the natural volatile oil present in the spice or in carefully prepared oleoresin extracts.

Cardamom oil: This is obtained upon steam distillation of the spice as a colourless or pale-yellow oil which darkens on exposure to light. Arctander (1960) has described the odour as warm-spicy and aromatic and it initially possesses a penetrating camphoraceous, cineole-like note, reminiscent of eucalyptus. Later, the odour becomes balsamic woody and increasingly sweet and almost floral on dry-out. He describes the flavour as rich-aromatic, warm and spicy, somewhat pungent at high concentrations, and fairly bitter if not diluted. The oils obtained from the Malabar and Mysore types have distinctly different organoleptic properties. Mysore cardamom oil has a pronounced harsh camphoraceous odour while that of the Malabar oil is more mellow and agreeable. The flavour of both types of oil deteriorates on prolonged storage even when air is excluded.

The yield and properties of the oil obtained upon distillation are dependent upon the spice type used, its age and to some extent upon the care taken during the distillation operation. The best distillation yields are usually achieved with freshly decorticated seeds from Alleppey greens. The physicochemical properties of various types of cardamom oil have been well reported in the literature (Rao *et al.*, 1925; Fischer *et al.*, 1945; Krishnan and Guha, 1950; Guenther, 1952; Gildemeister and Hoffmann, 1956; Nigam *et al.*, 1965; Lewis *et al.*, 1966; Baruah *et al.*, 1973) and the current standards are given in the 'Standard specifi-cations' section. Clevenger (1934) has reported that the physico-chemical properties of oil obtained from decorticated seeds and from whole fruit are virtually identical. The best-quality oils exhibit refractive index, optical rotation and ester-content values at the higher end of the normal range (Wellendorf, 1966). On storage, cardamom oil deteriorates in quality, and this change is accompanied by a decrease in the refractive index and optical-rotation values (Moudgill, 1924).

The composition of cardamom oil was first examined by Dumas and Peligot in 1834 who isolated terpin-hydrate, but later workers have regarded this compound as an artefact. Subsequent investigations by the Schimmel Co. (1897), Parry (1899), Wallach (1908) and Moudgill (1924) led to the identification of 1,8-cineole, alpha-terpinyl acetate, limonene, sabinene, alpha-terpineol and borneol as components of the oil. Little further progress was made with composition studies until the advent of gas-chromatography analysis in the 1960s. At the time of writing this review, some 40 compounds had been reported in the literature as constituents of cardamom oils (see Table 10.1).

The major components of cardamom oils are 1,8-cineole (20–60 per cent) and alpha-terpinyl acetate (20–53 per cent). The normal maximum contents for other principal components of cardamom oils are as follows: linalyl acetate, linalol and borneol (each up to 8.0 per cent); alpha-terpineol (4.3 per cent); alpha-pinene, limonene and myrcene (each up to 3 per cent). The relative abundance of individual components varies between samples and this is dependent upon a number of factors which are discussed below.

The total content of monoterpene hydrocarbons is usually less than 10 per cent and is frequently below 5 per cent in commercially distilled oils. The lower values found in some commercial oils possibly arise from evaporation losses of these low-boiling-point components during storage of the spice prior to distillation. There have been some exceptionally high values reported, however, where monoterpene-hydrocarbon contents of 15–23 per cent, associated with a particularly high limonene abundance, were found in commercial oils (Ikeda *et al.*, 1962; Nigam *et al.*, 1965; Chou, 1974). Bernhard *et al.* (1971) have suggested that in such cases there are grounds for suspecting adulteration of the distillation material with 'false cardamoms' (*Amomum* species or wild *Elettaria* species).

A number of changes can be wrought in the oil composition during distillation if the operation is not undertaken with due care. Incomplete distillation can lead to an unnaturally high cineole-to-terpinyl acetate ratio (Baruah *et al.*, 1973) and failure to recover some high-boiling-point components of considerable flavour significance (Lewis *et al.*, 1974). Lewis *et al.* (1966) have also suggested that enhanced terpene alcohol contents arise through hydrolysis during distillation. Commercial oils often contain up to 2 per cent *p*-cymene whereas Bernhard *et al.* (1971) found very little present in oils prepared by cold-pressing of seeds, and these authors have suggested that this compound is an artefact produced during distillation.

Studies of intrinsic differences between the volatile-oil compositions

Table 10.1 *Constituents identified in the essential oils of* Elettaria *species*

	True cardamom (E. cardamomum var. cardamomum)	Wild Indian cardamoms ('Ceylon type')	Wild cardamom of Ceylon (E. cardamomum var. major)
Monoterpene hydrocarbons			
p-cymene	(5,6,8,9,11–13)	(8)	–
camphene	(10,12,13)	–	(10)
d-limonene	(2,5,6,8–13)	(8)	(10)
myrcene	(5,6,8–10,12,13)	(8)	(10)
α-phellandrene	(10)	–	(10)
α-pinene	(5–13)	(8)	(10)
β-pinene	(5,10,12)	–	–
sabinene	(4,6–13)	(8)	(10,14)
α-terpinene	(5,10,12)	–	(10)
γ-terpinene	(5,10,12)	–	(10,15)
α-thujene	(5)	–	–
Monoterpene epoxides & carbonyls			
1,4-cineole	(9,13)	–	–
1,8-cineole	(1,6–13)	(8)	(10)
ascaridole	(10)	–	(10)
dl-camphor	(10,12)	–	(10)
cis-citral	(10)	–	(10)
trans-citral	(10)	–	(10)
citronellal	(10)	–	–
Monoterpene alcohols			
dl-borneol	(4,6,8,10,12,13)	(8;?)	(10)
citronellol	(10–12)	–	(10)
geraniol	(6,8,10–13)	(8)	(10)
linalol	(6,8–13)	(8)	(10)
cis-p.2-menthen-1-ol	(13)	–	–
trans-p.2-menthen-1-ol	(13)	–	–
nerol	(6,8,10,12,13)	(8)	(10)
trans-sabinene hydrate	(9,10)	–	(10)
α-terpineol	(1,6,8–13)	(8)	(10)
β-terpineol	(6,8,11,13)	(8)	(10)
4-terpinenol	(9,10,12,13)	–	(10,14,15)
Monoterpene esters			
geranyl acetate	(10,13)	–	(10)
neryl acetate	(6,8–10,13)	(8)	(10)
linalyl acetate	(6,8–13)	(8)	(10)
α-terpinyl acetate	(1,3,6–13)	(8)	(10)
4-terpinenyl acetate	(10)	–	(10)
Sesquiterpenes			
bisabolene	(10)	–	(10)
farnesol	(10)	–	(10)
cis- and *trans*-nerolidol	(6,8–10,12,13)	(8)	–
Misc.			
methyl heptanone	(6,8,11–13)	(8)	(10)
heptacosane	(6,8,11)	(8)	(10)
2-undecane	(6)	–	–
3-tridecane	(6)	–	–

References for Table 10.1
1. Schimmel & Co. (1897)
2. Parry (1899)
3. Wallach (1908)
4. Moudgill (1924)
5. Ikeda *et al.* (1962)
6. Nigam *et al.* (1965)
7. Wellendorf (1966)
8. Lewis *et al.* (1966)
9. Brennand and Heinz (1970)
10. Bernhard *et al.* (1971)
11. Baruah *et al.* (1973)
12. Chou (1974)
13. Miyazawa and Kameoka (1975)
14. Weber (1887)
15. Wallach (1906)

of Malabar-type and Mysore-type cardamoms have been undertaken
by Nigam *et al.* (1965), Wellendorf (1966), Lewis *et al.* (1966) and
Baruah *et al.* (1973) using distilled oils, and by Bernhard *et al.* (1971))
using cold-pressed oils. These investigations included examination of
the following named types: Mangalore, Coorg greens, Alleppey greens
and Guatemalan – Malabar. The results obtained indicate that the differences in oil composition between Malabar and Mysore cardamoms is
quantitative rather than qualitative. Mysore-type oils generally possess
a rather higher cineole content than Malabar-type oils, while the reverse
situation holds in regard to the alpha-terpinyl acetate (see Table 10.2).
In addition, the linalol and linalyl acetate contents are usually somewhat greater in Malabar oils than in Mysore oils. The differing contents
of these components is thought to account in a large part for the
organoleptic distinctions made between two types of oils.

Table 10.2 *Cineole and alpha-terpinyl acetate contents in the essential oil of some commercial types of true cardamom*

	1:8-cineole (per cent)	alpha-terpinyl acetate (per cent)	Ref.
Mysore	41–49	30–45	(1)
Mysore	41	30	(2)
Mysore-type Ceylon	44	37	(3)
Coorg greens	41	30	(4)
Mangalore	51–56	23–35	(1)
Alleppey greens	27	35	(4)
Alleppey	38	33	(1)
Alleppey	34	37	(5)
Malabar	28–43	45	(1)
Malabar	27	35	(2)
Malabar-type Ceylon	31	52	(3)
Malabar-type Guatemala	23	50	(3)
Guatemalan	36–38	31–38	(1)

References
1. Wellendorf (1966)
2. Lewis *et al.* (1966)
3. Bernhard *et al.* (1971)
4. Lewis *et al.* (1967)
5. Baruah *et al.* (1973)

In the past, uncertainty existed over whether the processing of freshly harvested fruit into either the green or the bleached forms of the spice resulted in any marked differences in the volatile-oil compositions of the products. Lewis *et al.* (1967) investigated this question and found that in two grades of Malabar-type cardamoms, Coorg greens and Saklespur bleached, there were only slight differences in the compositions of their distilled oils. Any pronounced differences observed in the volatile-oil composition and organoleptic properties of samples of green and bleached cardamoms from a recent harvest are, therefore, more likely to be a consequence of intrinsic cultivar characteristics (i.e. Malabar or Mysore) than to changes wrought by processing. Although no studies appear to have been undertaken to determine whether the volatile-oil composition changes during maturation of the fruit, one might infer from the work of Lewis *et al.* that the composition is stable in fruit containing black seeds harvested when the husk is green or yellowish in colour.

It has been mentioned earlier that the organoleptic quality of the spice and the distilled essential oil deteriorates on storage. With the spice, these changes are largely associated with evaporation losses while with the distilled essential oil, chemical transformations are solely responsible. These detrimental changes are frequently accentuated under common utilization conditions when the spice or the distilled essential oil are employed as flavourings. For example, cardamom in baking products may be exposed to oven temperatures of 149–205 °C for 5–90 minutes and in the preparation of some beverages and pickles to a pH as low as 2.8 with simmering for 15–25 minutes. Brennand and Heinz (1970) have reported that under these conditions considerable changes in the volatile-oil composition can occur, involving hydrolysis, isomerization and oxidation. Temperatures greater than 149 °C were found to result in a marked reduction in the contents of sabinene, linalyl acetate and alpha-terpinyl acetate and to an enhancement of the *p*-cymene content with a corresponding deterioration in flavour. In acid media, especially with a pH below 4 and at elevated temperatures, considerable changes were also found to occur but these probably result in rather more subtle flavour changes: alpha-terpinyl acetate is hydrolysed to its alcohol and linalyl acetate is suspected to isomerize to neryl acetate.

Interested readers should refer to papers by Anon. (1973) and Salzer (1975b) for the gas-chromatography conditions recommended for cardamom-oil analysis.

The capsule pigments

The chemistry of the pigments present in the capsule of cardamom fruit has received little attention. The major pigment is assumed to be chlorophyll and the colour fading is thought to be analogous to that of peas and other green vegetables. In this process the magnesium ion of the chlorophyll molecule is substituted by hydrogen ions, donated by organic acids present in the fruit, which results in an irreversible conversion to pheophytin (Campbell, 1937, 1950; Mackinney and Weast, 1940; Dutton *et al.*, 1943; Gold and Weckel, 1959).

The initial colour of dried cardamom fruit is dependent upon the intrinsic characteristics of the cultivar, the time of harvesting and the method of preparing the dried spice. Cardamom fruits gradually turn a pale green on ripening and if left until full maturity on the vine they change to a deep yellow colour and are susceptible to splitting during drying. If a good green colour is required in the dried spice, the optimum time for harvesting is when the fruits are still green but the seeds have acquired a black colour. The stage of development at which the fruit commences to turn from green to yellow is not uniform among the different cultivars, however, and this acounts for the specialization in the production of green or bleached cardamoms in the various producing regions of India (Natarajan *et al.*, 1967). In Kerala State, where the main variety grown is the Mysore type, most of the fruits are still green when at a suitable stage of development for harvesting and this region is renowned for its green cardamoms, epitomized by Alleppey greens. By contrast, in certain areas of Karnataka (e.g. Saklespur and Mudigere), where Malabar-type cardamoms are grown, the majority of fruits begin to turn yellow before they mature, and a uniformly coloured product can only be achieved by bleaching.

The retention of a good green colour in cardamoms after harvesting is dependent upon the care taken during the drying operation and in the subsequent handling and storage conditions. The pigmentation is initially fixed by subjecting the harvested fruit to a sudden rise in temperature to about 60 °C which kills the chloroplast. The subsequent rate of the fading of the colour during storage of the dried spice is influenced by the moisture content, the temperature and the exposure to light (Thomas and John, 1966). Under suitable storage conditions, which are discussed in the 'Processing and manufacture' section, the colour of conventionally dried green cardamoms remains good for up to 3 months. The recently introduced pre-drying alkali treatment for green cardamoms has the advantage of delaying fading for up to 10 months (Natarajan *et al.*, 1967, 1968). The effect of the alkali dip is believed to be twofold: (*a*) it accelerates drying by removing the waxy bloom on the capsule; and, more importantly, (*b*) it impregnates the capsule with sodium carbonate and thereby installs a delaying barrier to hydrogen ions attacking the chlorophyll.

Related species ('False cardamoms')

Of the numerous species closely related botanically to true cardamom, most of which are employed in the growing areas as spices or in the preparation of medicines, there are only two which normally enter

Western trade as low-grade substitutes for true cardamom: the Nepal or large cardamom (*A. subulatum* Roxb.) and the Korarima cardamom from Ethiopia (*A. korarima* Pereira). The wild cardamom of Ceylon (*E. cardamomum var. major* Thwaites) could perhaps be included in this grouping as it probably enters trade to some extent as an adulterant in consignments of decorticated seeds of true cardamom or true cardamom oil.

In general, the chemical information available on the various *Amomum* and *Aframomum* species is rather limited, and that which has been reported is summarized in the following paragraphs. These species differ principally from true cardamom in that the composition of their volatile oils, which determine their aroma and flavour, contain very little alpha-terpinyl acetate. Some of the *Aframomum* species also contain pungent principles.

Readers interested in obtaining further background information on *Amomum* and *Aframomum* species are recommended the accounts by Parry (1918), Winton and Winton (1939), Viehover and Sung (1937), Bouquet and Kerharo (1950), Ferrara (1957), Guenther (1952), Gildemeister and Hoffmann (1956), Berger (1964), Kulkarni and Pruthi (1967), Melchior and Kastner (1974) and Singh *et al.* (1978).

The wild cardamom of Ceylon (*Elettaria cardamom* var. major Thwaites)

The wild cardamom of Ceylon possesses a similar general composition to that of true cardamom but its aroma and flavour is considered inferior. On steam distillation, the dried fruit yields 2−6 per cent of a rather viscous essential oil which has a low optical-rotation value (+ 12 ° to + 16 °) in comparison with true cardamom oil (Sage, 1924; Guenther, 1952; Gildemeister and Hoffmann, 1956).

The composition of the distilled essential oil was first investigated by Weber (1887) and Wallach (1906), who reported the presence of the following as components: sabinene, terpinene, 4-terpinenol and terpineol esters. No further detailed composition studies appear to have been undertaken until Bernhard *et al.* (1971) carried out a gas-chromatography analysis of cold-pressed oil prepared from authenticated Sri Lankan seeds. These authors reported that the composition of the volatile oil of wild cardamon of Ceylon is qualitatively similar to that true cardamom (see Table 10.1) but that it is substantially different in quantitative terms. Their oil was characterized by an extremely high monoterpene hydrocarbon content (42 per cent) and very low 1,8-cineole and alpha-terpinyl acetate contents of 3.3 and 0.14 per cent respectively. The major individual components of the oil were found to be *trans*-sabinene hydrate (22 per cent), 4-terpinenol (15 per cent), alpha-pinene (13 per cent) and gamma-terpinene (11 per cent). Bernhard *et al.* commented that adulteration of true cardamom oil with the oil from the wild cardamom of Ceylon would be indicated by a marked enhancement of the monoterpene hydrocarbon content.

Investigations of wild Indian cardamoms, described as 'Ceylon type', by Moudgill (1924) and Lewis *et al.* (1966) provided oils on distillation in yields of 6–9.5 per cent which possessed properties very similar to those of true cardamom oils (e.g. optical rotation values of + 23 ° to + 35 °). Lewis *et al.* found also that their oil was qualitatively and quantitatively similar in composition to that of true cardamom oils – the 1,8-cineole and alpha-terpinyl acetate contents being 36 and 30 per cent respectively. Both Sage (1924) and Bernhard *et al.* (1971) have commented that this type of wild Indian cardamom is probably a larger-fruited form of the true cardamom and has lesser affinities with the authentic wild cardamom of Ceylon.

The Nepal or large cardamom (*Amomum subulatum* Roxb.)

The Nepal cardamom, which is grown in Nepal, Sikkim, Bhutan and Bengal, possesses a rather flat, cineole-like aroma and occasionally the traditional drying process introduces a smokey-note. Its flavour is much inferior to that of true cardamom. On steam distillation, the fruit yields 1–3.5 per cent of an essential oil. Quantitative chromatographic analyses of the composition of the distilled essential oil have been reported by Nigam and Purohit (1960) and by Lawrence (1970) and the constituents identified by these workers are listed in Table 10.3. A number of samples obtained from Nepal have also been examined at the Tropical Products Institute (unpublished results), and gas-chromatography analysis of the distilled essential oils confirmed the conclusions of the aforenamed workers that the composition is qualitatively similar to that of true cardamom oil. The major constituent of Nepal cardamom oil is 1,8-cineole (65–80 per cent) while the content of alpha-terpinyl acetate is low (traces to 5 per cent). The monoterpene hydrocarbon content is in the ranges 5–17 per cent, of which limonene, sabinene, the terpinenes and the pinenes are significant components. The terpineols comprise some 5–7 per cent of the oil. The high cineole content and the low terpinyl acetate content probably account for the very 'harsh' aroma of this spice in comparision with that of the true cardamom.

A number of flavonoids have also been identified in the seeds (Bheemasankara Rao *et al.*, 1976; Laksmi and Chauhan, 1977).

The Korarima or the Ethiopian cardamom (*Aframomum korarima* Pereira.)

As in the case of the Nepal cardamom, the Korarima cardamom from Ethiopia possesses a rather flat, cineole-like aroma and has an inferior flavour when compared with true cardamom. The distilled essential oil is obtained in yields of 1–4.5 per cent and it exhibits a negative optical-rotation value. Early investigations of the oil by the Schimmel Co. (1878), Haensel (1905) and Holmes (1914) yielded little information on its composition, other than that cineole was thought to be present. Lawrence (1970) has reported a gas-chromatography study of the distilled essential oil in which a number of constituents were identified (see Table 10.3). Similar results have been obtained at the Tropical Products Institute (TPI) (unpublished results) with samples obtained direct from Ethiopia. The oil composition is qualitatively similar to that of true cardamom and the major component is 1,8-cineole (35–41 per cent). The presence of alpha-terpinyl acetate was not reported by Lawrence but 5–8 per cent was found in the TPI samples. The mono-terpene hydrocarbon content is high (30–40 per cent), of which limonene, sabinene and alpha- and beta-pinene are the principal components. Monoterpene alcohols comprise some 7–14 per cent of the oil.

The round, Java or Siam cardamom (*Amomum kepulaga* Sprague and Burkill syn. *A. cardamomum* L.)

The dried fruit of this species has a strong camphoraceous odour and an aromatic flavour. The Schimmel Co. (1897b) reported obtaining a semi-solid essential oil in a yield of 2.4 per cent on steam distillation. This oil had an odour reminiscent of camphor and borneol, an optical rotation value of + 38 °, and was found to contain *d*-borneol and *d*-camphor is roughly equal proportions as the major constituents. Later, de Jong (1911) reported the preparation of a rather different type of oil from spice grown in Java. This exhibited a very low negative optical rotation and contained cineole (12 per cent).

No further composition studies appear to have been undertaken until Lawrence *et al.* (1972) carried out a gas-chromatography analysis of an oil distilled from fruit grown in Thailand. This oil, which was said to have an aroma reminiscent of true cardamom, contained 1,8-cineole as the major component (67 per cent) but no alpha-terpinyl acetate. Of the other 14 identified constituents (see Table 10.3), the following were present in significant quantities: beta-pinene (16 per cent), alpha-pinene (4 per cent), alpha-terpineol (5 per cent) and humulene (3 per cent). This study casts doubt on the botanical identity of Schimmel's sample, which appears to have closer affinities with *A. globosum*.

The large round Chinese cardamom (*Amomum globosum* Lour.)

This spice from southern China possesses an aromatic aroma and a camphoraceous and cooling flavour. Descriptions of the distilled essential oil, obtained in yields of 4–6 per cent, and its physico-chemical constants have been reported by the Schimmel Co. (1913) and Viehover and Sung (1937). More recently, Lawrence *et al.* (1972) have reported a gas-chromatography analysis of a distilled oil obtained in a yield of 2.5 per cent from fruit grown in Thailand. Twenty-six consti-tuents were identified in this oil (see Table 10.3), of which the major components were camphor (39 per cent) and bornyl acetate (39 per

Table 10.3 *Constituents identified in the essential oils from the fruits of some* Amomum *and* Aframomum *species*

	Amomum subulatum	*Aframomum korarima*	*Amomum kepulaga*	*Amomum globosum*	*Amomum xanthioides*	*Aframomum mala*	*Aframomum angustifolium*
Monoterpene hydrocarbons							
p-cymene	(2)	(2)	(5)	(5)	–	–	–
camphene	–	(2)	–	(5)	(7)	–	–
limonene	(2)	(2)	(5)	(5)	(7)	(9)	(10)
myrcene	(2)	(2)	(5)	–	–	–	–
α-phellandrene	–	(2)	–	(5)	(7)	(9)	–
α-pinene	(2)	(2)	(5)	(5)	(7)	(9)	(10)
β-pinene	(2)	(2)	(5)	–	–	(8,9)	(10)
sabinene	(1,2)	(2)	–	–	–	(9)	–
α-terpinene	(1,2)	(2)	–	–	–	–	–
γ-terpinene	(1,2)	(2)	–	–	–	–	–
terpinolene	–	(2)	–	(5)	–	–	–
Monoterpene epoxides and carbonyls							
1,8-cineole	(1,2)	(2)	(4,5)	(5)	–	(8,9)	–
d-camphor	–	–	(3)	(5)	(6)	–	–
carvone	–	–	(5)	–	–	–	–
geranial	–	–	–	(5)	–	–	–
geranyl acetone	–	–	–	(5)	–	–	–
myrtenal	–	–	(5)	–	–	–	–
Monoterpene alcohols							
d-borneol	–	–	(3)	(5)	–	–	(10)
geraniol	–	(2)	–	–	–	–	–
linalol	–	–	–	(5)	(6)	–	–
nerol	–	–	–	(5)	–	–	–
α-terpineol	(1,2)	(2)	(5)	–	–	(8)	(10)
γ-terpineol	(1,2)	(2)	(5)	–	–	–	–
terpinen-4-ol	(1,2)	(2)	(5)	–	–	–	–
Monoterpene esters							
bornyl acetate	–	–	–	(5)	(6)	–	–
fenchyl acetate	–	–	–	(5)	–	–	–
geranyl acetate	–	–	–	(5)	–	–	–
neryl acetate	–	–	–	(5)	–	–	–
α-terpinyl acetate	(1)	–	–	–	–	–	–
Sesquiterpenes							
α-amorphene	–	–	–	(5)	–	–	–
trans-α-bergamotene	–	–	–	(5)	–	–	–
bisabolene	(1)	–	–	–	–	–	–
δ-cadinene	–	–	–	(5)	–	–	–
caryophyllene	–	–	(5)	–	–	–	(8)
copaene	–	–	–	(5)	–	–	–
ar-curcumene	–	–	–	(5)	–	–	–
farnesol	–	–	–	(5)	–	–	–
humulene	–	–	(5)	–	–	–	–
humulene epoxide II	–	–	(5)	–	–	–	–

Table 10.3   (*Continued*)

	Amomum subulatum	Aframomum korarima	Amomum kepulaga	Amomum globosum	Amomum xanthioides	Aframomum mala	Aframomum angustifolium
nerolidol	(2)	–	–	(5)	(6)	–	–
δ-selinene	–	–	–	(5)	–	–	–
α-ylangene	–	–	–	(5)	–	–	–

References
1. Nigam and Purohit (1960)
2. Lawrence (1970)
3. Schimmel and Co. (1897)
4. De Jong (1911)
5. Lawrence *et al.* (1972)
6. Kariyone and Yoshida (1930)
7. Chau (1975)
8. Worsley (1934)
9. Eglington and Hamilton (1965)
10. Coomes *et al.* (1955)

cent). The 1,8-cineole content was 1 per cent and alpha-terpinyl acetate was absent.

The bastard cardamom (*Amomum xanthioides* Wallich.)

The bastard cardamom from Thailand possesses a distinctive, peculiar and camphor-like taste. Kariyone and Yoshida (1930) reported preparing two essential oils which exhibited somewhat different properties on distillation of two samples of the spice (yields of 1.7–3 per cent). One oil had a pronounced camphoraceous odour and contained an unidentified terpene, bornyl acetate and *d*-camphor. The second oil contained linalol, nerolidol and *d*-camphor. More recently, Chau (1975) reported identifying *d*-limonene, camphene, alpha-pinene and phellandrene as constituents of the monoterpene hydrocarbon fraction of the oil. A detailed examination and characterization of the volatile oil from an authenticated sample of this species is yet awaited.

The Bengal cardamom (*Amomom aromaticum* Roxb.)

This spice, which is grown in Bengal and Assam, possesses a strong camphoraceous and cineole-like aroma and flavour which is markedly different from that of true cardamom. The Schimmel Co. (1897a) prepared an essential oil in a yield of 1 per cent which exhibited a negative optical rotation and contained cineole. This spice appears to have been ignored in more recent times by chemists.

The melegueta pepper or grains of paradise (*Aframomum melegueta* (Rosc.) K. Schum.)

This spice from West Africa possesses a faint aromatic odour and a strong pungent taste. The Schimmel Co. (1897c, 1915) reported preparing an essential oil in yields of 0.3 − 0.75 per cent, which exhibited a negative optical-rotation value and was thought to contain phenolic components. No further work appears to have been undertaken on the essential oil composition in subsequent years.

The pungent principles, which comprise up to 3 per cent of the seeds, were first isolated in a crude form by Thresh (1884) and were given the name 'paradol' in subsequent investigations. A more detailed chemical study was carried out later by Nelson (1917), who drew attention to the similarities in properties between 'paradol' and 'gingerol', the pungent principle of ginger. Interest appears to have lapsed on the problem, apart from one study by Griebel (1943), until recent years when Connell (1970) succeeded in elucidating the structure of the pungent principles. Connell isolated the 'paradol' fraction from a commercial seed sample of unspecified origin and demonstrated that it consisted of a series of 1-(4-hydroxy-3′-methoxyphenyl)-alkan-3-ones related to the pungent principles of ginger (see Chapter 8 on Ginger). The major pungent constitutents were found to be [6]-paradol and (+)-[6]-gingerol, and these were accompanied by trace amounts of [8]-gingerol, [8]-paradol and [6]-shogaol.

Tackie *et al.* (1975) have reported an examination of seeds of Ghanaian origin in which [6]-paradol, [7]-paradol and [6]-shogaol were identified as the major constituents of the pungent-principle fraction, but the gingerols were absent. The differences in the pungent-principle composition found in these two investigations may arise from intrinsic cultivar differences or from the difficulties of botanical identification, which have been described by Harten (1970).

Aframomum mala K. Schum.

This species from East Africa was first examined by the Schimmel Co. (1905). Steam distillation provided an essential oil in a yield of 0.76 per cent which contained terpineol and cineole. Later, Worsley (1934) reported preparing an essential oil in yield of 3.2 − 3.4 per cent by distillation of seeds which exhibited slightly different physicochemical properties from those recorded by the Schimmel Co. This oil was found to contain 1,8-cineole (41 per cent) and an unidentified monoterpene, named 'kayene' (37 per cent), as the major components and terpineol, caryophyllene and beta-pinene as minor components.

The compostion of the essential oil was reinvestigated by Eglinton and Hamilton (1965), who suggested that Worsley's kayene was an unresolved mixture of beta-pinene and sabinene. In their oil, the monoterpene content was 85 per cent with 1,8-cineole (39 per cent) as the major component. Alpha-pinene, beta-pinene, limonene and sabinene were present in significant quantities (10−21 per cent) together with a little alpha-phellandrene.

The Madagascar cardamom (*Aframomum angustifolium* (Sonn.) K. Schum.)

The first study of this species was made by the Schimmel Co. (1912) in which an essential oil, possessing a cajeput-like odour and a negative optical rotation, was obtained in a yield of 4.5 per cent from seeds. Much later, Coomes *et al.* (1955) distilled seeds collected in Zanzibar and obtained an essential oil in a yield of 1 per cent which possessed an unattractive odour and somewhat different physicochemical constants from those recorded by the Schimmel Co. Analysis of the Zanzibar seed oil revealed a monoterpene hydrocarbon content of 41 per cent with beta-pinene (23 per cent) as the major component and alpha-pinene and limonene/dipentene present in significant quantities. Other constituents included cineole (18 per cent), alcohols (11 per cent, mainly of *d*-borneol and *l*-alpha-terpineol) and sesquiterpenes (13 per cent; probably mainly sesquibenihen). These authors suggested that the seeds examined by the Schimmel Co. may have been of different botanical identity.

The Madagascar cardamom is used as a substitute for pepper in the areas where it is grown, but the identity of the pungent principles has not been investigated.

The Cameroons cardamom (*Aframomum danielli* K. Schum.)

The Schimmel Co. (1897d) reported preparing an essential oil in a yield of 2.3 per cent which had a negative optical-rotation value and contained cineole. No further work appears to have been undertaken on this species in more recent times.

Standard specifications

True cardamom (*Elettaria cardamomum* var. *cardamomum*)

Most Western consuming countries specify cardamom in terms of density per litre and the extent of extraneous matter present. These are minimum standards but act as a protection against adulteration and establish a level of cleanliness.

By far the greatest influence, and one which is not generally appreciated, on the quality of spices are the standards imposed by the source country. The Indian 'Agmark' standards and the 'Ceylon Standards' of Sri Lanka both have the backing of government legislation. This has resulted in significant improvements in recent years in the quality and packaging of spices exported from these countries.

Indian Standards

The standard grading for cardamoms either whole green, or bleached and as seed are shown in the following definitions and tabulated quality requirements. Export quality control is maintained by pre-shipment inspection, analysis and certification.

Alleppey green cardamoms: The cardamoms shall be the dried capsules of *Elettaria cardamomum* grown in South India, kiln-dried; having a reasonably uniform shade of green colour, three-cornered and having a ribbed appearance. A tolerance of grey and cream-coloured capsules up to 25 per cent is permitted. Special characteristics are listed in Table 10.4.

Table 10.4 *Alleppey green cardamoms: Agmark requirements*

Grade designation	Trade name	Empty and malformed capsules, per cent by count, maximum	Immature and shrivelled capsules, per cent by weight, maximum	Size (diameter of holes in mm of the sieve on which retained) Tolerance ± 5 per cent	Weight, g/l minimum
AGS	Cardamom Superior	4.0	0.0	5.0	385
AGS 1	Shipment Green 1	3.0	7.0	4.0	350
AGS 2	Shipment Green 2	5.0	7.0	4.0	320
AGL	Light	...	...	...	260

Coorg clipped cardamoms: The cardamoms shall be the dried capsules of *Elettaria cardamomum* grown in Mangalore and Mysore; colour ranging from pale yellow to brown, global shape, skin ribbed or smooth; the pedicels separated. Special characteristics are listed in Table 10.5.

Table 10.5 *Coorg clipped cardamoms: Agmark requirements*

Grade designation	Trade name	Empty and malformed capsules, per cent by count, maximum	Unclipped capsules, per cent by count, maximum	Immature and shrivelled capsules, per cent by weight, maximum	Size (diameter of holes in mm of the sieve on which retained) Tolerance ± 5 per cent	Weight g/l minimum
CC 1	Bold	5.0	0.0	0.0	8.5	435
CC 2	Coorg Green or Notta Green	5.0	3.0	4.0	6.0	385
CC 3	Shipment	3.0	5.0	7.0	4.0	350
CC 4	Light	...	...	...	3.5	260

Bleachable white cardamoms: The cardamom shall be the fully developed dried capsules of *Elettaria cardamomum* grown in Mysore State to a reasonably uniform shade of white, light green or light-grey colour and suitable for bleaching. Special characteristics are listed in Table 10.6.

Table 10.6   *Bleachable white cardamoms: Agmark requirements*

Grade designation	Trade name	Empty and malformed capsules, per cent by count, maximum	Immature and shrivelled capsules, per cent by weight, maximum	Size (diameter of holes in mm of the sieve on which retained) Tolerance ± 5 per cent	Weight g/l minimum
BW 1	Mysore/ Mangalore Bleachable Cardamom A. Clipped	1.0	0.0	7.0	460
BW 2	Mysore/ Mangalore Bleachable Cardamom A. Unclipped	1.0	0.0	7.0	460
BW 3	Mysore/ Mangalore Bleachable Bulk Cardamom. Clipped	2.0	0.0	4.3	435
BW 4	Mysore/ Mangalore Bleachable Bulk Cardamom. Unclipped	2.0	0.0	4.3	435

Table 10.7   *Bleached or half-bleached cardamoms: Agmark requirements*

Grade designation	Empty and malformed capsules, per cent by count, maximum	Immature and shrivelled capsules, per cent by weight, maximum	Size (diameter of holes in mm of the sieve on which retained) Tolerance ± 5 per cent, maximum	Weight g/l, maximum
BL 1	0.0	0.0	8.5	340
BL 2	0.0	0.0	6.0	340
BL 3	0.0	0.0	4.0	280

Bleached or half-bleached cardamoms: The cardamom should be the
fully developed dried capsules of *Elettaria cardamomum* bleached or
half-bleached by sulphuring; colour ranging from pale cream to white,
global or three-cornered with skin ribbed or smooth. Special characteristics are listed in Table 10.7.

The terms used in Tables 10.4–10.7 are defined as follows:

Empty and malformed capsules – Capsules which have no seeds or
are scantily filled with seeds. For this purpose 100 capsules selected at
random from the sample shall be opened out and the number of empty
and malformed capsules counted.

Immature and shrivelled capsules – Capsules which are not fully
developed.

The grade designations and definitions of quality for Indian
cardamom seed are as follows:

Alleppey cardamom seeds: These should be the decorticated and dry
seeds of any variety of *Elettaria cardamomum* grown in Kerala State
and the southern districts of Tamil Nadu. Special characteristics are
listed in Table 10.8.

Table 10.8   *Alleppey cardamom seeds: Agmark requirements*

Grade designation	Trade name	Extraneous matter, per cent by weight, maximum	Light seeds, per cent by weight, maximum	Weight, g/l, minimum
AS 1	Prime	1.0	3.0	675
AS 2	Shipment	2.0	5.0	460
AS 3	Brokens	5.0	…	…

Mangalore cardamom seeds: These should be the decorticated and dry
seeds of any variety of *Elettaria cardamomum* grown in Mangalore
and Coorg districts of Karnataka. Special characteristics are listed in
Table 10.9.

Table 10.9   *Mangalore cardamom seeds: Agmark requirements*

Grade designation	Trade name	Extraneous matter, per cent by weight, maximum	Light seeds, per cent by weight, maximum	Weight g/l, minimum
MS 1	Prime	1.0	3.0	675
MS 2	Shipment	2.0	5.0	460
MS 3	Brokens	5.0	…	…

The terms used in Tables 10.8 and 10.9 are defined as follows:

Brokens – Include brown, red, immature and shrivelled seeds.

Extraneous matter – Includes calyx pieces, stalk bits and other foreign matter.

Light seeds – Include seeds brown or red in colour and broken, immature and shrivelled seeds.

For all grades of cardamom capsules and seeds there should be no visible mould and insect infestation.

Sri Lankan Standards

The specification for Ceylon-grown whole cardamoms is contained in Ceylon Standard 166 (1972) which states pre-shipment conditions for flavour and colour. In addition to a minimum volatile-oil content of 4 per cent, the requirements set out in Table 10.10 are specified.

Table 10.10   *Requirements of the Sri Lankan Standard*

Grade	Colour	Empty capsules, per cent by count, max.	Immature, shrivelled or malformed capsules, per cent by count, max.	Splits, per cent by count max.	Numerical value of sum of 'defective capsules' mentioned in preceding columns
LGS	Green	Nil	1	1	2 max
LG	Green	1	1.5	2	4 max
LLG 1	Light green	2	3	5	8 max
LLG 2	Light green	3	5	6	13 max
LB	Pale buff	4	7	8	18 max
LNS	Off colour	←————— not specified —————→			25 min

United Kingdom Standards

The United Kingdom Standard BS 4596:1970 for whole cardamom and seeds is identical in scope and requirement to the ISO R882 (1968) International Standard. The limits for extraneous matter, empty and malformed capsules, and light seeds are 5, 5, and 7 per cent respectively.

The chemical requirements should be in accordance with those listed in Table 10.11.

Table 10.11   *Chemical requirements of the British Standard*

Moisture, per cent, not more than	13
Volatile oil, expressed as ml per 100 g, not less than	4.0
Total ash, per cent, not more than	9.2

The *British Pharmacopoeia*, 1973, states that cardamom fruit shall consist of the dried nearly ripe fruit of *Elettaria cardamomum* Maton var. *miniscula* (var. *cardamomum*) Burkill and should conform to the requirements listed in Table 10.12.

Table 10.12 *Requirements of the British Pharmacopoeia*

Total ash of the seeds, per cent, nor more than	6.0
Acid-insoluble ash of the seeds, per cent, not more than	3.5
Foreign matter: of fruit, per cent, not more than	1.0
of the separated seeds, per cent, not more than	3.0
Volatile oil in the seed, per cent, not less than	4.0

United States Standards

The United States Government Standard lists chemical requirements for cardamom seed as shown in Table 10.13.

Table 10.13 *US Government Standard requirements*

Moisture, per cent, not more than	11.0
Volatile oil, per cent, not less than	3.0
Total ash, per cent, not more than	7.0
Acid-insoluble ash, per cent, not more than	3.0

From: U.S. Federal Specification: *Spices, ground, whole and spice blends,* No. EE-S-631H, June 5, 1975.

The limits of the various contaminants in cardamom consignments permitted under the Cleaniness Specifications of the American Spice Trade Association, are shown in Table 10.14.

Table 10.14 *ASTA Cleanliness Specifications*

Extraneous matter, per cent by weight	0.50
Excreta, rodent, pellets per lb	2
Excreta, other, mg per lb	1.00
Whole insects, dead, per lb	4
Insect-defiled, per cent by weight	1.00
Mould, per cent by weight	1.00

Canadian Standards

The Food and Drug Act 1954 stipulates that cardamom seed shall be the dried seed of cardamom and shall contain not more than 8 per cent total ash and 3 per cent ash insoluble in hydrocholoric acid.

The essential oil

The *British Pharmaceutical Codex* and the Essential Oil Association of the USA have standards for the essential oil distilled from cardamom spice. The oil is described as colourless or very pale yellow and should conform to the specifications listed in the Table 10.15.

There are no published specifications for cardamom oleoresin or for 'false' cardamoms.

Table 10.15   *Cardamom oil specifications*

	BPC 1973	EOA No. 289
Optical rotation, at 20 °C	+ 20 ° to + 44 °	+ 22 ° to + 44 °
Refractive index at 20 °C	1.461 to 1.467	1.463 to 1.466
Apparent density at 20 °C weight per ml	0.917 to 0.940	–
Specific gravity, at 25 °C	–	0.917 to 0.947
Ester value	90–150	–
Solubility in alcohol (70 per cent)	1 volume in 6	1 volume in 5

Production, trade and markets

When considering the production, trade and markets for cardamoms, it is necessary to make a clear distinction between 'true cardamom' (*Elettaria cardamomum* var. *cardamomum*) and the related species which for convenience will be collectively described here as 'false cardamoms'. The latter are comprised of a number of Asian *Amomum* species, together with the wild *Elettaria* varieties of India and Sri Lanka, and several African *Aframomum* species. Descriptions of these various types are provided in the 'Products and end-uses' section and other technical sections of this chapter.

Production and international trade is dominated by 'true cardamom' which is one of the highest-priced spices on the market and ranks second only to vanilla. The major suppliers of 'true cardamom' in the post – Second World War period have been, in order of import-ance, India, Guatemala, Sri Lanka and Tanzania. Annual total exports during the first half of the 1970s ranged between 3 000 to 3 500 tonnes, of which India provided about two-thirds. The main flow of trade in 'true cardamoms' is to the Arab countries of the Middle East, where almost two-thirds of world imports are consumed, and to Europe and North America. The Scandinavian countries form the largest consumer grouping after the Middle East market, and among the other importers the Federal Republic of Germany and the USSR are prominent. Strong preferences exist in a number of the consuming countries as to the geographical source and the physical form of the spice, and this is reflected in the prices obtained for the various types entering trade.

International trade in 'false cardamoms' is rather more difficult to estimate but was probably in excess of 1 000 tonnes in some years during the first half of the 1970s, of which Asian *Amomum* species accounted for over 90 per cent. Trade in *Amomum* species is charac-terized by being almost exclusively restricted to the Asian region, with Thailand, and more recently Nepal, as the principal suppliers and China and Pakistan as the main importers. Asian and African 'false cardamoms' are generally regarded as very different and inferior in quality to 'true cardamom' in the Arab countries of the Middle East, Western Europe and North America and imports are consequently very small. In the past, the limited demand in Western markets had mainly been for small quantities of specific types, such as the melegueta pepper or grains of paradise (*Aframomum melegueta*), for incorporation in certain specialist pharmaceutical preparations. However, during the early 1970s the Nepal cardamom (*Amomum subulatum*) and the Korarima cardamom (*Aframomum korarima*) from Ethiopia made some incursions into the Scandinavian market as low-priced, low-grade substitutes for true cardamom, probably as a consequence of the prevailing high prices for true cardamom.

Production

'True cardamom'

India is the longest-established 'true cardamom' producer and, in terms of land area given over to the crop, devotes far more resources to it than any other country, although higher yields are recorded elsewhere. The area under cardamom at the beginning of the 1940s was around 75 000 ha, of which about 55 000 – 60 000 ha were cultivated as distinct from semi-wild. In 1960 the total area appeared to have diminished somewhat from the 1940 level, but by the early 1970s it had sharply re-expanded to over 90 000 ha. Production has gradually increased over the decades, from around 1 000 tonnes per annum at the beginning of the 1930s to 2 500 tonnes in the mid-1940s and between 3 500 and 4 000 tonnes in the early 1960s. 'Katte' disease set back production levels during the middle and late 1960s, but a slow recovery ensued and the 3 000-tonne mark was re-attained in the mid-1970s. The main producing areas are located in the States of Karnataka, Kerala and Tamil Nadu. A considerable proportion of the crop is consumed domestically but the higher grades, especially green cardamoms, are reserved for export. Of the recorded exports between 1971 – 2 and 1975 – 6, Alleppey greens (Mysore type) accounted for 80 – 93 per cent, Coorg greens (Malabar type) for some 2 – 10 per cent, and the remainder consisted largely of bleached cardamoms. Exports of decorticated seeds during this period was of the order of 2 – 3 per cent of the total. Production of cardamoms in India is mainly undertaken by small farmers, and marketing is carried out under conditions of private enterprise. There existed a body entitled the Cardamom Co-operative Sale Society Ltd in the 1930s and 1940s but it was not until the mid-1960s that comprehensive measures were taken to improve the marketing system. The 1965 Cardamom Act gave rise to the formation of the Cardamom Board in 1966. Four years earlier the Indian Ministry of Food and Agriculture had drawn up the Cardamom Grading and Marking Rules which laid down, among other things, a system of compulsory inspection for all shipments leaving India. The formation of the

Cardamom Board gave a powerful impetus to the rationalization of the cardamom industry and strengthened its influence over the world market. The Agmark grading system for Indian cardamoms is described in the 'Standard specifications' section.

'True cardamom' production in Sri Lanka has been at a fairly constant level since the early 1930s with exports averaging 150 tonnes a year. Unlike India, domestic consumption of 'true cardamom' is low (estimated at only 2–3 per cent of the crop) and the export statistics may therefore be taken as guide to overall production (see Table 10.16). Cultivation is mainly on tea estates where both crops are grown together under natural forest shade on the steeper slopes of the estate periphery. Although the area under cardamom has been estimated to have increased from 2 800 ha in 1938 to 4 500 ha by 1970, production levels have not changed markedly. This is attributed to the general senility of many of the cardamom plants, leading to lower yields. During the mid-1970s, however, greater attention has been given by the Government to increasing production and quality. The number of

Table 10.16   *'True cardamoms': Exports from the main producing countries, 1931–76 (tonnes)*

	India[1]	Sri Lanka	Guatemala	Tanzania[2]
1931–35 (annual average)	510	140	...	...
1936–40 (annual average)	580	150	...	...
1941–45 (annual average)	580	150[2]	...	...
1946–50 (annual average)	790	100	...	...
1951–55 (annual average)	880	130	...	...
1956–60 (annual average)	1 530	140	190	...
1961	2 360	160	560	...
1962	2 260	150	1 040	...
1963	2 310	150	380	...
1964	1 780	140	395	...
1965	1 390	145	430	...
1966	1 720	125	445	...
1967	1 540	125	530	...
1968	1 450	125	560	...
1969	1 230	160	...	103
1970	1 760	200	980	146
1971	2 130	185	720	170
1972	1 450	215	640	160
1973	1 910	186	...	...
1974	1 700	145	...	...
1975	2 032	335	...	...
1976	...	162	...	...

Sources: Annual Trade Statistics of the countries mentioned
Plantation Crops, published by Commonwealth Secretariat.

[1]   From April of year stated to March of following year.
[2]   From July of year stated to June of following year.
...   not available

smallholders growing 'true cardamom' has increased and new plantings have been established on old and uneconomic tea estates as part of a rehabilitation programme. In addition, quality control is being exercised by the Government with the imposition of the pre-inspection export scheme operated by the Bureau of Ceylon Standards.

Guatemala has attained the position of the world's second largest exporter of 'true cardamoms' and since domestic consumption is negligible, the export statistics given in Table 10.16 are a good guide to production levels. The spice was introduced into Guatemala early in the twentieth century by German settlers and between the two world wars there was a small export of decorticated seeds. During the Second World War, the German plantations were expropriated and for a number of years thereafter production declined owing to the inexperience of the new managers. However, production levels slowly rose and a new stimulus entered the situation in the mid-1950s when coffee producers, who were dissatisfied with the world prices for their commodity, took the opportunity to diversify into this high-value spice. From 1956 onwards, production and exports grew rapidly and Guatemala attained a reputation as a supplier of high-quality green cardamom and decorticated seeds. To a lesser extent a similar development took place in El Salvador in the 1950s, but this country never achieved an established position on the world market.

Tanzania, like Guatemala, probably had 'true cardamom' introduced from quite an early date but it did not achieve prominence as a regular, if very small supplier until the late 1960s. During the mid-1970s marketed production was of the order of 300–350 tonnes per annum.

Among several other countries which have expressed interest in entering the 'true cardamom' trade, Papua New Guinea is worthy of mention in having established a small export-oriented industry in recent years. Both Papua New Guinea and Sri Lanka have expressed intentions to expand 'true cardamom' production and these two countries could make a significant impact on the world supply situation if their plans come to fruition.

Related species ('False cardamoms')

A number of cultivated and wild-growing *Amomum* species are exploited and traded throughout the Indian subcontinent, Indonesia, Indochina and mainland China. Precise production levels are not known for most countries, however, since a substantial proportion of the crops is consumed domestically. Thailand appears to have had the largest surplus production in the post – Second World War period and has been by far the biggest and most regular supplier to neighbouring Asian markets. The most notable development in this region has been the dramatic expansion of production and exports from Nepal since the early 1970s. Domestic consumption in Nepal is less than 100 tonnes per year. Production of the Nepal cardamom has also increased in Bhutan and Sikkim in recent years.

Table 10.17   *'False cardamoms': Exports from selected producing countries, 1956–76 (tonnes)*

	Thailand	Nepal[a]	Laos	India[b]	Ethiopia[c]
1956–60 (annual average)	170	...	...	...	...
1961	120	...	...	...	...
1962	150	...	...	...	...
1963	90	...	...	...	...
1964	225	...	...	...	...
1965	140	...	...	...	...
1966	115	...	...	...	...
1967	125	...	...	...	...
1968	155	261	...	...	...
1969	85	149	...	...	...
1970	120	398	31	...	4
1971	325	313	49	65	118
1972	355	298	29	68	29
1973	260	246	8[d]	95	61
1974	500	334	19[d]	70	...
1975	357	685	55[d]	92	...
1976	283	602	...	106	...

Sources: Annual Trade Statistics of Thailand and India.
Plantations Crops (Commonwealth Secretariat).
International Trade Centre (1977), *Spices, a Survey of the World Market*, Geneva: ITC. UNCTAD/GATT.
Trade Promotion Centre, Kathmandu.
Agricultural Development Bank of Nepal.

(a) From mid-July of year stated to mid-July of the following year.
(b) From April of year stated to March of the following year.
(c) Imports into Sweden and Finland only.
(d) Imports into Hong Kong only.
... not available

A similar situation exists with the various *Aframomum* species in Africa, although production is probably more dependent upon harvesting from the wild and trade is considerably smaller than for the *Amomum* species of Asia. The most notable development in this region has been the increase in Ethiopian production of the Korarima cardamom and of the exports to Scandinavia during the early 1970s.

Trade

'True cardamom'

The traditional supplier of 'true cardamom' has been India with Sri Lanka as a smaller but regular exporter. India has retained its dominant position in the post-Second World War period but the supply situation has changed substantially with the emergence of Guatemala as a very important exporter and to a lesser extent with the development of the Tanzanian industry (see Table 10.16). Export levels from these four countries between 1965–75 ranged as follows:

	tonnes
India:	1 200–2 100
Guatemala:	400–1 000
Sri Lanka:	125– 335
Tanzania:	100– 170 (figures for 1969–73 only)

The import situation for 'true cardamom' is characterized by the existence of two large and geographically distinct consumer groupings – the Arab countries of the Middle East and the Scandinavian countries. An approximate breakdown of world imports for 'true cardamom' during the first half of the 1970s is given in Table 10.18.

Table 10.18

	Approximate intake of world imports	Of which
The Arab countries of the Middle East	55–60 per cent	Saudi Arabia takes 55 per cent of regional imports
Scandinavia	16 per cent	Sweden and Finland take 60 and 30 per cent, respectively, of total
Other Western European countries	8 per cent	West Germany and the UK take 50 and 25 per cent of the total
Eastern European Socialist countries	5 per cent	The USSR accounts for 75 per cent
USA	2.5 per cent	
Iran	2 per cent	
Japan	3 per cent	

Recent annual imports into selected countries are provided in Table 10.19.

'True cardamom' enters international trade in three main forms: green whole fruit, bleached whole fruit and decorticated seeds. As is the case with a number of other spices, preferences are expressed by some consumers as to the origin and physical form of the spice when used in certain applications. Such preferences are most strongly expressed in the major world market of the Middle East and this aspect is discussed in the following paragraph. The bulk of world supplies consists of green cardamoms, with India as the leading supplier and with Guatemala in second place. This type has a wide field of applications. Half-bleached and wholly bleached cardamoms are more specialized in application

Table 10.19 Imports of 'true cardamom'* into selected countries, 1964–76 (tonnes)

	1964	1965	1966	1967	1968	1969	1970	1971	1972	1973	1974	1975	1976
Saudi Arabia	...	...	...	...	421	547	588	845	1 100	1 200	...	...	...
Kuwait – imports	...	...	321	505	629	532	463	705	758	686	386	...	...
re-exports[a]	...	...	...	...	(31)	(8)	(29)	(136)	(170)	(510)	...	...	...
Sweden	327	210	216	252	274	249	233	223	253	296	257	243	258
Finland	122	117	128	126	127	134	142	169	132	125	148	156	141
Denmark	34	31	28	31	31	31	33	25	34	33	34	27	25
Norway[b]	34	31	27	32	32	33	31	31	37	31	33	25	40
USSR[c]	...	...	...	...	...	...	74	140	110	160	203	...	...
German Federal Republic	97	86	50	66	91	79	70	110	112	126	123	117	108
United Kingdom[b]	...	...	...	...	...	...	...	...	...	19	31	44	59
USA	83	52	94	85	53	43	66	74	80	65	110	62	79
Iran[d]	...	...	...	...	29	...	37	82	49	27	61	72	39
Japan	25	27	41	34	64	79	79	107	84	112	145	77	64

Sources: Annual Trade Statistics of the countries mentioned
International Trade Centre: 'Spices, a survey of the world market'. (Geneva, 1977)

* Totals for true cardamom imports obtained by summing imports originating from India, Guatemala, Sri Lanka, Tanzania and Papua New Guinea. The actual imports of true cardamom may slightly exceed these figures owing some supplies arriving via intermediary countries.

... not available
(a) Figures for re-exports to Saudi Arabia only
(b) Whole cardamom imports only
(c) Imports from India only
(d) Includes supplies from Dubai

and are used in the Western consuming countries mainly for culinary purposes and in the preparation of mixed spices. The 'prime seed' grade is traded in considerable quantities and is used mainly for distillation of cardamom oil, while the 'light seed' is used mainly for grinding.

The principal and traditional use of 'true cardamom' in the Middle East market is for the flavouring of coffee. Consumption of the spice in this application is particularly high in Saudi Arabia, Kuwait and Bahrain. This market area is characterized by its insistence on small cardamoms which possess an intense and uniform green colour, and the demand for other forms of the spice is very small. India, as the major world source of high-quality green cardamoms, has been and remains the principal supplier to the Middle East market. However, Guatemala has achieved a substantial foothold in this regional market since the 1960s. Sri Lankan and Tanzanian green cardamoms are less favoured in the Middle East. Nevertheless, this region remains the principal market outlet for the Sri Lankan product.

In the Scandivanian market, the major application for 'true cardamom' is in the flavouring of baked goods and pastries. In Sweden, Denmark and Norway, the preference is mainly for green cardamoms, while in Finland decorticated seeds and bleached cardamoms comprise a large proportion of imports. India's former dominance as a supplier to this market has been eroded by the successful marketing techniques of Guatemala and on a much smaller scale by Tanzania. In all four Scandinavian countries, Guatemala supplied over 50 per cent of total imports during the first half of the 1970s.

In other importing countries outside the two major market areas discussed above, the uses of 'true cardamom' are more diverse and the principal application is in the preparation of spice blends. In the West German and United States markets, Guatemala has attained the dominant position, while the United Kingdom, Japan and Iran are more dependent upon Indian supplies. Iran is of interest in that virtually all Indian cardamoms imported are of the bleached type.

The encroachment of other exporting countries on India's traditional markets has been offset to a limited extent by the growth of its trade in cardamoms with the USSR and East Germany in recent years. The USSR in particular could come to occupy a prominent position among importers, as it already appears to be doing in respect of some other spices.

Generally speaking, however, world trade in 'true cardamom' does not appear to be expanding strongly; indeed the picture is one of fairly small, but steady long-term growth in consumption with occasionally pronounced short-term fluctuations. This spice is perhaps more vulnerable than many others to the onset of disease, and indeed the high prices induced by the 'katte' outbreak and subsequent tight supplies of the mid-1960s acted as a powerful damper on any likely expansion of the trade, and there is evidence that as a result, consumption in some

Western countries was quite sharply reduced, at least temporarily. In Scandinavia, the high price for 'true cardamom' is the probable reason for the imports of 'false cardamoms' from Ethiopia and Nepal in the early 1970s. By contrast, price increases appear to have had very little impact on demand levels or preferences in the Middle East, particularly in the cases of Saudi Arabia, Kuwait and Bahrain.

Related species ('False cardamoms')

The trade in *Amomum* species is largely contained within Asia, only very small volumes entering the Middle East, European and North American markets. Mainland China has been and remains by far the principal importer while smaller volumes have been regularly imported by a number of other countries, including Pakistan, Vietnam, Korea and Japan. Up until 1970, the major supplier was Thailand, while minor supplies emanated from Laos, Cambodia (Kampuchea), Nepal and India. Since 1970, Nepal has rapidly increased exports and soon matched Thailand in importance (see Table 10.17). The total recorded exports of Thailand, India, Nepal, Laos and Cambodia ranged between 400 and 1 000 tonnes per annum in the period 1970−5.

Thailand's exports have traditionally been comprised of 'best' and 'bastard' cardamoms. 'Best cardamoms' are believed to consist mainly of cultivated *Amomum kepulaga* and *Amomum krervanh*, while 'bastard cardamoms' consist of several wild-growing species, including *Amomum xanthioides*. Up until the early 1970s, it was usual for the greater part of annual exports to be in powdered or ground form, but during the mid-1970s there was a decline in trade in this form. As Table 10.17 shows, exports increased substantially during the first half of the 1970s, largely through an increase in production of 'bastard cardamom' which came to account for about 75 per cent of the total.

Nepal's exports of the Nepal cardamom (*A. subulatum*) were fairly small prior to 1970 and the major outlet was India. During 1970−6, exports rose from 200 to 700 tonnes per annum, of which only a fraction was destined for India. The vast bulk of Nepal's production, and a proportion of Bhutan's, is shipped to Pakistan via Singapore. Pakistan in the major importer of the Nepal cardamom in the region. China is believed to have bought small consignments. Some trial shipments of Nepal cardamom were also sent to Scandinavia during this period.

Very scanty information is available on the trade in African *Aframomum* species, but Ethiopia is notable in having achieved penetration of the Scandinavian market in the early 1970s with the Korarima cardamom (*Aframomum korarima*). Exports to Sweden for the years 1970−3 were 4, 118 and 18 tonnes respectively. Finland also took 5−11 tonne lots in the same period.

The incursion of Korarima and Nepal cardamoms into the

Scandinavian market, which had previously been highly discerning, was undoubtedly a reaction to the prevailing high prices for 'true cardamom'. It is questionable whether these 'false cardamoms' will be able to retain their foothold in this market should supplies of 'true cardamom' improve and prices stabilize.

Market structure

'True cardamom'

Trade in 'true cardamom' is mainly conducted directly between the producing and importing countries but in the case of the Middle East market there is a degree of reliance on entrepôts. South Yemen (formerly Aden) was of importance at one time as an entrepôt for the Middle East market but its function has now been superseded by Bahrain and Kuwait (see Table 10.19).

Apart from the degree of central-government influence over the production end of the trade in India and Sri Lanka, trade in cardamoms is conducted mainly on the basis of private enterprise, via the familiar network of collectors and exporters in the producing countries, the shipping companies, and spice merchants and dealers in the importing countries. The commission-earning broker or agent plays a full part in the trade, and a small amount of speculation takes place, although cardamom is not a sufficiently important spice to attract much interest from speculators. It is possible that the number of traders in cardamom, particularly at the importing end, is contracting slightly and that an increasing number of direct links are being established between the exporters and the processing and grinding factories, in common with other spices.

Related species ('False cardamoms')

By contrast to 'true cardamom', trade in Asian *Amomum* species is dominated by the dependence upon entrepôts. Traditionally, Hong Kong has overshadowed Singapore in this role and it has handled the vast bulk of exports from Thailand, Laos and Cambodia. Hong Kong's re-exports have been mainly absorbed by mainland China, although smaller volumes have been regularly shipped to other neighbouring countries, including Japan. Singapore has latterly attained importance, however, by handling Nepal's and Bhutan's exports, which were comparable in volume with those of Thailand in the mid-1970s.

Prices

'True cardamom'

The price of 'true cardamom' has been subject to very substantial fluctuations. In many of the importing countries it would appear that

Alleppey greens set the price trend and that other types of green cardamoms, bleached cardamoms and seeds follow this trend. As an indicator of the price differences between sources of green cardamoms in a market where strong preferences are expressed, prices (c.i.f.) of Sri Lankan and Tanzanian material were 20 to 25 per cent lower than for Indian and Guatemalan material in Kuwait in 1976. Bleached cardamoms fetch lower prices than green cardamoms, and decorticated seeds are distinguished into top-priced 'prime seed' and lower-valued 'light seed'.

London (c.i.f.) prices for Alleppey greens since the early 1960s are given in Table 10.20. The onset of 'Katte' disease in the mid-1960s might have given rise to a sharper and longer-term price increase had not the formation of the Indian Cardamom Board brought about a recovery in supplies earlier than expected. However, the widely expected return to the low price levels of the early 1960s has not occurred except very briefly in 1972, after which the commodity boom swept the price back up to high levels. Monsoon irregularities in India in 1975–6, together with indirect effects of the Guatemalan earthquake which occurred at about the same time, forced prices up still further and at the time of writing they stood at an all-time high, although the effect this would have on the trade had yet to become apparent.

Table 10.20 *Cardamoms: Annual average prices, c.i.f. London, 1961–77 (£ per tonne)*

	Alleppey green	*Seeds No. 1*
1961	1 200	1 830
1962	805	1 337
1963	1 019	1 288
1964	1 260	1 521
1965	2 363	3 135
1966	2 732	3 789
1967	1 725	3 261
1968	1 927[1]	3 156
1969	3 577	4 018
1970	4 156	5 153
1971	2 161	2 860
1972	1 868	2 072
1973	2 954	2 822
1974	3 996	3 996
1975	4 343	3 924
1976	7 661	6 735
1977[2]	14 073	14 881

Sources: Public Ledger
[1] The prices quoted in the third and fourth quarters of 1968 were 'spot' prices.
[2] First two quarters only.

Related species ('False cardamoms')

Prices for 'false cardamoms' are less readily available, but the material entering Western markets as a low-grade substitute for 'true cardamom' generally fetched less than 50 per cent of the price of top-grade 'true cardamom'. By way of comparison, Ethiopian Korarima cardamoms entering the Scandinavian market were priced at around US$9/kg in early 1978. Prices quoted for the Nepal cardamom (*A. subulatum*) on the Singapore market in January 1980 were US$2 500 – 3 000 per tonne, according to origin.

Trends in consumption and demand

'True cardamom'

A growth in demand has been experienced in most of the major importing countries in the post – Second World War period, but aside from population and income effects, there is not likely to be a substantial long-term growth in the market for this spice. The steady increase in price for 'true cardamom' in recent years has made an impact on demand in some markets and the significance of this price movement and some other factors are discussed in the following paragraphs.

In the major world market of the Arab countries of the Middle East, the demand for 'true cardamom' appears to be price-inelastic and recent price increases have had little effect. However, a more significant factor is that there has been a marked decline in the consumption of cardamom-flavoured coffee. Between 1965 and 1975, the proportion of Saudi Arabian imports used for flavouring coffee has been estimated to have fallen from 95 per cent to 70 per cent. This trend is associated with the transition from a traditional nomadic and rural society to one which is becoming more urban-centred. The decline in the consumption of cardamoms in coffee has so far been offset by a growth in use of the spice as a flavouring for confectionery and sweets. However, a further severe decline in coffee flavouring usage would obviously be of great significance not only to the regional demand but also to total world consumption.

In the Scandinavian market, where *per capita* consumption is second only to the Middle East market, there seems no reason to suppose that there will be any decline in the traditional use of 'true cardamom' in baked goods and pastries. The limited substitution of 'true cardamom' by 'false cardamoms' from Ethiopia and Nepal during the early 1970s was probably a short-term reaction to the high prices of the traditionally used, higher-quality spice.

With the possible exception of the German Federal Republic, there does not appear to be much sign of an increase in the popularity of the spice in Western European countries or in the USA, although the boom in domestic spice usage which occurred in the early 1970s almost certainly gave rise to a once-for-all increase. It is not one of the more popular culinary spices and even immigrant communities of Asian origin in Western Europe use it less than expected. It is very difficult to estimate the proportion of total imports destined for domestic consumption but it is probable that the proportion is small. The cardamom flavour has so far eluded satisfactory synthesis, and the effect in these markets of any prolonged period of high prices is more likely to be that of reduced domestic consumption, and outright omission from prepared food products, than of substitution by other materials of natural or synthetic origin. Any reduction of demand in this manner is likely to be only temporary, however, and the recent very high price levels need not be expected to bring about any long-term adverse effects on demand unless such peaks become frequent.

The food industry in Western markets uses the bulk of imports in three main forms: ground spice, oleoresin and distilled essential oil. The ground spice is used in the preparation of curry powder, baked goods, prepared savoury dishes, and a range of beverages

Cardamom oleoresin has been used in gradually increasing quantities in recent years, but it is clear that it is one of the less important products of its type. Usage in the United Kingdom, for example, is believed not to exceed one tonne per annum. It has a short shelf-life and this is imparted to the products in which it is used; consequently these products are necessarily those in which turnover is relatively rapid, for example sausages and salamis. Its price has generally been in the range of £150−225 per kilogramme, which is equivalent to £3.50−£5 per kilogramme dispersed on bases such as flour, rusk and dextrose.

Cardamom oil is the one cardamom product for which there appear to be possible substitutes, and therefore the maintenance of acceptably low and stable prices is of some importance. Distilled both in India and in certain of the Western consuming nations, many Western users nonetheless prefer an oil distilled domestically from the imported spice to their exact specification, and they seem prepared to pay rather more for this very high-quality oil. However, as cardamom oil is only used in very small quantities it is doubtful whether its price is of any consequence to the users. An estimate of the world market for this oil is precluded by lack of information, but there is no doubt that it is small by the standards of spice oils, although the oil is certainly used more widely than the oleoresin. The oil is increasingly being distilled in the cardamom-producing countries, particularly India, and there is a steady market for producer-distilled oils in the West, at any rate for the less demanding applications. Table 10.21 gives the recent trend in prices for cardamom oil.

Cardamom oil more closely resembles cardamom oleoresin than other spice oils resemble the corresponding oleoresins, and it may well be for this reason that the oil is used relatively so much more frequently than the oleoresin, which is the more expensive product. Cardamom oil

Table 10.21 *Cardamom oil: Annual average prices, London market, 1961–77 (£ per kg)*

	English (spot)	Sri Lanka[1]	Indian (c.i.f.)
1961	39.05	40.45	–
1962	37.21	33.26	28.00
1963	36.30	30.86	26.18
1964	36.05	30.86	24.47
1965	83.86	30.86	44.23
1966	120.73	30.86	46.85
1967	90.47	30.86	48.01
1968	66.83	30.86	59.25
1969	84.00	30.86	69.53
1970	120.57	30.86	101.14
1971	66.25	33.62	70.00
1972	54.88	36.38	42.81
1973	–	–	–
1974*	96	48	55
1975*	96	50	58
1976*	96	52	58
1977*	96[2]	65[2]	68[2]

Sources: *Perfumery and Essential Oil Record; Soap, Perfumery and Cosmetics* (after June 1969)
The Flavour Industry (after 1972)
  * *Cosmetic World News* (from mid-1974 to March 1977)
     No specifications as to f.o.b., c.i.f. or spot.
[1] 'Spot' for first four months of year, 'forward' from May.
[2] First quarter only
– not quoted

is mainly used in canned soups and meats and other savoury products which tend to be sold and consumed fairly shortly after manufacture, the oil presenting the same problems of short shelf-life as the oleoresin. It is also used in bun-spice flavour mixes for the Scandivanian market. The oil appears to be gaining acceptance in perfumery, although, unlike many spice oils, it is used more in perfumes and scents for women. Other uses include artificial fruit flavours, cordials, liqueurs and bitters, but the quantities so used are very small indeed.

Some so-called 'cardamom oils' are in use which in fact consist of a mixture of several materials. For example, one recently encountered oil was said to consist of 20 per cent 'true cardamom oil', 30 per cent 'other oils' and 50 per cent 'synthetics', although the latter items may have been obtained from other oils or natural materials. It is possible that some of the 'false cardamoms' entering the Scandinavian market were used for this purpose. Most flavour houses and perfumery manu-factures claim that a proportion of the cardamom oil they use is true oil, but it is clear that there is little prospect of much expansion in the market for cardamom oil.

'True cardamom' and its products can therefore be said to have a secure market without much prospect of any dramatic increase in consumption. Furthermore, the planned expansion of production in Sri Lanka and Papua New Guinea should have the effect of stabilizing supply levels and prices.

Related species ('False cardamoms')

An analysis of possible trends in consumption in the major Asian market is precluded by lack of reliable information. With regard to the prospects in Western markets, it has been mentioned earlier that the recent incursions of 'false cardamoms' into the Scandinavian market may well be a temporary phenomenon and that the foothold gained may be lost if the supply of 'true cardamoms' improves and prices stabilize.

References

Aiyadurai, S.G. (1966) *A Review of Research on Spices and Cashewnut in India*, Ernakulam-6: Indian Council of Agric. Res.

Anon. (1973) Essential Oils Sub-Committee, Soc. for Anal. Chemists: 'Application of gas liquid chromatography to the analysis of essential oils. Part II. Determination of 1,8-cineole in oils of cardamom, rosemary, sage and spike lavender', *Analyst*, **98**, 616–23.

Arctander, S. (1960) *Perfume and Flavour Materials of Natural Origin*, Elizabeth, N.J.: Published by the author.

Baruah, A.K.S., Bhagat, S.D. and Saika, B.K. (1973) 'Chemical composition of Alleppey cardamom oil by gas chromatography', *Analyst*, **98**, 168–71.

Berger, F. (1964/5) 'Neue Erkenntnisse auf dem Gebiet der Kardomomen-forschung', *Gordian*, **64**, 836–9, 885–8, 922–4, 956–61; **65**, 24–7.

Bernhard, R.A., Wijesekera, R.O.B. and Chichester, C.O. (1971) 'Terpenoids of cardamom oil and their comparative distribution among varieties', *Phytochem.*, **10**, 177–84.

Bheemasankara Rao, C., Namosiua Rao, T. and Suryaprakasam, S. (1976) 'Cardamonin and alpintin from seeds of *Amomum subulatum*', *Planta medica*, **29**, 391–2.

Bouquet, A. and Kerharo, J. (1950) 'Les vegetaux condiments de l'Afrique du Nord dans l'alimentation, la therapeutique et la magie', *Acta Tropica*, **7**, 237–74.

Brennand, C.P. and Heinz, D.E. (1970) 'Effects of pH and temperature on volatile constituents of cardamom', *J. Food Sci.*, **35**, 533–7.

Burkill, I.H. (1966) *A Dictionary of the Economic Products of the Malay Peninsula*, Kuala Lumpur: Ministry of Agriculture and Co-operatives.

Campbell, H. (1937) 'Undesirable colour changes in frozen peas stored at insufficiently low temperature', *Food Res.*, **2**, 55–77.

Campbell, H. (1950) 'Colour deterioration in peas during freezing storage', *Quick-Frozen Foods*, **12**, 129–32.

Chattopadhyay, S.B. (1967) *Diseases of Plants Yielding Drugs, Dyes and Spices*, New Delhi: Indian Council of Agric. Res.

Chau, L.T. (1975) 'Major monoterpene hydrocarbons from the essential oil of the fruit of *Amomum xanthioides*', *Tap. San, Hoa Hoc* (Vietnam), **13**, 29–32. (*Chem. Abs.* **83**,

103135r).

Chou, J.S.T. (1974) 'Cardamom oil, caraway oil and coriander oil', *Koryo*, **106**, 55–60.

Clevenger, J.F. (1934) 'Volatile oil in cardamom seed', *J. Assoc. Offic. Agric. Chemists*, **17**, 283–5.

Connell, D.W. (1970) 'Natural pungent compounds. III. The paradols and associated compounds', *Aust. J. Chem.*, **23**, 369–76.

Coomes, T.J., Islip, H.T. and Matthews, W.S.A. (1955) '*Aframomum angustifolium* seed from Zanzibar', *Col. Plant Animal Products*, **5**, 68–77.

Darlington, C.D. and Wylie, A.P. (1955) *Chromosome Atlas of Flowering Plants*, London: George Allen and Unwin.

De Jong, A.W.K. (1911) 'Monster kapolie (*Amomum cardamomum*)', *Jaarb. Dep. Landbouw Ned-India*, 48.

Dumas, M.M.J. and Peligot, E. (1834) 'Sur un Hydrate d'Essence de Terebenthine', *Ann. Chim. Phys.*, **57** (2), 334–5.

Dutton, H., Bailey, G. and Kohake, E. (1943) 'Dehydrated spinach. Changes in colour and pigment during processing and storage', *Ind. Eng. Chem.*, **35**, 1173–7.

Eglinton, G. and Hamilton, R.J. (1965) 'A reinvestigation of the essential oil of *Aframomum mala* (Zingiberaceae)', *Phytochem.*, **4**, 197–8.

Ferrara, A. (1957) 'Tecnologia delle spezie: Cardomomi', *Riv. Agric. Subtrop. e Trop.*, **51**, 393–400.

Fischer, L., Tornow, P.A. and Proper, B.L. (1945) 'The content and physical properties of certain volatile oils', *Bull. Nat. Formulary Comm.*, **13**, 6–10.

Gerhardt, U. (1968) 'Routine examination of spices for volatile oils and other constituents. II: Cardamom, coriander, caraway, juniper berries, celery, cloves, aniseed', *Fleischwirtschaft*, **48**, 1482–4.

Gerhardt, U. (1972) 'Changes in spice constituents due to the influence of various factors', *Fleischwirtschaft*, **52**, 77–80.

Geus, J.G. de (1973) *Fertilizer Guide for the Tropics and Sub Tropics*, 2nd edn, Zurich: Centre d'Étude de l'Azote.

Gildemeister, E. and Hoffmann, Fr. (1956) *Die Aetherischen Oele*, Vol. IV, Berlin: Akademie Verlag.

Gold, H.J. and Weckel, K.G. (1959) 'Degradation of chlorophyll to pheophytin during sterilization of canned green peas by heat', *Food Technol.*, **13**, 281–6.

Griebel, C. (1943) 'Ueber zwei afrikanische Erstazpfefferarten: Paradieskoerner und Mohrenpfeffer (Kani)', *Zeits. Untersuch der Lebensmittel* **85**, 426–36.

Griebel, C. and Hess, G. (1940) 'Die Haltbarkeit abgepackter gemahlener Gewurze', *Zeits. Untersuch der Lebensmittel*. **79**, 184–91.

Guenther, E. (1952) *The Essential Oils*, Vol. V, New York: D. Van Nostrand Co.

Haensel, H. (1905) 'Westafrikanische Kardamomen', Pharmaz. Ztg., **50**, 929.

Harten, A. M. van (1970) 'Melegueta pepper', *Econ. Bot.*, **24**, 208–16.

Holmes, E.M. (1914) 'The greater or Korarima cardamom', *Perf. Essent. Oil Record*, **5**, 302–4.

Holttum, R.E. (1950) 'The Zingiberaceae of the Malay Peninsula', *Gardens' Bull. Singapore*, *13*, 1–249.

Ikeda, R.M., Stanley, W.L., Vannier, S.H. and Spitler, E.M. (1962) 'The monoterpene hydrocarbon composition of some essential oils', *J. Food Sci.*, **27**, 455–8.

Kariyone, T. and Yoshida, Y. (1930) 'Constituents of *Amomum xanthioides* Wallich', *J. Pharm Soc. Japan*, **50**, 545–52.

Kasturi, T.R. and Iyer, B.H. (1955) 'Fixed oil from *Elettaria cardamomum* seeds', *J. Indian Inst. Sci.*, **37A**, 106–12.

Koller, W.D. (1976) 'Die Temperatur, ein wesentlicher Faktor bei der Lagerung von gemahlen Naturgewurzen', *Z. Lebensm. Unters. Forsch*, **160**, 143–147.

Krishnamurthy, M.N., Padma Bai, R. and Natarajan, C.P. (1967) 'Chemical composition of cardamom', *J. Food Sci. & Technol.* (India), **4**, 170.

Krishnan, P.P and Guha, P.C. (1950) 'Mysore cardamom oil', *Curr. Sci.* (India), **19**,

157.

Krishnan, P.P. (1951) Brochure containing the report of investigations carried out by Krishnan. Published by the Government of Mysore, 22–6.

Kulkarni, B.M. and Pruthi, J.S. (1967) 'A simple and rapid test for the detection of adulteration in cardamom seeds', *Indian Food Packer*, **21**, 14–19.

Laksmi, V. and Chauhan, J.S. (1977) 'Structure of a new aurone glycoside from *Amomum subulatum* seeds', *Indian J. Chem.*, **15B**, 814–15.

Lawrence, B.M. (1970) 'Terpenes in two *Amomum* species', *Phytochem.*, **9**, 665.

Lawrence, B.M., Hogg, J.W., Terhune, S.J. and Pichitakul, N. (1972) 'Terpenoids of two *Amomum* species from Thailand', *Phytochem.*, **11**, 1534–5.

Lewis, Y.S., Nambudri, E.S. and Philip, T. (1966) 'Composition of cardamom oils', *Perf. Essent. Oil Record*, **57**, 623–8.

Lewis, Y.S., Nambudri, E.S. and Natarajan, C.P. (1967) 'Studies on some essential oils', *Indian Perfumer*, **11**, 5–9.

Lewis, Y.S., Nambudri, E.S. and Krishnamurthy, N. (1974) 'Flavour quality of cardamom oils', *Proceedings of the 6th International Congress on Essential Oils*, San Francisco, Sept. 1974.

McConnell, D.J. and Upawansa, G.K. (1972) 'The spice industries of Sri Lanka', *UNDP/FAO Farm Management Report*, No. 5.

Mackinney, G. and Weast, C.A. (1940) 'Colour changes in green vegetables. Frozen-pack peas and string beans', *Ind. Eng. Chem.*, **32**, 392–5.

Marsh, A.C., Moss, M.K. and Murphy, E.W. (1977) *Composition of Foods, Spices and Herbs. Raw. Processed. Prepared*, Washington, DC: USDA, Agric. Res. Serv., Agric. Handbook No. 8–2.

Mayne, W.W. (1942) *Report on Cardamom Cultivation in South India*, Misc. Bull. No. 50, Imperial Counc. Agric. Res. India.

Mayne, W.W. (1954) 'Cardamoms in South Western India', *World Crops*, **6**, 397–400.

Melchior, H. and Kastner, H. (1974) *Gewurze*, Berlin: Paul Parey.

Miyazawa, M. and Kameoka, H. (1975) 'The constitution of the essential oil and non-volatile oil from cardamom seed', *J. Japanese Oil Chemists Soc.* (Yukaguku), **24**, 22–6.

Moudgill, K.L. (1924) 'Travancore essential oils. I. Oil from seeds of *Elettaria cardomomum* (cardamoms)', *J. Soc. Chem. Ind.*, **43**, 137T–138T.

Mukherji, D.K. (1973) 'Large Cardamoms', *World Crops*, **25**, 31–3.

Natarajan, C.P., Kuppuswamy, S., Krishnamurthy, M.N., D'Souza, T. and Gopalan, K.K. (1967) 'Preservation of green colour in cardamom', *Indian Spices*, **1**, 5–7.

Natarajan, C.P., Kuppuswamy, S. and Krishnamurthy, M.N. (1968) 'A study of the maturity, regional variations and retention of green colour of cardamoms', *J. Food Sci. Technol.* (India), **5**, 65–8.

Naves, Y.R. (1974) *Technologie et Chimie des Parfums Naturels*, Paris: Masson & Cie.

Nelson, E.K. (1917) 'Gingerol and paradol', *J. Amer. Chem. Soc.*, **39**, 1466–9.

Nigam, S.S. and Purohit, R.M. (1960) 'Chemical examination of the essential oil derived from seeds of *Amomum subulatum*', *Perf. Essent. Oil Record*, **51**, 121–3.

Nigam, M.C., Nigam, I.C., Handa, K.L. and Levi, L. (1965) 'Examination of oil of cardamom by gas chromatography', *J. Pharm. Sci.*, **54**, 799–801.

Ogzewalla, C.D. and Willms, M. (1962) 'Volatile oil in cardamom seed', *Proc. Okla. Acad. Sci.*, **43**, 57–60 (*Chem. Abs.*, **60**, 7867b).

Parameswar, N.S. (1973) 'Floral Biology of Cardamom (*Eletttaria cardamomum* Maton)', *Mysore J. Agric. Sci.*, **7**, 205–13.

Parry, E.J. (1899) 'Oil of cardamom', *Pharmac. J.*, **53**, 105.

Parry, E.J. (1918) *The Chemistry of the Essential Oils and Artificial Perfumes*, Vol. 1, 3rd edn, London: Scott, Greenwood & Son.

Pattanshetti, H.V. and Prasad, A.B.N. (1973a) 'September is the most suitable month for sowing cardamom seeds', *Current Res.*, **2**, 26.

Pattanshetti, H.V. and Prasad, A.B.N. (1973b) 'Two season seedlings are most suitable for planting in the field', *Current Res.*, **2**, 67–8.

Pritzer, J. and Jungkunz, R. (1944) 'Beitrag zur Kenntnis der Freuchte-Drogen der Ph.

H. V.', *Pharm. Acta Helv.*, **19**, 106–11.

Rao, B.S., Sudborough, J.J. and Watson, H.E. (1925) 'Notes on some Indian essential oils', *J. Indian Inst. Sci.*, **8A**, 155–8.

Ridley, H.N. (1912) *Spices*, London: Macmillan.

Rosengarten, F. Jr., (1969) *The Book of Spices*, Wynnewood: Livingston Publishing Co.

Sage, C.E. (1924) 'Oil of wild cardamoms', *Perfum Essent. Oil Record*, **15**, 150.

Salzer, U.-J. (1975a) 'Uber die Fettsaurezussamensetzung der Lipoide einiger Gewurze', *Fette, Seifen, Anstrichmittel*, **77**, 446–50.

Salzer, U.-J. (1975b) 'Analytical evaluation of seasoning extracts (oleoresins) and essential oils from seasonings', *Flavours*, **6**, 151–7.

Samarawira, I. (1972) 'Cardamom', *World Crops*, **24** (2), 76–8.

Sastri, B.N. (ed.) (1952) *The Wealth of India: Raw Materials. Vol. III*, New Delhi: Council of Scientific and Industrial Research.

Schimmel & Co. (1878) '*Amomum korarima* Oel', *Ber. Schimmel*, Jan., 8.

Schimmel & Co. (1897a) '*Amomum aromaticum* Oel', *Ber. Schimmel*, Apr., 48.

Schimmel & Co. (1897b) '*Amomum cardamomom* Oel', *Ber. Schimmel*, Oct., 9.

Schimmel & Co. (1897c) '*Aframomum melegueta* Oel', *Ber. Schimmel*, Oct., 10.

Schimmel & Co. (1897d) '*Aframomum danielli* Oel', *Ber. Schimmel*, Oct., 10.

Schimmel & Co. (1905) '*Amomum mala* Oel', *Ber. Schimmel*, Apr., 85.

Schimmel & Co. (1912) '*Aframomum angustifolium* Oel', *Ber. Schimmel*, Apr., 132.

Schimmel & Co. (1913) '*Aframomum globusum* Oel', *Ber. Schimmel*, Apr., 108.

Schimmel & Co. (1915) '*Aframomum melegueta* Oel', *Ber. Schimmel*, Apr., 38.

Shankaracharya, N.B. and Natarajan, C.P. (1971) 'Cardamom – Chemistry, technology and uses', *Indian Food Packer*, **25**, 28–36.

Shankaracharya, N.B. and Natarajan, C.P. (1975) 'Technology of spices', *Arecanut and Spices Bull.*, **7**, 27–43.

Siddappaji, C. and Reddy, D.N.R.N. (1972) 'A note on the occurrence of the aphid, *Pentalonia nigronervosa* form *caladii* Vanda Goot (Aphididoe-Homoptera) on Cardamom *(Elettaria cardamomum Salisb.)*', *Mysore J. Agric. Sci.*, **6**, 194–5.

Siebert, G. (1976) 'Der gegenwartige Stand der Standardisierung von Importgewurzen', *Die Lebensmittel – Industrie*, **23**, 558–61.

Singh, G.B., Pant, H.G. and Gupta, P.N. (1978) 'Large cardamom. A foreign exchange earner from Sikkim', *Indian Farming*, March 3–6, 21.

Strauss, D. (1977) 'Der Gehalt an aetherischen Oel bei Gemahlen Gewurzen', *Deut. Lebensmittel – Rundschau*, **73**, 332–4.

Tackie, A.N., Dwuma-Badu, D., Ayim, J.S.K., Dabra, T.T., Knapp, J.E., Slatkin, D.J. and Schiff, P.L. (1975) 'Hydroxyphenyl-alkanones from *Amomum melegueta*', *Phytochem.*, **14**, 853–4.

Thomas, A.I. and John, J. M. (1966) 'Before cardamom goes to the market', *Indian Farming*, **16** (7), 51–2.

Thresh, J.C. (1884) 'Proximate analysis of the seeds of *Amomum melegueta* (Roscoe)', *Pharm. J.*, 798–801.

Viehoever, A. and Sung, L.K. (1937) 'Common and oriental cardamoms', *J. Amer. Pharm. Assoc.*, **26**, 872–87.

Wallach, O.E. (1908) 'Zur Kenntniss der Terpene und der aetherischen Oele', *Liebigs Ann.*, **360**, 82–104.

Weber, E. (1887) 'Ceylon – Cardamomoel', *Liebigs Ann.*, **238**, 98.

Wellendorf, M. (1966) 'Gaschromatographic investigation of cardamom types', *Dansk. Tidsskr. Farm.*, **40**, 156–63.

Willis, J.C. (1966) *A Dictionary of the Flowering Plants and Ferns*, 7th edn (rev. by H.K. Airey Shaw), Cambridge Univ. Press.

Winton, A.L. and Winton, K.B. (1939) *The Structure and Composition of Foods*, New York: John Wiley & Sons.

Worsley, R.R. le G. (1934) 'Some East African essential oils. I. *Aframomum* spp.', *Bull. Imp. Inst.*, **32**, 253–63.

Yegna Narayan Aiyer, A.K. (1944) *Field Crops of India*, Bangalore: Govt. Press.

Chapter 11

Vanilla

Vanilla, an important and popular flavouring material and spice, is the fully grown fruit of the orchid *Vanilla fragrans* (Salisb.) Ames (syn. *V. planifolia* Andrews) harvested before it is fully ripe, after which it is fermented and cured. The fruits are usually referred to as vanilla beans. Vanilla extract is obtained by macerating the cured beans in alcohol. Vanilla is used extensively to flavour ice-cream, chocolate, beverages, cakes, custards, puddings and other confectionery. It is also used in perfumery and to a small extent in medicine. *Vanilla fragrans* is a native of Mexico and Central America, but is now cultivated in other parts of the tropics, especially in the Malagasy Republic (Madagascar), Réunion and the Comoro Islands.

The fragrance and flavour of vanilla beans is due to numerous aromatic compounds produced during the curing operation, among which vanillin is the most abundant. The flavour of vanillas from different parts of the world varies due to climate, soil, extent of pollination, degree of ripeness at harvesting and method of curing.

Vanillin was first isolated from vanilla by Gobley (1858). It was first produced artificially by Tiemann and Haarmann in 1874 from the glucoside coniferin, which occurs in the sapwood of certain conifers. Vanillin can now be produced synthetically, and is much cheaper than natural vanilla flavour. It is produced from the waste sulphite liquor of paper mills, from coal-tar extracts and from eugenol obtained from clove oil. Nevertheless, the flavour of vanilla beans from *V. fragrans* is far superior to that of synthetic vanillin, due to the presence of other flavour compounds in the natural product. This seems to be the deciding factor in favour of the natural product as a flavouring by the gourmet.

The natural-vanilla industry has been strengthened and stabilized to some extent by the United States' Drug Administration's labelling regulations for frozen desserts, which came into operation on 31 December 1965, according to which it is necessary to state whether natural or synthetic vanilla has been used. 'In the EEC, French law has decreed since May 1966 that the nature of the vanilla used in flavouring should be specified, a clear distinction being made between the natural and the synthetic product. More recently the EEC Commission has spent several years in trying to resolve difficulties in drawing up and issuing a Community directive in this matter, but though a draft proposal was issued in September 1970, by 1972 there were still no definite regulations for the flavour industry' (Commonwealth Secretariat, 1973).

History

Vanilla fragrans is indigenous to south-eastern Mexico, Guatemala and other parts of Central America, growing wild as a climber in the forests. Its use by the Aztecs was recorded by the Spanish conquistadors. Correll (1953) states that 'Bernal Díaz, a Spanish officer under Hernándo Cortés was perhaps the first white man to take note of this spice when he observed Montezuma, the intrepid Aztec emperor, drink "chocolatl", a beverage prepared from pulverized seeds of the cacao tree, flavoured with ground vanilla beans which the Aztecs call "tlilxochitl", derived from "tlilli", meaning "black", and from "xochitl" interpreted here as meaning "pod". Vanilla beans were considered to be among the rarer tributes paid to the Aztec emperor by his subject tribes.' Legend has it that Cortés in 1520 was given chocolate flavoured with vanilla by Montezuma, served in golden goblets.

Bernardino de Sehagún, a Franciscan friar, who arrived in Mexico in 1529, wrote about vanilla, saying that the Aztecs used it in cocoa, sweetened with honey, and sold the spice in their markets, but his work, originally written in the Aztec language, was not published until 1829–30. The Spaniards early imported vanilla beans into Spain, where factories were established in the second half of the sixteenth century for the manufacture of chocolate flavoured with vanilla. Francisco Hernández, who was sent to Mexico by Philip II of Spain, gave an illustrated account of vanilla in his *Rerum Medicarum Novae Hispaniae Thesaurus*, which was first published in Rome in 1651. In it he translates 'tlilxochitl' as 'black flowers', a fallacy which Correll (1953) says remained in the literature for many years, although the flowers are greenish-yellow in colour.

Hugh Morgan, apothecary to Queen Elizabeth I of England, suggested vanilla as a flavouring in its own right. He gave some cured beans to the Flemish botanist Carolas Clusius in 1602 and the latter describes them in his *Exoticorum Libri Decem* of 1605. William Dampier observed vanilla growing in 1676 in the Bay of Campeche in southern Mexico and in 1681 at Boco-toro in Costa Rica. Formerly, vanilla was used in medicine, as a nerve stimulant, and along with other spices had a reputation as an aphrodisiac. It was also used for scenting tobacco.

The plant appears to have been taken to England prior to 1733 and was then lost (Purseglove, 1972). It was re-introduced by the Marquis of Blandford at the beginning of the nineteenth century and flowered in

Charles Greville's collection at Paddington in 1807. Greville supplied cuttings to the botanic gardens in Paris and Antwerp. Two plants were sent from Antwerp to Buitenzorg (Bogor), Java, in 1819, only one of which survived the journey. It flowered in 1825, but did not fruit. Plants were taken to Réunion and from there to Mauritius in 1827. Vanilla was taken to the Malagasy Republic about 1840.

Although the plants grew well in the Old World tropics, fruits were not produced because of the absence of natural pollinators. It was not until Professor Charles Morren of Liége discovered the artificial means of pollination for the production of capsules in 1836 and Edmond Albius, a former slave in Réunion, developed a practical method of artificial pollination in 1841, and which is still used, that commercial production was possible in the eastern hemisphere away from the centre of origin.

Vanilla cultivation on a systematic basis was introduced into Java in 1846 by Teysmann, Director of the Buitenzorg (now Bogor) Botanic Gardens. It was the discovery of a satisfactory method of hand pollination and the failure of the sugar-cane crop in 1849–56 that gave impetus to cultivation of the crop in Réunion. Vanilla cuttings are said to have been first introduced into the Seychelles in 1866 and Lionnet (1958) says that vanilla was one of the earliest agricultural industries of the islands, the first exports being made in 1877, expanding rapidly towards the end of the century, and which have since declined. Vanilla was introduced from Manila to Tahiti by Hamelin in 1848, where an important industry developed. Cultivation of the crop began in the Comoro Islands in 1893 and soon spread throughout the islands. Vanilla was cultivated as early as 1839 in Martinique in the West Indies and probably about the same time in Guadeloupe. The plant was introduced into Uganda from Ceylon in 1912 and now has a small production. Former French island possessions are now the main producers of vanilla, with the Malagasy Republic as the major producer. Mexico still exports some of the spice.

Vanilla has been widely introduced throughout the tropics where climatic conditions are suitable, but has achieved little importance, except in the countries mentioned above. USA is the largest importer, followed by France and West Germany.

Botany

Systematics

Portères in Bouriquet (1954) describes 110 species of *Vanilla*, distributed in the tropics of both the Old and the New World. They belong to the orchid family, Orchidaceae, which is the largest family of flowering plants, with about 700 genera and 20 000 species. The Orchidaceae comprises a very natural, distinctive and highly advanced group of monocotyledons. They are perennial herbs which are widely distributed throughout the world with the greatest number in the tropics. They exhibit a wide range of life forms and have terrestrial, climbing, epiphytic and saprophytic species. Apart from the large number of ornamental species which are grown for their flowers, *Vanilla* is the only genus which has species of economic importance.

The correct name of the commonly cultivated vanilla of commerce is *Vanilla fragrans* (Salisb.) Ames, syn. *V. planifolia* Andrews, *Epidendrum vanilla* L., *Myrobroma fragrans* Salisb.

Two other species are occasionally cultivated, but yield an inferior product. They are:
1. *V. pompona* Schiede, West Indian vanilla, which occurs wild in south-eastern Mexico, Central America, Trinidad and northern South America. It is cultivated to a small extent in Guadeloupe, Martinique and Dominica. It resembles *V. fragrans*, but the leaves are larger, being 15–30 cm long and 5–12 cm wide. The greenish-yellow flowers are larger and more fleshy, with perianth lobes up to 8.5 cm long. The lip has a tuft of imbricate scales, instead of hairs in the centre of the disc. The cylindrical pods are shorter and thicker, being 10–17.5 cm long and 2.5–3.3 cm in diameter.
2. *V. tahitensis* J.W. Moore, Tahitian vanilla, indigenous to Tahiti and cultivated there and in Hawaii. This species is less robust than *V. fragrans* with more slender stems and narrower leaves which are 12–14 cm long and 2.5–3.0 cm wide. The lip is shorter than the sepals. The pods are 12–14 cm long and about 9–10 mm wide, tapering towards each end.

Cytology

The basic chromosome number for the genus is $x = 16$ and *V. fragrans* is a diploid with $2n = 32$, as are *V. pompona*, *V. tahitensis* and other species examined.

Structure

V. fragrans is a fleshy, herbaceous perennial vine, climbing by means of adventitious roots up trees or other supports to a height of 10–15 m; in cultivation it is trained to a height which will facilitate hand-pollination and harvesting.

Roots

Long, whitish, aerial, adventitious roots, about 2 mm in diameter, are produced singly opposite the leaves and adhere firmly appressed to the support up which the plant climbs. The roots at the base ramify in the humus or mulch layer. An endotrophic mycorrhiza is present. The outer parchment-like sheath or velamen is rather poorly developed.

Stem

The long, cylindrical, monopodial stems are simple or branched, and are succulent, flexuose and brittle. They are 1 – 2 cm in diameter and are dark green and photosynthetic with stomata. The internodes are 5 – 15 cm in length.

Leaves

The large, flat, fleshy, subsessile leaves are alternate, oblong-elliptic to lanceolate, and are 8 – 25 cm long and 2 – 8 cm broad. The tip is acute to acuminate and the base somewhat rounded. The veins are numerous, parallel and indistinct. The petiole is short, thick and canalized above.

Inflorescence

The stout inflorescences are axillary, usually simple, and only rarely branched. They are usually borne towards the top of the vine and are 5 – 8 cm long, with up to 20 – 30 flowers, but more usually 6 – 15, opening from the base upwards, generally with only 1 – 3 flowers open at one time and each lasting one day. The rachis is stout, often curved, and 4 – 10 mm in diameter. The bracts are rigid, concave, persistent, 5 – 15 mm long and about 7 mm wide at the base.

Flowers

The large, waxy, fragrant, pale greenish-yellow flowers are about 10 cm in diameter and are fugacious. The pedicel is very short. The inferior, cylindrical, tricarpillary ovary is often curved, 4 – 7 cm long and 3 – 5 mm in diameter. There are three oblong-lanceolate sepals, obtuse to subacute, slightly reflexed at the apex, 4 – 7 cm long and 1 – 1.5 cm wide. The two upper petals resemble the sepals in shape, but are slightly smaller. The lower petal is modified as a trumpet-shaped labellum or lip, which is shorter than the other perianth lobes and is 4 – 5 cm long and 1.5 – 3 cm broad at its widest point. It is attached to the column which it envelops. The tip of the lip is obscurely three-lobed and is irregularly toothed on its revolute margin. There are longitudinal verrucose darker-coloured papillae forming a crest in the median line and with a tuft of hairs in the middle of the disc. The column or gynostemium is 3 – 5 cm long and is attached to the labellum for most of its length. It is hairy on the inner surface, bearing at its tip the single stamen containing the two pollen masses or pollinia covered by a cap, and below is the concave sticky stigma, which is separated from the stamen by the thin flap-like rostellum.

Fruit

The capsule, known in the trade as a bean, is pendulous, narrowly cylindrical, obscurely three-angled, 10 – 25 cm long and 5 – 15 mm in diameter. It is aromatic on drying, containing when ripe myriads of very minute globose seeds, about 0.3 mm in diameter, which are

Fig. 11.1 *Vanilla fragrans:* Vanilla. A, portion of plant with inflorescence ($\times \frac{4}{5}$); B, column from front ($\times 4$); C, column from side ($\times 4$); D, lip opened out ($\times 1\frac{1}{2}$); E, fruit ($\times \frac{2}{5}$); F, seeds, ($\times 23$).

liberated by the capsule splitting longitudinally. In commercial production the capsules are harvested before they are quite ripe.

Pollination

The flower is so constructed that self-pollination of the individual flower is impossible, unless hand-pollinated, due to the separation of the stamen from the stigma by the rostellum.

In Mexico and Central America, where vanilla is indigenous, some of the flowers are pollinated by bees of the genus *Melapona*. Nectar is secreted by the base of the lip and the flowers are sweet-scented. Humming birds have been observed visiting the flowers and it has been suggested that they may also be pollinating agents. Elsewhere hand-pollination is necessary to provide fruits. Even in Mexico only a small percentage of the fruits set naturally and hand-pollination is carried out. In Puerto Rico natural pollination was about 1 per cent (Childers and Cibes, 1948). The method of hand-pollination was discovered by Morren in Liége in 1836, and Edmond Albius, a former slave in Réunion, discovered a practical method of artificial pollination in 1841, which is still used.

V. fragrans usually flowers only once a year over a period of about two months. In Mexico this is usually in April and May and in the Malagasy Republic, Réunion and the Comoro Islands between November and January. As already stated, the flowers open from the base of the raceme upwards and usually one, or more rarely two or three flowers are open on the inflorescence at one time. The flowers open early in the morning; they are receptive for eight hours and wither the following day. Fruit-set is highest when pollination is done early on a bright morning following rain. If fertilization has been successfully achieved the flowers remain on the rachis; if unsuccessful, the flowers drop off in two or three days. Thus it is possible to judge the number of fruits which have set and to discontinue pollination when the desired number have been obtained.

Hand-pollination is done with a splinter of bamboo or other material about the size of a toothpick. The flower is held in one hand and the labellum is pushed down with the thumb releasing the column. The stamen cap is removed by the stick which is held in the other hand, which exposes the pollinia. Then the flap-like rostellum is pushed up under the stamens with the stick and, by pressing with the thumb and finger, the pollinia are brought into contact with the sticky stigma to which the pollen mass adheres.

When fertile cross-pollinated seed is required, it is, of course necessary to obtain the pollinia from another plant.

Cultivars

Except in the countries of origin, introduction of material which is propagated vegetatively, is likely to be of very limited clonal origin and so little variation can be expected. As far as it can be ascertained there are few, if any, cultivars of *V. fragrans* recognized. According to Dupont, quoted by Lionnet (1958), the vanilla plantations of Réunion, Mauritius, the Seychelles and the Malagasy Republic all derive from a single cutting which was introduced into Réunion from the Jardin des Plantes in Paris.

Ecology

Climate and soils

In a wild state *V. fragrans* usually grows climbing on trees in wet tropical lowland forests from sea-level to 600 m. It thrives best in hot, moist, insular climates, with frequent, but not excessive rain. The optimum temperature is 21–32 °C, with an average around 27 °C, and with an evenly distributed rainfall of 2 000–2 500 mm per annum, but with two drier months to check vegetative growth and bring the vines to flower. Regions with a prolonged dry season should be avoided.

The monthly rainfall and maximum and minimum temperatures at stations in Mexico and the Malagasy Republic, taken from Bouriquet (1954), are given in Table 11.1.

Table 11.1 *Rainfall in Mexico and the Malagasy Republic (Madagascar)*

	Tecolutla: Mexico			Antalaha: Malagasy Republic		
	Rainfall (mm)	Maximum temperature (°C)	Minimum temperature (°C)	Rainfall (mm)	Minimum temperature (°C)	Minimum temperature (°C)
January	62	30.0	5.0	215	32.2	22.5
February	50	30.0	10.0	204	31.8	23.1
March	67	31.5	11.0	249	31.4	23.0
April	15	32.5	12.9	235	30.2	22.3
May	48	31.5	13.5	110	29.0	21.1
June	201	31.5	17.5	140	27.6	19.5
July	142	32.5	19.0	136	26.4	18.8
August	123	32.0	19.0	113	26.7	18.6
September	281	29.3	18.0	85	27.5	19.1
October	384	27.8	15.0	50	29.0	20.0
November	84	25.6	12.0	79	30.4	21.3
December	74	22.6	10.0	181	31.3	22.4
Total	1 531			1 797		

The most suitable land for vanilla is gently sloping with light friable soil, adequate but not excessive drainage, and a thick surface layer of humus or mulch in which the roots can spread. Waterlogging is harmful.

Partial shade is necessary and this is usually provided by the shrubs or small trees up which the vines are grown.

Cultivation

Propagation

Commercial vanilla is always propagated by stem cuttings. For breeding purposes the orchid can be grown from seeds, which is a long and complicated procedure and is briefly described below. Further details will be found in Purseglove (1972). The seed should be disinfected before sowing by shaking in 10 g of bleaching powder in 150 ml of distilled water. Knudson (1950) recommends a previous momentary treatment with 95 per cent alcohol to get rid of fatty material, followed by several washings in distilled water. The seeds are then grown on a sterilized medium containing basic salts and sugar, to which growth substances may be added. The formula used by Knudson (1950) for growing vanilla seeds was:

$Ca(NO_3)_2 4H_2O$	1.00 g
KH_2PO_4	0.25 g
$MgSO_4 7H_2O$	0.25 g
$(NH_4)_2SO_4$	0.50 g
$FePO_4 4H_2O$	0.025 g
Sucrose	20.00 g
Agar	12.00 g
Distilled water	1.0 litre

The pH was adjusted to $5-5.5$. Knudson reported that dormancy in vanilla seeds may be prolonged and under greenhouse conditions may continue for several years. He found that germination of seeds of *V. fragrans* is possible if the cultures are maintained in a dark incubator at 32 °C and that exposure of the seeds to greenhouse conditions before incubation resulted in a higher percentage of germination. Seeds of *V. fragrans* × *V. pompona* required a minimum temperature of 34 °C.

Hybridization and production from seed has been carried out in Puerto Rico and the Malagasy Republic.

In vegetative propagation, the cuttings should be taken from healthy vigorous plants and may be cut from any part of the vine. The length of the cutting is usually determined by the amount of planting material available. Short cuttings, 30 cm in length, will take 3 to 4 years to flower and fruit. Cuttings, 90–100 cm in length, are usually preferable. In some regions, cuttings 2–3.5 m in length may be used, when available, with their free ends hanging over supports; these will flower and fruit in 1 to 2 years. It is usual to remove two to three leaves from the base, which is inserted into the humic layer and mulch. With short cuttings, at least two nodes should be left above ground. The portions above ground should be tied to the support until the aerial roots have obtained a firm grasp. Cuttings are usually planted *in situ*, but they can be started in nursery beds when necessary. Because of their succulent nature, cuttings can be stored or transported for periods of up to two weeks if required.

Supports

The vines of vanilla require some form of support up which to climb, and also light shade; too dense shade and full sunlight are both deleterious. If new forest land is being cleared for planting, this may be partially cleared, leaving some small trees at the required distances. Usually small trees are planted and, where possible, these should be established before the vanilla. The ideal tree should be quick-growing, providing light, checkered shade; have sufficient low branches over which the vines can be trained to hang down, with the type of growth providing easy access to the vanilla; be strong enough to support the vines in strong winds; and be easily pruned when necessary. It is an advantage if it can be planted from large cuttings and it may be possible that it can provide an economic product as well as the vanilla. Among the latter are: Liberica coffee, *Coffea liberica* Bull; avocado, *Persea americana* Mill.; jackfruit, *Artocarpus heterophyllus* Lam.; annatto, *Bixa orellana* L.; cashew nut, *Anacardium occidentale* L.; hog plum, *Spondias mombin* L.; and white mulberry, *Morus alba* L. The two trees most commonly used in the Malagasy Republic are the physic nut, *Jatropha curcas* L., which can be propagated from cuttings or grows rapidly from seeds, and *Casuarina equisetifolia* L. Other trees which have been tried and recommended include: *Bauhinia* spp.; calabash, *Crescentia cujete* L.; *Croton tiglium* L.; *Dracaena* spp.; *Erythrina* spp.; *Ficus* spp.; *Gliricidia sepium* (Jacq.) Walp.; and *Pandanus* spp.

In the early stages, lateral shade may be provided by bananas or maize. Windbreaks should be planted where necessary. If vanilla is grown up posts or trellises, it will also be necessary to supply some form of partial shade. The woodwork is subject to decay and damage by termites, necessitating its replacement at regular intervals. Where wire is used for supports, the tender succulent vines can easily be damaged, especially in a strong wind.

Planting and after-care

The cuttings (see 'Propagation' above) are usually planted about 3 m apart at the foot of the supporting trees or poles. A spacing of 1.2–1.5 m in rows 2.5–3 m apart is also sometimes recommended. In the early vanilleries, the plants were often planted so close together that they became entangled. This usually gave very high initial yields, but presented grave problems of access and disease control later. The planting holes are best filled with humus and mulch, which should be raised above the soil surface. On account of the very superficial roots, cultivation is not done after planting. Clean-weeding of the vanillery is not recommended, but rank growth of climbers and other weeds should be controlled. Mulching has a very beneficial effect and should be done regularly. The application of guano and bonemeal has been found useful. Under good conditions the growth of the vine is very rapid and may range from 50 to 100 cm per month.

It is usually stated that as long as the vine can climb upwards it will not flower, but Irvine and Delfel (1961) did not find this to be so in Puerto Rico. However, it is necessary to train the vines so that they may grow at a convenient height for pollination and harvesting. The vines are twisted round the lower branches of the supporting tree or over the lattice of the trellis so that they may hang down. Care is required so as not to tear or bruise the leaves, branches or roots. The top 7.5 – 10 cm of the vine is usually pinched out 6 – 8 months before the flowering season to encourage the production of inflorescences in the axils of the leaves on the hanging branches. Vanilla usually starts flowering in its third year after planting, the time taken depending on the size of the original cuttings. The maximum production of flowers is reached in 7 to 8 years. Given proper care this may continue for several years, but in some vanilleries the production period is shorter. Correll (1953) says that in Mexico a small crop is gathered at the end of the third year and for 4 or 5 years the vines continue to increase in size and productivity; at the end of 9 or 10 years the vines have lost their commercial value and are abandoned.

As the flowers open, the requisite number are hand-pollinated, details of which are given under 'Pollination' above. Only the flowers on the lower side of the raceme are pollinated in order that the fruits may hang perpendicularly to produce straight beans; those on the upper side would produce crooked beans of inferior quality. Usually only one flower opens in each inflorescence in one day and is receptive for about 8 hours. Consequently, most of the pollination must be done in the mornings and is continued for 1 or 2 months until the required number of fruits have set. The number of inflorescences and flowers per vine, and the number which are pollinated and allowed to produce mature beans, depends upon the vigour of the plant. Usually on vigorous plants, 8 – 10 flowers on 10 – 20 inflorescences are pollinated, of which 4 – 8 capsules are allowed to grow to maturity on each raceme. If pollination has been successful, the perianth withers, but remains attached to the ovary, which then increases in size. If pollination has been a failure, the flowers drop off the next day.

When the desired number of fruits has set, the remaining buds are removed, which may be done by clipping off the tip of the inflorescence. Damaged and malformed capsules are removed during growth. The final number of beans per vine varies greatly and is usually about 30−150. Hand-pollination is usually done by women and children, who can make 1 000−2 000 pollinations each per day.

Gregory *et al.* (1967) have shown that the growth-regulating chemicals 2,4-D (2,4-dichlorophenoxyacetic acid), dicamba (2-methoxy-3, 6-dichlorobenzoic acid) and IAA-IBA (indoleacetic acid-indolebutyric acid) will induce the development of parthenocarpic fruits and give a high percentage of fruit-set. Dicamba and 2,4-D were translocated from the treated flower to buds in the same inflorescence, inducing them to set fruits, and dicamba was translocated from one raceme to another, inducing fruit set. The application of 0.1 mg of 2,4-D in lanolin paste around the base of the calyx resulted in pods, which, although weighing less, were similar in size to those from hand-pollinated flowers. Chromatograms made of extracts of cured parthenocarpic pods showed that vanillin was present in almost all samples. Thus, it may be possible to obtain vanilla beans without the need for hand-pollination.

The aim is to produce pods as long as possible, as these provide the highest grade; it also saves time in pollinating, picking and handling.

Harvesting and yields

The time between flowering and harvesting is 6−9 months. The pods are harvested rotationally when they are fully grown and as they begin to ripen, as shown by the tips becoming yellow. It is essential to pick the pods at the right stage as immature pods produce an inferior product and if picked too late they will split during curing. The plantations should be visited daily so that the pods can be picked as soon as they are ready. They may be harvested by sideways pressure of the thumb at the base or by cutting with a sharp knife. About 6 kg of green pods produce 1 kg of cured beans. Curing should begin within a week of harvesting the beans. This process is discussed in detail in the 'Processing and manufacture' section.

After fruiting, the old stems and weak branches are pruned off. The tree supports or shade should be pruned to provide 30−50 per cent of full sunlight and to induce branches at the correct height for training the vines. In some countries it is customary for the owners to prick distinguishing marks on the green pods on the vines to ensure against theft.

Yields are very variable. A good vanillery is said to yield about 500−800 kg of cured beans per hectare per annum during a crop life of about 7 years. Much lower yields are reported by Lionnet (1958−9) in the Seychelles.

Diseases

Anthracnose, *Calospora vanillae* Massée, is the most serious disease of vanilla in most countries. It attacks the stem apex, leaves and roots and results in wilting and falling of the fruits, which turn black at the ends and in the middle and fall off in one or two days. Excess of moisture, prolonged rainy weather, insufficient drainage, too much shade and overcrowding all favour the disease. Great damage was caused in the Seychelles in the 1890s, when the vines were planted too close together.

A root rot, *Fusarium batatis* Wollenw. var. *vanillae* Tucker, has been a limiting factor to vanilla production in Puerto Rico and has also been reported from other countries. In the early stages of the disease there is first a browning and death of the underground roots and later of the aerial roots. The plant ceases shoot growth and begins to send out numerous aerial roots, many of which die before or after coming into contact with the soil. The stems and leaves become flaccid and the stems begin to shrivel and eventually droop and dry out. Childers and Cibes (1948) state that the plants are less capable of resisting the disease when weakened by drought, by lack of important nutrients, too much sun, and over-pollination and fruit production. To control the disease, plants should be kept in a vigorous condition by the maintenance of adequate shade and a heavy mulch, especially during the dry season, by moderate to light pollination and by providing irrigation during extended dry periods. *Vanilla pompona, V. phaeantha* Rchb.f. and *V. barbellata* Rchb.f. are resistant and they can be hybridized with *V. fragrans*.

Mildew attacks the developing fruits. Bouriquet (1954) states that the fungus responsible in the Malagasy Republic is *Phytophthora jatrophae* Jens., which is also a pathogen on *Jatropha curcas* on which the vanilla is grown. Mildew has also been reported from Puerto Rico and elsewhere.

Correll (1953) records the following diseases attacking vanilla: *Phytophthora parasitica* Dast., causing a fruit rot; *Glomerella vanillae* (Zimm.) Petch, attacking the roots; *Vermicularia vanillae* Delacr. in Mauritius; *Gloeosporium vanillae* Cooke in Colombia, Mauritius and Sri Lanka; *Uredo scabies* Cooke in Colombia; *Macrophoma vanillae* Averna and *Pestalozzia vanillae* Averna in Brazil; *Physalospora vanillae* Zimm. in Java; and *Atichia vanillae* (Pat.) V Hoeh. in Tahiti.

Sunburn has also been reported, as has a tip die-back due to water deficiency.

Pests

Ridley (1912) states that one of the most destructive pests is the bug *Trioza litseae* Giard. in Réunion, which attacks the buds and flowers, puncturing them and producing spots of decay. The emerald bug, *Nezara smaragdula* (Fabr.) which is cosmopolitan throughout the tropics, lays its eggs on the leaves and stalks of the vanilla and the insects when hatched suck the sap of the flower-buds and stalks. The bug *Memmia vicina* Sign. has been reported by Bouriquet (1954) as damaging vanilla in the Malagasy Republic.

Two weevils, *Perissoderes oblongus* Hustache and *P. ruficollis* Waterh., attack the crop in the Malagasy Republic; the latter also occurs in the Comoro Islands. An ashy-grey weevil, *Cratopus punctum* Fabr., which bites holes in the flowers and can destroy the column, occurs in the Malagasy Republic, Réunion and Mauritius. Small lamellicorn beetles, *Hoplia retusa* Klug. ar.d *Enaria malanichtera* Klug., also damage the flowers in the Malagasy Republic.

Two moth caterpillars cause damage: *Conchylis vanillana* de Joannis in Réunion, and *Phytometra* (*Plusia*) *aurifera* (Hb.), which has a wide distribution, including tropical Africa.

Insects causing minor injuries in Puerto Rico are: a black weevil, *Diorymerellus* sp., which causes injury to the tips of the vanilla shoots; a small leaf tyer, *Platynota rostrana* Walker; an aphis *Cerataphis lataniae* (Boisd.), which also occurs in the Seychelles and Réunion; an earwig *Doru* sp.; and a woolly bear caterpillar *Ecpantheria incasia* Cramer.

Among the most serious pests in Puerto Rico, Childers and Cibes (1948) give the snail, *Thelidomus lima* Fér., and the slug, *Veronicalla kraussii* Ferussac, which damage the plants by the removal of the outer portions or entire sections of buds, leaves, shoots and immature fruits. They cause most damage during warm damp weather and the mulch forms an ideal harbouring place for them. They may be controlled by a metaldehyde bait.

Chickens cause much damage by scratching among the mulch and in so doing tear and expose the roots. Predial larceny may be a serious source of loss; some growers scratch the beans with their own small brand marks to try to prevent it.

Improvement

Comparatively little work has been done on the improvement of vanilla by breeding. As much of the vanilla in the Old World originated from a single clonal source there is little variation. Now that satisfactory methods exist for growing orchid seeds and the culture of orchid seedlings (see 'Propagation' above), it should not be too difficult to make, raise and test vanilla hybrids, which would then be increased rapidly by meristem culture. It has been suggested that vanilla seed should be inoculated with *Rhizoctonia repens* to ensure the survival of the seedlings. With modern techniques this would appear to be unnecessary.

As with many orchid genera, inter - and intraspecific *Vanilla* hybrids are relatively easy to make. *Vanilla fragrans* has been crossed with other species, including *V. phaeantha* Rchb.f., which is resistant to *Fusarium* root rot.

If new clonal material could be obtained from Central America with adequate quarantine precautions provided, it seems likely that the production of new hybrid material would be well worth while.

Products and end-uses

Vanilla beans which enter international trade are the cured fruit pods obtained from *V. fragrans* (true vanilla), *V. tahitensis* (Tahiti vanilla) and *V. pompona* ('vanillons', Guadeloupe or Antilles vanilla). True vanilla is by far the most important and is mainly employed for food flavouring, either in the powdered state or in the form of solvent extracts; it is also used to a limited extent in pharmacy and perfumery. Tahiti vanilla is used both for flavouring purposes and in perfumery, while vanillons is employed almost exclusively in perfumery.

Vanilla is exported from the producing countries in the whole or cut forms and end-processing is carried out in the consuming centres. The export of ground vanilla by the producing countries is rare.

The predominant form in which vanilla is employed for food flavouring varies from country to country. In the United States and the United Kingdom, both the domestic consumer and the processed-food manufacturers mainly use vanilla solvent extracts in flavouring applications, whereas retail sales for domestic culinary use in Continental Europe are largely of whole or powdered vanilla. The main demand for vanilla in the major importing countries is for the flavouring of ice-cream, but it is also extensively used in the flavouring of chocolate and other confectionery products, biscuits and other baked goods, and in alcoholic and non-alcoholic beverages.

The various types of vanilla products employed in flavouring applications are briefly described below using the terminology current in the United States:

'Vanilla extract'

This is a hydroalcoholic solution containing the extracted aroma and flavour principles of vanilla beans and may also contain added sweetening/thickening agents such as sugar and glycerine. Conventional vanilla extracts have a minimum ethyl alcohol content of 35 per cent and contain the soluble extractives from 1 part by weight of vanilla beans in 10 parts by volume of aqueous alcohol. In the United States, the largest market for vanilla extract, the composition requirements are strictly defined (see the 'Standard specifications' section). Vanilla extract may be prepared by direct extraction (maceration) or by dilution of concentrated vanilla extract, concentrated vanilla flavouring or vanilla oleoresin (see below). The direct extraction procedure provides a product with the best aroma and flavour, closely resembling that of vanilla beans.

'Vanilla flavouring'

This is similar to 'vanilla extract' but contains less than 35 per cent ethyl alcohol by volume.

'Vanilla tincture' (for pharmaceutical use)

This is prepared by maceration from 1 part of vanilla beans by weight to 10 parts of aqueous alcohol by volume and contains added sugar. It differs from 'vanilla extract' in having an ethyl alcohol content of at least 38 per cent.

'Concentrated vanilla extract' and 'concentrated vanilla flavouring'

These products are prepared by stripping off a part of the solvent from solvent extracts to concentrate the vanilla constituent content. They have the same alcohol content as the corresponding 'vanilla extract' or 'vanilla flavouring'.

'Vanilla oleoresin'

This is a semi-solid concentrate obtained by complete removal of the solvent from a vanilla extract. Aqueous isopropanol is frequently used instead of aqueous ethyl alcohol for the extraction step. Owing to unavoidable evaporation losses during the solvent stripping step, 'vanilla oleoresin' is inferior in aroma–flavour character to conventional, unconcentrated 'vanilla extract' prepared by maceration.

'Vanilla–vanillin extract and flavouring'

These products are fortified with synthetic vanillin and the natural component is usually obtained by dilution of 'vanilla oleoresin'.

'Vanilla powder'

This may be pure powdered vanilla but it is more usually a mixture of vanilla powder or vanilla oleoresin with sugar, food starch or gum acacia.

'Vanilla–vanillin powder'

This product is fortified by the incorporation of synthetic vanillin.

For perfumery applications, a number of solvent-extracted products are employed; the main types being:

'Perfumery vanilla tincture'

This is prepared by maceration of vanilla beans with perfumery alcohol, and has an ethyl alcohol content of around 90 per cent.

'Vanilla absolute'

This is prepared by direct alcohol extraction of vanilla beans followed by solvent stripping or by alcohol washing of an oleoresin prepared by extraction with a hydrocarbon solvent. It is the most concentrated form of the vanilla aroma, being 7 to 13 times stronger than good-quality vanilla beans, but it has a less well-rounded character.

The major types of vanilla

Vanilla beans differ in chemical, physical and organoleptic properties not only according to the species, but also within a species, depending on the geographical source and the physical form or grade. Consequently, preferences are expressed by consumers for particular types for certain applications.

The trade in true vanilla (from *V. fragrans*) in the twentieth century has been dominated by Madagascar (Malagasy Republic), the Comoro Islands and Réunion, producers of 'Bourbon' vanilla. Mexico and Indonesia have been next in importance, followed by the West Indies and South America. Other minor and intermittent suppliers have included Rodriguez, Mauritius and Seychelles—all three exporting 'Bourbon' type vanilla; Uganda, Fiji, Tonga and Sri Lanka.

Fig. 11.2   Cured vanilla beans (*Vanilla fragrans* (Salisb.) Ames). (Crown copyright).

Vanilla beans are supplied in three physical forms:
1. Whole beans.
2. Splits – Whole beans which have partially split open longitudinally from the blossom-end owing to dehiscence.
3. Cuts – Beans which have been cut into short lengths to accelerate the curing process, or portions of cured beans remaining after cutting away mouldy or damaged sections. This category may also include very small whole beans.

The higher grades of whole beans, which possess the best appearance, are preferred for domestic retail sales. Lower grades of whole beans and cuts, which have a lower moisture content, are more suitable for extraction purposes; but in practice, blends are made from the various grades to obtain an extract or oleoresin with the desired properties.

The characteristics of the major types of vanilla entering trade are summarized below. Further information on grading and packaging differences are provided in the 'Processing and manufacture' section under the appropriate country headings:

Mexican vanilla

Mexico has traditionally been regarded as the supplier of true vanilla possessing the finest aroma and flavour. Consumers who are accustomed to artificial vanilla, however, often dislike the fine flavour of Mexican vanilla and consider it deficient in 'body'. It is supplied in five grades (or seven if intermediate grades are included) of whole beans and in the form of cuts. The top grades of Mexican beans are rarely 'frosted' with a surface coating of naturally exuded vanillin.

Bourbon vanilla

This has a deeper 'body' flavour than Mexican vanilla but a less fine aroma. Of the three main sources of Bourbon vanilla – Madagascar, the Comoro Islands and Réunion – the last is regarded as providing the best quality. Réunion vanilla is, however, somewhat moister than the other sources and is less suitable for extraction purposes.

Bourbon vanilla is frequently 'frosted' and is marketed in five main grades of whole and split beans and a category known as 'bulk' (*'en vrac'*), comparable to Mexican cuts.

The major source of Bourbon vanilla, Madagascar, distinguishes vanilla produced on the north-east coast, which includes the major growing area of Antalaha prefecture, from vanilla produced on the island of Nossi-Bé and the neighbouring coastal area of the north-west mainland. A large proportion of Madagascan vanilla is now prepared by artificial drying.

Indonesian vanilla

This is produced principally on the island of Java and has traditionally been of mixed quality with little attention paid to grading. Java vanilla possesses a deep, full-bodied flavour and is frequently used for blending with synthetic vanillin. Exports from Java now include artificially dried, cut vanilla.

South American and West Indian vanilla

The small volume of true vanilla entering trade from this region is more similar in properties to Bourbon vanilla than Mexican vanilla, if frequently of a poorer quality.

Tahiti vanilla

The vanilla produced in French Polynesia is obtained from *V. tahitensis* and possesses a characteristic aromatic odour and usually has a lower vanillin content than true vanilla. It is generally less favoured for flavouring purposes than true vanilla owing to its somewhat rank flavour and to its relatively high volatile-oil content which can result in cloudy extracts. Tahiti vanilla is exported in five main grades which rarely 'frost'.

Vanillons (Guadeloupe vanilla or Antilles vanilla)

This is produced from *V. pompona* on certain of the former French West Indian islands, principally on Guadeloupe. Vanillons has a low vanillin content and possesses a characteristic floral aroma, bearing similarities to Tahiti vanilla. It is mainly employed in perfumery as its flavour is considered to be poor and it tends to provide gummy aqueous alcohol extracts. Vanillons is exported in three grades.

Processing and manufacture

1. Curing of Vanilla Beans

Quality requirements

The primary quality determinant for cured vanilla beans is the aroma/flavour character. Other factors of significance in quality assessment are the general appearance, flexibility, the length and the vanillin content. The relative importance of these various quality attributes is dependent upon the intended end-use of the cured beans.

Traditionally, the appearance, flexibility and size characteristics have been of importance since there is a fairly close relationship between these factors and the aroma/flavour quality. Top-quality beans are long, fleshy, supple, very dark brown to black in colour, somewhat oily in appearance, strongly aromatic and free from scars and blemishes. Low-quality beans are usually hard, dry, thin, brown or reddish-brown in colour and possess a poor aroma. The moisture content of top grade beans is high (30–40 per cent), whereas it may be as little as 10 per cent in the lower grades. At one time, the presence of a surface coating of naturally exuded vanillin crystals ('frosting') was regarded as an indicator of good quality. However, this is no real guide and Mexican vanilla, which has the best reputation for quality, rarely 'frosts'. A high vanillin content is desirable but this value is not directly commensurate with the overall aroma/flavour quality of the bean.

Much of the vanilla entering Western markets is used for the preparation of vanilla extract, and for this purpose the appearance of the beans is not of prime importance. In recent years, there has been a tendency for some of the larger extracting firms to encourage the production of artificially dried cut vanilla which possesses a good aroma/flavour character and a high vanillin content.

Traditional curing methods

A number of procedures have been evolved for the curing of vanilla but they are all characterized by four phases:
(*a*) 'Killing' or wilting: this stops further vegetative development in the fresh bean and initiates the onset of enzymatic reactions responsible for the production of the aroma and flavour. Killing is indicated by the development of a brown coloration in the bean.
(*b*) 'Sweating': This involves raising the temperature of the killed beans to promote the desired enzymatic reactions and to provoke a first, fairly rapid, drying to prevent harmful fermentations. During this operation, the beans acquire a deeper brown coloration and become quite supple, and the development of an aroma becomes perceptible.
(*c*) The third stage entails slow drying at ambient temperature, usually in the shade, until the beans have reached about one-third of their original weight.
(*d*) In the final stage, known as 'conditioning', the beans are stored in closed boxes for a period of three months or longer to permit the full development of the desired aroma and flavour.

The various traditional procedures for curing vanilla beans are described in the following paragraphs. The two most important methods are those of Mexico and the Indian Ocean islands producing 'Bourbon' vanilla.

Mexican curing methods

The two main traditional forms of curing employed in Mexico are the sun-wilting and the oven-wilting procedures (Ridley, 1912; Chalot and Bernard, 1920; Bouriquet, 1954; Theodose, 1973). The former is the oldest known method of curing vanilla and the latter was introduced around 1850. Both methods are still widely used by the specialist curing firms in Mexico which process the vast bulk of the vanilla crop (Mallory and Walter, 1942; Correll, 1953; Merory, 1968). The harvesting period in Mexico extends from November to January and curing by either method takes around five to six months before the product is ready for the market.

'Sun-wilting': On arrival at the curing house, the fresh beans may be set aside in a store for a few days until required and during this time the beans start to shrivel.

The fresh beans first have their peduncles removed and are then sorted according to their degree of maturity, size and into unsplit and split types. This is done as the various sorts cure at different rates. Beans which are already beginning to darken are removed, wiped with castor oil and are cured separately.

The beans are killed by exposing them to the sun for a period of about five hours on the day after sorting. The fresh beans are spread out on dark blankets resting on a cement patio or on wooden racks. In the afternoon, the beans become too hot to hold by hand and are then covered by the edges of the blanket. In the mid- to late-afternoon before the beans have begun to cool, the thick ends of the beans are laid towards the centre of the blanket which is then rolled up. The blanket rolls are immediately taken indoors and are placed in blanket-lined, air-tight mahogany boxes to undergo their first 'sweating'. Blankets and matting are placed over the sweating boxes to prevent loss of heat. After 12–24 hours, the beans are removed and inspected. Most of the beans will have begun to acquire a dark-brown colour indicating a good 'killing'. Beans which have retained their original green colour or which have an uneven coloration are separated and are subjected to oven-wilting (see later).

Those beans which have been properly killed are next subjected to a process involving periodic 'sunnings' and sweatings. 'Sunning' entails spreading the beans on blankets and exposing them to the sun for two to three hours during the hottest part of the day when weather conditions are favourable. During the remaining part of the day, unless a sweating is to be undertaken, the beans are stored indoors on wooden racks in a well-ventilated room. There are two distinct phases to this sunning/sweating stage. The first phase involves a fairly rapid drying in which the beans are given 'sunnings' virtually every day and several overnight sweatings until they become supple. This takes about five to six days. A preliminary sorting into lots corresponding to the various grades is usually carried out at this juncture. This is followed by further 'sunnings' and additional but less frequent sweatings. In practice, 'sunnings' are not carried out every day in this second phase since, apart from constraints imposed by the weather, too rapid drying is considered to be detrimental to quality. Some 20–30 days after killing, most of the beans become very supple and acquire characteristics close to those of the final product and are ready for the next stage of very slow drying indoors. The total number of sweatings undertaken during the 'sunning/sweating' operation can vary between four and eight.

Those beans which require a large number of sunnings and sweatings generally provide a low-quality product.

Very slow drying indoors lasts for approximately one month and a further sorting into grades is usually carried out during this time. The beans are regularly inspected and those which have achieved the requisite state of dryness are immediately removed from the racks for 'conditioning'. The overall sweating and drying operation may take up to eight weeks from the time of 'killing', according to the prevailing weather conditions. Small and split beans are usually ready for conditioning earlier than perfect, large beans.

Beans removed for conditioning are sorted again and are straightened by drawing them through the fingers. This operation is also useful in that it spreads the oil which exudes during the curing process and gives the beans their characteristic lustre. The beans are next tied into bundles of about fifty with black string. The bundles are wrapped in waxed-paper and are placed in waxed paper lined, metal conditioning boxes. Conditioning lasts for at least three months and during this period the beans are regularly inspected. Mouldy beans are removed for treatment (see later) and those which are not developing the required aroma may be re-subjected to 'sunnings and sweatings'. At the end of the conditioning period, the beans are given a final grading and are packed for shipment (see later).

'Oven-wilting':   In this procedure, use is made of a specially constructed brick or cement room, known as a *calorifico*, which serves as an autoclave. The room measures approximately $4 \times 4 \times 4$ metres and incorporates a wood-fired heater which is stoked from the outside. It is fitted with a small access door and has wooden racks fitted along the walls.

The beans to be killed by this method are divided into piles of up to 1 000 and are then rolled up in a blanket which is finally covered with matting to form a *malleta*. The *malletas* are moistened with water and are placed on the shelves in the *calorifico*. Water is poured onto the solid floor to maintain a high humidity, the door is closed and the heating fire is lit.

In about 12 hours, the temperature inside the *calorifico* reaches 60 °C. After a further 16 hours, a temperature of 70 °C is attained and this is maintained for another 8 hours. The *malletas* are removed after a total of 36 hours in the *calorifico*. If the temperature cannot be raised above 65 °C, then the total period of autoclaving is extended to 48 hours.

On removal from the *calorifico*, the matting is quickly stripped from the *malletas* and the blanket wrapped beans are placed in sweating boxes. After 24 hours, the beans are removed and inspected.

The killed beans are then subjected to repeated sunnings and sweatings, as described above under 'Sun-wilting'. Should the weather be overcast, the killed beans are stored on racks indoors in a well-ventilated room until sunning is possible. However, if the weather does not improve within three days, the batch is reprocessed through the *calorifico* and sweating box.

The Bourbon method

Bourbon vanilla is the name given to the product from the former French possessions in the Indian Ocean which employ a curing technique first developed on the island of Réunion, formerly known as Bourbon. Production of Bourbon-type vanilla is now dominated by Madagascar, with the Comoro Islands and Réunion as smaller but important sources.

The Bourbon curing technique is distinguished from those of Mexico in that 'killing' is achieved by scalding the beans in hot water and fewer sweatings are undertaken. The Bourbon product usually has a higher moisture content than the corresponding Mexican grade and is frequently frosted. As in Mexico, curing of vanilla is carried out by specialist firms rather than by the vanilla growers. Slight variations in the curing technique are practised in the various producing islands (Chalot and Bernard, 1920; Correll, 1953; Bouriquet, 1954; Lionnet, 1959; Hibon, 1966) and the following is a description of the procedure evolved on Madagascar.

On arrival at the curing factory, the beans are sorted according to the degree of maturity, size, and into split and unsplit types. Batches of beans, weighing 25–30 kg, are loaded into open-work cylindrical baskets which are then plunged into containers full of hot water heated to 63–65 °C over a wood fire. Batches of beans which will eventually make up the top three qualities are immersed for 2–3 minutes, while smaller and split beans are treated for less than 2 minutes. The warm beans are rapidly drained, wrapped in a dark cotton cloth and are placed in a cloth-lined sweating box. After 24 hours, the beans are removed and inspected to separate those which have not been properly killed.

The next stage of sun-drying is carried out on a plot of dry, easily drained ground, at some distance from roads to avoid contamination by dust. The killed beans are spread out on dark cloths resting on slatted platforms, constructed from bamboo and raised 70 cm above the ground. After one hour of direct exposure to the sun, the edges of the cloth are folded over the beans to retain the heat. The cloth-covered beans are then left for a further two hours in the sun before the blanket is rolled up and taken indoors. This procedure is repeated for 6–8 days until the beans become quite supple.

The third stage involves slow drying in the shade for a period of 2–3 months. The beans are spread on racks, mounted on supports and are spaced 12 cm apart in a well-ventilated room. During this slow drying operation, the beans are sorted regularly and those which have dried to the requisite moisture content are immediately removed for conditioning.

In some localities in the Bourbon producing areas, where the weather is frequently inclement during the sun- and indoor-drying periods of curing, ovens set at 45–50 °C have traditionally been used.

Conditioning of the beans is carried out in a similar manner to that described for Mexico and takes about 3 months for completion. The overall curing process for Bourbon vanilla lasts for 5–8 months. The main harvesting season in Madagascar extends from June to early October.

A modification to the traditional Bourbon curing method was devised in Puerto Rico in the 1940s and was adopted by the vanilla co-operative at Castaner (Childers and Cibes, 1948; Jones and Vincente, 1949a). On arrival at the factory, the beans are sorted into split and unsplit types and are then killed as soon as possible. Prior to killing, the beans are wiped with a damp cloth. Scalding entails three 10-second immersions at 30-second intervals in a water bath at 80 °C. After draining, the beans are wrapped in a blanket and are placed in a sweating box. Killing is followed by daily two-hour sunnings and overnight sweatings for about seven days until the beans become supple. The next stage of indoor air-drying is continued until the beans reach one-third of their original weight. The beans are then bundled and conditioned in tin boxes until they dry to one-quarter of their original weight. By contrast to Bourbon vanilla from the Indian Ocean producers, Puerto Rican vanilla scalded at 80 °C rarely frosts. When the weather is unsuitable for sunning, the beans are sweated in a closed oven at 45 °C containing a pan of water.

Other methods for *V. fragrans*

The Guadeloupe technique entails killing by making scars with a pin along the faces of the bean and then exposing the beans, wrapped in a blanket, to the sun for a few hours. The pin, which should be sterilized regularly, is fitted into a cork to protrude no more than 2 mm. After killing, the curing process is similar to that of Mexico (Chalot and Bernard, 1920; Arana, 1945).

Two other methods, which tend to provide a poor-quality product, have been described by Ridley (1912). The 'Guiana method' involves killing the beans by placing them in the ashes of a fire until they begin to shrivel. On removal, the beans are wiped clean, rubbed with olive oil, the lower ends are tied with string to prevent splitting, and they are then left to dry in the open air. In the 'Peruvian process', the beans are killed by immersion in boiling water and are then tied at the ends and hung up in the open air. After drying for about twenty days, the beans are lightly smeared with castor oil and are tied in bundles a few days later.

No distinctive local method of curing appears to have been evolved in Java (Hoover, 1926). Modifications of the Mexican and Bourbon methods were commonly used but in general less care seems to have been taken in curing and grading. The quality of the Java product has never compared favourably with those of Mexico or the Bourbon producers.

Curing of Tahiti vanilla

Since *V. tahitensis* is indehiscent, the beans are not killed artificially but are harvested when mature. This is characterized by the tip of the bean turning brown. The curing is carried out by specialist firms which employ a method bearing similiarities to the Mexican procedure (Correll, 1953; Hibon, 1966; Theodose, 1973).

On receipt by the curing firms, the beans are placed in piles which are turned daily. Beans which are entirely brown, indicating that vegetative life has ceased, are removed for sweating and drying. The 'killed' beans are spread out on blankets resting on raised, wooden racks and are exposed to the sun for three to four hours. The warm beans are then rolled up in the blanket and are placed in a sweating box overnight. This operation is repeated for fifteen to twenty days with progressively less frequent overnight sweatings. Finally, the beans are left outside in layers 10 cm deep to dry in the wind. When at the requisite state of dryness, beans are removed from the racks and are placed in large crates.

Most beans are sorted and sold shortly after drying has been completed and without any lengthy 'conditioning' period. The main harvest is collected during February and March and drying is usually completed during July and August. If the beans are kept for a long period before sale, they are stored in tins.

Investigations of improvements to traditional curing methods

During the 1940s and early 1950s, an extensive series of investigations were carried out at the US Department of Agriculture Federal Experiment Station, Mayaguez, Puerto Rico, which laid a firm foundation of knowledge for the improvement of vanilla-curing methods.

Harvesting and maturation

Arana (1944) and Jones and Vincente (1949c) showed that the common practice of harvesting green beans does not favour the production of cured vanilla with a fine aroma and flavour or a high vanillin content. The best results are obtained with beans harvested at the blossom-end yellow phase.

Killing methods

Comparisons were made for overall product quality between various killing methods: Mexican sun- and oven-wilting, Bourbon scalding, Guadeloupe scarification, exposure to ethylene gas and freezing (Arana, 1944, 1945; Jones and Vincente, 1949a). All of these methods were considered to provide satisfactory products but the effect of ethylene gas was more that of a maturing agent than a killing agent. The Guadeloupe scratching technique was found to be superior to other methods in some respects: the degree of splitting was low, sweating and drying times were comparatively short and vanillin contents were enhanced. However, beans killed by this technique were susceptible to mould infection and a poor flexibility in the stem ends which detracted from their appearance. A modification of the Bourbon scalding technique was eventually advocated for ease of use and consistent end-product quality. Scalding temperatures in the range of 60–80 °C were recommended, as higher temperatures adversely affect quality.

Sweating and drying

Arana (1944) compared traditional sun-drying/sweating procedures with an electric oven set at 45 °C in which the humidity was kept high. Oven sweating and drying was found to have advantages in that the incidence of mould was less, a shorter time was required and the procedure was less labour-intensive. In a later investigation, Rivera and Hageman (1951) suggested that a lower temperature of 38 °C was probably optimum for sweating. However, in more recent commercial developments, temperatures of around 60 °C have been employed in the sweating stage (see later).

The use of infra-red lamps has been studied by Cernuda and Loustalot (1948), but this costly method of heating was found to have no marked advantages and could initiate considerable deleterious oxidations. Similar conclusions were drawn in a later investigation in Madagascar (Theodose, 1973).

Moisture content

Arana (1944, 1945) examined the relationship of moisture content to the quality of cured beans. Fresh green or blossom-end yellow beans have a moisture content of about 80 per cent. The major moisture loss in curing occurs during the sweating/drying stages but some moisture reduction also occurs during the first three months of conditioning, after which it becomes negligible. Arana considered the optimum moisture content for cured beans to be 30–35 per cent. Also, he provided a nomograph showing the weights to which 100 pound (45 kg) lots of fresh beans should be reduced during curing to obtain a given moisture content.

Conditioning

This is normally carried out at ambient temperature and a study of the conditioning temperature effects on quality was made by Jones and Vincente (1949a). Temperatures in the range of 35–45 °C were found to accelerate conditioning and to provide a product which was considered to have a superior aroma to those conditioned at 13 °C or

27 °C. Broderick (1956) has suggested, however, that 45 °C may be rather too high for conditioning and that 38 °C might be safer.

Cut vanilla

Jones and Vincente (1949a) also investigated the curing of cut beans. The quality of extracts prepared from cured cut beans was found to be satisfactory and the vanilla content could be enhanced. It was pointed out that processing of cut beans was simpler than for whole beans and would be advantageous for material intended for extraction purposes.

Commercial innovations in curing methods

Artificially dried whole beans (Madagascar)

Since the end of the Second World War, much effort has been devoted to improving vanilla production in Madagascar and in 1954 the Station de la Vanille of the Institut de Recherches Agronomiques was established at Antalaha. One of the main areas of research was artificial drying methods to overcome the problems associated with traditional sun-drying. A hot-air drying system was devised and had been widely introduced in the early 1970s. Theodose (1973) has described a unit capable of producing 40 tonnes of dry vanilla in one season and taking 3 tonnes of fresh vanilla per day. The procedure is as follows:

On arrival at the factory, the fresh beans are weighed and then stored in 3 tonne heaps under cover. The heaps should be no more than 1 m deep and storage should not last longer than 48 hours to avoid fermentation. The beans are next sorted on a conveyor belt (5 m long and manned by 10 workers) into splits, small beans (less than 12 cm), first and second grade, and immature beans; the last type is rejected. Output is of the order of 600–700 kg/hr.

After sorting, the beans are loaded according to the grade into 0.6 m diameter open-work cylindrical baskets taking 50 kg. The loaded baskets are plunged into metal containers full of water heated to 63–65 °C, for a period of 2–3 minutes. The hot-water containers are 0.8 m in diam, 0.8 m deep and three-quarters full of water, installed in a stone base and heated by a wood-fire. Two containers enable 3 tonnes of beans to be scalded in 4–5 hours.

The scalded beans are allowed to drain for one minute and are then placed in blanket-lined sweating boxes. Beans at the bottom of the box receive a three-minute scalding and those at the top only two minutes. With good insulation, a temperature of about 50 °C is maintained for the 48-hour sweating period.

The chests are unloaded and the beans are placed on trays (1.25 m × 0.9 m) with a wire-mesh base, each taking 11–12 kg, fitted into a trolley. Each trolley is fitted with pivoting wheels and 22 trays separated by 6 cm spacing, and takes a total load of around 250 kg.

The plant is equipped with two hot-air drying tunnels, each capable of taking 6 trolleys or 1.5 tonnes of killed beans. One trolley enters the tunnel every 30 minutes and the transit time is 3 hours. The thermostat is set at 65 °C at the exit-end of the heat exchanger and the temperature decreases by 6 °C on transit through the tunnel. Each batch of beans spends 3 hours daily in the drier for 8 days, except split and small beans which are treated for only 4 to 5 days.

After completion of artificial drying, the supple and oily beans are slowly dried on racks in a well-ventilated room for one to two months. Sorting is carried out during this period and beans are removed for conditioning when sufficiently dry.

Artificially dried cut vanilla

A system for the preparation of artificially dried cut vanilla has been developed and patented by the American spice firm, McCormick and Co. (British Patent: 1−205−829; 1970 — 'Vanilla bean drying and curing'). The process involves cutting fresh beans into 1 cm lengths, killing and sweating on trays in an oven at 60 °C for 70−78 hours and then drying in a rotary hot-air drier at 60 °C to reduce the moisture content to 35−40 per cent. Finally, the cuts are air-dried in layers about 10 cm deep on perforated trays at ambient temperature with the aid of a fan to achieve a 20−25 per cent moisture content. All parts of the equipment in contact with beans are made of stainless steel and the oven is heated by a hot-water jacket. In 1965, McCormicks set up a plant in Uganda in co-operation with the Uganda Company (Jensen, 1970). The whole curing operation was reported to take only 4 days and five men could handle 1 tonne of green beans per week. The product was shipped in sealed cans to the United States for extraction. Some years later, McCormicks established a similar co-operative venture with a major vanilla exporter in Java. The product from this unit has a high vanillin content and is frosted.

Theodose (1973) has reported that pilot trials of a similar process have been carried out at the Antalaha Station in Madagascar. In this case, the beans are not chopped until after killing by scalding and an initial sweating. The killed beans are then sliced into 2−3 cm lengths and are subjected to hot-air drying at 65 °C in a tunnel drier. The warm cut beans are then sweated in boxes for 24 hours where the temperature is held at 50 °C. The process is repeated for 12 days, after which a product with a moisture content of 20−25 per cent is obtained. Sweating in the boxes is regarded as an essential since it prevents too rapid a drying which is detrimental to aroma development.

Grading and packaging

After conditioning, the cured beans are given an airing and are re-straightened by drawing through the fingers. The beans are then subjected to a final sorting into grades and according to their length, prior to bundling and packaging for shipment. The length of the beans is an important determinant of the price which the whole beans will fetch.

Grading systems differ somewhat between producing countries but beans are generally classified into three categories: unsplit beans, split beans and 'cuts'. The last type has traditionally consisted of beans which have been attacked by mould and have had the infected portion cut away. Very small and broken beans of poor aroma quality are usually combined with the 'cuts' from mouldy beans. It should be noted, however, that 'cuts' do not always consist entirely of poor-quality beans. In Mexico, 'cuts' usually comprise 10–20 per cent of production in a normal year but, in years of good prices, the smaller curing firms would often cut all their beans prior to curing because drying times were shortened. Also, the artificially dried cut beans which have entered the market in recent years are of a good aroma and flavour quality and are produced specifically for extraction.

Mexico

Prior to the early 1950s, Mexican vanilla was exported in five grades but the system was then extended to embrace seven grades (Correll, 1953; Bouriquet, 1954). The seven grades for whole beans in descending order of quality are 'Extra', 'Superior', 'Good-Superior', 'Good', 'Medium-Good', 'Medium' and 'Ordinary'. This grading is on the basis of moisture content, colour, general appearance and aroma quality. The moisture content of top-grade beans is around 35–40 per cent and that of the poorest grades can be as low as 10 per cent.

'Extras' are thick beans which have a dark-brown to black colour, glisten with oil, and are free from warts and other blemishes. They are entirely flexible along their whole length. The aroma is clean and delicate.

'Superiors' are similar in properties to 'Extras' but are not quite so thick and are of a less exceptional appearance. 'Extras' and 'Superiors' rarely have a coating of vanillin crystals.

The 'Good' grade consists of beans of a slightly paler colour and which have a poorer lustre and flexibility. The body is less thick than the top grades and there are some slight surface defects. The aroma is suave.

The 'Ordinary' grade beans have a poorer colour, dull appearance, surface blemishes and a weak aroma. The body is thin, tending towards rigidity and is rather desiccated.

These seven grades are further reclassified into various sizes ranging in length from 16.5 cm to 24 cm. The beans are then made up into bundles with the stem-ends together and the bundles are tied with black string at the top, middle and bottom. The straightest beans are placed in the centre of the bundle and those with the best appearance on the outside. Bundles of 'Extras' contain about 70 beans, 'Good' about 95, and 'Ordinary' about 130. The weight of the bundles ranges between 350 to 500 g according to the grade and length of the beans.

The bundles are packed into tin boxes lined with waxed paper which take 40 bundles in rows of 10. The boxes are marked with the grade and the length of the beans, and 4 tin boxes are then placed in a wooden case for shipment.

'Cuts' are graded into qualities corresponding to those of whole beans and are also classified into 'longs' and 'shorts'. 'Superior cuts' are regarded as comparable in quality to the corresponding whole beans and often have a surface coating of vanillin crystals. 'Ordinary cuts' include not only true cuts of lower grade beans but also very small beans (less than 15 cm) and broken beans of poor aroma quality. They are packed in loose layers in tin boxes lined with waxed-paper.

Bourbon vanilla

The vanilla of Madagascar, the Comoro Islands and Réunion is classified into five main grades of whole and split beans plus an additional category known as 'bulk' which is comprised of cuts. The grades of whole and split beans are also sub-divided according to size and the various producing regions have the following characteristics (Merory, 1968):

	Av. length *(cm)*	*Normal maximum* *(cm)*
Réunion	18−20	25−26
Madagascar		
(a) main producing area on north-east coast	16−18	22−23
(b) Nossi-Bé (north-west coast area)	14−15	20
Comoro Islands	15−16	21−22

The minimum acceptable length for the top five grades in the major producing area of Madagascar is 12 cm while for Nossi-Bé and the Comoro Islands it is 10 cm (Frere, 1954).

Madagascan beans are first sorted to separate beans below 12 cm in length and then the whole and split beans are classified into grades according to their aroma, moisture content and appearance. The five main categories for Madagascan whole beans are as follows:

'Extra': Whole, supple, unsplit beans, free of blemishes, possessing a uniform chocolate-brown colour and an oily lustre. The aroma is clean and delicate.

'1st': Similar to the 'Extra' grade but not quite so thick and of a less exceptional appearance.

'2nd': Somewhat thinner beans with a chocolate-brown colour but with a few skin blemishes. The aroma is good.

'3rd': Thinner, more rigid beans with a slightly reddish chocolate-brown colour. The aroma is fair.

Table 11.2 Moisture contents of commercial vanilla bean consignments according to source and grade

Quality	Mexico	Madagascar	Comoro Islands	Réunion	Uganda	Java	Tahiti	Vanillons
Grade unspecified	38–40(a)	31(a)	35(a)	–	–	–	31–38(a,c,e)	15–18(a)
Firsts	–	27–42(d,e)	33(d)	42(d)	–	–	35(d)	
Seconds	–	26–35(c,d,e)	20(c)	43(d)	23(c)	–	–	
Thirds	31(b)	23–32(d,e)	22–29(c,d)	27(d)	–	–	29–33(c,d)	15(d)
Fourths	–	19–22(c,d,e)	18(d)	16(d)	12(c)	18(c)	–	
1st Splits	–	36(d)	–	45(d)	–	–	–	
2nd Splits	–	33(d)	–	45(d)	–	–	–	
3rd Splits	–	23(d)	–	29(d)	–	–	–	
Superior cuts	11–12(b,c)	–	–	–	17(c)	–	–	
Ordinary cuts	10–12(b,c)	11–18(c)	10(c)	–	–	–	–	

References: (a) Arana, (1945); (b) Bouriquet (1954); (c) Morison-Smith (1964); (d) Garros-Patin and Hahn (1954); (e) Kleinert (1963).

'4th': Rather dry beans with a reddish colour and numerous skin blemishes. The aroma is ordinary.

Splits are sorted into categories corresponding to those for whole beans. Foxy splits are thin, hard and dry, short types with a reddish-brown colour.

After sorting into qualities, the whole and split beans are re-classified according to length into various sizes between 12 and 26 cm and are then made up into bundles. Each bundle contains 70 to 100 beans and weighs between 150–500 g. The bundles are packed into tin boxes lined with waxed paper which take between 20 to 40 bundles, weighing 8–10 kg. Six tins are fitted into a wooden case for shipment. More recently, cardboard boxes have been widely used for the external packaging instead of wooden cases (Theodose, 1973).

Beans remaining over from the sorting and grading described above are combined to form an additional category called 'bulk'. This consists of cuts, broken and very short beans and those with sub-standard colour and aroma. The constituents of the 'bulk' category are not tied up in bundles prior to packaging.

A batch of Bourbon vanilla consisting of the various categories may be sold as a 'head to tail' lot. An example of a 'head to tail' lot consisting of 50 per cent of the top qualities, i.e., 'Extras' and '1st', is as follows:

50 per cent	– whole 1st grade
20 per cent	– 1st splits or whole 2nd grade
25 per cent	– 2nd splits or whole 3rd grade
5 per cent	– 4th or 'bulk'.

Bourbon vanilla tends to have a somewhat higher moisture content than the corresponding Mexican grades and it is often 'frosted' with vanillin crystals. The moisture contents quoted in the literature for various types of Bourbon vanilla are listed in Table 11.2.

Tahiti vanilla

The beans are sorted into whole and splits and are then graded accord-

Table 11.3 *Grades of Tahiti vanilla*

Label	Quality	Characteristics	Size
Blue	Extra	Exceptional appearance and of a superior quality	min. 20 cm
Red	1st	Similar to Extra	min. 18 cm
White	2nd	Good-quality beans	min. 14 cm
Yellow	3rd	Fair quality	less than 14 cm
Green	4th	Inferior quality, thin or recured beans of any length.	

ing to quality and size (Frere, 1954). There are five main categories of whole and split Tahitian vanilla which are distinguished by the colour of the label, as shown in Table 11.3.

A sixth category exists, distinguished by a black label, which comprises badly damaged and very poor quality beans.

The top five grades of beans are made up into bundles and are tied at the top and bottom. The bundles are packed according to the grade into a waxed-paper lined, large tin box which weighs about 40 kg when full. One tin box is placed in a wooden crate for export.

Guadeloupe vanilla

'Vanillons' is packed separately from true vanilla and is sorted into three categories: Firsts, Seconds and Reddish. The beans are short in length (8–14 cm) and broad (up to 2.5 cm). The bundles are tied with string at each extremity. A distinguishing feature of vanillons used to be that each bean had a string tied around its middle to prevent splitting but this practice has become less prevalent (Frere, 1954; Merory, 1968).

Spoilage of vanilla

Moulds

Vanilla beans are quite susceptible to infection by *Penicillium* and *Aspergillus* moulds and this generally occurs during the conditioning and subsequent storage periods (Bouriquet, 1954). In appearance, there are two types of mould: one is white at first and turns green later, while the other is black and spreads rapidly. Infection always begins at the stem-end of the bean and, if left uncontrolled, the whole bean becomes wrinkled, dry, and acquires a disagreeable odour. It is virtually impossible to eliminate the odour once the mould takes hold and this considerably detracts from the market value.

Mould infection most frequently occurs with beans which have been harvested before they are mature. Development of mould is also encouraged if the beans are not killed properly as then they do not dry uniformly, and if the beans have an excessive moisture content on conditioning. Sweating and drying the beans in the sun also leads to a higher incidence of moulds than when an oven is used. Other contributors are dirty blankets and a general lack of cleanliness and ventilation in the curing room.

Apart from ensuring that the curing is carried out properly, other preventive measures include regularly sterilizing equipment in boiling water and blankets in antiseptic solutions. If mould attack becomes severe, it may be necessary to paint and disinfect the curing room with 1 : 1 000 solution of formaldehyde (Childers and Cibes, 1948). Another form of transmitting moulds is by packers who place the binding string in their mouths.

Beans should be examined weekly during conditioning and storage to permit removal and treatment of mouldy ones. If mould infection is identified and treated immediately, its spread can be checked. A common treatment for beans suffering from initial attack by moulds is to clean the bean with a cotton swab soaked in 95 per cent alcohol. The use of dilute formaldehyde solutions is not favoured as the US Food and Drug Administration forbids entry of beans treated in this way. With cases of slight infection in Mexico, it is customary after cleaning the beans to wipe them with the 'balsam' or oily secretion of any mature beans; and when the mould has taken a good hold, the beans are often immersed in hot water for an hour (Chalot and Bernard, 1920).

When mould attack is severe, it is usual to cut away and discard the infected portion; the remaining part of the bean is known as a 'cut'.

Infestation

Vanilla beans are prone to attack by mites of the *Tyrophagus* species (Chalot and Bernard, 1920; Mallory and Cochran, 1941; Bouriquet, 1954) which imparts a disagreeable odour to the beans. The mites appear during conditioning, shipment or subsequent storage and may be detected by the small holes which they produce in the beans.

In cases of limited infestation prior to shipment, alcohol treatment or sunning is often effective. With more serious attacks, Childers and Cibes (1948) recommend fumigation of equipment and the curing and conditioning rooms with flowers of sulphur.

If serious infestation is discovered on receipt of a shipment, it may be necessary to cut away the infected parts and sell the remaining portions as 'cuts'.

Creosoted vanilla

Some beans develop a creosote-like aroma which is impossible to eliminate once formed. This off-aroma generally becomes apparent at quite an early stage in the sweating process and results from an abnormal fermentation due to poor handling and curing practices. The principal cause is believed to be improper storage methods for fresh beans prior to killing. This undesirable fermentation can be avoided if fresh beans are stored in well-ventilated small piles, and by commencing curing as soon as possible (Bouriquet, 1954).

Vanilla poisoning

'Vanillism' is the term given to a form of poisoning which sometimes appears in persons who work with vanilla (Arana, 1945). There are two phases at which vanilla poisoning occurs: during handling of the green plant, i.e., during planting and harvesting the green beans, and during the later stages of curing, especially during the conditioning operation. Poisoning by the green plant usually arises from contact with the latex juice and this results in skin inflammation. Contact with the eyes must be avoided. During curing, symptoms include skin eruptions, headaches, fever and intestinal disorders. Similar symptoms have been recorded in persons handling synthetic vanillin and this compound is believed to be responsible for 'vanillism' during the curing operation (Chalot and Bernard, 1920). The effects in both cases usually disappear within 2 to 3 days and it has been observed that resistance appears to build up as a person becomes used to handling vanilla.

If a person is very susceptible, then rubber gloves should be used and hands and other exposed parts should be washed after work, preferably with dilute alcohol. Readers interested in a more detailed discussion of vanillism are recommended to refer to the article by Bui-Xuan-Nhuan (1954).

2. The preparation of vanilla products

Vanilla extract

In the United States, Government regulations require that vanilla extract should have an ethanol content of no less than 35 per cent by volume and that 1 gallon* (3.79 litres) of extract should contain the soluble extractives from a minimum of 13.35 ounces (377.8 g) of vanilla beans of not more than 25 per cent moisture content (or their equivalent). The only other permitted ingredients are water and glycerin or propylene glycol or sugar or dextrose or corn syrup. An extract conforming to this specification is known as 'singlefold' and one prepared from double the quantity of beans is known as 'doublefold'. The maximum concentration possible by straightforward aqueous ethanol extraction is fourfold.

In practice, many manufacturers use 16 ounces of beans to make up a gallon extract (approximately 12 g in 100 ml). The most economical concentrations are considered to be 2 pounds and 4 pounds of beans to a gallon, which provide extracts of just over 'twofold' and 'fourfold' strength. These extracts are then diluted, if necessary, to the customers' specific requirements.

Glycerine and sugar are frequently included in the formulation as they lend smoothness and viscosity to the extract and also help to 'fix' the aromatic constituents, thereby extending the shelf-life. Inclusion of these additives in the initial extraction solvent, known as the menstruum, is believed to assist the extraction of the flavouring constituents and glycerine also increases the colour of the extract. One gallon (3.79 litres) of twofold extract would commonly have 1 pound (0.45 kg) of sugar and 0.06 gallon (ie 6 per cent v/v) of glycerin included in the initial menstruum.

The quality of a vanilla extract is dependent upon a number of factors which include:
1. Careful handling and storage of the beans prior to extraction.

---

* 1 US gallon = 0.833 Imperial gallons

2. Appropriate selection and blending of beans.
3. The degree of comminution of the beans.
4. The method and conditions of extraction. Two extractions methods are practised: maceration and percolation.
5. Proper ageing of the extract to permit full flavour development.

Bean storage

Even after completion of curing, vanilla beans often continue to develop a desirable aroma and flavour if stored under suitable conditions, and it is usual for extract manufacturers to store beans for a period after importation. Merory (1956) has recommended that vanilla beans should be stored in open containers at a temperature of about 10 °C and at a low humidity. Moisture contents of 25–30 per cent are preferred for extraction purposes, and storage temperatures may be raised to 15–21 °C without detriment to flavour·quality if some moisture loss is desired in the beans.

Selection and blending of beans

The properties of vanilla beans can differ considerably according to their source and to the grade. Mexican vanilla is generally considered to possess the finest aroma but the 'body' of the flavour is relatively weak in comparison with other commercial sources of *V. fragrans*. Bourbon vanilla has a greater 'body' and fullness of flavour and the 'body' strength is even more pronounced in Java vanilla. The extractable colour is also variable and dry beans give a darker colour than moist ones. Consequently, extract manufacturers select and blend various types of beans, with due regard to the price and availability to obtain an end-product with the desired properties. Merory (1968) has provided a number of examples of blends preferred in the United States and one of these is reproduced below as an illustration:

50 per cent – Madagascan Firsts
15 per cent – Mexican Cuts
25 per cent – Madagascan Foxy Splits

If a stronger vanilla flavour is required, the proportion of Bourbon vanilla in the blend may be increased. Madagascan Foxy Splits and similar dry types are useful in enhancing the colour of the extract.

The menstruum

In addition to the aromatic constituents, the aqueous alcohol menstruum co-extracts some of the non-aromatic constituents of the beans: resins, sugars, waxes, gums, etc. Their presence in an extract assists in providing a certain depth of flavour and body. However, if present in too large a quantity, these compounds detract from the flavour by giving a woody, somewhat bitter taste which masks the desired vanilla flavour. The relative proportion of non-aromatic constituents extracted is largely dependent upon the ethanol content of the menstruum.

With ethanol contents greater than 70 per cent, a considerable quantity of fixed oil is obtained which will precipitate in a fine cloud and cannot be removed when the extract is diluted to the normal 35−40 per cent ethanol content. Menstruums with ethanol contents below 35 per cent readily dissolve gum, and this causes difficulties in percolation and filtration operations.

The colour of the extract is dependent upon a number of factors which include the quality of the bean, the duration of extraction and the presence of glycerine, but the ethanol content of the menstruum is also of importance. The colour of the extract progressively darkens as the ethanol content of the menstruum is increased up to 60 per cent. With ethanol contents greater than 70 per cent, the colour lightens, and with 95 per cent ethanol very little colour is extracted. In the past, some manufacturers have added alkali to the water wash after the aqueous ethanol menstruum extraction in order to enhance colour and resin values, but this practice is considered detrimental to flavour quality.

Ethanol contents of 50−60 per cent in the menstruum yield extracts with a good flavour and colour and sufficient water-soluble extractives to provide 'body', but little, if any, of the undesirable oils and waxes. An ethanol content of 60 per cent in the menstruum is considered optimal (Gnadinger, 1927; Broderick, 1955b; Merory, 1956).

Comminution of the beans

Extraction is carried out on beans sliced into short lengths (about 1−2 cm) rather than with powdered vanilla, which is difficult to prepare and involves the risk of aroma loss by evaporation, or with pulped vanilla, which tends to yield an opaque extract. The comminution is generally done in a machine fitted with revolving blades (e.g. a FitzPatrick comminuting machine). Prior to slicing, the beans are washed with a portion of the menstruum to dissolve any surface vanillin. During the cutting operation, a little of the menstruum is allowed to flow over the beans to prevent overheating and evaporation losses.

Extraction by maceration

This is the traditional method of preparing vanilla extract and involves placing the chopped beans in a vessel where they are allowed to steep in the menstruum for up to one year. In the past, wooden barrels and a 50 per cent ethanol content menstruum were used. This technique provided a product with a good flavour but of a non-standard quality owing to seepage, evaporation losses and to the variable moisture content of the beans. Modern macerators are air-tight vessels, constructed from stainless steel, tin or lined with glass, which permit slow agitation by stirring, rocking or tumbling. With a menstruum containing about 60 per cent ethanol, modern maceration extractors provide a good-quality product in 1−3 months. It should be appreciated that the beans contain some moisture which immediately dilutes the alcohol content of the menstruum and the requisite initial ethanol content of the menstruum should be calculated according to the moisture content of the beans. As a guideline, a menstruum containing 60 per cent ethanol would be added to beans with a 30 per cent moisture content to provide a near-optimum extraction medium (Broderick, 1955b). After the requisite time has elapsed for extraction, the liquid is slowly drained off and filtered.

The maceration procedure is very lengthy and has a low throughput in terms of equipment utilization compared with the percolation method (described below) but it is considered by some to provide a superior-quality product.

Extraction by percolation

The bulk of vanilla extract is now prepared by this method. The equipment consists of a stainless-steel or tin vessel fitted with a series of perforated trays to hold the chopped beans. The menstruum is sprayed on to the top tray, percolates down from the tray to tray, collects in the base of the vessel and is then recirculated by a pump. The trays are designed so that the menstruum continually covers the beans and percolation is aided by a slight positive pressure maintained by the pump. Some vessels are fitted with hot-water jackets to permit extraction at a slightly elevated temperature of 38−49 °C as this is considered to assist extraction without detriment to flavour properties. Merory (1956) has recommended three consecutive extractions, each for at least five days, using a menstruum with a 60 per cent ethanol content for the first extraction, 30−35 per cent ethanol in the second, and 15 per cent ethanol content in the third extraction. The beans are finally washed with water and this is done without circulation, to avoid extraction of gums.

Merory (1968) has described an operation to prepare 100 US gallons (379 litres) of twofold vanilla extract (26.7 ounces of beans per gallon or 20 g per 100 ml) with a 35 per cent ethanol content. The extraction vessel has a capacity of 200 gallons and is fitted with ten trays, each capable of holding about 18 lb (approx 8 kg) of cut beans. The initial menstruum (62 gallons at 65 per cent ethanol content) is made up by mixing 95 per cent ethanol (42 gallons), water (14 gallons) and glycerin (6 gallons). The beans (166.9 lb or 75.7 kg of 30 per cent moisture content) are first washed in a portion of the menstruum and are then comminuted. The cut beans and the menstruum are then loaded into the extractor and the menstruum is circulated twice daily for 8 to 10 days. After a few circulations, the ethanol content is diluted to 60 per cent by the moisture present in the beans. The extractor is then drained slowly until 40 gallons (152 litres) of extract has been collected. The draining takes about two days.

For the second extraction, warm water (22 gallons or 83.4 litres) at 60 °C is poured into the extractor. The temperature drops to 45 °C after the first circulation. After three days, the temperature drops to 35 °C and the ethanol content of the menstruum is about 30 per cent. Draining is commenced on the fourth day and 20 gallons (76 litres) of extract are collected.

For the third extraction, warm water (20 gallons) is added and the process is repeated. The ethanol content of the menstruum is about 15 per cent and 20 gallons are drawn off.

Finally, the beans are washed with cold water (20 gallons) by adding 5 gallon portions at 30 minute intervals. The washes are collected in 5 gallon volumes until 20 gallons are obtained. This extract is then combined with those from the previous three extractions to provide 100 gallons of twofold extract of approximately 35 per cent ethanol content. After 'ageing' has been completed, the extract is filtered or centrifuged.

The exhausted beans are expressed, centrifuged or washed with water without circulation and the recovered dilute aqueous ethanol solution is used for a subsequent extraction operation.

Ageing of extracts

In order to permit a full development of the flavour, extracts should be 'aged'. According to Broderick (1955b), the greatest modification to the flavour occurs in the first 30 days after extraction but a definite improvement is discernible for at least 90 days. Three months is generally regarded as the minimum time for ageing and six months is preferable. With extracts prepared by the lengthy maceration procedure, the product is usually well-aged when tapped off. However, this is not the case with the more rapid percolation process and a separate storage period is required to develop the full aroma/flavour. This is necessarily costly and material intended for the retail trade is often bottled immediately after preparation since ageing can occur during normal shelf-life.

Ethanol contents of 42–45 per cent are known to accelerate ageing of extracts and this fact can be applied to the problem of ageing percolated extracts. On combining the extracts from the percolator, all or a portion of the final water wash can be withheld to provide an extract with a near optimum ethanol content for ageing. The withheld wash water is set aside in cool storage until required to adjust the ethanol content of the aged extract (Merory, 1956).

Storage containers

Vanilla extracts are best stored in stainless-steel, tin or glass vessels. Wooden barrels are inferior owing to the risk of seepage and evaporation losses, and new wooden barrels are to be avoided as tannins and other undesirable flavours can be absorbed. Aluminium, nickel, copper and zinc are unsuitable for storage vessels and for extraction equipment.

Vanilla oleoresin

The preparation of vanilla oleoresin intended for flavouring purposes involves solvent extraction of chopped beans (usually 'cuts'), followed by removal of the solvent by distillation under vacuum. The oleoresin remaining after solvent stripping is a dark, viscous mass. Extraction is carried out either in a percolation vessel or in a sealed vessel in which the beans, placed in baskets, are continuously immersed in the solvent. The preferred solvents for extraction are warm, 50 per cent (v/v) aqueous ethanol or warm, 50 per cent aqueous isopropanol. These menstruums are considered to provide oleoresins with the optimum combination of flavour properties, yield and solubility in aqueous ethanol (Garros-Patin and Hahn, 1954; Merory, 1968; Cowley, 1973). Duty is payable with ethanol and there are cost-saving advantages in the use of isopropanol for the extraction.

For use in flavouring, the oleoresins are diluted to one-, two- or tenfold strength as required. However, the flavour of vanilla oleoresins is not as full-bodied or well-rounded as those of vanilla extracts owing to the loss of some aromatic constituents during the solvent stripping operation. Vanilla oleoresin best fulfils the role of a 'vanilla base' and is often used for compounding with synthetic vanillin.

Cowley (1973) prepared oleoresins from a number of types of vanilla beans by extraction with 50 per cent aqueous alcohol and obtained products with a specific gravity of approximately 1.3 in yields as shown in Table 11.4.

Merory (1968) has described a procedure for the preparation of vanilla oleoresin as follows: chopped vanilla beans (200 pounds; 91 kg) are placed in the baskets of an extractor and a menstruum of 50 per cent

Table 11.4

Source	Bean length (cm)	Moisture content (%, v/w)	Vanillin content (%, w/w) dry basis	Oleoresin yield (%, w/w)		Non-volatile residue of oleoresin (%)
				on moist basis	on dry basis	
Réunion	18	37.0	2.1	35.2	55.8	79.5
Comoro Is.	16	23.6	2.42	38.7	50.7	84.1
Madagascar	17	38.8	2.28	29.9	48.9	79.8
Seychelles	14	36.0	2.32	37.9	59.2	81.2
Uganda	14	22.6	1.63	47.0	60.8	77.2
Tahiti	9	40.6	1.52	38.5	64.5	66.4

aqueous isopropanol (200 US gallons; 658 litres) is added. During the extraction, continuous heat of not higher than 46 °C is applied for 2 days. On the third day, extraction is continued without heat and on the fourth day the extract is drained off. For the second extraction, another menstruum of 50 per cent aqueous isopropanol (80 gallons; 304 litres) is used and the same procedure is followed. A third and final extraction is carried out with cold water (100 gallons; 379 litres) for one day and the extract is draned off on the second day. Residual menstruum is recovered by pressing the beans. The extracts from the three extraction steps are combined and the solvent is stripped off by distillation under vacuum. A viscous mass of vanilla oleoresin is obtained in a yield of about 100 pounds (45 kg).

Vanilla absolute and tincture for perfumery

For perfumery purposes, a very concentrated form of the vanilla aroma, known as an 'absolute', is required which is soluble in pure ethanol and perfume oils. Extraction of vanilla with hot, 60−80 per cent ethanol, followed by removal of the solvent, provides a semi-solid absolute in a yield of about 10−12 per cent (w/w). However, this type of absolute has limited applications in perfumery since it has a high resin content and will not completely redissolve in pure ethanol. In order to minimize this solubility problem, some manufacturers have devised selective extraction techniques in which the vanilla is first extracted with a hydrocarbon or chlorinated hydrocarbon solvent to remove resinous material, and is then extracted with aqueous ethanol or acetone. An alternative approach involves first preparing an oleoresin by hot benzene extraction (yield: 6−9 per cent, w/w) and then washing the oleoresin with ethanol to obtain the aromatic constituents. On evaporation, this absolute is obtained in a yield of about 60−70 per cent (w/w) from the oleoresin in the form of a very dark-brown, highly viscous mass. The absolute prepared by direct ethanol extraction is the most concentrated form of the vanilla aroma but it lacks the full-rounded character of aqueous ethanol vanilla extracts owing to a loss of some of the constituents during solvent stripping. The absolute prepared from the benzene-extracted oleoresin is even less rich in aroma (Garros-Patin and Hahn, 1954; Arctander, 1960; Naves, 1974).

Vanilla tinctures used in perfumery differ from those employed in flavouring in that the ethanol content is much higher (approx. 90 per cent v/v) and they are prepared with perfume alcohol, i.e., alcohol denatured with diethyl phthalate, etc. Perfumery tinctures are frequently made by maceration of vanilla beans (10 g) in 95 per cent ethanol (100 ml).

Finally it should be appreciated that the aroma character of perfumery vanilla absolutes and tinctures is dependent upon the species, geographical source and grade of the vanilla extracted. The aroma can be modified by appropriate blending.

Vanilla powder

Owing to the high fat and moisture content of vanilla beans, they are difficult to powder alone and this operation is usually carried out in the presence of sugar or a similar suitable blending material. Consequently, 'vanilla powder' is normally a mixture of ground vanilla and a carrier. A minimum of 30 per cent sugar in the mixture is necessary during the powdering to obtain a satisfactory product. Care must be taken during the operation to avoid overheating which can result in the loss of volatile constituents by evaporation. An anti-caking agent, such as aluminium calcium silicate, may be incorporated in the ground mixture at a level of up to 2 per cent by weight.

Chemistry

The chemistry of the three commercially exploited vanilla species, *Vanilla fragrans* (true vanilla), *V. tahitensis* (Tahiti vanilla) and *V. pompona* (Guadeloupe vanilla or 'vanillons'), has been the subject of many investigations since the middle of the nineteenth century. Although vanillin, the most abundant of the aroma/flavour constituents of cured vanilla beans, has been known for over a century, the characteristic, well-rounded and subtle aroma of natural vanilla has not yet been reproduced synthetically. This is due to the fact that numerous other constituents, present in minor or trace quantities, are very important contributors to the organoleptic character of natural vanilla and they also determine the aroma/flavour differences between the three species. The identification of the aroma/flavour constituents of vanilla beans and investigation of their relative importance remains an active field of chemical research.

General composition of cured vanilla beans and their solvent extracts

Cured vanilla beans contain vanillin, organic acids, fixed (fatty) oil, wax, gum, resins, tannins, pigments, sugars, cellulose and minerals. The cured beans contain very little steam-volatile (essential) oil. The relative abundance on a dry-weight basis of certain constituents of the cured beans can vary somewhat between individual samples and this arises from a number of factors. These factors include the species and the environmental conditions of growth, differences in harvesting, curing and ageing procedures, and on the grade of bean. Analytical data on the general composition of vanilla beans has been reported in the literature by Winton and Winton (1939), Bouriquet (1954), Kleinert

(1963) and Morison-Smith (1964); and the characteristics of the main commercial types entering the market are summarized in the 'Products and end-uses' and 'Processing and manufacture' sections. There are no official analytical standards for vanilla beans.

Although the appearance of the cured bean is regarded as important by some consumers, the quality is primarily assessed by a subjective organoleptic evaluation of the aroma and flavour. The organoleptic distinctions made between the three vanilla species, individual sources of supply and individual grades are due to the qualitative and quantitative differences in the occurrence of the various aromatic constituents. While the vanillin content alone cannot be directly correlated with the aroma/flavour quality of cured vanilla beans, this figure is, nevertheless, used as an indicator of quality in laboratory analysis. Difficulties are encountered in the collation and comparison of data published in the literature on vanillin contents, however, owing to differences in the vanillin determination methods employed, and since the moisture contents of the samples are not always specified. Moisture contents can range from 10 to 40 per cent according to the grade of the vanilla. The vanillin contents on a dry-weight basis for some samples have been reported in the literature by Bouriquet (1954), Kleinert (1963) and Cowley (1973), but the majority of reports are for vanilla beans as received, i.e., while still containing some moisture (Tiemann and Haarmann, 1874, 1876; Pritzer and Jungkunz, 1928a and b; Winton and Winton, 1939; Correll, 1953; Morison-Smith, 1964). From the published data, it appears that the vanillin content on an as-received basis for commercial consignments of *V. fragrans* can range from 1.3 to 3.8 per cent with Mexican beans averaging around 2 per cent and Bourbon vanilla averaging between 2.1 and 2.3 per cent. Java vanilla has a reputation for a rather higher average vanillin content, but exceptionally high and low values have also been reported (Hoover, 1926; Martin *et al.*, 1975). Tahiti vanilla has been reported to have vanillin contents ranging from 0.9 to 3.3 per cent, averaging somewhat lower than Mexican or Bourbon beans, while Guadeloupe vanilla or 'vanillons' (*V. pompona*) usually has an even lower vanillin content of below 1 per cent. Winton and Winton (1939) and Jones and Vincente (1949c) have observed that there is a trend for increasing vanillin content with bean length and that a similar trend is encountered with improving grade quality.

The term 'resins' is loosely applied to non-vanillin extractives of cured beans which are soluble in alcohol and alkalis but which are insoluble in water. The resin content of cured vanilla beans is variable, ranging around 1 per cent on an as-received basis. The fat content has been reported to range from about 4.5 to 15 per cent, and the major component fatty acids have been identified as oleic and palmitic acids (Garros-Patin and Hahn, 1954; Salzer, 1975). The sugar content of cured beans has been reported to range from 7 to 20 per cent, and

Kleinert (1963) has identified glucose and fructose as the main constituents with sucrose present in smaller quantities.

The organoleptic properties, chemical composition and the yield obtainable for the various types of solvent extracts of vanilla beans are dependent upon the raw material used, the solvent and extraction method employed, as has been described in the preceding 'Processing and manufacture' section. 'Vanilla extract' when prepared by the traditional maceration technique in aqueous ethanol provides the closest resemblance to cured vanilla beans in terms of aroma and flavour. 'Vanilla oleoresin' and 'vanilla absolute' are more concentrated but are less well-rounded in aroma and flavour owing to the loss of some organoleptically important constituents through evaporation losses or to solubility problems. The vanillin content of a conventional, single-fold vanilla extract, containing the soluble extractives of 1 part of beans by weight to 10 parts of solvent by volume, is usually around 0.2 per cent.

The aroma and flavour of cured vanilla beans

The organoleptic properties of cured vanilla beans are primarily determined by the volatile constituents, of which vanillin is the most abundant. However, some of the non-volatile constituents may play a role in modifying the flavour perception. The resins possess no aroma but have a pleasant taste, and are also beneficial in 'fixing' the volatile aromatic constituents in solvent extracts (Merory, 1968).

The aroma and flavour of the main commercial types of vanilla are quite distinctive and Arctander (1960) has given the following descriptions:

Bourbon vanilla (V. fragrans *from Madagascar, Réunion and the Comoro Islands*):   The aroma is extremely rich, sweet, tobacco-like, somewhat woody and animal, and possesses a very deep balsamic, sweet-spicy bodynote. The odour of vanillin is not one of the characteristics of Bourbon vanilla. However, the odour varies considerably according to the moisture content of the beans. Very moist beans have a stronger vanillin character while the higher-boiling aromatic constituents are more perceptible in drier beans.

Mexican vanilla (*also from* V. fragrans):   This has a somewhat sharper and more pungent aroma than the Bourbon type.

Tahiti vanilla (*from* V. tahitensis):   The aroma is almost perfumery sweet and is not tobacco-like, not very deep woody, nor distinctly animal.

Guadeloupe vanilla or 'vanillons' (*from* V. pompona):   This has a peculiar floral-sweet fragrance of the anisic, heliotropin-isosafrol type, and it is more perfumy than all other vanilla types. It is considered poor for flavouring purposes.

Broderick (1955a) has commented that Java beans (from *V. fragrans*) possess a very heavy and woody flavour in most instances. The occurrence of numerous non-vanillin aroma and flavour contributors present in minor or trace quantities in vanilla beans is the reason for their organoleptic superiority over synthetic vanillin and synthetic blends. Natural vanilla has a delicate, rich and mellow aroma, while that of synthetic material tends to be heavy and grassy. The natural extract has a delicate and mellow after-taste, while the after-taste of synthetic material is less pleasant.

The volatile constituents of vanilla

Vanillin, the most abundant volatile aromatic constituent of vanilla beans, was first isolated and identified by Gobley (1858), and its structure was confirmed by synthesis by Tiemann and Haarmann (1874). It was quickly appreciated that vanillin was not solely responsible for the characteristic aroma and flavour of cured vanilla beans and Tiemann and Haarmann initiated the protracted search for other volatile constituents with the isolation of benzaldehyde and vanillic acid in 1876.

Walbaum (1909) examined Tahiti vanilla and identified anisyl alcohol, anisaldehyde and anisic acid as constituents. Later, Gnadinger (1925) confirmed that anisyl alcohol was the major component of the steam-volatile oil of Tahiti vanilla and reported that it was also present in Guadeloupe vanilla. The presence of this compound could not be detected in Mexican, Bourbon, Java or South American vanilla beans (*V. fragrans*). Gnadinger found that the Bourbon vanilla contained aromatic cinnamic acid esters and its steam-volatile oil was about one-tenth of that of Tahiti vanilla (0.006 per cent as compared to 0.06 per cent). Busse (1900) and Pritzer and Jungkunz (1928a and b) reported detecting the presence of piperonal (heliotropin) in Tahitian and Guadeloupe vanillas, but this compound was not found in these two species by Walbaum or Gnadinger, and its occurrence has remained in dispute until relatively recently.

vanillin   anisyl
                alcohol

piperonal
(heliotropin)

Further progress on identifying the volatile constituents of vanilla beans languished until after the Second World War, and Bohnsack (1965, 1967, 1971) is notable in making a substantial contribution to the subject using classical methods. Most other investigators in the post-war period have employed chromatographic techniques, and gas chromatography analysis has been particularly fruitful. Using the gas chromatography approach, Klimes and Lamparsky (1976) have identified some 170 volatile constituents of Bourbon (Madagascan) vanilla, of which only 26 were found to occur in concentrations greater than 1 ppm in their sample of beans. The four most abundant volatile constituents were found to be vanillin (about 2 per cent), *p*-hydroxy benzaldehyde (0.2 per cent), *p*-hydroxy benzyl methyl ether (0.02 per cent) and acetic acid (0.02 per cent). The remaining 22 more abundant constituents were present in the 1 – 10 ppm range. The relation between the small number of 'major volatile components' to the numerous volatile components present in trace quantities clearly indicates the importance of the latter in contributing to the overall aroma and flavour of vanilla. Schulte-Elte *et al.* (1978) have reported identifying two diastereoisomeric vitispiranes (2, 10, 10-trimethy 1-6-methylidene-1-oxaspiro (4.5) dec-7-enes) at 1 ppm level in an oleoresin prepared from *V. fragrans* and stated that these two compounds were important contributors to the vanilla aroma.

p-hydroxy
benzaldehyde

p-hydroxy
benzyl methyl
ether

vitispirane

Tables 11.5 and 11.6 list the volatile constituents identified in the three important vanilla species at the time of compiling this review. Comment is necessary on this table in that the absence of a particular compound in the list for one of the species does not necessarily imply that it does not occur naturally. Madagascan (Bourbon) vanilla is the only type which has as yet been subjected to 'in-depth' gas chromatography analysis, while Guadeloupe vanilla has received only perfunctory examinations. It is possible, therefore, that a larger number of compounds may yet be found to occur as common components in all three species but in differing abundance. Furthermore, it should be appreciated that the majority of these analyses were carried out on solvent extracts which may not accurately correspond to volatile-

Table 11.5 Volatile constituents identified in vanilla beans and vanilla extracts

	V. fragrans	V. tahitensis	V. pompona
Aromatic carbonyls			
vanillin	+	+	+
anisaldehyde	+(1,2,8)	+(2,17,22)	–
acetophenone	+(8)	–	–
benzaldehyde	+(1,8,18)	–	–
p-hydroxybenzaldehyde	+(1,5, 6,11,15,20)	+(15,20)	–
piperonal (heliotropin)	+(1)	+(4,16,19, 20,22)	+(16,19)
salicylic aldehyde	+(1)	–	–
Aromatic alcohols			
anisyl alcohol	+(1,6)	+(2,12,15, 17,22)	+(12,14)
benzyl alcohol	+(1)	–	–
coniferyl alcohol	?(5)	–	–
p-hydroxy benzyl alcohol	+(3,7,9,25)	+(3)	+(3)
phenyl ethyl alcohol	+(1,2)	–	–
vanillyl alcohol	+(3,23,25)	(3)	(3)
Aromatic acids			
anisic acid	+(8)	+(12,17)	–
benzoic acid	+(8,24)	–	–
cinnamic acid	+(12)	–	–
p-hydroxy benzoic acid	+(5,13,21)	+(13,21)	+(13)
salicyclic acid	+(1,5)	–	–
vanillic acid	+(5,8, 13,18,24)	+(13)	+(13)

	V. fragrans	V. tahitensis	V. pompona
Aromatic esters			
anisyl acetate	+(10)	+(2)	–
benzyl acetate	+(1)	–	–
benzyl benzoate	+(10)	–	–
benzyl butyrate	+(10)	–	–
benzyl cinnamate	+(10)	–	–
benzyl formate	+(1)	–	–
cinnamyl benzoate	+(10)	–	–
cinnamyl cinnamate	+(10)	.	–
diethyl phthlate	+(1)	–	–
di-n-butyl phthalate	+(1)	–	–
di-n-propylphthalate	+(1)	–	–
di-nethyl benzoate	+(1)	–	–
furfuryl acetate	+(10)	–	–
furfuryl benzoate	+(10)	–	–
methyl anisate	–	+(2)	–
methyl benzoate	+(1)	–	–
methyl-cis-cinnamate	+(1,2, 10,12)	–	–
methyl-trans-cinnamate	+(1,2, 10,12)	+(2)	–
methyl phenyl acetate	+(1)	–	–
methyl salicylate	+(1)	–	–
methyl vanillate	+(1)	–	–
mono ethyl phthalate	+(1)	–	–
phenyl ethylacetate	+(1)	–	–

References on p. 694

Table 11.6 *Additional volatile constituents identified in* V. fragrans

	Ref.
Phenols and phenol ethers	
anisole	(1)
p-cresol*	(1, 2, 9)
creosol	(1, 2)
p-cresyl isopropyl ether	(1)
p-cresyl methyl ether	(10)
1, 2-dimethoxy benzene	(1)
diphenyl ether	(1)
p-ethyl guaiacol	(1)
eugenol	(2)
guaiacol	(1, 2, 9)
p-hydroxybenzyl ethyl ether	(1, 27)
p-hydroxybenzyl methyl ether	(1, 27)
phenol	(1)
vanillin 2, 3-butylen glycol acetal	(1)
vanillyl ethyl ether*	(2, 27)
vanillyl methyl ether*	(20, 27)
p-vinyl guaiacol	(1)
p-vinyl phenol	(1)
(* also identified in *V. tahitensis*)	
Aliphatic alcohols	
butan-2, 3-diol	(1)
dedecan-1-ol	(1)
heptan-1-ol	(1)
hexan-1-ol	(1)
2-methyl-butan-1-ol	(1)
3-methyl-butan-1-ol	(1)
3-methyl-pentan-1-ol	(1)
nonan-2-ol	(1)
octan-1-ol	(1)
1-octen-3-ol	(1, 2)
pentan-1-ol	(1)
pentan-2-ol	(1)
prenol	(1)
Aliphatic carbonyls	
acetaldehyde	(8)
decan-2-one	(1)
diacetyl	(8, 20)
heptan-2-one	(1)
hexan-2-one	(1)
3-hydroxy-butan-2-one	(1)
1-hydroxy-heptan-2-one	(1)
1-hydroxy-pentan-2-one	(1)
5-hydroxy-heptan-2-one	(1)
octan-2-one	(1)
octa-4, 6-dien-3-one	(1)
3-octen-2-one	(1)
pentan-1-al	(1)
3-penten-2-one	(1)
nonan-2-one	(1)

Table 11.6　*(Continued)*

	Ref.
Aliphatic acids	
acetic	(1, 8)
butyric	(1)
capric	(1, 9)
caproic	(1, 2)
caprylic	(1, 2, 9)
formic	(1)
glycolic	(1)
n-heptanoic	(2)
isobutyric	(8)
isovaleric	(1, 8)
lactic	(1)
lauric	(1)
myristic	(1)
methoxyacetic	(1)
n-nonanoic	(2)
Aliphatic esters and lactones	
n-amyl acetate	(1)
γ-butyrolactone	(1)
butyl valerate	(1)
dihydroactinolide	(1)
ethyl caproate	(1)
ethyl lactate	(1)
ethyl levulinate	(1)
ethyl methoxyacetate	(1)
ethyl-2-methyl butyrate	(1)
ethyl palmitate	(1)
n-hexyl acetate	(1)
isobutyl valerate	(1)
isopropyl valerate	(1)
methyl caproate	(1)
methyl cyclohexancarboxylate	(1)
methyl glycolate	(1)
methyl heptadecanoate	(1)
methyl heptanoate	(1)
methyl lactate	(1)
methyl laurate	(1)
methyl myristate	(1)
methyl nonanoate	(1)
methyl palmitate	(1, 2)
methyl pentadecanoate	(1)
methyl valerate	(1)
γ-nonalactone	(1)
propyl valerate	(1)
Aromatic hydrocarbons	
benzene	(1)
toluene	(1)
dimethyl benzene	(1)
trimethyl benzene	(1)
ethyl benzene	(1)
propyl benzene	(1)

Table 11.6 *(Continued)*

	Ref.
p-ethyl toluene	(1)
styrene	(1)
naphthalene	(1, 10)
Terpenoids	
α- and β-pinene	(1)
limonene	(1)
myrcene	(1)
β-phellandrene	(1)
α-terpinene	(1)
p-cymene	(1)
α-curcumene	(1)
δ-cadinene	(1)
α-muuroleene	(1)
myrtenol	(1)
α-terpineol	(1)
terpinen-4-ol	(1)
linalol	(1)
citronellol	(1)
nerol	(1)
geraniol	(1)
β-bisabolene	(1)
β-cyclocitral	(1)
6, 10, 14-trimethyl-pentadecan-2-one	(1)
Aliphatic hydrocarbons	
nonane	(1)
decane	(1)
undecane	(1)
dodecane (two isomers)	(1)
pentadecane	(1)
tetradecane (two isomers)	(1)
hexadecane (two isomers)	(2)
heptadecane (branched)	(1)
docosane (branched)	(1)
χ-decane (branched)	(1)
χ-dodecene	(1)
χ-tetradecene	(1)
χ-eicosene	(1)
eicosane (branched)	(1)
Heterocyclics	
furfural	(1, 2, 8)
furfuryl alcohol	(1)
furfuryl hydroxy methyl ketone	(1)
2-acetyl furan	(1)
5-methyl furfural	(1)
2-pentyl furan	(1)
2, 5-dimethyl furfural	(8)
2-hydroxy-5-methyl furan	(1)
thiophene	(1)
2-acetyl pyrrole	(1)
methyl nicotinate	(1)
vitispirane (2 diastereo-isomers)	(26)

References for Tables 11.5 and 11.6

1. Klimes and Lamparsky (1976)
2. Shiota and Itoga (1975)
3. Prat and Subitte (1969)
4. Lhugenot *et al.* (1971)
5. Anwar (1963)
6. Bohnsack (1965)
7. Bohnsack and Seibert (1965)
8. Bohnsack (1967)
9. Bohnsack (1971a)
10. Bohnsack (1971b)
11. Chovin *et al.* (1954)
12. Gnadinger (1925)
13. Stoll and Prat (1960)
14. Simony (1953)
15. Bonnet (1968)
16. Pritzer and Jungkunz (1928)
17. Walbaum (1909)
18. Tiemann and Haarmann (1876)
19. Busse (1900)
20. Kleinert (1963)
21. Morison-Smith (1964)
22. Cowley (1973)
23. Goris (1924)
24. Goris (1947)
25. Chevalier *et al.* (1972)
26. Schulte-Elte *et al.* (1978)
27. Galetto and Hoffmann (1978)

component composition of the original vanilla beans owing to differences in extraction efficiencies and to ageing effects on the extracts. Aqueous ethanol extracts, in particular, undergo quantitative, and perhaps even qualitative, changes on ageing. These changes include oxidation of aldehydes such as vanillin and *p*-hydroxy benzaldehyde to their corresponding acids; by contrast, the corresponding alcohols are relatively stable to oxidation (Stoll and Prat, 1960; Chevalier *et al.*, 1972). Also, it should be noted that ethyl vanillin, whose natural occurrence in vanilla has been doubted (Thaler, 1959), has been detected as a trace component in *V. fragrans* and *V. tahitensis* by Shiota and Itoga (1975).

Comparisons of the volatile-component compositions of the three vanilla species have been reported by Chovin *et al.* (1954), Stoll and Pratt (1960), Kleinert (1963), Jackson (1966), Prat and Subitte (1969), Lhugenot *et al.* (1971), Cowley (1973), Oliver (1973), Shiota and Itoga (1975), Bonnet (1968), Anwar (1963), Morison-Smith (1964) and Tabacchi *et al.* (1978), of which the last four cited provided quantitative estimations of the relative abundance of certain components. Drawing on the information available at the time of writing this review, it seems that the differences in volatile-component composition between species are probably quantitative rather than qualitative, and of the various non-vanillin volatile constituents, those listed in Table 11.7 are significant as distinguishing features.

Hence, the main distinction between *V. fragrans* and *V. tahitensis* is the pronounced content of anisyl alcohol in the latter. Guadeloupe vanilla (*V. pompona*) has received less attention but may be distinguished from Tahiti vanilla on the basis of the relative abundance of anisyl alcohol, *p*-hydroxy benzoic acid and possibly piperonal. The relative abundance of piperonal in these two species is disputed, however, and it may be that it is naturally variable.

With regard to distinctions between the various sources of *V. fragrans*, Shiota and Itoga (1975) have made an interesting gas-chromatography comparison of Mexican and Madagascan vanillas

Table 11.7   *Distinguishing features for vanilla species*

Compound	V. fragrans	V. tahitensis	V. pompona
anisyl alcohol	absent or traces	very abundant and main distinguishing feature[1, 2, 3]	present as a minor component
anisaldehyde, anisyl ethers and anisic acid esters	traces	relatively abundant[4]	?
piperonal (heliotropin)	absent or traces	minor component[9] to relatively abundant[5]	minor component to relatively abundant[6]
p-hydroxy benzoic acid	relatively little	relatively abundant, 2× more than in other species[7, 8]	relatively little

References: (1) Gnadinger, 1925; (2) Bonnet, 1968; (3) Cowley, 1973; (4) Prat and Stoll, 1968; (5) Lhugenot *et al.*, (6) Prat and Stoll, 1968; (7) Morison-Smith, 1964; (8) Stoll and Prat, 1960; (9) Kleinert, 1963; (10) Tabacchi *et al.* (1978).

which is a useful first approach to the problem. A more extensive screening of a larger number of samples using 'in-depth' gas-chromatography analysis is probably necessary, however, before distinctions between sources can be made with certainty and explanations can be provided for the subtle differences in organoleptic properties. Studies of the composition of Java vanilla appear to be limited to those reported by Gnadinger (1925) and Morison-Smith (1964).

Development of the aroma and flavour

Green vanilla beans (or more accurately, pods) contain very little, if any, free vanillin and are substantially odourless and flavourless. If left to ripen on the vine, the beans gradually turn from green to yellow with the colour change commencing at the blossom-end, then split open and acquire a dark brown or chocolate colour. The beans develop aroma and the resin and free vanillin content increases as they darken but, if left, the mature beans eventually become brittle and finally almost odourless owing to evaporation of the volatile components.

Normally, beans are harvested when in the green state and are then subjected to the process of 'curing' to arrest vegetative development and to accelerate the formation of the desired aroma and flavour.

Traditional curing methods essentially consist of four steps, as has been described in the 'Processing and manufacture' section: wilting or killing; sweating; drying; and finally conditioning or ageing – this last step may take six months or longer. The aroma and flavour of the beans progressively develops from the sweating stage but the fully rounded, characteristic aroma and flavour is only acquired during the lengthy 'conditioning' stage. Accompanying the development of the aroma and flavour, there is an associated change in the colour of the beans from green to brown. This starts immediately after killing the green bean and is largely completed by the end of the sweating stage.

Aroma and flavour development may continue for a protracted period if the cured beans are stored under appropriate conditions and users generally prefer well-aged material to newly cured beans. Further modifications and desirable changes in the aroma and flavour occur with vanilla extracts on their ageing.

The aroma and flavour precursors

The development of the aroma and flavour during curing was appreciated to be a type of fermentation process from quite an early date but it took many years to substantiate the hypothesis scientifically. In 1885, Tiemann reported the isolation of an heteroside, which he named glucovanillin, by the oxidation of a water extract of green vanilla beans. Subsequently, Busse (1900) showed that vanillin could be obtained by the action of acid or emulsion on an unknown component of green beans. This compound was concluded to be an heteroside or, more specifically, a glucoside. In 1913, Lecompte postulated that the vanillin precursor present in green vanilla beans was coniferoside which, under the action of an oxidase, would first split to vanilloside (glucovanillin) and this is turn would yield vanillin and glucose on hydrolysis by acid or emulsin.

Goris (1924) isolated three glucosides from green vanilla beans. The most abundant of these was thought to be the glucovanillin of Tiemann and a second was postulated as a glucoside of vanillyl alcohol. Goris could not detect any coniferoside, and he questioned the role and occurrence of this compound in green vanilla beans. He suggested an alternative mechanism of vanilla formation in which the glucoside of vanillyl alcohol was oxidized to yield glucovanillin which would then hydrolyse to vanillin. Later, Goris (1947) confirmed that green vanilla beans contain at least four glucosides which yield vanillin and other aroma and flavour components on their cleavage. The most abundant glucoside was identified as glucovanillin while glucovanillyl alcohol was found in lesser quantities and a third was thought to be a glucoside of protocatechuic acid (3, 4-dihydroxy benzoic acid).

Readers who are interested in a more detailed discussion of these early studies are recommended to refer to the review by Janot (1954).

The mechanism of aroma development

Our present knowledge of this process resides largely on a series of investigations of *V. fragrans* carried out at the US Department of Agriculture Experiment Station at Mayaguez in Puerto Rico. These studies confirmed that vanillin is formed by the action of an hydrolytic enzyme on glucovanillin and that hydrolysis of other glucosides yield additional volatile compounds which contribute to the overall aroma and flavour. Further transformations of the liberated vanillin and other substrates subsequently occur by the action of a complex of oxidizing enzymes and during the conditioning stage non-enzymatic transformations play a very important role in aroma development (see Table 11.8).

Arana (1943, 1944) demonstrated that the glucovanillin content of vanilla beans on the vine gradually increases with maturity and that it is not uniformly distributed longitudinally. The relative abundance of glucovanillin is greatest at the blossom-end and least at the stem-end of

Table 11.8   *Transformations of glucovanillin and vanillin during the curing of vanilla beans*

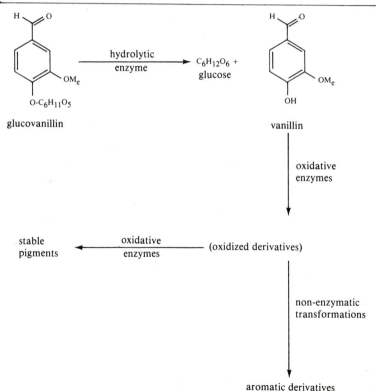

the bean. This distribution parallels the pattern of colour changes from green, through yellow to brown on maturation. This fact also accounts for the observation that crystallization of vanillin on the surface of cured beans is greater at the more mature blossom-end than at the stem-end. Most of the glucovanillin is located in the fleshy wall of the bean but a substantial quantity is also present in the central segment surrounding the seeds and placenta.

The presence of an hydrolytic enzyme capable of splitting gluco-vanillin to vanillin, first noted by Lecompte (1913), was confirmed by Arana (1943), who considered it to be of a beta-glucosidase type. The glucosidase is entirely located in the fleshy wall of the bean and is absent from the central segment. In order to achieve complete hydrolysis of the glucovanillin present in the bean, it is therefore essential that the gluco-vanillin in the central segment should migrate to the glucosidase in the pod wall, or vice versa. The process of artificial curing is believed to facilitate this diffusion by rupturing the enzyme cell walls; and free vanillin is in fact found in the dark-brown oleoresin secretion surround-ing the seeds of cured beans (Small, 1942).

Arana found that the content and activity of the glucosidase increases as the bean matures, closely paralleling the build-up of gluco-vanillin. At the green-bean stage, the activity of the glucosidase and the content of free vanillin is negligible. Maximal activity of the glucosidase is encountered at the split blossom-end yellow phase and the free vanillin content is highest at the subsequent chocolate-brown stage. The glucosidase activity is apparently partially inactivated when the bean becomes chocolate-brown for half its length but it can be reactivated during curing. Green beans exhibit very low glucosidase activity throughout the artificial curing process and this results in a very low vanillin content in the product compared with beans harvested at a later stage of maturity. However, since cured green beans are normally acceptable, this further reinforces the observation that aroma/flavour quality is not directly related to vanillin content. The hydrolysis of other glucosides is presumed to parallel that of glucovanillin.

After hydrolysis of the glucosides, the vanillin and other liberated phenols undergo transformations by the action of oxidizing enzymes to yield other aromatic compounds, quinones and, eventually, stable pig-ments. Balls and Arana (1941a) have shown that when beans are aged under conditions which do not permit sublimation, the vanillin content gradually decreases while the phenol value remains virtually constant. Two enzymatic oxidation systems have been identified: a peroxidase using hydrogen peroxide (Arana, 1940, Balls and Arana, 1941b) and an oxidase using atmospheric oxygen (Arana, 1940; Jones and Vincente, 1949b; Rivera and Hageman, 1951). The oxidase is believed to be responsible for the major oxidative transformations in vanilla during curing, including much of the browning. Some methods of killing beans cause damage to the outer tissue, which accelerates the initial rate of oxidase/atmospheric oxygen reactions.

The peroxidase/hydrogen peroxide system is notable in that it can survive the sweating process and has been found intact in some completely cured beans; and it may, therefore, play some role in the transformations occurring during the conditioning phase. Jones and Vincente (1949b) are of the opinion, however, that the principal changes wrought by the oxidative enzymes in vanilla beans occur during the first two weeks of the curing process. Towards the end of the sweating process and throughout the conditioning phase, during which the full, well-rounded aroma and flavour develop, non-enzymatic reactions assume the dominant role.

More recently, a number of workers have made proposals on the origin of some of the non-vanillin volatile constituents present in cured vanilla beans. It has been demonstrated by Chevalier *et al.* (1972) that vanillic acid and *p*-hydroxy benzoic acid can be formed in vanilla extracts by oxidation of the corresponding aldehydes, but quantities of these two acids are also present in the cured beans prior to extraction. Anwar (1963) has suggested that the main route to *p*-hydroxy benzoic acid during curing may be by the hydrolysis of anthocyanins, while Zenk (1965) has proposed that vanillic acid and vanillin arise separately from a common precursor. Prat and Subitte (1969) have reported finding considerable quantities of *p*-hydroxy benzyl alcohol present in extracts of green beans of *V. pompona* and have suggested that this compound may be an important intermediary in aroma development in this species.

Factors influencing aroma development and quality

Investigations on *V. fragrans* at the US Department of Agriculture Experiment Station at Mayaguez in Puerto Rico have also provided useful information on the influence of harvesting and curing methods on the aroma quality of cured beans.

Vanilla beans ripen and are harvested over a period of several months and the bean length at harvest steadily increases as the season progresses. Jones and Vincente (1949c) harvested pods during the early-, mid- and late-season when they were at a similar stage of maturity and then subjected them to identical curing procedures. The aroma/flavour quality of the cured product from the short pods harvested in the early-season was found to be superior to that of the mid- and late-season crops, even though the vanillin content on a moisture-free basis was lower. This experiment demonstrated once again that a high vanillin content is not necessarily a prerequisite of high aroma quality.

Maturation studies carried out by Arana (1944) and Jones and Vincente (1949c) have shown that pods harvested at the blossom-end yellow stage provide a superior aroma in the cured product than beans which are harvested at the green, blossom-end brown or fully brown phases.

Jones and Vincente (1949c) also found that diseased plants do not appear to provide cured beans which are markedly inferior in aroma and flavour to the products of healthy plants, although bean yields per plant are reduced. These workers could not find any definite correlation between aroma/flavour quality and the altitude of plant cultivation, but commented that this may have been masked by other variables such as rainfall and soil.

With regard to curing methods, Jones and Vincente (1949a) found that curing of ground fresh beans resulted in a higher vanillin content than by the curing of whole or cut beans, and that this process did not cause any aroma/flavour deterioration. This phenomenon is believed to arise from the more intimate contact between the glucovanillin and glucosidase achieved by grinding.

Although atmospheric oxygen is essential for some of the oxidative transformations during curing, excessive aeration during the sweating stage can lead to the formation of an undesirable prune-like aroma (Jones and Vincente, 1949a).

Temperature control during the sweating and conditioning stages is also considered important in providing a cured bean with a fine aroma and flavour (Jones and Vincente, 1949a; Rivera and Hageman, 1951). Elevated temperatures during the sweating stage adversely affect the oxidase system.

The moisture content of the beans during conditioning appears to have some influence on aroma/flavour quality. Arana (1944) found that beans with a high moisture content (50−54 per cent) tended to have a slightly fermented aroma and were less suave than those conditioned at lower moisture contents.

Aroma/flavour development in vanilla extracts

During the ageing of vanilla extract, the dissolved vanilla extractives continue to undergo chemical transformation which results in further development of a desirable aroma and flavour. These transformations involve hydrolysis, oxidation and trans-esterification of certain components. It has already been mentioned that oxidation of vanillin and *p*-hydroxy benzaldehyde to their corresponding acids is a common feature with aqueous ethanol extracts but that vanillyl alcohol and *p*-hydroxy benzyl alcohol are relatively stable.

The most important reaction in organoleptic terms during ageing of aqueous ethanol extracts is the so-called 'alcoholysis of esters' (Merory, 1968). This involves the hydrolysis of esters of higher alcohols and re-esterification of the liberated acids with lower alcohols. The liberated higher alcohols slowly oxidize to aldehydes. A slow rate of oxidation is believed to provide a product with a superior aroma and flavour.

It is of interest that vanilla oleoresin, which is solvent-free, also undergoes flavour modification on ageing.

Authenticity determination of vanilla extract

Vanilla extract is an important food flavouring in the United States and its composition is strictly defined by Government regulations (see the 'Standard specifications' section). These regulations specify that vanilla extract may be prepared only from *V. fragrans* and *V. tahitensis* and state the minimum levels for the vanilla constituent and ethanol content. Optional permitted additives to vanilla extract are limited to glycerine, propylene glycol, sugar, dextrose and corn syrup. Consequently, considerable attention has been devoted to devising analytical methods for checking the authenticity of vanilla extract. It should be stressed, however, that the analytical methods described in the following paragraphs are means of determining vanilla extract composition while the aroma and flavour quality can only be assessed by subjective organoleptic tests.

Traditionally, the authenticity of a vanilla extract has been evaluated on the basis of the content of ethanol, vanillin and resins, the colour value and on the lead number, which is a test for the organic acid content. Deviations from the accepted values for authentic extracts would indicate that the extract in question was deficient in vanilla constituent or that adulterants had been added. Adulterants which have been used to mask weak extracts include foreign vegetable matter as a colour enhancer, organic acids to boost the lead number, and synthetic aroma and flavour chemicals such as synthetic vanillin, ethyl vanillin (which has a flavour strength $4 \times$ that of vanillin), methyl vanillin, vanitrope (propenyl guaethol), piperonal, coumarin and methyl coumarin. For historical analytical data on authentic vanilla extracts, the reader is referred to Winton and Winton (1939) and Blomquist *et al*. (1965) and for more recent data to the annual reports of the Flavour Extract Manufacturers' Association of the United States.

In recent years, a number of new methods have been devised to improve on the traditional authenticity tests, several of which have been accepted by the Association of Official Analytical Chemists (1975). A summary is provided below on developments in analytical techniques, some of which permit an identification of the type of vanilla used in the preparation of the extract.

Organic acids

The techniques of paper chromatography (Fitelson, 1963), ion exchange gradient elution chromatography (Sullivan *et al*., 1960; Fitelson, 1963; Blomquist *et al*., 1965) and gas chromatography (Fitelson and Bowden,

1968; Schoen, 1972) have all been applied to the analysis of vanilla organic acids. These chromatographic studies have shown that vanilla extracts contain at least twenty organic acids, among which malic acid is one of the major components, and that distinctions can be made between the three vanilla species on the basis of the total acid content and their composition pattern. In addition, it is possible to distinguish between Mexican and Bourbon (Madagascan) beans. Chromatographic analysis of the organic acids of vanilla extracts, is, therefore, not only useful in detecting gross deficiencies in acid content or adulteration, but also in identifying the type of beans used.

Amino acids

Stahl *et al.* (1962) have developed a paper chromatography method for vanilla amino acid analysis and have shown that Bourbon, Mexican and Tahitian beans can be distinguished from one another. In addition to being a useful method for the qualitative separation of extracts prepared from these different types of vanilla, the technique also provides a means of differentiating between extracts which differ significantly in their blend mix. More recently, gas chromatography methods have been applied to vanilla amino acid analysis (Anon., 1977; Martin *et al.*, 1977).

Vanillin

Martin *et al.* (1975) have devised a method for differentiating between a true vanilla extract and one which has been adulterated by synthetic vanillin. The method involves determining the vanillin content of the extract by gas chromatography, the content of potassium, inorganic phosphate and nitrogen by specified methods, and then calculating the ratios of these constituents one to another. The adulteration of an extract by the addition of synthetic vanillin is indicated when the ratios for vanillin to potassium, etc., are higher than those of standard authentic extracts.

Other synthetic flavour additives

Thin-layer chromatography (Kleinert, 1963; Kahan and Fitelson, 1964) and gas chromatography (Bonnet, 1968; Potter, 1971; Meili and Chaveron, 1976) techniques have been reported for detecting the presence of common synthetic flavour additives in vanilla extracts.

In addition to some of the techniques described above, the species of vanilla bean contained in an extract can be checked also by determining the abundance of certain natural aroma/flavour constituents, e.g., anisyl alcohol and piperonal, using the chromatographic methods described in the preceeding sub-section concerned with the aroma/flavour constituents of vanilla.

Standard specifications

The United Kingdom

The British Standards Institution has published a specification for vanilla (BS 5432, 1976: *Vanilla* – Part 1 – Vocabulary) which is identical with the International Standards Organization specification, 'Vanilla – Vocabulary' (ISO 3495; 1976). The standard specifies that it applies to the following species of vanilla plants: '*Vanilla fragrans* (Salisbury) Ames, syn. *V. planifolia* Andrews, commercially known under various names such as Bourbon Vanilla, Mexican Vanilla, Indonesian Vanilla and Seychelles Vanilla; *Vanilla tahitensis* J.W. Moore commercially known as Tahiti Vanilla; and to certain forms obtained from seeds, possibly hybrids of *Vanilla fragrans* (Salisbury) Ames. It does not apply to *Vanilla pompona* Schiede (Antilles Vanilla).' The standard defines such terms as green, prepared and cured vanilla, vanilla pods, split vanilla, and provides a qualitative classification of vanilla types – supple, dry, frosted, mouldy, creosoted vanilla, etc.

A further part to the ISO Standard, entitled '*Vanilla fragrans* – Specification', is in the course of preparation and a British Standard will be based on this International Standard.

Vanilla is no longer included in the *British Pharmacopoeia*, the *British Pharmaceutical Codex* or the *British National Formulary*. The Martindale '*Extra Pharmacopoeia*' (27th edn) definition for vanilla tincture is identical with that given in the *US National Formulary*.

France

Regulations were issued in 1966 which forbid the use of the word 'vanilla' or a derivative of the word unless in reference to a product made from the properly dried and cured fruit of *Vanila planifolia* or similar species of the orchid family. The regulations also stipulate that if the vanilla flavour used is synthetic or artificial then this must be stated on the label of the product.

La Reglementation des Produits Alimentaires (8th edn) states that the term 'pure vanilla powder' ('Poudre de vanille pure') is reserved for vanilla in powder form. Vanilla sugar is defined in two forms: 'Poudre de vanille sucré' is a mixture of vanilla powder and sucrose in which the vanilla content is at least 25 per cent; 'Sucre vannille' is a product comprised of sucrose and the total aromatic and sapid constituents obtained from at least 10 g of vanilla to 100 g of the product to be sold.

The International Standard, 'Vanilla – Vocabulary' (ISO 3495; 1976), was drawn up in collaboration with the Association Francais de Normalisation.

The United States

The *US Dispensatory* (26th edn, 1967) defines vanilla as 'the cured, fully-grown unripe fruit of *Vanilla planifolia* Andrews, often known in commerce as Mexican or Bourbon vanilla, or of *V. tahitensis* J.W. Moore, known in commerce as Tahiti vanilla. Vanilla yields not less than 12 per cent of anhydrous extractive soluble in diluted alcohol.'

The *US National Formulary* states that vanilla tincture intended for flavouring purposes contains the soluble extractives of 1 part by weight of vanilla beans and 2 parts by weight of sugar in 10 parts by volume of aqueous ethanol and is prepared by maceration. The ethanol content of vanilla tincture should be 38−42 per cent by volume.

There are no US Federal standards for vanilla beans, but the composition and labelling of vanilla products fall within the scope of the Food and Drug Administration Regulations. The definitions and requirements for vanilla products described in Part 169 of Volume 42 of the *Federal Register* (issued 15 March 1977) are summarized below:

Vanilla beans are defined as 'the properly cured and dried fruits of *Vanilla planifolia* Andrews and of *Vanilla tahitensis* Moore.'

Unit weight of vanilla beans

This term is defined as 'in the case of vanilla beans containing not more than 25 per cent moisture, 13.35 ounces of such beans; and in the case of vanilla beans containing more than 25 per cent moisture, it means the weight of such beans equivalent in content of moisture-free vanilla-bean solids to 13.35 ounces of vanilla beans containing 25 per cent moisture.' The moisture content is determined by a specified method.

Unit of vanilla constituent

This term is defined as 'the total sapid and odorous principles extractable from one unit weight of vanilla beans by an aqueous alcohol solution in which the content of ethyl alcohol by volume amounts to not less than 35 per cent.'

Vanilla extract is 'the solution in aqueous ethyl alcohol of the sapid and odorous principles extractable from vanilla beans. In vanilla extract the content of ethyl alcohol is not less than 35 per cent by volume, and the content of vanilla constituent is not less than one unit per gallon*. The vanilla constituent may be extracted directly from vanilla beans or it may be added in the form of concentrated vanilla extract or concentrated vanilla flavouring or vanilla flavouring concentrated to the semi-solid form called vanilla oleoresin. Vanilla extract may contain one or more of the following optional ingredients: glycerin, propylene glycol, sugar (including invert sugar), dextrose, corn sirup.'

---

* US gallon = 0.833 Imperial gallon

Vanilla flavouring

This differs from vanilla extract in that the ethyl alcohol content is less than 35 per cent.

Concentrated vanilla extract and concentrated vanilla flavouring

These products conform to the requirements for vanilla extract and vanilla flavouring, respectively, except that they are concentrated to remove part of the solvent, and each gallon contains two or more units of vanilla constituent. The ethyl alcohol content on concentrated vanilla extracts is not less than 35 per cent and for concentrated vanilla flavouring is less than 35 per cent.

Vanilla powder is defined as 'a mixture of ground vanilla beans or vanilla oleoresin or both, with one or more of the following optional blending ingredients: sugar, dextrose, lactose, food starch, dried corn sirup, gum acacia.' Vanilla powder may contain one or any mixture of two or more certain specified anticaking ingredients provided that their content in the finished products does not exceed 2 per cent by weight. 'Vanilla powder contains in each 8 pounds not less than one unit of vanilla constituent.'

Vanilla–vanillin extract

This conforms to the requirements for vanilla extract 'except that for each unit of vanilla constituent contained therein, the article also contains not more than 1 ounce of added vanillin.'

Vanilla–vanillin flavouring

This differs from vanilla-vanillin extract in that the ethyl alcohol content is less than 35 per cent.

Vanilla–vanillin powder

This conforms to the requirements for vanilla powder 'except that for each unit of vanilla constituent, the article contains not more than 1 ounce of added vanillin.'

The regulations for the products listed above also include their specified names and detailed requirements for labelling.

Production, trade and markets

Vanilla is notable among spices for its rapid acceptance and popularity following its first introduction to the European markets, and it is still one of the most widely used flavouring materials. Over 95 per cent of world demand for the vanilla flavour is satisfied by relatively inexpensive synthetic substitutes, principally synthetic vanillin, but nonetheless world production and consumption of natural vanilla have been rising during the last decade after half a century of stagnation. In 1975 world exports of vanilla beans amounted to around 1 400 tonnes valued at nearly £10 million.

Vanilla, which is indigenous to Central America, has been introduced into many tropical countries in several geographical areas but the number of suppliers of importance in international trade is relatively small. The characteristics of vanilla produced in the various growing areas differ significantly and as with other spices preferences are expressed according to the geographical source by certain users for particular applications. The primary sub-division of vanilla in international trade is according to the species: true vanilla from *V. fragrans* is far the most important and the most widely cultivated; Tahiti vanilla from *V. tahitensis*, produced in French Polynesia, is less favoured for flavouring purposes and is traded in comparatively small volumes; and the product of *V. pompona*, known as 'vanillons', 'Guadeloupe vanilla' or 'Antilles vanilla', cultivated on some of the French West Indian islands, is of very minor importance in trade. True vanilla is classified into four main geographical categories: Bourbon vanilla, produced in the Indian Ocean Islands, principally by Madagascar, the Comoro Islands and Réunion; Mexican vanilla; Indonesian or 'Java' vanilla; and South American/West Indian vanilla. Production and trade in true vanilla is dominated by the Indian Ocean producers, with Madagascar accounting for over 75 per cent of world exports.

The major consumers are the USA (accounting for 60 per cent of the market), France, the Federal Republic of Germany and Japan. However, these countries are also important producers of synthetic vanillin, using as starting materials eugenol from clove leaf oil, lignin obtained as a by-product of the wood-pulp industry, and guaiacol from coal-tar.

Domestic consumption of vanilla beans by the producers is negligible. Almost all production therefore enters world trade, although on certain occasions in Madagascar deliberate destruction of vanilla bean stocks took place. Vanilla, though insignificant in value terms in the total imports of the consuming countries, constitutes an important source of foreign exchange earnings to the Indian Ocean producers, and it was partly for this reason that in Madagascar there was a move towards centralized government control of production and marketing after independence in 1960.

Production

Annual production figures for vanilla are no more readily available than for any other spice, and those that do exist have to be carefully interpreted in the light of certain problems. For example, some statistics include both green vanilla and cured vanilla under the one heading, yet the latter is 70 per cent lighter than the former. Another problem is that the length of processing time may render accurate identification of the year of production uncertain, while unreported changes in stock levels can give rise to distortions. For the same reason, export and import figures may only be used as rough guides to average production levels over a number of years, and in any case the export figures by no means always agree with the corresponding import figures. Tables 11.9−11.11 show the exports of the leading producers, and Tables 11.12−11.17 the sources of imports of some of the large consumers.

Although in the past vanilla production was undertaken to some degree in large, generally foreign-owned, plantations, this form of production is now of negligible importance and foreign investment in vanilla production and curing is unusual. It is now a skilled labour-intensive activity carried out by small-scale producers. However, these producers generally have secondary occupations, since the time-lag between initial investment and the first harvest is quite lengthy. Even the curers, to whom it is usual for the growers to sell the crop, have to undertake their investment one year in advance of the first sale. On the other hand, in Madagascar and one or two other producing countries new methods of artificial curing−providing vanilla suitable for use in the manufacture of extracts−have been developed and these, besides speeding up processing, could render some of the current labour-intensive grading and marketing practices redundant. The widespread introduction of these new curing techniques could have serious socio-economic repercussions.

In all producing countries vanilla production has been and remains prone to great fluctuations. For example, production in Madagascar during 1960−75 varied from estimated lows of 550 and 600 tonnes, in 1962 and 1973 respectively, to highs of approximately 1 700 tonnes in 1964 and 1972. The two major causes of these fluctuations are climate and the producers' responses to price changes. Vanilla cultivation in most of the producing countries tends to be concentrated in single areas and the cyclones prevalent in the ocean islands generally cause extensive damage to both growing and harvested crops in terms of quality as well as quantity. To give just one example, about two-thirds of Madagascar's 1976 crop and about 20 per cent of the stored 1974 and 1975 crops were lost as a result of one cyclone, and the gestation period for new plantings added further difficulties to the supply problem. Such variations in supply and the time required to make good the losses so caused give rise to considerable fluctuations in the price, which in turn affect production levels. Like most primary producers, the relatively large number of vanilla growers base their individual, unco-ordinated production plans on the prevailing market price, a high price encouraging an increase in the area planted and vice versa. However, an increase in area arising from high prices will not be reflected in increased market supplies until the time needed for maturing, harvesting and curing has elapsed; and it can well happen that during this period a disequilibrium in the market will cause the price to fall back from its peak and the eventual increase in market supplies will only serve to drive the price down still further. Producers then respond by cutting back production and thereby bring about another price rise and subsequent plan for increased production. This cycle is familiar in many types of agricultural production and has become known as the 'cobweb cycle'.

This form of instability provides a sound argument for the creation of a marketing board, or similar organization, with the object of neutralizing such fluctuations, and some producers, for example, Madagascar, have taken steps in this direction. Some growers and curers have tried to counteract the cobweb cycle by harvesting green beans long before maturity so as to take advantage of high prices and to avoid theft, but quality and quantity are adversely affected.

Historical development

Vanilla cultivation was well established in Mexico under the Aztec empire and its commercial potential on the European market was quickly appreciated by the Spaniards soon after the Conquest. However, attempts at cultivation outside Mexico were initially unsuccessful owing to problems of fertilizing the flowers, and this ensured a Mexican monopoly in the vanilla trade well into the nineteenth century. The ending of the Mexican monopoly resulted from the discovery of a method of artificial fertilization by a native of Réunion (formerly Bourbon) and the French initiative in developing production in their overseas possessions. Cultivation of vanilla in Réunion became important between 1849 and 1856 and attained sizable proportions by 1874. The crop was introduced into Madagascar and the Comoros in the years 1840 and 1893, respectively. During the latter half of the nineteenth century, vanilla was also introduced into many other tropical countries. Production of vanilla in these other countries has never matched that of the Bourbon vanilla producers, comprising Madagascar, the Comoro Islands and Réunion, who outstripped Mexican production by the end of the nineteenth century and have subsequently dominated the trade.

Vanilla production in the individual producing countries is discussed in the following paragraphs.

Mexico

Cultivation and processing of vanilla in Mexico is limited to a well-defined area on the first rising ground of the coastal plain of the Gulf of Mexico and encompasses part of central Veracruz and northern Puebla. All of the growing districts and the principal trading/curing centres lie within a radius of about 65 km from the town of San José Acateno. Cultivation of vanilla has traditionally been carried out by Totonoco Indians on small plots of land. Few of the growers cure their own vanilla and the majority sell their crop to traders who specialize in this operation. The main curing centres are San José Acetano, Papantla and Gutierrez Zamora.

As mentioned above, the Mexican monopoly in the vanilla trade was virtually undisturbed from the sixteenth until the mid-nineteenth century. The development of artificial pollination transformed the situation and by the mid-1880s the combined production of Réunion, Java and Mauritius exceeded that of Mexico, which thereafter continued to lose ground in spite of the introduction there of artificial pollination. Early Mexican production figures are not available, but it would seem that from about 1900 to the late 1930s annual production fluctuated, sometimes dramatically, around 100 tonnes. During the Second World War the temporary disappearance from the market of the lower-priced Bourbon vanillas induced an increase in Mexican production through a trebling of the price in relation to pre-war levels. In 1944, 300 tonnes were shipped to the USA alone. After the war an attempt was made to use Mexican production to disrupt Madagascar's attempts to maintain and stabilize price levels, but without success. The reappearance of the Bourbon vanillas at low prices caused production in Mexico to be largely abandoned, the period 1949–52 being disastrous to growers and curers alike. The number of people involved in the Mexican vanilla industry in 1950 was about 10 000, one-fifth of the 1920 total.

After 1952 there was some recovery and annual production varied around an average of 80–100 tonnes until the early 1960s, when a further decline set in. Between 1969 and 1974 annual average exports were less than 20 tonnes. Vanilla production is comparatively unremunerative in Mexico, and the citrus, stockbreeding and petroleum oil industries, among others, have drawn labour away.

Madagascar

Vanilla production in Madagascar is concentrated along the north-east coast. The main area of production in this belt is the most northerly prefecture of Antalaha around the trading centres of Antalaha, Andapa, Sambava and Vohémar where vanilla monoculture is practised. The scale of vanilla production gradually decreases down this belt through the prefectures of Fénérive and Tamatave and is least around the most southerly towns of Vatomandry and Mahanoro. In the southern section of the belt, vanilla competes with the production of cloves, coffee and rice. A small quantity of vanilla is also produced on the island of Nossi-Bé and on the neighbouring mainland coast of north-west Madagascar around the towns of Ambanja and Ambilobe. In the early years of production, Madagascan vanilla was almost wholly in the hands of European landowners but by the 1960s the bulk of the crop was grown by smallholders. In 1973, 37 604 planters were recorded as actively engaged in vanilla cultivation but annual output varied immensely from grower to grower – in some cases being as low as 50 kg of green vanilla. As is the case in Mexico, few vanilla growers cure their own crop of beans. The curing has traditionally been carried out in the local towns by intermediary specialist firms, which were formerly often owned by Chinese and other Asian groups or Réunionnaire Creoles. Final sorting and packaging of the cured beans is carried out by exporting firms in Antalaha, which is the world's largest vanilla shipping port. Since Madagascar obtained independence, the role of intermediaries of immigrant origin in the local vanilla trade has declined owing to government intervention and reorganization of the industry.

The 1960s saw the introduction of far-reaching government legislation, mainly with the object of guaranteeing the producer a minimum price and protecting him against monopoly buying, speculation and other malpractices.

In 1900 Madagascar's production was about 15 tonnes, but it increased rapidly and was 233 tonnes in 1915. Immediately after the First World War demand boomed, production lagged and prices rose. Malagasy planters responded dramatically, exports reaching 298 tonnes in 1924, 619 tonnes in 1926 and 1 091 tonnes in 1929, at which point Madagascar was supplying over 80 per cent of the world's vanilla needs. The industry was badly hit by the depression of the 1930s, prices spiralled downwards, and large stocks accumulated. Production, down to 875 tonnes in 1930, averaged 640 tonnes per year for the remainder of the decade, and quality also deteriorated. In 1933, however, in order to restore the quality of exports and retain the interest of buyers, the colonial government introduced and rigorously enforced standard specifications for the export of vanilla, the value of which totalled 75 million francs for 1938.

In the Second World War Indian Ocean producers were cut off from their main markets, initially by the Allied blockade and later by the shortage of shipping space. Stocks accumulated in consequence, and after the war attempts were made to stabilize the trade through price control and the destruction of stockpiles. However, prices slumped and this, together with the impact of cyclones in 1950, 1959 and 1960, created severe problems for the producers. Between 1952 and 1958 production averaged not more than 400 tonnes per annum, with dips to around 300 tonnes in the wake of the cyclones. After 1960, however, production exhibited a rising trend, with an annual average of 900 tonnes for the period 1964–8 and 1 200 tonnes for the period 1969–73.

This period of growth can be attributed mainly to certain government policies: firstly, a regeneration policy instituted in the 1960s, and secondly, a growing willingness to adopt strenuous measures to rationalize the marketing of vanilla and to combat speculation. To these ends, price-fixing schemes and a system of export quotas and buffer stocks have been evolved. The largely ineffective Price Support Fund of 1953 was overhauled in 1961 when a price stabilization board, the 'Caisse de Stabilisation des Prix de la Vanille' came into being under the independent new government. This organization sets minimum prices, supervises production and monitors the world market. All planters and exporters have to be registered and the Prefecture of Antalaha is the only recognized production zone. In spite of early success there was a slump in exports which led to the formation in 1964 of the Vanilla Alliance 'Univanille', of which Madagascar, the Comoro Islands and Réunion were founder members. A subsequent conference convened by the Government of Madagascar brought together for the first time representatives of vanilla planters, traders and consumers. A series of meetings was thereby inaugurated, as a result of which a greater measure of market stabilization was achieved.

Another reorganization occurred in 1966, involving the creation of an interprofessional group consisting of all vanilla planters, processors and exporters, for whom membership was to be compulsory. It was to be governed by representatives of government ministries, the afore-mentioned Caisse and the 'Institut d'Emission Malgache', although this body supplemented rather than supplanted the functions of the Caisse. All other organizations previously involved in the vanilla industry ceased to function.

The maintenance of stocks at an appropriate level has been the most difficult problem facing the Vanilla Alliance. The main object of the stocks was to provide a form of insurance against crop failures, but stock conservation is expensive and the very existence of stocks can in certain circumstances threaten the stability of the market. For example, in 1974 the level of stocks was 3 000 tonnes, or nearly three years' consumption of vanilla, and although some subsequent reduction in stocks was to be expected, deliberate destruction of stocks in the interests of market stability is far from unknown. However, on balance, the government's actions have clearly improved matters and in Table 11.20 the guaranteed prices paid to Malagasy growers are shown. For the future, it is possible that newly developed techniques of artificial drying and the creation of a new disease-resistant strain with a higher vanillin content could have a profound effect upon Madagascan production.

The Comoros

The Comoro Islands archipelago, which lies to the north-west of Madagascar, is the world's second major producer of vanilla. Production, originally undertaken by Europeans, is now carried out by numerous small growers whose individual annual outputs range from 2 to 200 kg of green beans, although Europeans continued to participate in curing into the 1960s. Over 75 per cent of production takes place in Grande Comore Island, with minor contributions from Anjouan, Mohéli, and Mayotte.

The Comoros' production and trade statistics have often been shown aggregated with those of Madagascar, for which reason the situation prior to 1940 is unclear, although there is no doubt that the

Comoro contribution to world supplies was substantial. After the war, annual production declined to a level of 50–60 tonnes in the mid-1950s and then recovered to an average of 158 tonnes in 1965–9. In 1971 and 1972 exports exceeded 200 tonnes but a drastic slump occurred in 1973 and 1974 (see Table 11.10).

Réunion

This territory has been historically important in the development of vanilla production. It was the first country to introduce artificial fertilization of vanilla flowers and subsequently Réunion disseminated vanilla to other Indian Ocean islands. At one time vanilla production on Réunion flourished but by the mid-1950s its contribution to world supplies had diminished to near insignificance. Production rose from about 2 tonnes in 1851 to around 200 tonnes in 1895; but the average annual exports for the period 1955–9 were 53 tonnes; for 1960–4, 42 tonnes; for 1965–9, 30 tonnes; and for 1970–4, 26 tonnes.

Production has tended to decline owing to cyclone damage to the plantations, competition from other cash crops such as sugar and, during the French colonial period, the labour laws applied resulted in labour costs of production exceeding those of Madagascar and the Comoros. Production of vanilla is carried out along the north-east coast of the island and is undertaken by families on small plots of up to 1 ha in size. Réunion vanilla has traditionally been, and remains, the most highly regarded for quality among the Bourbon-type vanilla sources in the Indian Ocean; and the French authorities, reluctant to see the industry disappear completely, offered the producers financial aid during the 1970s and this appears to have achieved positive results. Production in 1974 was 74 tonnes and in 1975, 104 tonnes.

Indonesia

The development of vanilla production in Indonesia has not been well documented but up to the 1940s the main producing areas were in West and Central Java. These areas remain important but in recent years small-scale production has developed in South Sumatra and Sulawesi as a result of government-encouraged migration and resettlement. In former years, vanilla cultivation was undertaken both on European-owned plantations and by small farmers and the curing was often undertaken by Chinese traders. The quality of Indonesian or 'Java' vanilla has always been variable and quality was often sacrificed for quantity. Vanilla production is now almost exclusively in the hands of smallholders, and recently one major trader in Central Java has established an artificial curing plant to supply the American market with material for vanilla extract. In the next few years Indonesia could become a major force in the world vanilla trade, for it is estimated that annual production in the mid-1970s was in excess of 400 tonnes. Until the 1940s, when exports almost completely ceased, the then Dutch East

Indies provided about 1.5 per cent of world supplied. Production during the 1950s remained low and it was not until the 1960s that a sustained increase was evident.

French Polynesia

In contrast to Indonesia, French Polynesia has been declining in importance. Once introduced, vanilla production progressed rapidly from 11 tonnes in 1883 to 73 tonnes in 1891. From 1900 until the late 1950s average annual production was maintained at around 100 tonnes with substantial short-term fluctuations. During the period 1936−45 an annual average of 133 tonnes was exported (see Table 11.9), mainly in response to a sharp peak in demand from the USA, whose normal supplies had been cut off during the war. After the late 1950s, production declined to an average of 86 tonnes in the period 1965−7 and 26 tonnes in the period 1970−4, exports in 1974 being a mere 12 tonnes (Table 11.10).

The vanilla produced in French Polynesia is the so-called 'Tahiti vanilla' from *V. tahitensis*, which differs considerably in its characteristics from true vanilla produced in Mexico, by the Bourbon vanilla suppliers and by Indonesia, and it is not as well regarded for flavouring applications. The post-war decline in production of Tahiti vanilla is probably associated with the increasing supply of true vanilla from other sources.

All French Polynesian vanilla is grown in the Society Islands, particularly Tahiti. Vanilla cultivation is mainly carried out by Polynesian farmers on small plots of land and, as elsewhere, curing is undertaken by middlemen, who are often of Chinese origin. The harvesting, curing and export of Tahiti vanilla is strictly regulated by the authorities.

Other producers

Vanilla was introduced into a number of Indian Ocean territories from Réunion during the latter half of the nineteenth century. The Seychelles, Mauritius and Rodriguez were all significant suppliers of Bourbon-type vanilla in former years but their contribution to world supplies in recent years has become negligible. At the turn of the century, exports from the Seychelles of around 70 tonnes were equal to those of Réunion and were greater than the combined vanilla production of all other British territories. However, the advent of synthetic vanillin and disease problems resulted in production falling to below 1 tonne per annum in the mid-1930s. Interest in the crop was rekindled after the Second World War but by the early 1970s exports had ceased owing to continued disease problems, high production costs and competition for labour by the tourist industry.

Elsewhere in the Indian Ocean and Pacific Ocean regions, vanilla has been exported in small quantities by countries such as India, Sri

Lanka, Tonga and Hawaii. Vanilla was introduced into Uganda as an estate crop in the 1930s but annual exports rarely exceeded a few tonnes. In the early 1970s, an American spice company set up an artificial curing plant in co-operation with the Uganda Company, but the impact on production does not seem to have been great and the future of Ugandan vanilla is uncertain.

In the Western Hemisphere, a number of countries have at various times undertaken vanilla production. These include the West Indian islands of Guadeloupe, Dominica, Puerto Rico, St Lucia and St Vincent, the first named being the major source of 'vanillons' or 'Guadeloupe vanilla' from *V. pompona*. However, with the notable exception of Mexico, the volume of exports from the countries in this region has never amounted to very much owing to agronomic and weather problems, production costs and competition from other cash crops.

Trade

Almost all vanilla production enters trade, which is dominated on the supply side by Madagascar, from where over half of the world's requirements of natural vanilla have been obtained since the First World War, and on the demand side by the USA, which has consistently accounted for over half of total world imports. During the nineteenth century, by contrast, European countries took the major portion. The first quarter of the twentieth century saw rapid growth of the world's vanilla trade, US imports increasing from an annual average of 175 tonnes in 1900–04 to about 460 tonnes in 1920–4. Between 1925 and 1938, US imports were more stable at around 500 tonnes per annum. Before the Second World War world consumption was approximately 850 tonnes per year, of which Western and Central Europe (notably the UK, France, Germany, the Netherlands, Switzerland, Austria and Czechoslovakia) accounted for 300 tonnes and other countries 50 tonnes, in comparison with the USA's 500 tonnes. Exporters during the same period were Madagascar (435 tonnes), Tahiti, the Comoros, Mexico (100 tonnes each), Réunion (50 tonnes) and Guadeloupe (12 tonnes), with some others (40 tonnes).

After the war the trade soon re-established itself at pre-war levels and maintained them until the mid-1960s, since when there has been an increase in world trade. This increase is partly due to the greater stability made possible by the Vanilla Alliance, but is mainly because of the legislative measures in the USA and France, which had the effect of reversing the trend whereby any growth in demand for the vanilla flavour tended to be met by synthetic substitutes, rather than by a growth in the natural vanilla trade. Although synthetic vanilla does enter international trade – Canada, for example, exporting large

Table 11.9 *Vanilla beans: Exports of major producing countries, 1915–60 (tonnes)*

	Madagascar and the Comoros[1]	Réunion	Tahiti (French Polynesia)	Mexico	Guadeloupe
1915	234	61	163		
1916	217	66	146		
1917	279	121	166		19
1918	283	87	87		45
1919	357	115	183		17
1920	533	122	102		24
1921	491	83	97		21
1922	518	105	172		12
1923	283	63	76		11
1924	298	83	85		24
1925	411	61	77		31
1926	619	92	47		22
1927	494	87	82		9
1928	681	116	65		10
1929	1092	98	81		3
1930	655	30	72		1
1931	797	50	69		1
1932	866	33	55		3
1933	659	21	52		5
1934	457	34	103		6
1935	463	19	87	115	8
1936	542	64	94	144	13
1937	313	69	107	157	15
1938	376	63	125	177	10
1939	335		206	177	
1940	263	50	120	170	
1941	358		211	209	
1942	18		55	53	
1943	107		104	92	
1944	361		154	181	
1945	486				
1946					
1947					
1948					
1949					
1950					
1951					
1952					
1953	372				
1954	244				
1955	301				
1956	387				
1957	418				
1958	438				
1959	398				
1960	270				

Source: US Foreign Service Reports
      G. Bouriquet: *Le Vanillier et la Vanille* (Paris, 1954)

[1] From 1947 the figures relate solely to Madagascar

quantities to the USA – a very large proportion of synthetic production is consumed in the countries of origin.

The major individual exporters and importers will now be studied in turn. Tables 11.9 and 11.10 show the exports of the major producing countries and their relative share of the world's vanilla trade.

Madagascar, Réunion and the Comoros

Réunion beans usually have a high moisture content and are therefore not well suited to extraction purposes. For this reason exports from this source are destined mainly for France and Central Europe for applications other than extraction, while the majority of exports from Madagascar and the Comoro Islands are destined for the USA (see Table 11.11). In practice, the proportion reaching the USA from these sources is even greater than the figures suggest, since there are some re-exports from France to the USA. Direct shipments to the USA from Madagascar only became of importance towards the end of the Second World War although these had begun ten years earlier. Early in the Second World War, shipping restrictions gave rise to the accumulation of large stocks, which remained high until well after the war. In September 1947 the level of stocks was 1 660 tonnes and steps had to be taken to assure importers of the stability of the Madagascan vanilla market. The setting of a minimum price of $17 per kg for best quality beans, however, induced US importers to place a virtual embargo on Madagascan vanilla. This situation continued until May 1949 when price control was abolished after several price reductions had failed satisfactorily to resolve the deadlock in spite of the burning of 600 tonnes of low-quality beans by the Malagasy Government as a precaution against threatened price collapse. The Government in this instance paid compensation, and arising from this incident the idea of stabilization funds was first conceived as a method of stabilizing the vanilla market. Various minor attempts at stabilization were made in the 1950s, with varying degrees of success, but a more aggressive price-fixing policy in the early 1960s led to the 'Vanilla War', US importers again boycotting Madagascan vanilla imports, which were nearly halved in 1962–3. Price-fixing apart, the US importers resisted Madagascan attempts to by-pass them and create direct contacts with the end-users.

It was in response to the crisis that the aforementioned 1964 meetings were convened, with the formation of the Vanilla Alliance and the development of a rigorous system of production control involving export quotas and price control. After the 1964 St Denis conference, Réunion and the Comoros followed Madagascar in submitting their vanilla marketing to more rigorous control and in organizing co-operative systems and price stabilization funds.

Table 11.10 *Vanilla beans: Exports, by quantity and value, from major producing countries 1960—76*

		1960	1961	1962	1963	1964	1965	1966	1967	1968	1969	1970	1971	1972	1973	1974	1975	1976
Madagascar	Tonnes	269	585	639	290	628	982	885	666	960	1 097	1 216	1 160	1 215	720	1 353(a)	1 200(a)	1 000(a)
	£'000	2 384	2 740	3 137	1 516	2 314	3 556	3 230	2 446	4 262	4 898	5 408	5 280	6 054	4 372	7 960	8 102(a)	8 858
The Comoros(a)	Tonnes	80	90	48	207	175	167	134	145	138	207	144	206	207	34	160	211	210
	£'000	517	298	228	889	620	575	470	510	590	933	605	907	976	184	844	1 448	1 827
Réunion	Tonnes	31	42	33	60	44(a)	58	16	18	25	32(a)	26(a)	31(a)	21(a)	21(a)	4(a)	8(a)	70(a)
	£'000	234	186	171	276	161	207	64	70	122	149	122	148	119	129	24	63	178
Indonesia	Tonnes	13(a)	23(a)	45(a)	25(a)	39(a)	59(a)	56(a)	108	86	15	216	135	127(a)	317	60(a)	237	334
	£'000	...	39	93	43	72	107	100	118	89	16	277	123	129	327	59	323	560
Mexico	Tonnes	114(a)	103(a)	39(a)	22(a)	17(a)	70	22	39	54(a)	18(a)	22	23	18	19	15(a)	1(a)	–(a)
	£'000	...	282	104	71	50	217	57	113	193	65	70	3	64	48	37	1	–
French Polynesia	Tonnes	178	223	209	223	165(a)	132	115	59	67	55	33	27	25	25(a)	12(a)	8	8(a)
	£'000	743	711	580	477	425	500	461	291	348	290	195	166	153	155	117	97	122
Seychelles	Tonnes	8	4	7	2	1	1	5	2	1	...	1	...	1	–	–	–	...
	£'000	41	11	21	6	4	4	13	4	2	...	2	...	2	–	–	–	...
Uganda	Tonnes	2	3	1	1	2(a)	3(a)	6	3	3	8	2	1	1	–	–	–	–
	£'000	13	13	5	4	7	7	18	9	10	29	15	12	5	–	–	–	–
German Fed. Rep. (Re-exports)	Tonnes	1	1	12	7	13	20	29	51	59	92	72	68	62	78	92	72	127
	£'000	3	2	68	38	56	77	122	213	285	347	344	344	347	527	640	605	1 328

Source: Annual trade figures of above countries, except those marked (a) which are taken from *FAO Trade Yearbook*
– nil or negligible
... not available

Table 11.11 *Vanilla beans: Exports, by quantity and value, from Madagascar, 1960–76*

		1960	1961	1962	1963	1964	1965	1966	1967	1968	1969	1970	1971	1972	1973	1974	1975	1976
USA	Tonnes	227	483	498	257	561	813	683	423	675	746	753	803	821	340	...	...	...
	£'000	5 669	6 358	6 857	3 767	5 768	8 208	6 965	4 327	7 243	8 175	8 015	8 860	10 134	4 466	...	...	...
France	Tonnes	30	75	111	26	35	106	135	147	158	219	276	226	238	230	...	...	...
	£'000	734	974	1 523	424	359	1 101	1 383	1 509	1 709	2 255	2 960	2 546	3 037	3 318	...	...	...
German Fed. Rep.	Tonnes	10	23	28	5	14	54	58	71	106	109	135	91	116	102	...	...	...
	£'000	245	306	398	73	50	554	589	728	1 130	1 118	1 446	1 017	1 477	1 477	...	...	...
UK	Tonnes	2	3	1	–	4	6	3	–	–	–	2	–	2	–	...	...	...
	£'000	–	–	–	–	–	–	–	–	–	–	22	–	26	–	...	...	...
Canada	Tonnes	–	–	–	–	10	–	2	4	1	8	28	26	13	–	...	...	...
	£'000	–	–	–	–	104	–	21	41	11	86	298	295	165	–	...	...	...
Japan	Tonnes	...	.:	...	...	...	...	...	...	...	...	7	7	11	30	...	...	...
	£'000	...	...	...	...	...	...	...	...	...	...	92	81	144	431	...	...	...
Australia	Tonnes	...	...	...	...	...	...	...	...	...	...	13	6	13	17	...	...	...
	£'000	...	...	...	...	...	...	...	...	...	...	133	69	159	248	...	...	...
Total*	Tonnes	269	585	640	292	628	984	885	666	961	1 097	1 216	1 160	1 215	720	1 353	1 200[2]	1 000[1]
	£'000	6 703	7 695	8 821	4 279	6 961	9 946	9 045	6 825	10 326	11 768	12 979	12 871	15 142	9 956	...	...	...

Source: 1960–66 *Commerce Exterieur*
1966–70 *Tropical Products Quarterly*
1970– *Annual Trade Report of Madagascar*
FAO Yearbook, 1976

(1) FAO estimate

(2) Unofficial estimate

– nil or negligible

... not available

* In many cases, the total includes figures for countries not shown separately above

Other exporters

Mexico, as already indicated, was formerly a substantial producer of vanilla beans, mainly for the US market. Mexican vanilla, particularly during the 1960s, suffered strong competition from the cheaper but comparable Bourbon variety which, along with Indonesian production, gained some of the sales lost by Mexico. Most of Indonesia's production is absorbed by the US market, but the growing Asian market, Japanese particularly, will no doubt provide an increasing outlet for Indonesia's growing production. Vanilla beans from Tahiti are exported mainly to Europe.

Imports into the USA

The American market has long been distinguished by its relative stability as well as size. For example, imports in 1909 and 1959 were approximately equal at about 500 tonnes. The dominance of this importer is reinforced by the fact it imports vanilla from all the major producing countries, especially from Madagascar, and, following the decline of the Mexican trade, from Indonesia (see Table 11.12).

Table 11.12 *Vanilla Beans: Average annual imports into the USA, 1901–75 (tonnes)*

1901–05	208
1906–10	391
1911–15	437
1916–20	468
1921–25	446
1926–30	565
1931–35	568
1936–40	500
1941–45	501
1946–50	724
1951–55	569
1956–60	540
1961–65	707
1966–70	858
1971–75	984

Source: US Foreign Trade Statistics

Since the mid-1960s American imports have exhibited a gradual increase, annual imports increasing from 740 tonnes in 1964 to 1 500 tonnes in 1977 (see Table 11.13). This is mainly the effect of legislation by the US Congress regarding labelling requirements for frozen desserts, which has reflected the growing preference of American consumers for natural food additives and flavourings, particularly in ice cream. The *US Vanilla Extract Standard* of 1963 and the *US Frozen*

Table 11.13 *Vanilla beans: Imports into the USA, 1954–77 (tonnes)*

	1954	1955	1956	1957	1958	1959	1960	1961	1962	1963	1964	1965	1966	1967	1968	1969	1970	1971	1972	1973	1974	1975	1976	1977
Madagascar	272	293	425	422	432	319	332	457	579	391	620	792	716	457	866	780	880	653	866	...	867	652	587	1 049
Indonesia	19	6	6	3	22	14	19	25	59	25	39	60	56	59	66	25	111	106	129	...	59	197	290	405
The Comoros and Réunion	...	...	...	...	...	...	...	...	...	...	...	...	...	...	–	–	–	–	–	...	13	108	124	87
Mexico	98	96	82	99	88	132	97	91	34	14	11	30	14	41	36	34	14	12	12	...	10	–	–	2
France	...	...	1	5	9	7	12	3	3	17	8	27	5	4	1	–	–	–	4	...	...	–	10	–
Malaysia	...	...	...	...	...	...	...	...	...	2	21	45	15	5	7	13	3	3	–	...	25	–	–	–
French Polynesia	20	34	25	37	31	40	8	26	29	28	18	9	11	10	7	7	2	3	–	...	2	2	3	6
Uganda	1	...	6	1	2	2	3	1	6	...	...	2	4	2	3	1	6	4	2	...	...	...	–	1
Total*	423	434	571	591	591	510	474	615	716	483	740	979	841	582	992	863	1 016	850	1 073	1 056	977	962	1 014	1 553

Source: US Foreign Trade Reports
        USDA Foreign Agricultural Circulars

*   In some cases, the total includes figures for countries not shown separately above
–   nil or negligible
...   not available

Desserts Standards of 1965 were the main measures passed to this end. It is likely that the impact on the trade would have been even greater had it not been for lack of confidence regarding future price levels and supply stability. Not until 1966 did the long-expected boom begin, slowly, to appear. Thereafter growth was steady and by 1973 one estimate suggested that the consumption of natural vanilla by the ice-cream industry had at least doubled since the imposition of the Food and Drug Administration's new standards.

Another influence in the USA market was the 'Vanillamark' programme, sponsored by the Vanilla Alliance and operating in Europe from 1968 and in the USA from 1971. By early 1976 over 700 products had been licensed to display the 'Vanillamark', which assures the consumer that the produce is flavoured solely with natural vanilla. This measure did much to inform and educate the consumer, and made labelling less confusing.

Imports into France

For many years all the major vanilla bean producers, except Mexico, were part of the French Union, for it was the growing demand in the last century which encouraged production in the dependencies. Not only did domestic consumption increase substantially, but a large entrepôt trade developed. However, this entrepôt trade began to decline as consumers elsewhere increasingly began to import direct from producers, and, in comparison with a re-export trade of 500 tonnes in the inter-war years, the average in the mid-1950s was 150 tonnes and in the late 1950s it was 50 tonnes. France nevertheless remains the largest market for vanilla beans after the USA, with a considerable and consistent increase in imports since the early 1960s, as Table 11.14 illustrates. This growth has been facilitated by an Act passed in 1966–7 whereby the use of the word 'vanilla' is forbidden except in reference to the natural product, the use of synthetic vanilla being only permitted subject to clear labelling to that effect.

The source of French imports is also of interest in that Tahiti provided over 50 per cent of French imports in most of the 1960s, but imports from this source are now insignificant. The dominant source of French imports is Madagascar, followed by the Comoro Islands and Réunion.

Imports into the German Federal Republic

West Germany is now the third largest importer of vanilla beans. Up until 1939 the domestic market was supplied mainly by French re-exports, but after the war direct contacts with the producers, especially Madagascar and the Comoros, began to be made. Even an entrepôt trade began in Hamburg, the USA being the most common importer of German re-exports. Through the 1950s and 1960s there was a steady increase in imports, from 18 tonnes in 1954 to 120 tonnes in 1968. In the

Table 11.14 *Vanilla beans: Imports into France, 1954–77 (tonnes)*

	1954	1955	1956	1957	1958	1959	1960	1961	1962	1963	1964	1965	1966	1967	1968	1969	1970	1971	1972	1973	1974	1975	1976	1977[1]
French Polynesia	27	34	45	40	50	49	62	74	80	91	83	74	57	43	30	39	15	15	10	10	3	–	2	2
Madagascar	38	36	36	35	28	23	11	21	38	29	21	59	81	101	98	164	191	187	225	243	229	152	268	336
Réunion	7	9	16	22	16	11	12	10	9	9	16	16	9	8	16	22	22	28	16	18	3	8	18	13
The Comoros	–	–	–	–	–	–	10	15	5	9	7	10	8	17	30	7	6	13	11	10	41	37	30	56
Guadeloupe	–	–	–	–	–	1	1	–	1	3	2	–	–	–	–	–	–	–	–	–	–	–	–	–
Indonesia	–	–	–	–	–	–	–	1	3	2	–	–	–	–	–	–	–	–	–	–	–	–	–	–
Total*	75	81	99	97	96	88	96	125	136	144	130	159	155	171	174	233	234	243	262	296	277	199	325	417

Source: Statistiques du Commerce Exterieur
– nil or negligible
1 Preliminary
* In some cases, the total includes figures for countries not shown separately above

Table 11.15 *Vanilla beans: Imports into the Federal Republic of Germany, 1954–76 (tonnes)*

	1954	1955	1956	1957	1958	1959	1960	1961	1962	1963	1964	1965	1966	1967	1968	1969	1970	1971	1972	1973	1974	1975	1976
Madagascar	17	20	34	24	30	31	21	21	39	13	18	49	52	65	100	102	95	98	99	98	125	99	164
Réunion	1	2	1	2	3	6	2	7	13	29	35	20	36	32	3	1	1	2	1	–	–	–	–
French Polynesia							8	4	3	6	7	4	4	4	6	3	2	2	3	3	5	3	3
France									1	3	3	2	2	2	2	3	3	3	3	9	14	19	18
The Comoros															12	9	15	5	1	9	16	2	4
Total*	18	22	36	28	36	39	32	40	57	51	63	75	95	103	123	118	118	113	111	114	160	125	192

Source: Aussenhandel – Spezialhandel nach Waren und Ländern
* Where no figures is given statistics were unavailable. Totals include figures for some countries not listed separately.

Table 11.16 Vanilla beans: Imports into the UK, 1951–76 (tonnes)

	Average 1951–55	Average 1956–60	Average 1961–65	Average 1966–70	1970	1971	1972	1973	1974	1975	1976
Seychelles	0.3	3.6	2.3	1.7	0.6	0.5	0.2	–	–	–	–
Uganda	1.2	2.1	1.0	0.3	1.4·	–	0.7	–	–	2.3	1.5
Madagascar	1.5	0.8	2.6	4.7	2.1	–	0.6	–	1.4	–	0.7
Réunion	5.5	4.3	0.7	0.8	1.1	–	–	–	–	–	–
French Polynesia	1.7	2.3	2.0	1.5	1.0	0.4	0.3	0.4	–	0.2	–
France	20.5	8.1	4.7	7.5	9.1	12.0	14.4	15.7	17.2	2.4	14.6
German Fed. Rep.	–	6.3	7.1	5.4	3.7	3.0	1.3	4.5	8.6	7.8	9.1
Total*	31.3	27.7	20.4	22.2	20.2	16.0	17.6	22.0	28.1	16.2	27.9

Source: Tropical Products Quarterly
  UK imports statistics
– nil or negligible
* In many cases, the total includes figures for countries not shown separately above

early 1970s imports tended to stabilize in the region of 110–120 tonnes per annum, but since 1973 rose rapidly and averaged 159 tonnes per annum during the period 1974–6 (see Table 11.15). The main supplier is Madagascar, providing over 75 per cent of West Germany's requirements.

Imports into the UK

The UK has never been a major consumer of natural vanilla, imports fluctuating in the range of 15–30 tonnes per annum, or 2 per cent of world trade. Sizable quantities used to be imported from Réunion, and small quantities have been taken from French Polynesia and the Commonwealth, including the Seychelles and Uganda, but these are no longer of any significance. A trend towards increased supplies from Madagascar in the 1960s was reversed during the 1970s. France was the dominant supplier in the 1950s, but since then West Germany has also become important, accounting currently for one-third of the UK market (see Table 11.16).

Other importers

There appear to be several small but expanding markets for vanilla. The most important is Japan, whose imports rose from 10 tonnes in 1965 to 40 tonnes in 1970 and have averaged 35 tonnes annually between 1970 and 1974, rising to 62 tonnes in 1976. France used to be Japan's main supplier, but this is decreasingly true. Canada's annual imports averaged 40 tonnes between 1964 and 1969, the USA being the main supplier, since when average annual imports have risen to 63 tonnes for the period 1970–76 (see Table 11.17).

During the period 1971–75 average annual imports of other were: Denmark, 13 tonnes; Italy, 15 tonnes; the Netherlands, 14 tonnes; Switzerland, 18 tonnes; Poland, 12 tonnes; Saudi Arabia, 17 tonnes; and Australia, 20 tonnes.

Market structure

Prior to the intervention in the 1960s of the Malagasy Government in the marketing process, the structure of the vanilla market was similar in almost all producing countries, the marketing chain beginning with the grower and progressing through buyer, curer and exporter to the importers and processors in the importing countries. However, much was changed by the Malagasy Government, and in every year since 1964 there has been a meeting between the Vanilla Alliance and the representatives of vanilla importers and users (e.g. the Vanilla Bean Association of America, the Flavouring Extract Manufacturers' Association, and the Syndicat Européen du Commerce des Vanilles). The Vanilla Alliance forms a common position regarding quantities and prices, and the meetings thus take the form less of negotiations than

Table 11.17 *Vanilla beans: Imports into selected countries, 1960–76*

		1960	1961	1962	1963	1964	1965	1966	1967	1968	1969	1970	1971	1972	1973	1974	1975	1976
USA	Tonnes	474	615	716	483	740	979	841	582	992	863	1 016	850	1 073	1 056	977	962	1 014
	£'000	4 068	2 751	3 338	2 367	2 686	3 383	2 938	2 063	4 098	3 779	4 320	3 441	4 489	5 087	5 443	6 273	8 296
France	Tonnes	96	125	136	144	130	159	155	171	174	233	234	243	262	296	277	199	325
	£'000	635	551	587	538	416	611	614	714	850	1 125	1 164	1 257	1 369	1 827	1 782	1 631	3 242
German Fed. Rep.	Tonnes	32	40	57	51	62	75	95	103	120	118	118	113	111	114	160	125	192
	£'000	280	204	282	249	227	253	359	396	558	510	522	521	562	675	945	946	1 819
Canada	Tonnes	...	...	...	...	47	29	39	38	41	43	53	46	47	53	129	50	65
	£'000	...	...	...	...	179	103	152	148	190	202	249	219	235	295	365	358	612
Japan	Tonnes	...	...	...	...	10	10	13	14	17	22	40	30	27	38	39	23	62
	£'000	...	...	...	...	47	44	55	62	89	102	216	157	148	243	252	198	555
UK	Tonnes	26	24	24	14	21	19	24	20	23	25	20	16	18	22	28	16	28
	£'000	205	127	121	73	85	73	93	83	109	115	94	84	93	128	160	115	257
Australia[1]	Tonnes	...	...	...	...	...	20	11	17	18	18	19	18	28	18	28	23	14
	£'000	...	...	...	...	...	59	40	56	69	67	80	68	92	54	182	166	120

Source: Annual trade figures of above countries
(1) Not separately specified 1960–4.
... not available

of exchanges of information on world market movements. Conditions governing the timing of purchases, receipt of revenue, size of contracts, failure to fulfil obligations, and so on, are laid down with each agreement. It will therefore be clear that most of the vanilla trade is closely regulated by governmental and quasi-governmental agencies, and even the US importers, for a long time staunch opponents of controls, began to realize the advantages. Vanilla producers outside the Vanilla Alliance export *via* the normal network of shippers, brokers, dealers and merchants, which dominates the trade in other spices.

Imports into the consuming countries are controlled by a small number of dealers and processors, who keep in close contact with one another through their trade associations. In the USA McCormicks, the large spice distributor and processing company, is the major importer of vanilla, while commercial rules and regulations are administered by the aforementioned Vanilla Bean Association. Most of the vanilla beans are processed into extract by a few large firms. In West Germany the bulk of the vanilla trade is handled by two importing firms in Hamburg, while in France imports pass through one of four official brokers.

Until the Second World War a substantial entrepôt trade in vanilla existed, and France's role has already been mentioned. The reason it declined was that currency restrictions in the wake of the war made direct trade between producers and consumers more profitable, although the relatively small amount of re-export trade which remains seems to be stable both in France and in West Germany. Processed vanilla products, such as vanilla extract, tinctures and absolutes, are also exported from the major consuming countries but there are no available figures on the size of this trade.

Prices

It will already be clear that vanilla's history has been characterized by relatively stable demand and widely fluctuating supplies. The price of vanilla, for reasons discussed, is comparatively price-elastic but demand is inelastic, supply and a very low price may do nothing to help clear a glutted market although excessively high prices can damp down the demand, and have often been known to do so. The result of the cobweb cycle, as exhibited by the vanilla market, has caused vanilla to acquire a reputation for being more prone to fluctuations than many other tropical products and therefore to be subject to a greater degree of risk, both for grower and for exporter.

Until recently prices on the vanilla market have fluctuated severely. For example, Bourbon vanilla was marketed at $1.95 per kg in 1930 and $30 per kg in 1959 (f.o.b. Madagascar), in spite of the existence of synthetic substitutes whose prices have remained very low and stable; and in the 1960s vanillin derived from lignin was priced in the range

$6.60-7.20$ per kg, while vanilla bean prices varied between \$9 and \$35 per kg. In the early 1970s there was considerable overproduction of synthetic vanillin. New plants were opened in response to an anticipated increase in demand from the pharmaceutical industry but the demand failed to materialize at the expected time. The price of vanillin was thus forced downwards. In the late 1970s the opposite situation applied on account of production problems, such as mechanical difficulties and strikes, but in spite of the shortage the producers were still maintaining stable price levels of around $9-10$ per kg.

On the whole, the Vanilla Alliance's policies have helped stabilize natural vanilla prices (see Tables 11.18–11.20) and the price of vanilla from other sources has tended to follow the Bourbon prices. Vanilla price data must however be treated with great care, since vanilla can be traded in several forms. For example, synthetic vanilla formulations are often much more concentrated than natural vanilla, which in turn varies not only between sources but between grades. As an example of the price differential between the various grades of vanilla beans, the following were the prices fixed by the Vanilla Alliance at the 1974–5 annual conference:

	US	Europe
1st grade per kg f.o.b	\$14.90	71.25 francs
2nd grade per kg f.o.b.	\$14.70	70.25 francs
3rd grade per kg f.o.b.	\$14.50	69.00 francs

Table 11.18 *Vanilla beans: Quarterly and annual average prices, c.i.f. New York, 1964–77* (£ per tonne)

		Quarters				Annual
		I	II	III	IV	average
Madagascar	1964	5 027	4 420	4 4 332	4 034	4 472
	1965	4 034	3 946	4 090	4 233	4 078
	1966	4 233	4 332	4 332	4 332	4 322
	1967	4 263	4 263	4 263	4 263	4 263
	1968	5 029	5 067	5 144	5 144	5 096
	1969	5 144	5 144	5 144	5 144	5 144
	1970	5 144	5 144	5 144	5 144	5 144
	1971	5 076	5 394	5 394	5 394	5 315
	1972	5 243	6 068	6 058	6 058	5 854
	1973	6 181	6 181	6 181	6 234	6 198
	1974	6 645	6 645	6 763	6 763	6 704
	1975	6 615	7 700	8 457	8 812	7 896
	1976	9 000	9 961	10 529	11 992	10 298
	1977	11 555	12 759	...	...	...

Source: Oil Paint and Drug Reporter (now *Chemical Marketing Reporter*)

... not available

Table 11.19: *Vanilla beans: Approximate spot prices, New York, early March 1966–78 (cents per pound)*

	1966	1967	1968	1969	1970	1971	1972	1973	1974	1975	1976	1977	1978
Bourbon	525–550	520–535	550–575	550–560	550–560	560–570	560–570	660–680	675–700	785–810	900–950	900–950	1043
Mexican	...	...	...	625–650	625–650	800	800	700–750	700–750	700–750	...	...	...
Tahitian	625–650	625–650	725–750	775–800	700	950	950	925–950	950–975	1 125	1 600	1 600	1 800
Java	435–475	500–510	500–510	535–545	530	930	930	600–700	630–655	725–750	800	1 050	550

Source: USDA Foreign Agriculture Circular
... not quoted, or data not available

Table 11.20   *Green vanilla: Price received by Madagascan producers, 1952–77 (MG francs per kg.)*

1952	200
1953	250
1954	300
1955	375
1956	400
1957	450
1958	500
1959	1 000
1960	300
1961	275
1962	475
1963	350
1964	175
1965	175
1966	185
1967	130
1968	150
1969	...
1970	...
1971	...
1972	220
1973	220
1974	240
1975	250
1976	...
1977	...

Sources: *Marchés Tropicaux et Mediterranéens*—various issues

... not available

Sometimes a final processor may require vanilla beans of a specific grade from a specific source, but if the required supplies are short the quoted spot price can be strongly influenced. However, the vanilla trade is conducted mainly on a 'forward' basis, and therefore spot prices are not a reliable guide to the state of the market. In the late 1970s price trends have been upward, reflecting the Vanilla Alliance's policy of raising export prices in the face of inflationary pressures and currency instability; but the Alliance has also been flexible, having, for example, agreed in July 1973 to rescind a 20 per cent price increase after opposition from major importers. In mid-1976, however, the official price f.o.b. Madagascar was raised to $19.80 per kg, followed by further reported increases to $23.00 per kg in 1977 and $30.00 per kg in mid-1978.

Trends in consumption and prospects

The traditional applications of vanilla, as a food flavouring in industry and in the kitchen, are well known. In the USA, the UK and France vanilla-flavoured ice-cream accounts for over half the total ice-cream output, and, although only a relatively small proportion of the flavouring material so used is in fact natural vanilla, this proportion is growing as a result of the activities of the US Food and Drug Administration in the 1960s. In other uses too, such as chocolate, biscuit and confectionery manufacture, natural vanilla may be gaining ground slightly. In perfumery and pharmaceuticals Tahiti vanilla, which has a characteristic odour of heliotropin, is preferred.

Although overall usage is extensive, a precise breakdown of the pattern of natural and synthetic vanilla consumption as between the various end-users cannot be ascertained to any worthwhile degree of accuracy. Where domestic use of the vanilla flavour in extract form is concerned, it is likely that the synthetics hold the field almost exclusively, there being little or no natural vanilla in the familiar liquid household product. In Continental Europe, however, a large proportion of unprocessed natural vanilla is consumed domestically; in France the proportion is 50 per cent or higher, often in the form of vanilla pods. But despite the resurgence in the domestic use of many spices, the future growth of the market for natural vanilla in its domestic applications remains uncertain, the growth of the prepared-foods market having checked sales of vanilla extract.

During most of the twentieth century there has been a relatively stable demand for natural vanilla, but the aggregate demand has not kept pace with rising incomes and population. This initially seems surprising when one considers that demand for vanilla is governed by demand for the sort of final products, such as ice-cream, which are luxuries and which one would therefore expect to exhibit elastic demand in relation to income. The explanation lies simply in the advance of synthetic vanilla, particularly vanillin derived from lignin *via* the wood-pulping industry. However, the characteristic, well-rounded, subtle flavour of natural vanilla has ensured a continued demand in spite of the competition from the cheaper synthetic vanilla formulations, and indeed natural vanilla is often blended with synthetic vanillin in order to improve the overall aroma and flavour character of the synthetic product.

It will be clear that, with synthetic vanilla still dominating the market, only a very small degree of substitution of the natural product for a previously used synthetic would cause a major impact in demand for vanilla beans. The full force of this truth will be appreciated when it is realized that if the increased annual demand for the vanilla flavour is estimated at 5 per cent and this had to be satisfied entirely from natural sources alone, production would have to double in the first year and increase by as much in absolute terms in subsequent years: at this rate the whole of Madagascar's stocks, for example, could be liquidated in one year. Such an eventuality can certainly not be foreseen in practice, but an increasing number of consumers can detect the difference between natural and synthetic vanilla, so substitution is likely to continue to take place in favour of the natural product rather than the reverse. Provided that the Vanilla Alliance succeeds in smoothing out the worst of the trade fluctuations, there is no reason to believe that the future of the market for natural vanilla is other than secure.

References

Anon. (Ets. Mero et Boyveau — Bernard et Honnorat), (1977) 'Determination par chromatographie des amino-acides dans les extraits de vanille Bourbon (*Vanilla planifolia*)', *Parfums, Cosmetiques, Aromes*, **18**, 77–80.

Anwar, M.H. (1963) 'Paper chromatography of monohydroxyphenols in vanilla extract', *Analyt. Chem.*, **35**, 1974–6.

Arana, F.E. (1940) *Chemistry of Vanilla*, USDA Fed. Expt. Station, Mayaguez, Puerto Rico; Report for 1939, 2–14, Washington DC: USDA.

Arana, F.E. (1943) 'Action of beta-glucosidase in the curing of vanilla', *Food Res.* **8**, 343–51.

Arana, F.E. (1944) *Vanilla Curing and its Chemistry*, USDA Fed. Expt. Station, Mayaguez, Puerto Rico; Bulletin No. 42 (October), Washington DC: USDA.

Arana, F.E. (1945) *Vanilla Curing*, USDA Fed. Expt. Station, Mayaguez, Puerto Rico; Circular No. 25 (May), Washington DC: USDA

Arctander, S. (1960) *Perfume and Flavour Materials of Natural Origin*, Elizabeth, N.J.: Published by the author.

Association of Official Analytical Chemists (1975) *Official Methods of Analysis*, 12th edn, Washington DC: A.O.A.C.

Balls, A.K. and Arana, F.E. (1941a) 'Determination of the significance of phenols in vanilla extract', *J. Assoc. Offic. Agric. Chemists*, **24**, 507–12.

Balls, A.K. and Arana, F.E. (1941b) 'The curing of vanilla', *Ind. Eng. Chem.*, **33**, 1073–5.

Blomquist, V.H., Kovach, E. I and Johnson, A.R. (1965) 'Authentic vanilla extracts: Comparison of analyses of commercial samples with their laboratory prepared analogues', *J. Assoc. Offic. Agric. Chemists*, **48**, 1202–11.

Bohnsack, H. (1965) 'Uber die Inhaltstoffe der Bourbon-Vanillischote (1 Teil) und Vanillin — butylenglycolid', *Riechstoffe, Aromen, Koeperpflegemittel*, **15**, 284–7.

Bohnsack, H. (1967) 'Uber die Inhaltstoffe der Bourbon-Vanilleschote (4 Teil)', *Riechstoffe, Aromen, Koeperflegemittel*, **17**, 133–6.

Bohnsack, H. (1971a) 'Uber die Inhaltstoffe der Bourbon-Vanilleschote (5 Teil)', *Riechstoffe, Aromen, Koerperflegemittel*, **21**, 125–8.

Bohnsack, H. (1971b) 'Uber die Inhaltstoffe der Bourbon-Vanilleschote (6 Teil): Neutraloel', *Riechstoffe, Aromen, Koerperflegemittel*, **21**, 163–6.

Bohnsack, H. and Siebert, W. (1965) 'Uber Inhaltstoffe der Bourbon-Vanilleschote (2 Teil). p-Hydroxybenzyl-alkohol und p-hydroxybenzylmethyl aether', *Riechstoffe, Aromen, Koeperflegemittel*, **15**, 321–4

Bonnet, G. (1968) 'Separation chromatographique en phase gazeuse et sur couche mince de quelques composes a saveur vanillee', *Ann. Fals. Exp. Chim.*, **61**, 360–71.

Bouriquet, G. (ed.) (1954) *Le Vanillier et la Vanille dans le Monde*, Paris: Editions Paul Lechavalier.

Broderick J.J. (1955a) 'The chemistry of vanilla', *Coffee and Tea Ind.*, 59–60 (Feb.), 53–58 (March).

Broderick, J.J. (1955b) 'Vanilla extract manufacture. A guide to choice of method', *Food Manuf.* (Feb.), 65–68.

Broderick, J.J. (1956) 'The science of curing vanilla', *Food Technol.*, 184–7.

Bui-Xuan-Nhuan (1954) 'Le Vanillism', in *Le Vanillier et la Vanille*, (ed. G. Bouriquet).

Busse, W. (1900) 'Ueber die Bildung des Vanillins und der Vanillefrucht', *Zeits, Untersuch, Nahr, Genussmtl.*, **3**, 21–5.

Cernuda, C.F. and Loustalot, A.J. (1948) *Vanilla Curing*, USDA Fed. Expt. Station, Mayaguez, Puerto Rico; Report for 1947 (Oct. 1948), Washington DC: USDA.

Chalot, C. and Bernard, U. (1920) *Culture et Preparation de la Vanille*, Paris: E. Larose.

Chevalier, M., Prat, Y. and Navellier, P. (1972) 'Caracterisation par chromatographie en couche mince des constituents aromatiques de la vanille dans les glaces et creme glaces', *Ann. Fals. Exp. Chim.*, 12–16.

Childers, N.F. and Cibes, H.R. (1948) *Vanilla Culture in Puerto Rico*, USDA Fed. Expt. Station, Mayaguez, Puerto Rico; Circular No. 28 (June 1948), Washington DC: USDA.

Chovin, P., Stoll, S. and Bouteville, Y. (1954) 'Un compasant naturel de la Vanille: L'aldehyde p-hydroxybenzoique. Extraction, caracterisation', *Ann. Fals. Fraud.*, **47** 187–91.

Commonwealth Secretariat (1973) *Plantation Crops*, London: Commonwealth Secretariat.

Correll, D.S. (1953) 'Vanilla–Its botany, history, cultivation and economic import', *Econ. Bot.*, **7**, 291–358.

Cowley, E. (1973) 'Vanilla and its uses', *Proceedings of the Conference on Spices*, London, April 1972, pp 79–84, London: Tropical Products Institute.

Dupart, R. (1938), *L'Archipel des Seychelles. Ses Resources Naturelles, Sa Foune Entomologique et Son Evolution Economique*, Manartes.

Fitelseon, J. (1963) 'Organic acids in vanilla extract', *J. Assoc. Offic. Agric. Chemists*, **46**, 626–33.

Fitelson, J. and Bowden, G. L. (1968), 'Determination of organic acids in vanilla extracts by GLC separation of trimethylsylated derivatives', *J. Assoc. Offic. Agric. Chemists*, **51** 1224–31.

Frere, J. (1954) 'Le Conditionnement', in *Le Vanillier et la Vanille*, (ed. G. Bouriquet).

Galetto, W.G. and Hoffmann, P.G. (1978) 'Some benzyl ethers present in the extract of vanilla (*Vanilla planifolia*)', *J. Agric. Food Chem.*, **26**, 195–7.

Garros-Patin, J. and Hahn, J. (1954) 'Chimie de la Vanille', in *Le Vanillier et la Vanille*, (ed. G. Bouriquet).

Gnadinger, C.B. (1925) 'Identification of sources of vanilla extracts', *J. Ind. Eng. Chem.*, **17**, 303–4.

Gnadinger, C.B. (1927) *Vanilla*, Minneapolis, Minn.: McLaughlin, Gormley, King, Co.

Gobley, T.W. (1858) 'Recherches sur la principe odorant de la vanille', *J. Pharm. Chim.*, III, **34**, 401–5.

Goris, M.A. (1924) 'Sur la composition chimique des fruits verts de vanille et la mode formation du parfum de la vanille', *Compt. Rend.*, **179**, 70–2.

Goris, M.A. (1947) 'Formation du parfum de la vanille', *Ind. Parfumerie*, **2**, 4–12.

Gregory, L.E., Murray, H.G. and Colberg, C. (1967) 'Parthenocarpic pod development by *Vanilla planifolia* Andrews induced with growth-regulating chemicals', *Econ. Bot.*, **21**, 351–7.

Hibon, Th. E. (1966) 'Connaissance de la vanille', *J. Agric.Trop.*, **13**, 353–84.

Hoover, C.L. (1926) 'The vanilla industry of Netherlands India', *The Spice Mill*, **49**, 922–6.

Irvine, J.E. and Delfel, N.E. (1961) 'Flowering behaviour of vanilla', *Nature*, 190, 366.

Jackson, H.W. (1966) 'Gas chromatographic analysis of vanilla extracts', *J. Gas. Chromat.* May, 196–7.

Janot, M.M. (1954) 'Formation du Parfum de la Vanille', in *Le Vanillier et la Vanille* (ed. G. Bouriquet).

Jensen, W.V. (1970) 'Marketing of vanilla beans *Vanilla planifolia* Andrews and *V. tahitensis* J.W. Moore', *Acta Hort.*: 1st East African Hort. Symposium, Kampala, Uganda; 23–24 Feb. 1970, 158–166.

Jones, M.A. and Vincente, G.C. (1949a) 'Criteria for testing vanilla in relation to killing and curing methods', *J. Agric. Res.*, 78, 425–34.

Jones, M.A. and Vincente, G.C. (1949b) 'Inactivation and vacuum filtration of vanilla enzyme systems', *J. Agric. Res.*, 78, 435–43.

Jones, M.A. and Vincente, G.C. (1949c) 'Quality of cured vanilla in relation to some natural factors', *J. Agric. Res.*, 78, 445–50.

Kahan, S. and Fitelson, J. (1964) 'Chromatographic detection of flavour additives in vanilla extract', *J. Assoc. Offic. Agric Chemists*, 47, 551–4.

Kleinert, J. (1963) 'Vanille und Vanillin', *Gordian*, 53, 809–14, 840–54, 892–8.

Klimes, I. and Lamparsky, D. (1976) 'Vanilla volatiles – A comprehensive analysis', *Int. Flav. Food Additives*, Nov./Dec., 272–91.

Knudson, L. (1950) 'Germination of seeds of vanilla', *Amer. J. Bot.*, 37, 241–7.

Lecompte, H. (1913) 'Formation de la vanilline dans la vanille', *Agr. Prat. des Pays Chauds*, 13, 3–14.

Lhugenot, J.C., Maume, B.F. and Baron, C. (1971). 'Gas chromatographic and mass spectrometic study of vanilla related compounds', *Chromatographia*, 4, 204–8.

Lionnet, J.F.G. (1958–9) 'Seychelles vanilla', *World Crops*, 10, 441–4; 11, 15–17.

Mallory, L.D. and Cochran, W.P. (1941) 'Mexican vanilla production and trade', USDA *Foreign Agric.*, 5, 469–88.

Mallory, L.D. and Walter, K. (1942) 'Mexico's vanilla production', US. Dept. Commerce, *Foreign Commerce Weekly*, 7 (1), 8–10, 23.

Martin, G.E., Dyer, R., Jansen, J. and Sahn, M. (1975) 'Determining the authenticity of vanilla extracts', *Food Technol.*, 29, 54–9.

Martin, G.E., Ethridge, M.W. and Kaiser, F.E. (1977) 'Determining the authenticity of vanilla extracts', *J. Food Sci.*, 42, 1580–3.

Meili, M. and Chaveron, H. (1976) 'Examen des extraits de vanille et des produits et alimentaires aromatises a l'aide de ces extraits', *Ann. Fals. Exp. Chim.*, 69, 745–56.

Merory, J. (1956) '40% more flavour in improved vanilla process', *Food Eng.* (May), 91, 93, 160.

Merory, J. (1968) *Food Flavourings. Composition, Manufacture and Use*, Westport, Conn.: Avi Publishing Co.

Morison-Smith, D. (1964) 'Determination of compounds related to vanillin in vanilla extracts', *J. Assoc. Offic. Agric. Chemists*, 47, 808–15.

Naves, Y.R. (1974) *Technologie et Chimie des Parfums Naturels*, Paris: Masson et Cie.

Oliver, R. (1973) 'Methods for the study of the aromatic components of vanilla extracts', *Proceedings of the Conference on Spices*, London, 10–14 April, 1972, London: Tropical Products Institute.

Potter, R.H. (1971) 'Non-vanillin volatiles in vanilla extracts', *J. Assoc. Offic. Agric. Chemists*, 54, 39–41.

Prat, Y. and Stoll, S. (1968) 'Tests specifiques d'authenticite des extraits de vanille. Detection des resines et pigments par chromatographie en couche mince', *Ann. Fals. Exp. Chim.*, 61, 5–12.

Prat, Y. and Subitte, J. (1969) 'Contribution a l'etude des constituants aromatiques de la vanille. Detection de l'alcool p-hydroxybenzylique par chromatographie sur couche mince', *Ann. Fals. Exp. Chim.*, 62, 225–30.

Pritzer, J. and Jungkunz, R. (1928a) 'Analytisches uber Vanillin and Vanillinzucker', *Chem. Ztg.*, 52, 537.

Pritzer, J. and Jungkunz, R. (1928b) 'Uber Vanille, Vanillin und ihre Mischungen mit

Zucker', *Zeits. Untersuch Lebensmtl.*, **55**, 424–46.

Purseglove, J.W. (1972) *Tropical Crops: Monocotyledons*, London: Longman.

Ridley, H.N. (1912) *Spices*, London: Macmillan.

Rivera, J.G. and Hageman, R.H. (1951) *Vanilla Curing*, USDA Fed. Expt. Station, Mayaguez, Puerto Rico; Report for 1950, 30–3, Washington DC: USDA.

Salzer, U. -J. (1975) 'Uber die Fettesaurezussamensetzung der Lipoide einige Gewurze', *Fette, Seifen. Anstrichmittel*, **77**, 446–50.

Schoen, K.L. (1972) 'Organic acids in vanilla by gas-liquid chromatography: Interpretations of analytical data', *J. Assoc. Offic. Agric. Chemists*, **55**, 1150–2.

Schulte-Elte, K.H., Gautschi, F., Renold, W., Hauser, H., Frankhauser, P., Limacher, J. and Ohloff, G. (1978) 'Vitispiranes, important constituents of vanilla aroma', *Helv. Chim. Acta*, **61**, 1125–33.

Shiota, H. and Itoga, K. (1975) 'The study of the aromatic components of vanilla beans (*Vanilla planifolia* Andrews and *V. tahitensis* Moore)', *Koryo* (Japan), **113**, 65–71.

Simony, R. (1953) 'Etude Morphologique, Histologique et Chimique des Vanilles', Ph. D. Thesis, Univ. of Strasbourg.

Small, J. (1942) 'Vanilla: a pocket-lens study', *Food Proc., Packeting, Marketing*, 137–41.

Stahl, W.H., Voelker, W.A. and Sullivan, J.H. (1962) 'Analysis of vanilla extracts. IV. Amino acid determination', *J. Assoc. Offic. Agric. Chemists*, **45**, 108–13.

Stoll, S. and Prat, Y. (1960) 'Etude de la degradation de la vanilline, de l'ethylvanilline et de l'aldelyde p-hydroxybenzoic, par autoxidation', *Ann. Fals. Exp. Chim.*, **53**, 316–17.

Sullivan, J.H., Voelker, W.A. and Stahl, W.H. (1960) 'Analysis of vanilla extracts. I. Organic acid determination', *J. Assoc. Offic. Agric. Chemists*, **43**, 601–5.

Tabacchi, R., Nicollier, G. and Garnero, J. (1978) 'À propos de quelques particularites des extraits de vanille Tahiti', *Parfums, Cosmetiques, Aromes*, **21**, 79–81.

Thaler, H. (1959) 'Aethylvanillin, ein naturlicher Bestandteil der Vanille?', *Deut. Lebensmitl.-Rundschau*, **55**, 172–5.

Theodose, R. (1973) 'Traditional methods of vanilla preparation and their improvement', *Trop. Sci.*, **15**, 47–57.

Tiemann, F. (1885) 'Ueber·Glucovanillin and Glucovanillylalkohol', *Chem. Ber.*, **18**, 1595–1600.

Tiemann, F. and Haarmann, W. (1874) 'Ueber das Coniferin und seine Umwandlung in das aromatisches Princip de Vanille', *Chem. Ber.*, **7**, 608–23.

Tiemann, F. and Haarmann, W. (1876) 'Ueber Bestandtheile der naturlichen Vanille', *Chem. Ber.*, **9**, 1287–92.

Walbaum, H. (1909) 'Das Vorkommen von Anis-alkohol und Anisaldehyd in den Fruchten der Tahitivanille', *Wallachs Festschrift*, 649–53. (*Ber. Schimmel*, 1909, Oct., 140–1).

Winton, A.L. and Winton, K.B. (1939) *The Structure and Composition of Foods*, Vol. IV, New York: John Wiley & Sons.

Zenk, M.H. (1965) 'Biosynthese von Vanillin in *Vanilla planifolia* Andr.', *Z. Pflanzenphysiol.*, **53**, 404–14.

Chapter 12

Coriander

Coriander, *Coriandrum sativum* L., is an annual herb, belonging to the family Umbelliferae. It is a native of the Mediterranean region. It is one of the earliest spices used by mankind. It is extensively grown in India, the USSR, central Europe, Asia Minor and Morocco. The leaves are used for flavouring soups and other foods. The fruits are an important ingredient of curry powder, usually contributing the greatest quantity of all the spices, followed by turmeric. They are used as a pickling spice, in seasonings and sausages and also in pastries, buns, cakes and other confectionery. Ridley (1912) states that it is used in flavouring gin and other spirits. It is used medicinally for a number of purposes, particularly as a carminative. The fruits and the oil are used as a flavouring agent to cover the taste or correct the nauseating or griping qualities of other medicines. Coriander was used in love potions and according to Redgrove (1933) and Rosengarten (1969) its use as an aphrodisiac is mentioned in *The Thousand and One Nights*.

Its name is derived from the Greek *koris*, meaning bedbug, because of the unpleasant, fetid, bug-like odour of the green unripened fruits.

History

Coriander was used in Egypt for medicinal and culinary purposes as early as 1550 B.C. and is mentioned in the Ebers Papyrus. It was known to the ancient Israelites and is referred to in the Bible in *Exodus*, **16**:31 and *Numbers*, **11**:7. It is also mentioned in Sanskrit literature. It was one of the drugs employed by Hippocrates about 400 B.C. Ridley (1912) says that it is mentioned by Cato in the third century B.C., and Pliny states that the best came in his time from Egypt. In the first century A.D. its seeds were to be found in the shops of Pompeii. Coriander was introduced into England by the Romans. According to Redgrove (1933) it was a constituent of the *eau de Carmes* invented by the Carmelite monks in Paris in 1611, which achieved great popularity, both as a cordial and a toilet water. Rosengarten (1969) records that it was one of the first herbs grown in America by the colonists, having been introduced into Massachusetts before 1670.

Botany

Systematics

The genus *Coriandrum* L. has two species, which are native to the eastern Mediterranean region, and of which one, *C. sativum* L., is cultivated and is coriander.

Cytology

According to Darlington and Wylie (1955) the basic chromosome number of the genus is $x = 11$ and *C. sativum* is a diploid with $2n = 22$.

Structure

Coriander is an annual, erect, glabrous herb, 20–90 cm high. The stem, which is slender and smooth, is corymbosely branched in the upper part. The lower leaves, 2.5–10 cm long and 2–7.5 cm wide, are pinnate with long petioles, with nearly sessile rounded leaflets with crenate margins. The upper leaves are finely cut with linear lobes and are bi- or tri-pinnate. The small, white or pink flowers are borne in compound umbels about 4 cm across. The calyx is green, five-toothed, 2–3 mm long. The petals are unequal in size, with the two inner ones obovate with emarginate apex, and the three outer ones much longer, oblong, with the middle one bifid. There are five stamens with spreading filaments. Hermaphrodite and staminate flowers may occur in each umbel. The fruits are nearly globular, 3–4 mm in diameter, yellow-brown when ripe, ribbed, with two slender spreading styles on a short process. The fruits consist of two halves, the single-seeded mericarps. On separating, the inner surface is concave and the outer surface has sinuous ridges alternating with straight ridges. The unripe fruits smell of bedbugs, but become pleasantly aromatic on ripening.

Pollination

Aiyadurai (1966) states that flower opening and anthesis proceed from the periphery inwards both within the compound umbel and within the umbellets. Dehiscence of the anthers is spread over a period of ten hours or so, the anthers springing out one after the other and shedding pollen at intervals of up to three hours. The time taken for anthesis to be completed for all flowers of an umbel is three to four days. The flowers are protandrous, with the anthers maturing before the stigmas becomes receptive. As stated above, hermaphrodite and staminate flowers occur within the umbel. There is a considerable amount of cross-pollination, mainly brought about by bees.

Chaudhry (1961) says that the stigma is receptive for five days, the first three giving the highest set. Pollen remained viable for a maximum of 24 hours. For emasculation and hand pollination the buds should be at least four days old. Flower opening started at 6 a.m. and reached a maximum between noon and 2 p.m.

Cultivars

Some cultivars are recognized in the USSR and elsewhere and there is some variation in the amount of oil in the fruit. The Russian cultivar 'Lucs' gave the highest yield and essential-oil content. The cultivar 'CIMPO S-33' developed in Bangalore, India, from Bulgarian seed gave three times higher yields and an essential-oil content about seven times more than the local cultivar (Anon., 1976; Dimri *et al.*, 1977; Kumar *et al.*, 1977). Details are given under 'Improvement'.

Ecology

Climate and soils

Coriander grows under a wide range of conditions, but thrives best on a medium to heavy soil in sunny locations with good drainage and well-distributed moisture. It is usually grown as a rain-fed crop, although it can be grown with irrigation where required. It is grown in all the states of India. Yegna Narayan Aiyer (1944) says that the heavy, black, clayey cotton soils as occur in the Deccan and southern India are particularly suited to coriander cultivation. Coriander also grows on the rich silt loams of northern India.

In India, Sastri (1950) states that the time of sowing varies in different localities in India. In Bengal and Uttar Pradesh the seeds are sown during the cold season; in Bombay (Maharashtra), during the monsoon; and in Madras (Tamil Nadu), in autumn. In Mysore (Karnataka) and in certain parts of Madras coriander is grown in two seasons, from May to August and from October to January.

Burkill (1966) informs us that it can be grown throughout Malaysia to flowering, but if seed is wanted the crop must be raised in the hills. Ochse and van der Brink (1931) state that it is cultivated in mountainous regions of Indonesia for its fruit, but that it is mainly imported from elsewhere.

Cultivation

Coriander is always propagated by seed. Before sowing, the fruits are rubbed until the two mericarps are separated. A clean and reasonably fine seedbed is required. It is broadcast or drilled in rows. Yegna Narayan Aiyer (1944) gives the distance between rows as 23 cm; Rosengarten (1969) says 38–76 cm apart. It is usually grown in pure stand. The seed rate, according to Sastri (1950) varies from 16 to 25 pounds per acre (18−28 kg/hectare) in the Punjab and from 10 to 15 pounds per acre (11−17 kg/hectare) in southern India. The crop requires two or three weedings or the weeds may be chemically controlled. Prometryne has been found to be a suitable herbicide for coriander in Russia. The crop is rather slow to germinate and may take 10−25 days.

Sastri (1950) states that little attention appears to have been given to manurial treatment in India, but that experience in European countries has shown that manuring greatly improves the yields and that significant results have been obtained when nitrogenous, phosphatic and potash fertilizers are applied in the early stages of development. Aiyadurai (1966), reporting on manurial trials in India, states that a response to nitrogen alone was observed at Delhi and to nitrogen and phosphoric acid at Jamnagar. No improvement in the essential-oil content was brought about by the manurial treatments, although exceptions to this have been found elsewhere.

The crop matures in $3-3\frac{1}{2}$ months after sowing. It is advisable to pull or cut the crop when there is dew in order to avoid shattering. It is usually recommended that the crop should be harvested when fully ripe to ensure that the unpleasant odour of the unripe fruit has disappeared. This aspect is discussed under 'Chemistry'. The quality of the spice is highly dependent upon the stage of fruit maturity at harvest and on the methods used for its subsequent drying and handling, as is reviewed in the 'Processing and manufacture' section.

After threshing, the fruits should be further dried, winnowed and stored in bags. Under favourable conditions yields of 1 000−1 500 pounds per acre (1 120−1 700 kg/hectare) are obtained, but yields of 2 000 pounds per acre (2 240 kg/hectare) have been recorded.

Diseases

Chattopadhyay (1967) gives the following diseases of coriander in India:

A gall-forming fungus, *Protomyces macrosporus* Unger, causes small tumour-like swellings on all the herbaceous parts of infected plants, including the stems, petioles, veins of leaves and flower stalks. At Gwalior, where the disease was reported, the mean disease intensity was 23 per cent and the average amount of loss per plant was approximately 15 per cent.

A wilt disease, *Fusarium oxysporum* Schlecht. f. *corianderii* Kulkarni, Nikam & Joshi, has been found in parts of India and can cause serious and sudden damage to the crop. The plants are attacked at all stages of growth, the severity of infection increasing with age. It causes a drooping of the terminal portions, followed by withering and drying up of the leaves, eventually resulting in death. Partial wilting in which growth is arrested is also found and such plants are often sterile.

A powdery mildew, *Erysiphe polygoni* DC., and a stem rot, *Sclerotinia sclerotiorum* (Lib.) de Bary, have also been reported.

Pests

Sastri (1950) states that the crop is not subject to any serious pests, but occasionally stick-bugs, leaf-eating caterpillars and boring grubs are found on the plants. A chalcid fly, *Systole albipennis*, has been reported as damaging the fruits.

Improvement

A few cultivar trials have been carried out in the USSR and India. Tetraploid plants have been produced by colchicine which showed improved morphological development and increased oil content of the fruits.

The Central Indian Medicinal Plants Organization in Bangalore, India, introduced cultivars from Bulgaria and the USSR in 1969 and these were intensively selected over a period of 5 years. The plants were selfed and this did not result in any loss of vigour. The cultivar 'CIMPO S-33' from Bulgarian material proved outstanding. It yielded 2 117 kg/hectare of seeds compared with 750 kg/hectare from the local cultivar; it had an oil content of 1.3 per cent as against 0.18 per cent with the local, giving 27.52 kg/hectare of oil as compared with 1.35 kg/hectare from the local. It was a tall, late-maturing cultivar with small seeds (Anon., 1976; Dimri *et al.*, 1977; Kumar *et al.*, 1977).

Products and end-uses

The coriander plant yields two primary products which are employed for flavouring purposes: the fresh green herb and the spice. The latter is the dried form of the whole, mature seed capsule (fruit) but it is frequently and incorrectly termed 'coriander seed' in commerce. The odour and flavour of these two products are markedly different, and the herb is generally disliked and little used in Europe and North America, except in certain specialist applications. However, the herb is much appreciated for culinary flavouring purposes in Asia, the Middle East, Central and South America, where it is produced in substantial quantities for domestic consumption. By contrast, the spice is of considerable importance as an item of international trade and it is widely used in the whole or ground form for flavouring applications. The spice is also employed for the preparation of its steam-distilled essential oil and of its solvent-extracted oleoresin, both these products being utilized by the aroma and flavour industries. The residues remaining after distillation of the spice may be employed as a cattle feed, and interest has also been expressed in the USSR in the recovery of the fatty oil for possible use as a lubricant in the metallurgical industries.

The major use of the spice on a world-wide basis is in flavouring applications in the ground form and its main outlet is as an ingredient of curry powders, of which it comprises some 25 to 40 per cent of the spice mixture. The ground spice is also extensively used domestically as a flavouring agent and by manufacturers of processed foods in, for example, baked goods, sauces and meat dishes. The whole spice is employed in pickling and in flavouring of certain alcoholic beverages, particularly gin. The spice mainly enters trade in the whole form and is ground in the importing centres.

The steam-distilled spice oil is produced mainly in Eastern Europe, with the USSR as the traditional major supplier, although it is prepared in some Western European countries and in the USA from both domestically grown and imported spice. The essential oil has similar applications to the ground spice in the flavouring of processed foods and it is also employed to some extent in pharmaceutical products and perfumery formulations. In the USSR, the essential oil is fractionated to obtain its major component, linalol, which is employed as a starting material for the synthetic preparation of citral and ionones.

The oleoresin, prepared by solvent extraction of the spice, is prepared on a relatively small scale in the USSR and in some of the highly industrialized Western countries. It has similar applications to the essential oil in flavouring and perfumery.

The major types of the spice

The spice entering international trade varies considerably in its physical and chemical characteristics according to the geographical source and consequently some users express preferences for certain types in particular applications.

In commerce, coriander is broadly divided into two types according to the size of the fruit, which is an indication of its volatile-oil content and suitability for particular end-uses, as the var. *vulgare* (diameter 3−5 mm) or the var. *microcarpum* (diameter 1.5−3 mm). The large fruited types supplied mainly by tropical and subtropical producing countries, e.g., Morocco and India, contain a low volatile-oil content (0.1−0.35 per cent) and are used extensively for grinding and blending purposes. The smaller-fruited types are produced in temperate regions and usually have a volatile-oil content of greater than 0.4 per cent. The very small-fruited types grown in the USSR and some other countries of Eastern and Central Europe contain between 0.8 and 1.8 per cent

Fig. 12.1   Coriander (*Coriandrum sativum* L.) (× 1) (Crown copyright)

volatile oil and are highly valued as a raw material for the preparation of the essential oil. The classification of the spice according to its physical and chemical characteristics is described in more detail in the 'Chemistry' and 'Standard specifications' sections of this chapter.

Processing and manufacture

The spice

Quality requirements

The quality of the whole spice is primarily evaluated on the basis of the content and aroma/flavour character of its volatile oil and on its size and appearance. The relative importance of these quality attributes is dependent upon the intended end-use of the spice. For the preparation of the distilled spice oil and the solvent-extracted oleoresin, the general appearance of the spice is not of great significance and the principal requirement is for a high content of volatile oil which possesses a desirable aroma and flavour. The smaller-fruited types of the spice, which are rich in volatile oil, are mainly used in these applications. The appearance is rather more important when the spice is intended for direct use in the whole or ground form, and medium- to large-sized fruits are usually more suited for this purpose since their size and colour tend to be more uniform than the small types.

   The current standards for the spice are described in the 'Standard specifications' section of this chapter.

Factors influencing quality

The size, the volatile-oil content and the aroma/flavour character of dried, mature fruit are principally governed by the intrinsic properties of the cultivar grown; and improvement can be achieved by selection and propagation of cultivars which possess the optimum combination of the desired quality attributes together with a high fruit yield. This aspect is discussed in more detail in the 'Chemistry' section.

The stage of maturity of the fruit at harvest is also of paramount importance in determining the quality of the spice. Immature fruits contain a higher volatile-oil content than ripe fruits, but the aroma of the immature fruits is generally considered to be disagreeable by consumers in Western countries. The characteristic, sweet and spicy aroma of the spice does not develop until the fruit has attained maturity and commences to dehydrate on the plant. Thus, it is very important to harvest the fruits at the correct stage of maturity to avoid an excessive proportion of immature fruits in the crop, which would detract from its aroma quality. Since fruit ripening on the plant is not simultaneous but progressive, judgement is required in deciding the optimum time for harvesting. This is normally done when a fair proportion of the fruits on an umbel have changed colour from green to grey.

Various opinions have been expressed on the optimum stage for harvesting in relation to the quality of the final dried product. Crooks and Sievers (1941) proposed harvesting when half the fruits on the plant change from green to grey, but Willkie *et al.* (1940) suggested that the proportion should be one-half to two-thirds. More recently, Chikalov (1962) and Tsvetkov (1970) recommended harvesting when the fruits on the central and first-order umbels have attained ripeness, corresponding to a chestnut-like colour, in order to obtain a high-quality product.

Over-ripening of the fruits on the plant should also be avoided since this can reduce the proportion of whole, dried spice from the harvest. If the fruits are allowed to become too ripe there is a distinct risk of shattering during harvesting and in the subsequent cleaning and drying operations. To minimize breakages it is preferable to gather the fruits either very early in the morning when the plant is moist with dew, or in the late evening around sunset. Splitting of the fruit is undesirable for two main reasons: firstly, it spoils the appearance of the whole spice and, secondly, such a condition can lead to a considerable loss of the volatile oil during subsequent storage (Tanasienko, 1961).

At harvest, the moisture content of the fruits may be greater than 20 per cent and this must be reduced to 9 per cent or less during drying. If the fruits are not thoroughly dried, they absorb heat very readily and this can result in deterioration of both the colour and the flavour of the spice.

Cleanliness of the product is most important in marketing this spice, and after drying the spice should be thoroughly sieved to remove extraneous matter such as stalks, plant debris and dirt.

Drying

The traditional procedure for preparing the spice involves drying in two steps. After cutting the plants with scythes or mowing machines, they are piled into small stacks in the field to wither for two or three days. The fruits are then threshed out from the plant and are dried in partial shade. If the fruits are still rather moist after winnowing, they may be exposed to the sun for a period before final drying under cover. When judged thoroughly dry, the spice is cleaned by sieving.

In the USSR, artificial drying of coriander fruits is practised and several studies of the optimum conditions for this process have been reported by Shlyapnikova *et al.* (1972a, 1972b, 1974). These authors conclude that, contrary to general opinion, the fruits are fairly stable to heat and they may be dried artificially under controlled conditions without significant loss or quality deterioration of the volatile oil. The two principal factors in quality control during artificial drying are the temperature and the initial moisture content of the fruits. The optimum air temperature for drying was found to be 80–90 °C. At temperatures over 100 °C, the flavour of the volatile oil acquires a 'burnt note', while at temperatures in excess of 140 °C evaporation losses of the volatile oil become significant. It was also recommended that the fruits should be left to dry naturally to 18 per cent moisture or less prior to commencing artificial drying. Fruits with initial moisture contents greater than 18 per cent were found to suffer a loss of some volatile oil during artificial drying as a result of an internal steam-distillation process.

Storage

The whole, dried fruits are usually packed into sacks and stored in a cool, dry room. Although some loss of volatile oil is inevitable during prolonged storage, the extent of deterioration is slight if the spice has not been damaged and the air temperature is moderate. Lukyanov and Berestovaya (1973) found that carefully prepared whole coriander lost no more than 5 per cent volatile oil during a two-year storage period, irrespective of whether the material was kept in heaps, cotton bags or polythene bags. However, Rakova (1961) has recommended that the spice should be placed in hermetically sealed cans immediately after drying in order to ensure that quality deterioration during storage is minimal. In the case of the crushed or ground spice, fairly rapid volatile-oil losses are encountered if the material is left exposed to the air, and storage in air-tight containers is a necessity.

The essential oil

Coriander oil of commerce is prepared by steam distillation of the mature, dried fruits. The yield of the essential oil obtained upon distillation is dependent upon two factors: firstly, the type of the spice used and, secondly, on whether or not it has been crushed prior to distillation.

The small-fruited types of coriander grown in the USSR and certain other countries in Eastern and Central Europe possess the highest content of volatile oil and are, therefore, best suited to give high distillation yields. However, the chemical composition and organoleptic properties of the distilled oil are also governed by the type of spice used; and some distillers are prepared to sacrifice high distillation yields by selecting other types of the spice which provide oil with specific desired properties.

Distillation of the oil is hindered by the fact that the oil cells are located within the mericarp of the spice, protected by a thick cell wall, and also by the high fat content which tends to occlude the volatile oil and to reduce the vapour pressure. In order to obtain the maximum yield of essential oil and to reduce the processing time, it is necessary to crush the spice prior to distillation. Overheating of the spice during the crushing operation and undue delay in loading the crushed material into the still must be avoided since volatile-oil loss by evaporation can readily occur. The advantages of distilling the crushed spice were first noted by Chernukin (1928), who reported a distillation yield improvement of 17 per cent and also a saving of about 25 per cent in operational time and a reduction of 10 to 15 per cent in steam consumption. Similar results have been reported by Tanasienko and Mezinova (1939), Tucakov (1957) and Balinova-Tsvetkova and Kamburova (1975).

Guenther (1950) has reported that in commercial-scale distillations in Hungary, using stills of several thousand litre capacity, crushed coriander yielded 0.92 per cent oil after steam distillation for $9\frac{1}{2}$ hours. Whole seed from the same lot, distilled in the same still and with the same steam pressure, yielded only 0.88 per cent of oil after $12\frac{3}{4}$ hours.

The USSR is the largest producer of coriander oil, and continuous distillation equipment has been introduced to replace the conventional types of still operated on the batch system. According to Iakobakvili (1960), the new equipment, known as Ponomarenko and Pokolenko, consists of a column about 10 m high and 2 m in diameter, the total volume of the unit being 29 m^3, of which 21.3 m^3 are utilized in the extraction. The apparatus works on a countercurrent principle: the dried fruits are first crushed and then immediately introduced to the column by means of a feeder screw helix, at a high level. This allows the steam which enters the column from below to percolate through the depth of the charge, the vaporized oil and steam then being led to the condenser system. The contact time for the ground material in the apparatus is about 30 minutes. With this equipment the operations for the feeding of material and processing are completely automated and manual operations eliminated. Throughput is said to range from 100 to 320 tonnes of crushed coriander in 24 hours; while production of each kilogramme of the oil requires 41 – 48 kg of steam. The residual volatile oil in the distillation residue is 0.011 per cent. Smolianov (1964) also refers to this type of distillation equipment, in the context of the largest factory, Alexeev, in the USSR, which operates over the whole year and processes some 200 tonnes of coriander in 24 hours. Yields are said to approach 1.0 per cent and this represents an improvement of the order of 20 per cent over conventional steam-distillation equipment. The distillation waters are continuously extracted by means of an auto-cohobation system forming an integral part of the equipment. The residues from distillation are processed for their fatty oil by being first milled through rollers and then extracted with solvent (benzene) to yield 17–18 per cent of this product.

The oleoresin

Coriander oleoresin is prepared commercially on a relatively small scale and very little information has been published on the manufacturing methods used. The spice has a relatively low volatile-oil content in comparison to that of the fatty oil and the oleoresin extract may be regarded as a solution of the volatile oil in the fatty oil. The fat content may be lessened and the volatile-oil content enhanced to some extent by the use of selective extraction solvents, but it is common for the distilled essential oil to be added to the oleoresin to boost the aroma/flavour strength. The volatile-oil content of commercial oleoresins is in the range of about 5–40 per cent.

In the USSR, studies of the use of liquid carbon dioxide as the extraction solvent in oleoresin preparation have been reported (Meerov and Bykova, 1971; Bykova *et al*., 1971, 1974; Shtovkhan *et al*., 1977). Apart from higher acid numbers, the product extracted by carbon dioxide is said to be similar in properties to the oleoresins extracted by conventional solvents.

Chemistry

The chemistry of the coriander plant has been the subject of many investigations since the middle of the nineteenth century. The composition of the volatile oil, which determines the odour and flavour character, has been of particular fascination to chemists. In the unripe fruits and the vegetative parts of the plant, aliphatic aldehydes predominate in the steam-volatile oil and are responsible for the peculiar, fetid-like aroma. On ripening, the fruits acquire a more pleasant and sweet odour and the major constituent of the volatile oil is the monoterpene alcohol, linalol. Extensive research has been carried out in recent years in the USSR and neighbouring producing countries aimed at obtaining a better understanding of the mechanism of the oil composition transformation in the fruits and at controlling product quality.

General composition of the spice and the oleoresin

Dried, ripe coriander fruit contain steam-volatile oil, fixed (fatty) oil, proteins, cellulose, pentosans, tannins, calcium oxalate and minerals. The major constituents are fibre (23–36 per cent), carbohydrates (about 20 per cent), fatty oil (16–28 per cent) and proteins (11–17 per cent). The high fat and protein contents lend the residues remaining after distillation of the essential oil from the spice useful as animal feed. The relative abundance of the various components, particularly that of the volatile oil, can vary somewhat between different samples of the spice. These variations are principally a factor of the cultivar grown, but other factors of significance are the location and environmental conditions of growth, the state of fruit maturity at harvest, the drying procedure, and the conditions and duration of storage. Examples of the possible range in the general composition of the spice are given in the literature by Winton and Winton (1939), Willkie *et al.* (1940), Althausen *et al.* (1940), Kolachov (1940), Anon. (1950), Dublyanskaya (1964), Gerhardt (1968), Karow (1969), Shankaracharya and Natarajan (1971), Marsh *et al.* (1977) and Strauss (1977). In addition, Dublyanskaya *et al.* (1965) have reported composition analyses for nine cultivars grown at two different locations in the USSR. A summary of the characteristics of the major types of the spice entering the international market is provided in the 'Products and end-uses' section and the current standards are given in the 'Standard specifications' section.

The primary quality determinant of the spice is the content and composition of its steam-volatile oil. This subject is dealt with in detail in the following sub-section, but a summary of the salient points will be given at this juncture. The volatile-oil content of the spice can vary considerably according to the type and source, and usually ranges from 0.1 to 1.7 per cent for consignments entering trade, although some new cultivars have been reported to contain up to 2.7 per cent. Table 12.1 provides historical data for the volatile-oil contents of the spice grown in different countries. European coriander is mainly of the small-fruited type and usually has a volatile-oil content greater than 0.4 per cent, with the highest values exhibited by some Russian cultivars. Moroccan and Indian coriander are mainly large-fruited types, globular in shape in the former and egg-shaped in the latter, and their volatile-oil contents are usually less than 0.4 per cent. In addition to the variation in volatile-oil content, distinctions are made on an organoleptic basis between various sources of coriander. Indian and Moroccan coriander are generally regarded as inferior to European types, and the traditional Russian spice is regarded as the best. During storage, some of the volatile oil can be lost by evaporation but the rate of loss and the extent of organoleptic deterioration is dependent upon the physical form of the spice and on the conditions and duration of storage. Whole coriander fruits, which have been carefully dried, can normally be stored with minimal deterioration over a considerable period. However, significant oil losses can occur with damaged or split fruit during storage. The most serious problem is encountered with ground coriander, which undergoes a rapid volatile-oil loss and a marked organoleptic deterioration within a matter of weeks if left exposed to the atmosphere.

The composition of the fatty (fixed) oil of the spice has been studied by Dublyanskaya (1964), Kartha and Selveraj (1970), Vijayalkshmi and

Table 12.1   *Historical data on the volatile oil content of coriander spice by source*

Country	Percentage volatile oil	Ref.	Country	Percentage volatile oil	Ref.
Russian S.S.R.	0.8−1.8	1−8	Armenian S.S.R.	0.26−0.6	1
	(0.9−1.8)*	14*	Azerbaijan S.S.R.	0.18−0.41	1
Norway	1.4−1.7	9	Afghanistan	0.18−0.41	1
Poland	0.6−1.15	2,4		(0.45)*	14*
	(0.7−1.0)*	14*	Turkey	0.3−0.4	5
Germany	0.6−1.0	5,9	Syria	0.26−0.34	5
Czechoslovakia	0.65−1.0	2,5,8	'Palestine'	0.27−0.36	5
	(0.4−0.75)*	14*	North Africa	0.25−0.35	5
Hungary	0.4−1.1	4,5,8,10	Morocco	0.1−0.5	2−5,7,8,11
	(0.7−0.9)*	14*		(0.2−0.6;	
Bulgaria	(0.3−1.5)*	14*		av. 0.3)*	14*
Romania	0.3−0.8	2,8	Egypt	(0.3−0.35)*	14*
	(0.4−0.6)*	14*	Iran	0.1−0.35	1,4,6,12
Yugoslavia	0.4−0.5	2	'East Indies'	0.15−0.25	5,11
	(0.35−0.47)*	14*	Indian	0.1−0.6	2,3,13
England	0.5−0.85	2,4		(0.05−0.25)*	14*
	(0.65−0.85)*	14*	China	(0.3−0.7;	
Holland	0.5−0.6	5,8,11		av. 0.4)*	14*
France	0.4	8,11			
Italy	0.25−0.6	2,5,8,11			
	(0.25−0.35)*	14*			

References

1. Obuchow and Kondrazki (1946)
2. Althausen *et al.* (1940)
3. Anon. (1950)
4. Shellard (1963)
5. Willkie *et al.* (1940)
6. Lowman *et al.* (1949)
7. Gerhardt (1968)
8. Dimri *et al.* (1977)
9. Ramstad (1942)
10. Guenther (1950)
11. Gildemeister and Hoffmann (1961)
12. Kumar *et al.* (1977)
13. Puri *et al.* (1968)
14.* Results for commercial consignments imported into the UK in 1975−6. Private correspondence between TPI and consumers.

Rao (1972) and Salzer (1975a). Dublyanskaya *et al.* (1965) have also reported the fatty-oil compositions of nine cultivars grown in comparative trials in the USSR. The saponifiable portion of the fatty oil accounts for some 90 per cent of the total and is characterized by a very high content of octadecenoic acids (approx. 95 per cent of the total constituent acids listed in Table 12.2). Petroselinic acid and oleic acid occur at similar levels and jointly comprise 74–85 per cent, linoleic for 7–16 per cent and palmitic for 4–8 per cent of the constituent fatty acids. During prolonged storage of the spice, the free fatty-acid content gradually increases and, according to Viswanath and Ramaswamy Ayyar (1934), this value is a good indicator of the age of the material. More recently, changes occurring in the fatty oil of the spice during storage have been studied by Georgiev (1968).

A number of non-volatile, extractable minor constituents of the spice, some of which occur in the non-saponifiable portion of the fatty oil, have also been identified, and these are listed in Table 12.2.

Coriander oleoresin is prepared by solvent extraction of the spice as outlined in the 'Processing and manufacture' section. The oleoresin contains the volatile oil, fatty oil and some other extractives, but their relative abundance is dependent upon the raw material, the processing procedure and the particular solvent used. According to Salzer (1975b), coriander oleoresins commonly contain about 90 per cent fatty oil and about 5 per cent steam-volatile oil.

The volatile oil

Volatile oil canals are present in all of the organs of the coriander plant, but the fruit is remarkable in that the odour, composition and content of its volatile oil change during the course of fruit ripening. In the unripe fruit, two types of volatile oil canals are present. One type is located on the periphery of the fruit and these contain a volatile oil which is similar in composition to that of the vegetative organs in being comprised predominantly of aldehydes. The second type of canals are buried in the mericarp of the fruit kernel and the composition of their volatile oil is very different, containing linalol as the major component together with some other oxygenated monoterpenes and monoterpene hydrocarbons. As the fruit ripens on the plant, the peripheral canals become flattened, commence to lose their volatile oil, and the odour of the fruit changes. On drying to around 7 per cent moisture content, the outer canals completely lose their volatile oil but the inner canals remain intact and the characteristic odour and composition of the volatile oil of the spice are attained.

In the paragraphs immediately following, the volatile oil of the spice, obtained from fully ripe, dried fruits, will be discussed while the changes in the volatile oil of the plant during the course of development will be dealt with in the final part of this section.

Table 12.2   *Acid constituents of coriander fatty oil and some other minor constituents of the non-volatile oil*

	Ref.
Acid constituents of the fatty oil	
myristic	1
palmitic	1,2
stearic	1
arachinic	1
hexadecenoic	1
oleic	1,2
petrolselinic	1
linoleic	1,2
Minor constituents of the non-volatile oil	
triacontane	3
triacontanol	3
tricosanol	3
γ-sitosterol	4
β-sitosterol	3,5,6
coriandrinol (β-sitosterol-D-glucoside)	3,5
stigmastanol	5
glucose	5
fructose	5
sucrose	5
manitol	5,6
angelicin	3
psoralene	3
umbelliferone	4,7
scopeletin	4,7
querticin-3-glucoronide	8,9
iso-querticin	8
rutin	8
cis-ferulic acid	10
p-hydroxy benzoic acid	10
cis-and *trans-p*-coumaric acid	10
protocatechuic acid	10
vanillic acid	10
amino acids	11

References

(1) Salzer (1975a)
(2) Dublyanskaya (1964)
(3) Gupta *et al*. (1977)
(4) Kartnig (1966)
(5) Vaghani and Thakor (1958)
(6) Farooq *et al*. (1961)

(7) Sergeeva (1974)
(8) Kunzemann and Heermann (1977)
(9) Harbourne and Williams (1972)
(10) Gopala Rao and Sriramula (1977)
(11) Popescu and Tugui (1976)

The volatile-oil content of the spice

Varietal differences

According to Berger (1952) and Heeger (1956), the classification devised by Alefeld is recognized in commerce to distinguish coriander into two categories: the small-fruited *Coriandrum sativum* L. var. *microcarpum* DC. (diameter 1.5–3 mm) and the larger-fruited *C. sativum* L. var. *vulgare* Alef. (diameter 3–5 mm). The former is exemplified by the volatile-oil-rich Russian coriander while the latter include Moroccan, Indian and some other Asiatic types of coriander, all of which have very low volatile-oil contents (see Table 12.1).

A definite relationship between the size (or more precisely the surface area) of the spice and its oil content was first demonstrated by Varentzov (1927). His observation that smaller fruit contain more volatile oil has been subsequently confirmed by a number of other workers, including Althausen *et al.* (1940), Kolachov (1940), Guenther (1950), Tucakov (1957), Patakova and Chladek (1966) and Schratz and Qadry (1966a). In addition, several investigations have shown that the smaller-fruited, high oil-yielding types of coriander are generally late flowering and maturing (Lowman *et al.*, 1949; Heeger, 1956; Peneva and Krilov, 1977; Dimri *et al.*, 1977; Kumar *et al.*, 1977). Cultivars which flower and mature earlier generally have larger fruits with a lower volatile-oil content but have a better appearance and are more suited for spice usage than for distillation.

Even within the two broad classifications described by Alefeld, a considerable variation in the volatile-oil content and some other properties is found between different cultivars. In order to approximate or define the geographical origin of a consignment of the spice, Althausen *et al.* (1940) proposed characterization standards based on the fruit size and on certain physicochemical properties. Later, Harrod (1960) suggested a simpler and quicker method based on the appearance and number of fruits per gramme: samples with less than 75 (average 66.5) fruits per gramme and which exhibited purple patches include Moroccan and Mogadore coriander, while samples with 80–110 (average 98) fruits per gramme include English and Romanian, and samples with over 130 (average 161) fruits per gramme include German, Hungarian, Polish and Russian coriander.

Since the early 1940s, considerable attention has been devoted to screening trials in a number of countries with the aim of selecting cultivars with the optimum combination of fruit yield and volatile-oil content. Studies in the USA in the 1940s generally favoured Russian cultivars of coriander (Kolachov, 1940; Willkie *et al.*, 1940; Lowman *et al.*, 1949). More recently, extensive trials have been undertaken in the USSR and some other Eastern Bloc countries, for example, by Dublyanskaya *et al.* (1965), Patakova and Chladek (1966), Razinskaite (1966), Lorincz (1966), Zelenova (1973), Girenko (1974), and Kuzina

(1975). Among a number of well-tried Russian cultivars, which include 'Alekseevskii-247', 'Voznesenskii-60', 'Tminovidnii', 'Rous' and 'Novii', the cultivar 'Lucs' has generally been found to provide the optimum in fruit yield, volatile-oil content and volatile-oil composition. A new cultivar, 'Amber', has recently been reported which surpasses 'Lucs' in volatile-oil content, yielding 2.45−2.64 per cent as compared to 1.9−2.21 per cent in comparative trials (Glushenko *et al.*, 1977). In India, a new strain, named 'CIMPO S-33', derived from Bulgarian seed has shown considerable promise in possessing 1.3−1.6 per cent of volatile oil in combination with high fruit yields (Dimri *et al.*, 1977; Kumar *et al.*, 1977).

Influences of conditions of growth

In addition to intrinsic differences between cultivars in their fruit yield and volatile-oil content, these properties are also strongly influenced by the location and enviromental conditions of growth.

One of the most important influences is the site location or more precisely, the latitude of cultivation. It has been noted for some time that in the Northern Hemisphere there is a marked trend for volatile-oil contents to increase as one progresses from south to north (Ivanov *et al.*, 1931). Even in the extremely cold and short growing seasons in Norway (Ramstad, 1942) and Siberia (Lytkin, 1953), exceptionally good volatile-oil contents, superior to many areas in central and southern Europe, have been reported. More recently, Razinskaite (1966) carried out a study with 11 cultivars of coriander and showed that in each case higher volatile-oil contents were obtained when grown in Lithuania as compared to southern Russia.

The climatic and weather conditions during growth are regarded as more important than the nature of the soil with regard to the volatile-oil content. Bauer *et al.* (1942) and Kuzina (1975) have observed that the best oil yields are obtainable in cool, rather wet summers. Other factors have been studied by Khotin (1968) and by Peneva and Krilov (1977). The last-named workers carried out a detailed study of seven cultivars in three localities which differed in altitude, soil and climatic conditions. They reported that growth was slightly more affected by light than by temperature, while the environment affected the growing period, fruit yield, the total volatile-oil content and the linalol content of the fruit.

The judicious use of fertilizers has also been shown to benefit the volatile-oil content as well as the fruit yields (Defert and Rudolf, 1925; Turbina, 1945; Nosti Nava *et al.*, 1953; Heeger, 1956; Razinskaite and Slavenus, 1966a; Golz *et al.*, 1966; Khotin, 1968; Laza and Silva, 1970; Pillai and Boominathan, 1975).

Harvesting and drying influences

It has already been mentioned that the volatile-oil content of the fruit reaches a maximum while it is still unripe and that during ripening the volatile-oil content diminishes owing a collapse of the peripheral volatile oil canals. However, since the volatile oil present in the peripheral canals imparts a rather fetid, bedbug-like odour to the fruit, harvesting is delayed until the fruit has ripened and the characteristic, sweet odour of the spice has developed.

In fully ripe fruit, traces of the peripheral-canal volatile oil may be present but the bulk of the volatile oil is enclosed in four internal oil ducts which are located in pairs buried below the internal surface of each half-kernel, and facing one another. These internal volatile oil reservoirs are dead-ended with dense epithelial cells through which the oil penetrates with difficulty. Under conditions of natural drying on the plant or carefully controlled artificial drying, very little volatile-oil loss occurs owing to the structural characteristics of the fruit. Shlyapnikova *et al.* (1974) have shown in a study of the 'Lucs' cultivar that volatile-oil losses of 4−5 per cent can occur while fruits dehydrate under natural conditions from a moisture content of 35 down to 12 per cent. The main losses of volatile oil during natural drying were found to occur during the initial stages of dehydration. Changes in volatile-oil content during artificial drying were found to be dependent upon the initial moisture content and the temperature and duration of drying. With fruits harvested when their moisture content was below 18 per cent and then dried at temperatures below 90 °C, losses of volatile oil were insignificant. Interestingly, the volatile-oil content actually increased slightly under certain artificial drying conditions, reaching its maximum (2−5 per cent) at between 80 and 90 °C, as a result of an apparent stimulation of the biosynthetic pathways responsible for volatile-oil formation. However, fruits which were harvested with high initial moisture contents (greater than 18 per cent) were found to lose 5−12 per cent of their volatile oil during artificial drying and the losses increased progressively as the drying temperature increased beyond 100 °C. Since these losses exceeded those occuring during natural drying, Shlyapnikova *et al.* (1974) consider that the losses arose by evaporation of volatile oil from the internal reservoirs owing to the fruit walls and tissues being insufficiently dense in fruits with high moisture contents.

The optimum conditions for harvesting and drying coriander fruit are discussed in the 'Processing and manufacture' section.

Storage influences

Conflicting data are reported in the literature on the extent of volatile-oil loss from the whole spice. Lukyanov and Berestovaya (1973) found losses of only 3−5 per cent over a two-year period for whole, dried fruit stored in heaps or cotton bags, and they stated that the organoleptic quality deterioration was not great. Schratz and Qadry (1966a) have reported similar findings, although they did not provide quantitative data for oil losses. By contrast, Rakova (1961) reported losses of up to 23 per cent over one year for the whole spice stored in paper or cotton bags and noted that some organoleptic deterioration occurred even with samples in which oil losses were slight. These differences are probably related to the care given to harvesting and drying the fruit and possibly also to intrinsic differences between cultivars for resistance to oil permeation. Analytical data reported by Sankevich (1936) and Topalov and Kalichkov (1962) indicate that volatile-oil diffusion through the whole spice can be extensive. These authors found 40 per cent of the volatile oil in the husk and the remainder dissolved within the fatty oil of the kernel.

Fruits which have been damaged or split in the course of harvesting and drying can suffer considerable volatile oil losses during storage. Tanasienko (1961) found that halves from split fruit lost 50 per cent of their original volatile oil over a six-month storage period. Crushed or ground coriander deteriorates even more rapidly and substantial volatile-oil losses may occur within a matter of weeks on exposure to the atmosphere (Schratz and Qadry, 1966a; Shlyapnikova and Ponomarev, 1970).

The influence of various storage conditions and containers on spice quality retention has been studied by Torricelli (1937) and some of the workers listed above. Their conclusions are summarized in the 'Processing and manufacture' section.

Properties and composition of the spice oil

The essential oil obtained on steam distillation of the spice is a colourless or pale yellow liquid. Arctander (1960) has described its aroma as pleasant, sweet, somewhat woody-spicy aromatic, and says that the floral-balsalmic undertone and peppery-woody topnote are characteristic features. He describes the flavour as mild, sweet and spicy-aromatic yet somewhat warm and slightly burning. The organoleptic properties of the distilled oil tend to deteriorate during prolonged storage, as is the case with the spice especially if it is left exposed to light and air. The inclusion of unripe fruits or other overground parts of the plant during distillation of the spice imparts an obnoxious odour to the oil.

Variations have been noted in the literature between the odour characters of oils distilled from different types and sources of the spice. Moroccan and Indian coriander oils are generally regarded as inferior in odour quality to European spice oils. Furthermore, distinctions are made between the various European types of spice oils and some authors have remarked that traditional Russian oils possess a characteristic, spicy note.

Physicochemical properties

As in the case with the oil distillation yield, the physicochemical constants of the distilled oil tend to vary somewhat according to the type of spice used, its age, and to a certain extent upon the processing procedure followed. The current standards for the spice oil are given in the 'Standard specifications' section and it should be noted that these are based mainly on the properties of European spice oils. Historical data on the general ranges in the physicochemical properties of coriander oils have been reported by the Schimmel Co. (1909) and by Shankaracharya and Natarajan (1971).

The physicochemical properties of European spice oils fall within fairly close limits, with the optical-rotation value usually ranging between + 9 ° and + 13 °, while the ester number is normally well below the upper limit of the standard specifications (Althausen *et al.*, 1940; Guenther, 1950; Tucakov, 1957; Irintscheff, 1957; Gildemeister and Hoffmann, 1961; Shellard, 1963). Data in the literature for Moroccan spice oils indicate an upper limit of + 10 ° for the optical-rotation value, and ester numbers of up to 30 (Althausen *et al.*, 1940; Guenther, 1950). Traditional Indian spice oils are notable in exhibiting refractive-index values at or below the lower limit of the standard specifications and in possessing very high ester numbers (Anon., 1923; Rao *et al.*, 1925; Puri *et al.*, 1968; Gupta *et al.*, 1977).

The inclusion of unripe fruits or leaf and stalk material of the plant together with the spice during distillation results in a change of a number of the physicochemical constants. The specific gravity, optical rotation and alcohol (calculated as linalol) values are reduced somewhat, while the carbonyl value is enhanced. Provided that oil losses during storage of the spice prior to distillation are only slight, there are only small changes in the physicochemical properties of the distilled oil, mainly a slight increase in the linalol content and the ester value (Lukyanov and Berestovaya, 1973). Upon storage of the distilled oil in contact with the atmosphere, there is a gradual change in some of physicochemical properties, notably an increase in the specific gravity and the acid and ester numbers (Lukyanov and Berestovaya, 1973).

Composition

Studies of the composition of the spice oil were initiated early in the nineteenth century and the major constituent was first isolated by Kawalier (1852). This compound was subsequently characterized as an alcohol by Grosser (1881) and was named coriandrol by Semmler (1891) in a later investigation. The identity of coriandrol was eventually established by Barbier (1893) as an optically active form (dextrorotary) of the monoterpene alcohol, linalol.

Walbaum and Muller (1909) carried out a more detailed study of the coriander spice oil composition and reported that the *d*-linalol content ranged from 60 to 70 per cent and the hydrocarbon content was about

20 per cent. Alpha- and beta-pinenes, dipentene (limonene), *p*-cymene, alpha- and gamma-terpinenes, *n*-decanal, geraniol and *l*-borneol were also identified as constituents of the spice oil. Very little further advance was made on composition analysis during the following 50 years. However, the advent of chromatographic analysis techniques, especially gas chromatography, facilitated more detailed examinations and at the time of writing some 48 compounds had been identified in coriander spice oils (see Table 12.3).

The linalol content of coriander spice oils has been reported in the literature to range between 25 and 80 per cent, but values below 55 per cent have mainly been found with coriander indigenous to Asia. With regard to the linalol content and some other composition characteristics, European coriander spice oils may be placed at one end of the spectrum and Indian oils at the other end. For most European oils, the monoterpene hydrocarbon content is between 16 and 30 per cent, the linalol ranges between 60 and 75 per cent, and the remainder is largely comprised of other oxygenated monoterpenes. Russian oils have traditionally exhibited high linalol contents (69−75 per cent) and this feature has been maintained with the new cultivars selected for a combination of desirable characteristics (Obuchow and Kondrazki, 1946; Dublyanskaya *et al.*, 1965; Junkeviciene *et al.*, 1977; Glushenko *et al.*, 1977). The published data indicates that in European spice oils the major monoterpene hydrocarbon constituents are gamma-terpinene (up to 10 per cent), alpha-pinene, limonene and *p*-cymene (each up to 7 per cent), while the most abundant non-linalol oxygenated monoterpines are borneol (up to 7 per cent), geranyl acetate (up to 5 per cent), geranial and camphor (each up to 4 per cent), and geraniol (up to 2 per cent). An insufficient number of detailed analyses have as yet been reported to provide reliable quantitative data on the relative abundance of the minor constituents in European spice oils. However, it might be noted that anethole, which is present at up to 0.5 per cent levels in some Bulgarian oils, is absent in some other European oils (Rasmussen *et al.*, 1972). Also, *trans*-2-tridecenal reported by Schratz and Qadry, 1966a and b, (see also Reisch *et al.*, 1966) as a minor constituent present in the spice oils of two large-fruited coriander varieties (one German and the other Indian) had not been found in other oils at the time of compiling this review. A larger number of detailed analyses are necessary to establish the qualitative and quantitative composition differences between the various types of European spice oils before the distinctions made on organoleptic grounds can be rationalized.

Indigenous Indian coriander spice oils differ from European oils in possessing a lower linalol content and another distinguishing feature, recognized by early investigators (Anon., 1923; Rao *et al*, 1925), is the comparatively high ester content. Examination of the common, large-fruited type of Indian coriander by Gupta *et al.* (1977) revealed the presence of 21 per cent linalyl acetate and 42 per cent linalol in the

Table 12.3 *Constituents identified in coriander essential oils*

	Spice oils (from ripe, dried fruit)	Herb oil	
		Green herb prior to flowing	Flowering herb
Monoterpene hydrocarbons			
p-cymene	1, 4–8, 11, 12, 14–16, 18	—	—
camphene	4, 6–8, 12, 15, 16, 18	—	—
Δ-3-carene	4, 11, 12, 16	—	—
limonene (dipentene)	1, 2, 4, 6–8, 11, 12, 15–17	—	—
myrcene	2, 4, 6–8, 12, 15, 16	—	—
cis- and trans-ocimene	8, 12, 16	—	—
α-phellandrene	8, 12, 15, 16	—	—
β-phellandrene	1, 3, 4, 8, 12, 14, 16, 17	—	—
α-pinene	1, 2, 4–8, 11, 12, 14–18	—	—
β-pinene	1, 2, 4–8, 11, 12, 14–	—	—
sabinene	4, 12, 15, 16	—	—
α-terpinene	1, 2, 7, 8, 12, 14–16, 18	—	—
γ-terpinene	1, 4–8, 12, 15, 16	—	—
terpinolene	1, 12, 15, 16	—	—
α-thujene	12, 16	—	—
Monoterpene oxides and carbonyls			
camphor	6, 12, 15, 16	—	—
1,8-cineole	11, 15, 17	—	—
linalol oxide	16		
carvone	15	—	—
geranial	8, 16, 18	—	—

Table 12.3   (*Continued*)

	Spice oils (from ripe, dried fruit)	Herb oil	
		Green herb prior to flowing	Flowering herb
Monoterpene alcohols			
borneol	1, 5, 6, 10, 12, 14–18	20	20
citronellol	11, 12, 16, 17	–	–
geraniol	1, 2, 5, 6, 10–12, 15–17	–	–
linalol	1, 2, 5, 6, 8, 10–12, 14–18	–	20, 23
nerol	12, 16	–	–
α-terpineol	3, 12, 15, 16	–	–
4-terpinenol	12, 15, 16	–	–
Monoterpene esters			
bornyl acetate	1, 3	–	–
geranyl acetate	1, 3, 6, 8, 12, 15–17	–	–
linalyl acetate	1, 3, 6, 12, 17	–	–
α-terpinyl acetate	3	–	–
Sesquiterpenes			
β-caryophyllene	16, 17	–	–
caryophyllene oxide	17	–	–
elemol	17	–	–
nerolidol	15, 17	–	–
Phenols			
anethole	13, 15	–	–
myristicin	16	–	–
thymol	8, 17	–	–

Table 12.3 (*Continued*)

	Spice oils (from ripe, dried fruit)	Herb oil	
		Green herb prior to flowing	Flowering herb
Misc.			
acetic acid	15	—	—
α-*p*-dimethyl styrene	12	—	—
Aliphatic hydrocarbons			
heptadecane	16	—	—
octadecane	16	—	—
Aliphatic alcohols			
decanol	1, 16	—	—
dodecanol	16	—	—
Aliphatic aldehydes			
octanal	—	21	—
nonanal	16	—	23
decanal	8, 10, 14, 16, 18	19, 20, 21	20, 22, 23
undecanal	16	21	—
dodecanal	16	21	—
tridecanal	—	21	—
tetradecanal	—	21	—
3-octenal	—	21	—
2-decenal	16	—	22
5-decenal	—	21	—
8-methyl-2-nonenal	—	—	22
8-methyl-5-nonenal	—	21	—

Table 12.3 *(Continued)*

	Spice oils (from ripe, dried fruit)	Herb oil	
		Green herb prior to flowing	Flowering herb
6-undecenal	—	21	—
2-dodecenal	16	—	—
7-dodecenal	—	21	—
2-tridecenal	8, 9	20	20
8-tridecenal	—	21	—
9-tetradecenal	—	21	—
10-pentadecenal	—	21	—
3, 6-undecadienal	—	21	—
5, 8-tridecadienal	—	21	—

References

1. Walbaum and Muller (1909)
2. Marakova and Borisynk (1959)
3. Pertsev and Pivnenko (1962)
4. Ikeda *et al.* (1962)
5. Wellendorf (1963)
6. Akimov and Voronin (1965, 1968)
7. Avakova *et al.* (1966)
8. Schratz and Qadry (1966a)
9. Reisch *et al.* (1966)
10. Mahran *et al.* (1967)
11. Puri *et al.* (1968)
12. Karlsen *et al.* (1971)
13. Rasmussen *et al.* (1972)
14. Stankeviciene *et al.* (1973)
15. Chou (1974)
16. Taskinen and Nykanen (1975)
17. Gupta *et al.* (1977)
18. Jukneviciene *et al.* (1977)
19. Bryusova *et al.* (1940)
20. Schratz and Qadry (1966b)
21. MacLeod and Islam (1976)
22. Carlblom (1936)
23. Lesnov and Pekhov (1970)

distilled oil, while Puri *et al.* (1968) found that another sample contained only 25 per cent linalol. The last-named workers also examined a small-fruited coriander indigenous to the Kulu valley area in India and found the oil to contain 48 per cent linalol and, interestingly, a substantial proportion of citronellol. The large-fruited Indian coriander also appears to be distinct from other sources of the spice in the unique occurrence of the phenol, thymol (up to 7 per cent).

Only one detailed analysis has been reported for Moroccan coriander oil and the composition of this sample was found to be similar in most respects with European oils (Taskinen and Nykanen, 1975).

While the composition and the organoleptic properties of the spice oil are mainly determined by the intrinsic characteristics of the cultivar grown, they can be modified to some extent by other factors which include the stage of maturity at harvest, composition changes wrought during drying, storage and distillation of the spice, and on subsequent storage of the distilled oil. Premature harvesting of the fruit or the inclusion of stalk and leaf in the distillation charge results in an enhancement of the aldehyde components at the expense of most of the other constituents. Detailed composition data for the unripe fruits and the vegetative organs of the plant are given in the following sub-section ('Ontogenesis').

With fully ripe fruits which suffer only slight oil loss during drying and storage, the changes in oil composition appear to be minor and quantitative rather than qualitative. Shlyapnikova *et al.* (1974) have shown that under conditions of natural drying or carefully controlled artificial drying, a slight enhancement of the linalol content occurs but that the composition quickly stabilizes during the drying operation. Lukyanov and Berestovaya (1973) have observed similar changes during the storage of the whole spice. It was found that in the first year of storage the principal changes in the volatile oil were slight increases in the relative abundance of the linalol and the ester constituents, but no further changes in oil composition occurred during the second year of storage. In these cases, it seems likely that proportionately greater losses of the monoterpene hydrocarbons rather than of the oxygenated constituents are encountered. However, Shlyapnikova *et al.* found that artificial drying at temperatures over 100 °C results in the formation of a 'burnt-note' and a lowering of the linalol content. Tanasienko and Sobeleva (1961) and Shlyapnikova and Ponomarev (1970) found that substantial oil losses are entailed during storage of damaged, crushed or ground spice, and the changes in oil composition in the initial rapid-loss stage appear to parallel those encountered in high-temperature drying. The linalol content of the volatile oil then remains constant for a period, but prolonged exposure to the atmosphere eventually results in a further reduction in the linalol content and in a considerable organoleptic deterioration (Rakova, 1961). Schratz and Qadry (1966a) have reported that after storage of the whole spice for one year, only small quantities of artefacts could be detected in its volatile oil, whereas extensive artefact formation occurred with ground spice left in contact with the atmosphere. Changes in the volatile-oil composition of the spice during storage have also been studied by Georgiev (1968).

During distillation of the spice, a number of transformation may occur in the composition of the volatile oil. Small quantities of *p*-cymene may be produced as an artefact, linalyl acetate and some other esters may be hydrolysed, and *d*-linalol may rearrange to its optically inactive isomer geraniol. The maximum deterioration during storage of the distilled spice oil occurs when it is left exposed to light and air (Schratz and Qadry, 1966a; Lukyanov and Berestovaya, 1973). Oil storage transformations include those mentioned for distillation but oxidative changes, including the conversion of linalol to geranial, are the most important (Akimov and Voronin, 1968b).

In conclusion, readers who are interested in gas-chromatography analysis conditions and methods of determining the linalol content of coriander oil are recommended to refer to a review by Salzer (1975b).

Ontogenesis: Changes in the volatile oil during plant development

At the seedling stage, the coriander plant acquires a distinctive aroma, reminiscent of the stink-bug, and this is retained by the leaves and stalk throughout the period of plant development until the final phase of fruit ripening, during which the vegetative organs shrivel up. The immature fruits of the plant also possess the odour, but as they ripen their odour acquires a greater similarity to that of the dried spice. On full ripening and drying of the fruit, the bug-like aroma disappears. In Western markets, the odour and flavour of the herb is generally disliked and for this reason only fully ripe fruits are employed for distillation of the spice oil. In India, however, the leaves are appreciated for their flavouring properties and are incorporated into many dishes. The fresh leaves possess a high content of vitamin C and carotene, but the vitamin C content diminishes rapidly on storage. Composition analyses for the herb have been reported by Ranganathan (1935), Sarkar and Chavan (1963), Sergeeva (1974) and Gopala Rao and Sriramula (1977). According to Tucakov (1957), the odour of the green plant and flowers acts as an excitant and attractant for bees, which play an important role in fertilizing the flowers.

Volatile-oil content changes

Each of the vegetative organs of the plant (leaves, stalks and root) contain volatile oil which is detectable at an early stage of development of the seedling. The content of the volatile oil in the vegetative organs increases progressively with plant development and reaches a maximum (about 0.1–0.2 per cent on a fresh-weight basis) in the overground parts at the flowering stage (Schimmel and Co., 1895; Chiris, 1925; Spiridonova, 1936; Carlblom, 1936; Penka and Bacikova, 1960; Razinskaite, 1967; Razinskaite and Slavenus, 1966b; Lassanyi and Lorincz, 1968; Lukyanov and Berestovaya, 1971). During the fruit ripening phase, the vegetative organs progressively dehydrate and their volatile-oil content diminishes as the oil canals flatten. According to Razinskaite and Slavenus (1966b), the oil content in the various vegetative organs peaks at different stages of plant development: early on in the roots, at the flowering stage with the stems, and at plant maturity with the leaves.

In the reproductive organs, volatile oil is detectable in the umbels at the flowering stage, and its content rises steadily until the fruit commence to ripen (Penka and Bacikova, 1960; Razinskaite and Slavenus, 1966b; Lassanyi and Lorincz, 1968, 1969; Logvinov *et al.*, 1975). As the fruits develop to full ripeness, during which dehydration occurs, their volatile-oil content diminishes. According to Lukyanov and Berestovaya (1971), approximately one-third of the volatile oil present in the immature fruit is lost in the course of fruit ripening. The volatile oil of the fruits at maturity is dependent upon the position of the umbel in small-fruited varieties and it is highest in the central umbels, lower in the second-order, and lowest in the first-order umbels (Razinskaite and Slavenus, 1966b; Lukyanov, 1962; Yankulov, 1963; Tsvetkov, 1970). By contrast, Yankulov (1963) could find no such variation in a large-fruited coriander cultivar.

Physicochemical constant changes

With the exception of Ivanov *et al.* (1929), all of the early investigators agreed that the odour change during maturation was associated with a transition in the properties of the volatile oil. The Schimmel Co. (1895) and Spiridonova (1936) recorded the physicochemical constants of the essential oil distilled from the overground parts of the plant at various stages of development, and showed that the specific gravity increased gradually and the optical rotation increased dramatically between flowering and fruit ripening. Physicochemical constant determinations by Chiris (1924, 1925), Kopp (1929), Carlblom (1936) and, later, by Guenther (1950) and Miller (1952) are in accord with the findings of the Schimmel Co. and Spiridonova. At the young green herb stage, the distilled oil has a specific gravity (at 20 °C) of the order of 0.850, the optical rotation is less than + 1 °, the alcohol value is low and the aldehyde value is high. Oil distilled from fresh plants bearing fruits have intermediate values between these and those of the spice oil.

Composition of the herb oil

The composition in the vegetative organs of the plant was recognized to be aldehydic in character at least as early as 1928 by Chernukin. Carlblom (1936) examined an essential oil distilled from the flowering plant and provided the first reasonable composition analysis. This oil was found to contain about 95 per cent aldehydes, of which *n*-decanal comprised about 10 per cent. Myrcene and two isomers of decenal, 2-decenal and 8-methyl-2-nonenal, were also claimed to be present in this oil.

Bryusova *et al.* (1940) examined the essential oil distilled from the green parts of the plant and confirmed a total aldehyde content of about 95 per cent and an *n*-decanal content of around 10 per cent.

No further progress was made until the 1960s when thin-layer chromatography studies were undertaken by Lorincz and Tyihak (1965a and b), El-Hamidi and Ahmed (1966), Schratz and Qadry (1966b), Lassanyi and Lorincz (1967, 1968, 1969), and Lukyanov and Mukhanova (1964, 1968). These studies and those of the majority of subsequent workers confirmed that the volatile-oil composition in the vegetative organs was comprised mainly of aldehydes and differed little from organ to organ. However, the identity of the aldehydes remains in dispute.

In their series of papers, Lassanyi and Lorincz reported that linalol was absent in the vegetative organs at all stages of development of the 'Lucs' cultivar, but that it remains present in the rejected pericarpum of the seedling at virtually the same level as in the dormant fruit. These authors also observed that a non-aldehydic compound was present in the vegetative organs throughout their development and its proportion was almost equal to that of the aldehydes around the wilting phase.

Schratz and Qadry (1966b) carried out an examination of the volatile-oil composition of two large-fruited coriander cultivars (one German and the other Indian) which involved analysis of individual organs at one-week intervals during the complete cycle of development. Three compounds, *trans*-2-tridecenal, *n*-decanal and borneol, were stated to be present throughout the life cycle of the vegetative organs in high, medium and small quantities respectively. During the flowering and early fruiting period, small quantities of hydrocarbons and traces of linalol were detected in the vegetative organs but they disappeared on plant maturation. *Trans*-2-tridecenal was said to be responsible for the bug-like odour of the herb.

Lesnov and Pekhov (1970) reported a thin-layer chromatography examination of an oil distilled from a flowering Russian herb and detected the presence of decanal, nonanal and linalol. The specific sharp odour of the herb was attributed to nonanal while decanal was considered to contribute little to the characteristic odour.

MacLeod and Islam (1976) have reported an extremely detailed and thorough gas chromatography/mass spectrometry study of a solvent extract of fresh coriander leaf of unspecified type or source. Some thirty components were detected in the oil and the majority were identified (see Table 12.3). Over 90 per cent of the oil was found to be comprised of a series of aliphatic aldehydes, of which C_{12} aldehydes were the most abundant. Saturated straight-chain aldehydes constituted about 40 per cent of the oil and included *n*-decanal (10 per cent), undecanal (3 per cent), octanal (5 per cent), dodecanal (16 per cent) and tridecanal (4 per cent). Straight-chain monoenals accounted for about 39 per cent of the total oil and included 7-dodecenal (21 per cent), 9-tetradecenal (9 per cent) and 10-pentadecenal (3 per cent). Two straight-chain dienals were also identified: 3, 6-undecadienal (3.4 per cent) and 5, 8-tridecadienal (5.6 per cent). This study showed reasonable agreement with that of Carlblom (1936) in the total aldehyde and *n*-decanal contents, and differed only in that the early worker reported 2-decenal and 8-methyl-2-nonenal, whereas MacLeod and Islam found 5-decenal and 8-methyl-5-nonenal. By contrast, MacLeod and Islam's results are at considerable variance with those of Schratz and Qadry (1966b) and Lesnov and Pekhov (1970). Neither 2-tridecenal nor nonanal, claimed to be present by the earlier workers and attributed responsible for the bed-bug odour, were detected.

To further confuse the issue, Tschogowadse and Bachtadse (1977) have reported a gas-chromatography analysis of an essential oil distilled from the fresh herb of the 'Zwrilpotala' cultivar, harvested prior to blooming. In this sample some 37 components were detected and the following were identified: alpha-pinene (19 per cent), *p*-cymene (27 per cent), linalol (19 per cent), borneol (7 per cent), geraniol (9 per cent) and decanal (4 per cent). This composition seems to have closer affinities to that of the unripe fruit than the pre-blooming stage herb, although Chiris (1925) and Kopp (1929) have reported high linalol contents in the flowering herb.

Composition changes in the reproductive organs

During the development of the reproductive organs, the volatile-oil composition progressively transforms from being predominantly aldehydic to one in which linalol is the most abundant component. The stage of appearance of linalol is disputed, however, with Schratz and Qadry (1966b) and Lassanyi and Lorincz (1968) claiming that it is already present in the flowering bodies, while Lukyanov and Berestovaya (1971) state that it only appears in the fruits.

Schratz and Qadry (1966b) have reported that during fruit development the relative abundance of borneol and the aldehydes (identified as *trans*-2-tridecenal and *n*-decanal) progressively diminish, while linalol, the hydrocarbons, geranyl acetate and geraniol increase. On full ripening and drying of the fruit, the aldehydes and borneol, which characterize the volatile oil of the vegative organs, further decline to minor or trace quantities.

An explanation for the change in fruit-oil composition during ripening was first postulated by Chernukin (1928) who suggested that the aldehydes were reduced to linalol and the hydrocarbons. Later, Carlblom (1936) suggested that the linalol might be derived from myrcene. However, recent histochemical investigations have indicated that chemical transformations of the type described above play no more than a minor role in the process of fruit ripening.

Boratynskaya (1956) carried out a study of the various volatile oil canals in the plant and showed that the fruit possessed two distinct types. One set of canals located on the periphery of the fruit become flattened and lose their volatile oil during ripening while those located inside the kernel remain intact. Hotin (1957) observed that if the fruits ripen at high humidity, the peripheral canals do not completely flatten and the volatile-oil content of the fruit is high but its organoleptic quality is poorer. Tanasienko (1960) and Lukyanov and Mukhanova (1964) reported that the composition of the volatile oil in the two sets of canals in the fruit were quite distinct, and that the peripheral canals are rich in aldehydes while the internal canals contain mainly monoterpene hydrocarbons and alcohols.

Lassanyi and Lorincz (1968, 1970) re-examined the fruit canal structures, their oil composition and their fate during fruit development, and confirmed the conclusions of the earlier workers. These investigators noted that although the peripheral canals become flattened during the course of fruit development they still retain some oil at the ripe fruit stage and only lose all their oil during the drying process. The production of linalol in the internal canals was found to be rapid at first, but a plateau was reached at the waxy, ripe fruit stage when these canals had developed to their maximum size. Lukyanov and Berestovaya (1971) and Logvinov *et al.* (1975) have confirmed that the linalol content peaks at this stage. The variation in oil composition during fruit ripening has been examined also by Stankeviciene *et al.* (1973), using gas-chromatography analysis.

Tsvetkov (1970) has reported that when Bulgarian coriander is harvested at optimum maturity, the volatile-oil composition in the central, first- and second-order umbels was not markedly different, even though the oil content differs. Karlsen *et al.* (1971) undertook a similar gas-chromatography study with Bulgarian coriander, but examined individual fruits and found qualitative and quantitative differences between fruits from the same umbel.

Standard specifications

The spice

The United Kingdom

There are no statutory standard specifications in the UK for the coriander spice, other than the official pharmaceutical requirements. The *British Pharmaceutical Codex*, 1973, defines the spice as consisting

Table 12.4 *Characteristics quoted in the British Pharmaceutical Codex, 1973*

Variety	No of fruits/g	Appearance	Volatile oil (%, v/w)
English	av. 100	uniform buff colour, frequently split.	0.3–0.8
Moroccan	not less than 75	marked with purplish patches, rarely split.	0.3–0.6
Russian	av. more than 130	purplish-brown colour, usually whole.	0.8–1.2
Argentine	smaller than English	deep brownish buff coloured, some split fruits.	0.3–0.6

of the ripe and dried fruits of *Coriandrum sativum* L. It distinguishes several varieties according to their geographical origin in relation to the size, appearance and volatile-oil content of the fruits, as listed in Table 12.4.

The *Codex* requires that, in addition to satisfying macro- and microscopical conditions, the spice should comply with the specifications of the *British Pharmacopoeia*, 1973: the whole spice should contain not more than 1.5 per cent acid-insoluble ash, not more than 2.0 per cent foreign organic matter and not less than 0.3 per cent of volatile oil, determined by a specified method. For the powdered spice, the limits for acid-insoluble ash and foreign organic matter are the same as for the whole spice, but the minimum limit for volatile oil is reduced to 0.2 per cent.

The International Standards Organization, which has the active support of the United Kingdom, through its collaboration with the British Standards Institute, was preparing an International Standard for coriander at the time of writing this review. This Standard is expected to be the basis of a British Standard Specification.

The United States

The United States Government Standard requires that coriander shall be the dried fruit of *Coriandrum sativum* L., and shall satisfy the conditions enumerated in Table 12.5.

In addition, the American Spice Trade Association's Cleanliness Specifications are as listed in Table 12.6.

Canada

Canadian Government Standards require that the spice shall be the dried fruit of the coriander plant and shall contain not more than 7 per cent total ash and 1.5 per cent ash insoluble in hydrochloric acid (Canadian Food and Drug Regulations, 1969, Division 7 — Part B 07.022).

Table 12.5   *US Government Standards for coriander, whole and ground*

Moisture, not more than	9.0 per cent
Total ash, not more than	7.0 per cent
Acid insoluble ash, not more than	1.0 per cent
Volatile oil, ml per 100 g, not less than	'a trace'
Sieve test (for ground coriander only)	
US standard sieve size	No. 30
Percentage required to pass through, not less than	95

From: US Federal Specifications: *Spices, ground and whole, and spice blends*, No. EE-S-631H. June 5, 1975.

Table 12.6   *ASTA Cleanliness Specification for coriander*

	max.
Extraneous matter, per cent by weight	0.5
Rodent excreta, by count	4
Other excreta, mg per lb	10
Whole dead insects, per cent by weight	1.0
Mouldy spice, per cent by weight	1.0

Other countries

Standard specifications for coriander have also been published by a number of other countries, including Sri Lanka (Bureau of Ceylon Standards Specification, SLS 246:1973).

The essential oil

The *British Pharmacopoeia*, 1973 and the *United States Pharma-*

Table 12.7   *Requirements for the spice oil*

	British Pharmacopoeia Standard	United States Pharmacopoeia Standard
Optical rotation	+ 8° to + 12° at 20 °C	+ 8° to + 12° at 25 °C
Refractive index at 20 °C	1.462 to 1.472	1.462 to 1.472
Specific gravity at 25 °C	—	0.863 to 0.875
Wt. per ml at 20 °C	0.863 to 0.870	—
Solubility in 70 per cent alcohol	1 volume in 3 volumes at 20 °C	1 volume in 3 volumes
Heavy metals, max.	—	0.004 per cent

copoeia, 18th Revision (1970) have standards for the essential oil distilled from the spice which is described as a colourless to pale yellow liquid with the properties given in Table 12.7.

The British Standards Institution has also published a specification (BS 2999/33:1971) for coriander spice oil. The standard includes the property requirements listed in Table 12.8, which are to be determined by specified methods.

Table 12.8 *Requirements of the British Standard the spice oil*

	BS 2999/33:1971
Apparent density (mass/ml) at 20 °C	0.860 to 0.876
Optical rotation at 20 °C	+ 5° to + 13°
Refractive index at 20 °C	1.462 to 1.470
Solubility in 65% (v/v) alcohol at 20 °C	1 volume in 8 volumes
Acid value	not greater than 3.0
Ester value	not greater than 22.0
Ester value after acetylation	not less than 200.0

Production, trade and markets

Coriander, indigenous to southern Europe, is now grown in a large number of countries, of which India, Morocco, Pakistan, Romania and the USSR are the major producers of the spice. Other producers include Iran, Turkey, Egypt, Lebanon and Israel in the Middle East region; China, Burma and Thailand in the Asian region; the Netherlands, the UK, France, Italy, Hungary, Czechoslovakia, Poland, Bulgaria and Yugoslavia in Europe; and the USA, Argentina, Mexico and Guatemala in the Americas. Although annual production statistics are not available for most of the spice producers, it does not appear that world production is dominated by any particular country. As a result of the relative ease with which this crop can be cultivated as compared with many others, there is the potential in many countries for a substantially large increase in their production within very short periods. A probable case in which this has occurred is Mexico.

In several of the producing countries there is a large domestic demand for the spice, while the major foreign trade markets are Sri Lanka, the Middle East, Malaysia, Japan, Chile, Bolivia and the USA.

In addition to the spice, obtained by drying the mature fruits of the plant, considerable quantities of the fresh green herb are consumed domestically in the producing countries of Asia, the Middle East, Central and South America. The small, woody root of the plant is also used in certain countries, particularly China, as a vegetable. However, only the spice is of importance as an item of international trade.

Production

The small-scale nature of production, often on scattered, inaccessible and fragmented holdings, makes it difficult to obtain reliable estimates of area under cultivation, and production estimates, even when available, are very unreliable. Trade figures, which are generally more comprehensive and up to date, in the case of some spices are considered useful guides to production, but in other cases, of which coriander is an example, most producing countries have a large domestic market and thus export statistics are an unreliable guide to production levels. For instance, although India is a major coriander producer, her exports are negligible. However, some tentative production estimates are available for India (see Table 12.9). Average annual production was estimated at 79 000 tonnes in 1961/2–1965/6, and 92 000 tonnes in 1969/70–1972/3, whereas annual exports during approximately the same periods were about 2 600 tonnes and 700 tonnes respectively (i.e. approximately 3 per cent and 0.8 per cent of India's production). Since 1972–3 the situation has not changed significantly.

India is probably the world's largest coriander producer, with an annual production of around 100 000 tonnes. The plant is cultivated in all States, being grown on a field scale for seed purposes and on a smaller scale for its green leaves and stems. It forms an important subsidiary crop in the black cotton soils of the Deccan and South India and in the rich silt loam of North India. In 1952 it was estimated that about 40 000 ha were under coriander in Madras and 4 000 ha in Bombay, while in the Punjab it was grown in every district. In 1959 further estimates suggest areas of 45 000 ha in Madhya Pradesh, 26 000 ha in Bombay, 5 000 ha in Mysore and 4 000 ha in Bihar. Estimates of total area under coriander would suggest an expansion in the 1960s with a more rapid increase of about 8 per cent between 1972–3 and 1973–4. Production estimates suggest a rising trend but with wide yearly variation, e.g. 70 000 tonnes in 1970 and 115 000 tonnes in 1971. No specific reasons have been suggested for these fluctuations and thus one must assume that they are caused by the usual factors influencing spice production, namely climatic conditions, prices received and substitution by producers of more lucrative crops.

Limited production statistics are also available for Morocco and Pakistan (see Table 12.9), but data on other producers are either scanty or non-existent.

A comparison of Moroccan data in Tables 12.9 and 12.10 suggests that Morocco, unlike India, exports a large proportion of her output

Table 12.9: *Coriander: Area cultivated and spice production, 1961/2–1974/5[1]*

Country		Annual average 1961/2–1965/6	1964	1965	1966	1967	1968	1969–70	1970–1	1971–2	1972–3	1973–4	1974–5
India	ha	234 000						69 700	101 200	114 600	252 600	272 000	
	tonnes	79 000									83 000	92 000	
Pakistan*	ha					6 000	7 000				5 150	5 160	5 030
	tonnes					2 800	3 416				2 692	2 792	2 709
Morocco	ha		13 750	9 000	12 500	12 000		26 000					
	tonnes		9 020	4 900	8 070	3 165		13 380					

Source: Tropical Products Quarterly
Estimates of Area and Production of Principal Crops of India, 1972–3
 (Ministry of Agriculture, Government of India, 1974)
 Indian Spices
 Monthly Statistical Bulletin of Bangladesh, September 1975

*Bangladesh figures from 1972–3
[1]Where no figure is given statistics were unavailable

Table 12.10 *Coriander seed: Exports of selected countries 1957–77*

	1957	1958	1959	1960	1961	1962	1963	1964	1965	1966	1967	1968	1969	1970	1971	1972	1973	1974	1975	1976	1977
Morocco																					
tonnes	3 722	9 071	5 886	9 249	3 163	9 393	7 101	8 378	11 696	6 350	7 039	13 187	11 577	12 445	14 868	12 039	13 057	11 514	9 738	7 674	...
£'000	175.4	243.8	183.9	369.6	300.0	367.2	291.3	300	436.7	396.6	554.9	738.3	787.7	914.4	1 045.7	841.6	1 080.2	972.2	1 196.9	2 107.3	...
Iran(1)																					
tonnes	...	...	...	...	...	161	140	401	322	571	317	155	173	749	1 111	633	522	...(5)	...	...	...
£'000	...	...	...	...	...	10.0	9.9	26.2	22.8	48.8	30.6	14.9	15.2	63.3	91.4	51.4	62.6	...	...	...	...
India																					
tonnes	3 493	2 677	765(2)	...	1 858(3)	8 393	2 470	833	234	142	482	2 435	3 263	515	392	680	930	897	669	755	2 904
£'000	163.2	122.3	65.4	...	154	548.8	133.1	55.2	32.8	23.5	56.6	200.8	235.5	52.6	54.1	85.1	107.5	160.6	148.0	185.9	1 277.8
Argentina																					
tonnes	176	59	99	96	118	271	142	62	45	2 045	2 246	4 575	2 519	2 775	4 832	3 967	2 701	8 153	51	366	...
£'000	6.3	2.1	2.6	3.8	6.1	16.8	6.3	2.8	1.7	210.5	216.0	486.2	324.3	315.7	540.7	484.9	358.4	1 452	4	43	...
Pakistan																					
tonnes	...	315	...	338(4)	723	...	...	406	106	258	1 467	1 259	90	103	536	...	59	15	38	...	...
£'000	...	10.3	...	10.5	41.1	...	...	20.7	8.2	15.3	104.0	79.4	6.1	4.5	31.9	...	6.3	3.1	7	...	...

Sources: Annual Trade Statistics of countries shown above
USDA Foreign Agriculture Circular
TPI Report G37

–   nil or negligible
...   not available
(1)   21 March to 20 March of year shown
(2)   January 1959 to March 1960
(3)   From 1961, Indian figures are from April to March of year shown
(4)   From 1960 Pakistan figures are from July to June of year shown
(5)   Item not shown separately in trade statistics

and thus export figures can be taken as a reasonable guide to production levels. The available data would suggest an upward trend in production between the mid-1950s and late 1960s, but since then production has averaged around 10 000 tonnes per annum but with considerable yearly fluctuations.

Pakistan's production was estimated at 2 800 tonnes from 6 000 ha in 1967, of which just over 50 per cent was exported, and 3 400 tonnes from 7 000 ha in 1968, of which just under 40 per cent was exported. Production was probably disrupted by the 1971 war since export figures show a dramatic decline to negligible quantities in the 1970s (see Table 12.10). No current area, production or export figures are available for Bangladesh (formerly East Pakistan), but some 5 700 ha were under cultivation in the late 1960s with an annual out-turn of some 3 000 tonnes of the spice.

Production in Eastern Europe is known to be substantial. In the USSR, the spice is grown mainly for the production of the essential oil from which the major constituent, *d*-linalol, is isolated for use as a starting material for the production of citral and other derivatives. The production of the spice oil in 1940 amounted to 333 tonnes and in 1960 was 390 tonnes but rose to 750 tonnes in 1963. Zukov (1964) estimated that the domestic requirement for the oil would rise to around 2 000 tonnes by 1970. Assuming an average yield of 0.8−1.0 per cent of oil from Russian coriander, the minimum production of the spice in 1963 must have been of the order of 70 000 tonnes, in addition to which there was probably a large production for direct spice consumption. Romania is another major producer but the only guide to production can be derived from imports of coriander seed from Romania into Malaysia and Singapore (up to 1961), Sri Lanka (up to 1966) and the USA. Yearly exports from Romania to these countries have invariably exceeded 1 500 tonnes and in 1966 exports to Sri Lanka alone were just over 3 000 tonnes. When production for domestic use, the extraction of the essential oil and exports to other countries are taken into consideration, then it is likely that average annual production in Romania has been greater than 3 000 tonnes. Production of coriander in Yugoslavia became important during the Second World War when supplies of imported spices were cut off, and by 1945 around 1 000 ha of coriander were under cultivation. By the mid-1950s around 2 000 ha were under cultivation and Yugoslavia had become an exporter rather than an importer of coriander oil. Information is not available on recent production levels in other countries of Eastern and Central Europe.

In the USA coriander is produced in Kentucky, mainly for the liquor industry, and a limited quantity is grown in California as a winter crop and in the central states as a summer crop. It would seem, however, that American producers find it difficult to compete with many other producers who have lower labour costs. Coriander is a relatively low-value crop compared with other agricultural commodities. At one time the crop was extensively cultivated in the United Kingdom, particularly in East Anglia and Essex.

No information is available on production in other countries, except for Argentina and Iran, who publish export figures which give some guide to the order of magnitude of production. These are discussed in the following section on trade.

Trade

The spice enters international trade mainly in the whole form but substantial, if unquantifiable, amounts are also traded as a constituent of mixed spices, particularly curry powders. Few figures are available on the trade in the essential oil but it is thought to be relatively small, and trade in the oleoresin appears to be on a yet smaller scale. The major exporters of the spice in likely order of importance are Morocco, Argentina, Romania, Mexico, Iran and India, while the major purchasers are Sri Lanka, Malaysia and Singapore (which both have substantial re-export trades), the USA, Japan, Chile and Bolivia.

A major feature of the trade is the wide yearly fluctuations in quantity and values traded. As yet, no particular explanation for this has been proffered and the answer probably lies in the interaction of several variables, including fluctuations in production, prices and stocks. No data are available on stock levels, but the whole spice can be stored for several years, and so also can some of the products in which coriander is used.

A second related feature of the coriander trade is, with the probable exception of Morocco and Romania, the frequency with which the relative importance of countries shifts. This can best be seen by looking at the major exporting and importing countries.

Morocco

From the mid-1950s to the mid-1960s Moroccan exports showed considerable yearly fluctuations; for example, between 1957 and 1958 exports almost trebled, and then fell in the succeeding year by almost a third (see Table 12.10). An upward trend in exports can be discerned over the period 1957–71 by averaging over several years, but in the 1970s this stabilized as the following average annual export figures show: 1957–61, 6 218 tonnes; 1962–6, 8 586 tonnes; 1967–71, 11 823 tonnes; and 1972–5, 11 637 tonnes. Moroccan coriander seed is exported to many Asian, African, Middle Eastern and European countries, but by far the largest importer is Sri Lanka, taking approximately 40 per cent, followed by Malaysia, Japan and the USA.

Romania

Export statistics are not available for Romania but it is evident from the returns of importing countries that Romania is a major producer and probably the third largest exporter of coriander seed. Despite wide yearly fluctuations, US imports from Romania have shown a steadily rising trend, averaging 252 tonnes in 1957−60, 299 tonnes in 1961−4, 341 tonnes in 1967−70, and 481 tonnes in 1971−5. The main importer appears to be Sri Lanka, whose imports from Romania averaged nearly 1 500 tonnes between 1957 and 1966, while Romanian exports to Malaysia and Singapore averaged 275 tonnes in the period 1957−61. Unfortunately, except for the USA, these countries no longer record coriander seed imports separately and it is therefore unrealistic to make any firm observations on the computed total exports from Romania; suffice it to say that exports appear to have fluctuated widely over the last two decades, with a slight upward trend.

Argentina

There are no data to define the level of production and consumption of coriander in any part of South America, but the flavour of the spice and the herb is known to be highly popular. Argentine export statistics (see Table 12.10) show a massive expansion of exports from 1966 onwards to put Argentina as the second major world exporter of the spice. During 1957−65 the exports averaged almost 120 tonnes, and during 1966−73 they reached 3 200 tonnes. A record 8 153 tonnes were exported in 1974, falling to only 51 tonnes in 1975 but recovering to 366 tonnes in 1976. Although Argentina exports to many countries, her major markets are in South America and the Middle East, with Chile, Bolivia, Lebanon and Syria being the leading importers.

Iran

Iranian exports are approximately one-twentieth by volume of those of Morocco. The figures exhibit similar characteristics to those of Morocco, namely wide yearly variations and an upward trend. While the fluctuations are not synchronized, the trend appears to follow a similar pattern to that of Morocco, as illustrated by the following annual averages: 319 tonnes 1962−66, 501 tonnes 1967−71, and 577 tonnes 1972−3. Exports went almost entirely to Malaysia, Singapore and to Middle East countries, particularly Oman and Dubai.

India

It is difficult to make direct quantity comparisons between Indian exports and those of other countries owing to the use of different time periods in the trade statistics. However, in 1957 and 1961−2 India exported approximately the same quantity of coriander seed as Morocco, and like the latter country there have been wide annual divergences in quantities exported, but since the mid-1960s the trend has been downwards, as the following average annual export figures show: 2 069 tonnes 1957−61, 2 484 tonnes 1962−6, 1 457 tonnes

Tabel 12.11   *Coriander spice: Imports of selected countries, 1957–77*

		1957	1958	1959	1960	1961	1962	1963	1964	1965	1966	1967	1968	1969	1970	1971	1972	1973	1974	1975	1976	1977
Sri Lanka	tonnes	4 629	5 062	6 377	5 714	6 066	7 581	4 785	5 780	6 537	5 607	7 936	8 320	8 973	5 253	5 497	3 881	...	6 051	2 455	327	...
	£'000	258	235	282	313	456	435	261	316	367	353	684	545	708	479.3	468	575	...	607	297	53	...
United States	tonnes	1 090	847	1 168	1 294	1 126	1 222	735	1 672	1 158	1 572	1 244	1 612	1 214	1 401	1 264	1 587	1 524	1 575	2 471	2 857	2 507
	£'000	63	40	49	66	114	73	28	72	51	141	103	120	96	117	101	119	153	178	310	590	869
India	tonnes	2 394	112	5	—	—	—	—	—	102(1)	258	186	32	—	—	12	110	126	129	36	6	48
	£'000	60.5	2.6	0.5	—	—	—	—	—	5.5	16.2	12.6	2.5	—	—	0.9	1.1	5.2	13.9	3.3	1.3	13.4
Thailand	tonnes	...	...	...	107	10	108	63	98	105	94	70	103	166	...(4)	...	...	...	...	...	...	...
	£'000	...	...	...	14.6	1.6	18.1	10.9	16.8	16.0	16.2	12.1	15.9	16.3	...	...	...	...	...	...	...	...
Japan(2)	tonnes	197	505	294	523	726	430	649	703	937	1 021	...	966	1 123	1 563	1 464	1 722	1 736	1 608	1 833	...(5)	...
	£'000	14.3	15.6	10.8	28.9	63.6	20.6	26.2	26.1	30.8	...	...	66.4	76.6	113	104	110	139	145	228	...	...
Malaysia and Singapore	tonnes	4 271	3 554	3 106	4 030	2 976(3)	...	...	...	...	...	...	...	...	...	...	...	...	...	...	...	...
	£'000	267	188	151	228	232	...	...	...	...	...	...	...	...	...	...	...	...	...	...	...	...

Sources: Annual trade statistics of countries shown
USDA Foreign Agriculture Circular
TPI Report G37

— nil or negligible
... not available
(1) From 1965 Indian statistics are from April to March of year shown
(2) Japanese figures are calculated from the export returns of Malaya and Singapore (until 1961),
India and Morocco
(3) Not separately shown after 1961
(4) Not separately shown after 1969
(5) Not separately shown after 1975

1967–71, 832 tonnes 1972–4 and 712 tonnes in 1975–6 (see Table 12.10).

India is also an important importer of the spice but the quantities have diminished in recent years to just over 100 tonnes per annum. The importation of nearly 2 400 tonnes in 1957, almost exclusively from Pakistan, was an aberration from the usual pattern.

Sri Lanka

Sri Lanka was once the largest importer of coriander seeds. As Table 12.11 shows, however, imports fluctuated widely over the period 1957–75 around an average of 5 917 tonnes per annum, with a maximum of almost 9 000 tonnes in 1969. Average annual imports have been as follows: 5 570 tonnes 1957–61, 6 058 tonnes 1962–6, 7 196 tonnes 1967–71, and 4 129 tonnes 1972–75. Thus until the late 1960s imports showed an upward trend, after which there has been a dramatic decrease, reaching only 327 tonnes in 1976. The bulk of Sri Lanka's imports were supplied by Morocco and Romania with India (up to 1961) and Pakistan (during the 1960s) making important contributions. Sri Lanka has also re-exported small quantities of coriander seed, almost exclusively to the Maldive Islands.

The USA

The USA has for a long time been a substantial importer of the spice. Over the past two decades US imports have shown periods of both wide fluctuations and relative stability. Thus over the period 1957–1966 average annual imports were 1 146 tonnes, falling to 847 tonnes in 1958 and 735 tonnes in 1963, and rising to 1 672 tonnes in 1964. Between 1966 and 1974 imports remained relatively stable, with a high of 1 612 tonnes in 1968 and a low of 1 214 tonnes in 1969. In 1975, however, imports increased by 57 per cent over the 1974 levels to 2 471 tonnes and this level was maintained in 1976. In the past the bulk of coriander seed imports have been supplied by Morocco and Romania, with several other countries providing small quantities, but a major feature of the 1975 data is the upsurge in imports from Mexico, which supplied 33 per cent of the total.

Japan

Coriander seed is not listed separately in the import statistics of Japan but export statistics of producing countries show Japan to be an importer of substantial quantities, rivalling the United States. The known suppliers to Japan are Morocco, India, Argentina, Iran, and probably Malaysia, Singapore and Romania, although the trade statistics of the last three countries do not list coriander exports separately. The only significant Japanese supplier, however, is Morocco, supplies from all other countries being quite negligible. Moroccan coriander exports to Japan are therefore fairly representative of the total Japanese imports. From these statistics Japan appears to be the fastest-growing market for coriander, imports having increased from an annual average of around 400 tonnes in 1957−61 to around 1 700 tonnes in 1970−5.

Other importers

Despite relatively small populations, several Middle East countries, particularly Kuwait, Saudi Arabia, Lebanon, Syria, Oman, Dubai, Qatar, and Yemen, import substantial quantities of coriander seed. Coriander seed is an important ingredient of Arab cooking, and consumption of coriander per head must be the highest in the world. Unfortunately, no data are available on individual countries but the export statistics of Morocco, Argentina and Iran show a large proportion of coriander seed going to the Middle East.

Compared with the consumption of other spices, the countries of the EEC are relatively unimportant in the coriander trade. Probably the largest consumer in the EEC is West Germany, whose annual imports averaged 930 tonnes in the period 1964−8. Morocco and Romania generally account for 60−70 per cent of total supplies, with Bulgaria, Hungary, Yugoslavia and Poland sharing the remainder. UK trade in coriander has been estimated at around 500 tonnes per annum, but the UK, like most EEC members, fails to separate coriander seed from other spice seeds in its trade figures. From the export data of some producers it is possible to obtain some idea of the order of magnitude of imports. Thus average annual coriander seed exports from Morocco during 1968−72 to the UK were 403 tonnes, to West Germany 599 tonnes, to the Netherlands 860 tonnes, to France 252 tonnes and to Italy 82 tonnes, while exports to the EEC constituted approximately 17 per cent by volume of the total Moroccan coriander exports. Exports of coriander seed from Iran, Argentina, India and Pakistan to EEC members constituted an even smaller proportion of their total coriander exports than that of Morocco.

Pakistan used to be a major exporter, particularly in the mid-1960s, but owing to diminishing exports may now be a net importer. Iranian export statistics for 1972−3 (the last year for which data are available) show Pakistan as having imported 103 tonnes. The roles of Malaysia and Singapore in the coriander trade are particularly difficult to document, since trade figures for Malaysia and Singapore are only available up to 1961, after which coriander seed was not listed separately. Over the period for which data are available, 1957−61, both imports and exports averaged around 3 600 tonnes per annum, the main sources being India and Morocco with substantial quantities also coming from Romania, Burma, Iran and Pakistan while the main destinations were Japan, South Africa and Indonesia. Both Malaysia and Singapore still import substantial quantities but it is impossible to establish how much of this is re-exported. Export statistics from Burma are only available from 1957 to 1962, and show a rapid rise from 200 tonnes in 1957 to nearly 1 100 tonnes in 1959, followed by an equally rapid fall to nearly 150 tonnes in 1961. From the latest US import statistics it would seem that Mexico has become an important exporter of coriander seed, Mexican exports to the US having risen rapidly in the 1970s from 4 tonnes in 1971, 28 tonnes in 1972, 88 tonnes in 1973, 235 tonnes in 1974, to 835 tonnes in 1975. One must assume that this growth has been achieved through increased production, but as with all coriander-exporting countries one is never certain, because of the dearth of production statistics, whether changes in quantities traded are a result of shifts in domestic consumption levels or a result of actual increased production.

Market structure

Because of the large number of countries both exporting and importing coriander, it can be presumed that there must be considerable variations in the methods by which it is traded. No evidence has been seen, however, which would suggest that the methods of coriander trade in individual countries differ in any way from the methods by which those countries organize their trade in other spices. Thus in Western Europe, Asia, North America and the Middle East, coriander appears to enter international trade through the same distribution channels as other spices, involving the services of an exporter, an agent – broker and occasionally a dealer. In some countries, particularly in Eastern Europe, centralized marketing bodies undertake the export of coriander seed and oil. Except perhaps in Singapore, the re-exporting of coriander seed seems to constitute a relatively small proportion of the total coriander trade. However, the large import duty imposed on the USSR coriander seed oil into the US did lead to France acting as an entrepôt between the two countries in order to avoid paying the high import taxes.

Prices

In preceding sections of this chapter, attention has been drawn to the fact that characteristics of the spice vary considerably according to the cultivar and the geographical source, and that preferences are expressed by consumers for certain types in particular applications. The small-fruited cultivars produced in Europe, exemplified by Russian coriander, have a far greater volatile-oil content and flavour strength than the larger-fruited types, exemplified by Moroccan and Indian coriander, and the former fetch higher prices in the market. In addition to possessing a low volatile-oil content, Indian coriander has a distinctly different flavour from the Moroccan and Romanian spices, its competitors in general spice applications; and, in the UK at least, Indian coriander is normally bought only by immigrant Indian deale.

There has also been criticism that Indian material contains an unusually high proportion of extraneous matter and this too has kept prices lower. Consequently, in the last decade an attempt has been made to impose quality controls on Indian exports. In some years Indian coriander has been substituted for coriander from other sources which are more highly priced or in short supply.

From the available price series (see Tables 12.12 and 12.13) it would seem that Morocco, as the major trading country, acts as a price leader, while Romanian prices follow the Moroccan ones. The price of coriander seed has shown some instability, particularly in the mid-1970s, the causes being the usual ones of climatic variations, pests and diseases, low price-elasticity of demand and low responsiveness of production to changes in demand. Nevertheless, coriander seed prices do not seem to have exhibited the same range of price fluctuations as other spices. This can probably be explained by the fact that production is not concentrated solely in one or two countries and that production meant for domestic consumption can be relatively easily diverted into export markets if prices become sufficiently attractive.

Table 12.12   *Moroccan coriander spice: Quarterly and annual average prices, c.i.f. United Kingdom, 1966–77 (£ per tonne)*

	Quarters				Annual average
	I	*II*	*III*	*IV*	
1966	53.5	71.4	86.6	90.7	78.9
1967	103.6	90.3	83.4	99.4	94.2
1968	111.5	72.1	55.9	59.3	74.8
1969	67.2	73.5	90.3	92.7	80.9
1970	88.6	77.3	84.6	82.0	83.0
1971	82.0	79.0	83.2	74.3	80.0
1972	77.3	77.0	82.2	82.0	79.6
1973	82.0	105.0	103.0	105.0	98.8
1974	110.0	110.0	95.0	103.0	103.0
1975	125.0	135.0	155.0	182.0	149.0
1976	258.0	238.0	305.0	375.0	278.0
1977	650.0	660.0	673.0	660.0	662.0

Source: *Public Ledger*

Price variations of coriander seed were much wider between the mid-1950s and mid-1960s than they have been since then. In the former period, four rough trends may be discerned: prices fell slightly during 1957–9, rose throughout 1960 to a peak in 1961, fell in 1962, and remained steady during 1963–65 at a level somewhat higher than in 1957–9. Prices rose to a new peak in 1967 and fell in 1968. Since the late 1960s, prices have been more stable but have continued their upward trend, averaging around £100 per tonne in 1973 and 1974. During 1975

Table 12.13 *Coriander spice: Approximate New York spot prices, early March, 1966–77 (cents per lb)*

	1966	1967	1968	1969	1970	1971	1972	1973	1974	1975	1976	1977
Moroccan	11	17	17	13	14	14	17	18	20	18	30	60
Romanian	10	13	14	11	12	14	13	15	17	...	23	...

Source: USDA Foreign Agriculture Circular
... not available.

and 1976 prices rose fairly steadily but then doubled during the first quarter of 1977 and maintained this level throughout the year, producing an annual average of £662 per tonne in 1977.

Trends in consumption and prospects

The principal area of usage of the spice is for flavouring foods, but a limited amount is used for pharmaceutical and perfumery purposes.

The major individual outlet for coriander is in the ground form as an ingredient in curry powder and spice mixtures. Coriander is normally the major ingredient of curry powder, comprising up to 40 per cent by weight. Consequently, the spice is extensively used in Indian, Malay, Indonesian and Arab cooking. In English and North American kitchens, the spice is used mainly in the whole form as a pickling spice in combination with other spices. It is less popular in French and Italian kitchens. The spice is fairly extensively used in Western countries in the flavouring of processed foods, including breads, cakes, sauces and meat products (especially sausages and frankfurters), soups and confectionery. Coriander also forms an important ingredient for several alcoholic beverages, particularly gin.

The demand for the spice appears to be growing fairly steadily in line with population and income increases. An exception is in Japan where consumption has increased enormously, reflecting in the main the rapid growth of the production and consumption of curry powder. It will be the derived demand arising from changes in the consumption of curry powder that will be the major influence on the future pattern of coriander consumption. Given the relative ease of coriander production throughout most of the world, there are unlikely to be any supply shortages limiting future growth in consumption.

Very little information is available on the commercial essential oil. It has been mentioned earlier that the USSR produces substantial quantities of the oil for domestic use as a source of *d*-linalol. The essential oil is also distilled commercially in Poland, Hungary, Holland, France, the UK and the USA, and in these countries the product is mainly intended for flavouring usage in applications similar to those of the spice. Some essential oil is also employed in perfumery and pharmaceutical formulations. The scale of oil production outside the USSR is not known with certainty but Arctander (1960) has suggested a figure of around 20 tonnes per annum. There is some price variation between the oil from different sources, which partly reflects quality distinctions made by consumers.

Although several of the larger flavouring houses produce and market coriander oleoresin, the demand is thought to be considerably smaller than for the essential oil. Usage in the UK is no more than 5 tonnes per annum.

References

Aiyadurai, S.G. (1966) *A Review of Research on Spices and Cashewnut in India*, Ernakulam-6: Indian Council of Agric. Resc.

Akimov, Y.A. and Voronin, V.G. (1965) 'Analysis of coriander oil and products of its processing'., *Gaz. Kromatogr., Moscow*, **3**, 142–6. (*Chem. Abs.*, **66**, 98424b).

Akimov, Y.A. and Voronin, V.G. (1968a) 'Use of gas-liquid chromatography for the analysis of coriander oil', *Zh. Prikl. Khim., (Leningrad)*, **41** (11), 2561–3 (*Chem. Abs.* **70**, 50416f).

Akimov, Y.A. and Voronin, V.G. (1968b) 'Gas-liquid chromatography of coriander oil oxidation products', *Zh. Prikl. Khim. (Leningrad)*, **41** (10), 2344–6 (Chem. Abs. **70**, 228432).

Althausen D., Boruff, C.S., Gamlin, E.R., Koenig, C.J. and Landes, K.H. (1940) 'Coriander', *The Spice Mill*, **63**, Aug. 32–3, 39–40; Sept., 40–41; Oct., 39–40.

Anon. (1923) 'Coriander oil from Mysore fruits', *Perf. Essent Oil Record*, **14**, 121.

Anon. (1950) *The Wealth of India*, Vol. 2, (ed. B.N. Sastri), Delhi: Council of Sci. and Industrial Research.

Anon. (1976) 'The New Coriander Strain "CIMPO S-33" ', *Indian Spices*, **13** (1), 2–3.

Arctander, S. (1960) *Perfume and Flavour Materials of Natural Origin*, Elizabeth, N.J.: Published by the author.

Avakova, L., Kustova, S. and Shcedrina, M. (1966) 'Composition of the turpentine fraction obtained on rectification of coriander essential oil', *Zh. Prikl Khim*, **39** (3), 719–22.

Balinova-Tsvetkova, A. and Kamburova, K. (1975) 'Determination of the essential oil content in the seed of some Umbelliferaea', *Rasteniev dni Nauki*, **12** (5), 40–5 (*Hort. Abs.*, **46**, 43679).

Barbier, P.H. (1893) 'Sur le licaroel droit', *Compt. Rendu*, **116**, 1459–61.

Bauer, K.H., Rudorf, W. and Heeger, E.F., (1942) 'The cultivation relations of some drug and aromatic plant species with specific reference to the content of valuable constituents', *Landw. Jahrb.*, **92**, 1–52.

Berger, F. (1952) *Handbuch der Drogenkunde*, Vol. 3, Vienna: Verlag W. Maudrich.

Boratynskaya, W. (1956) 'Differential development of volatile oil canals in *Coriandrum sativum* L.' *Biuletyn Panstwowego Inst. Naukowego*, **2**, 13–23.

Bryusova, L.Y., Shagalova, R.U. and Novikova, N. (1940) 'Decaldehyde from the oil of blooming coriander', *Sintezy Dushistykh Veshchestv, Sbornik Statei*, 247–52 (*Chem. Abs.*, **36**, 3781).

Burkill, I.H. (1966) *A Dictionary of the Economic Products of the Malay Peninsula*, Kuala Lumpur: Ministry of Agriculture and Co-operatives.

Bykova, S.F., Popova, S.A. and Pekhov, A.V. (1971) 'Chemical composition of a CO_2 extract from coriander seeds', *Maslo-Zhir. Prom.*, **37** (9), 33–5 *(Chem. Abs.*, **75**, 154933k).

Bykova, S.F., Aleksandrov, L.G., Meerov, Y.S. and Anoshin, I.M. (1974) 'Effect of some factors on the yield of linalol from coriander seeds on extraction with liquid CO_2', *Izv. Sev. -Kavk. Nauchn. Tsentra Vyssh. Shk., Ser. Tekh. Nauk*, **2** (4), 18–19 *(Chem. Abs.*, **83**, 65311k).

Carlblom, A.J. (1936) 'Origin of linalol in coriander oil. Composition and structure of the components of the ethereal oil at the flowering stage of *Coriandrum sativum', J. Prakt. Chem.*, **144**, 225–41.

Chattopadhyay, S.A. (1967) *Diseases of Plants Yieldings Drugs, Dyes and Spices*, New Delhi: Indian Council of Agric. Resc.

Chaudhry, A.R. (1961) 'Receptivity of Stigma, Viability of Pollen and Opening of Flowers in *Coriandrum sativum* and *Foeniculum vulgare', Agric. Pakist.*, **12**, 29–41.

Chernukin, A. (1928) 'The importance of grinding seeds in the manufacture of coriander and anise essential oils', *Maslob Zhir. Delo*, **5**, 11–13. *(Chem. Abs.*, **23**, 3538).

Chernukin, A. (1928) 'Process of formation of ethereal oil in the coriander plant', *Maslob. Zhir. Delo*, **12**, 34–6.

Chikalov, P.M. (1962) 'The best time and method for the harvest of coriander'. *Maslob. Zhir. Prom.*, **28** (2), 26–9 *(Chem. Abs.*, **56**, 15621c).

Chiris, E.A. (1924) 'Oil of coriander flower', *Parfums de France*, **21**, 197.

Chiris, E.A. (1925) 'Oil of coriander flower', *Parfums de France*, **29**, 197.

Chou, J.S.T. (1974) 'Volatile components of cardamom, coriander and caraway', *Koryo*, **106**, 55–60.

Crooks and Sievers (1941) 'Condiment Plants', *USDA, Bur. Plant Ind.* (July). (Cited by Guenther, 1950.)

Dafert, O. and Rudolf, J. (1925) 'Influence of varied fertilizer on the quantity of useful constituents of coriander, anise, chamomile and paprika'. *Heil-und Gewurzpflanzen*, **8**, 83–92.

Darlington, C.D. and Wylie C.P. (1955). *Chromosome Atlas of Flowering Plants*, 2nd. edn, London: Allen and Unwin.

Dimri, B.P., Khan, M.N.A. and Narayana, M.R. (1977) 'Some promising selection of Bulgarian coriander (*Coriandrum sativum* Linn.) for seed and essential oil with a note on cultivation and distillation of oil', *Indian Perfumer*, **20** (1A), 14–21.

Dublyanskaya, N.F. (1964) 'Fatty and essential oils of cultivated plants', *Maslob. Zhir. Prom.*, **30** (5), 24–26 *(Chem. Abs.*, **54**, 8531d).

Dublyanskaya, N.F., Panfilova, V.M. and Chernysheva, S.L. (1965) 'Biochemical properties of fruits of coriander as related to the variety characteristics', *Maslob. Zhir. Prom.*, **31** (11), 25–7 *(Chem. Abs.*, **64**, 3961e).

El-Hamidi, A. and Ahmed, S.A. (1966) 'The content and composition of some umbelliferous essential oils', *Pharmazie*, **21**, 438–9.

Farooq, O., Varshney, I.P., Rahman, W. and Naim, Z. (1961) 'Constituents of the seeds of *Coriandrum sativum', Arch. Pharm.*, **294**, 138–40.

Georgiev, E.V. (1968) 'Changes in essential and fatty oils during storage of fruits of several *Umbelliferae', Mezhdunar Kongr. Efirnym Maslam,* (*Mater) 4th 1968*, **2**, 33–6 *(Chem. Abs.*, **81**, 68330).

Gerhardt, U. (1968) 'Routine examination of spices for essential oils', *Fleischwirtschaft*, **48**, 1482–4.

Gildemeister, E. and Hoffmann, Fr. (1961) *Die Aetherischen Oele*, Vol. VI, Berlin: Akademie Verlag.

Girenko, M.M. (1974) 'The variability of character in coriander', *Trudy po. Prikladnoi Botanike, Genetike i Selektsii*, **51** (3), 148–57. *(Hort. Abs.*, **45**, 8783).

Glushenko, N.N., Ponmarev, E.D., Silchenko, V.M., Lugovskaya, T.I., Semenchenko, T.D. and Smelchukova, V.G. (1977) 'Data from the industrial testing of a new coriander variety, amber', *Maslob. Zhir. Prom.*, **6**, 28 *(Chem. Abs.*, **87**, 73221).

Golz, L., Lehmann, L. and Zalecki, R. (1966) 'Reaction of coriander to late doses of nitrogen, phosphorous and potassium', *Herba Polon.*, **11**, 39–46 (*Chem. Abs.*, **66**, 10263k).

Gopala Rao, P. and Sriramula, M. (1977) 'Physiological characterisation of a spice (*Coriandrum sativum*) and a condiment (*Trigonella foenum graecum*) during vegetative and reproductive stages', *Curr. Sci.* (*India*), **46**, 615–16.

Grosser, B. (1881) 'Ueber das aetherische Oel der Fruechte von *Coriandrum sativum*', *Chem. Ber.*, **14**, 2485–508.

Guenther, E. (1950) *The Essential Oils*, Vol. IV, New York: D. Van Nostrand Co.

Gupta, G.K., Dhar, K.L. and Atal, C.K. (1977) 'Chemical constituents of *Coriandrum sativum* Linn. seeds', *Indian Perfumer*, **21**, 86–90.

Harbourne, J.B. and Williams, C.A. (1972) 'Flavanoid patterns in the fruits of the *Umbelliferae*', *Phytochem.*, **11**, 1741–50.

Harrod, D.C. (1960) 'A note on coriander of commerce', *J. Pharm. Pharmacol.*, **12**, 245–7.

Heeger, E.F. (1956) *Handbuch des Arznei-und Gewurzplanzenbaues Drogengewinnung*, Berlin: Deutscher Bauernverlag.

Hotin, A.A. (1957) 'Biological basis of essential oil development', Krasnodar: Dissertation (Cited by Lassanyi & Lorincz, 1968.)

Iakobakvili, N. (1960) 'La production USSR des huiles essentielles et leur composition', *La France et ses Parfumes*, **3**, 50.

Ikeda, R.M., Stanley, W.L., Vannier, S.H. and Spitler, E.M. (1962) 'The monoterpene hydrocarbon composition of some essential oils', *J. Food Sci.*, **27**, 455–8.

Irintscheef, I. (1957) 'Coriander oil', *Parfumerie u. Kosmet*, **38**, 200.

Ivanov, N.N., Grigoreva, V.F. and Ermakov, A.I. (1929) 'Content of essential oil during the process of maturation and germination of coriander', *Bull. Appl. Bot., Genetics & Plant Breeding* (Leningrad), **21** (4), 321–41 (*Chem. Abs.*, **26**–5605).

Ivanov, N.N., Laurova, M.N. and Gapockho, M.P. (1931) 'The chemical composition of the seed of oleiferous plants in relation to geographical distribution', *Bull. Appl. Bot., Genetics & Plant Breeding* (Leningrad), **25**, 1–86 (*Chem. Abs.*, **26**, 756).

Jukneviciene, G., Dagyte, S. and Stankevicience, N. (1977) 'Biological properties and essential oils of some spice plants grown at the Kaunas Botanical Garden', *Liet. T.S.R. Mokslu Akad. Darb.*, Ser C, **3**, 9–16. (*Chem. Abs.*, **88**–3090g).

Karlsen, J., Chingova, B., Zwetkov, R., and Baerheim Svendson, A. (1971) 'Studies on the essential oil of the fruits of *Coriandrum sativum* by means of gas-liquid chromatography. Terpenes and related compounds. XI', *Pharm. Weekbl.*, **106**, 293–300.

Karow, H. (1969) 'Qualitative determination of the composition of some spices. III. Composition and essential oils of some spices', *Riechstoffe, Aromen, Koerperflegenmittel*, **19**, 60–6.

Kartha, A.R.S. and Selveraj, Y. (1970) 'Occurrence of $\triangle^{5,6}$ — octadecenoic acid in some *Umbelliferae* seed fats', *Chem. Ind.*, 831–2.

Kartnig, Th. (1966) 'Ueber einige Lipoide-Inhaltstoffe aus den Fruchten von *Anethum graveolons* (L.) and *Coriandrum sativum* (L.)', *Fette, Seifen, Anstrichmittel*, **68**, 131–134.

Kawalier, A. (1852) 'Ueber das Corianderoel', *Liebigs Ann.*, **84**, 351–2.

Khotin, A.A. (1968) 'Role of external factors in accumulation of essential oils', *Tr. Vses. Nauch. Issled. Inst. Efirnomaslich Kult.*, **1**, 35–44 (*Chem. Abs.*, **72**, 35671h).

Kolachov, P. (1940) 'Domestic cultivation of coriander', *Spice Mill*, **63** (Nov.), 34–5.

Kopp, E. (1929) 'Roumanian coriander oil', *Pharm. Zentralhalle*, **70**, 789–91.

Kumar, C.R., Sarwar, M. and Dimri, B.P. (1977) 'Bulgarian coriander in India and its future prospects in export trade', *Indian Perfumer*, **21** (3), 146–50.

Kunzemann, J. and Heermann, K. (1977) 'Isolation and identification of flavan (ol)-o-glycosides in caraway, fennel, anise and coriander, and of flavan-o-glycosides in anise', *Z. Lebenzm. Unters-Forsch.*, **164**, 194–200.

Kuzina, E.F. (1975) 'Some biological and chemical characteristics of coriander grown in the Leningrad region', *Byulleten VNII Rastenievodsta*, **47**, 68–70 (*Hort. Abs.*, **46**,

7942).

Lassanyi, Zs. and Lorincz, C. (1967) 'Test on terpenoids present in parts of *Coriandrum sativum* L. I: Thin-layer chromatographic examination of the volatile oil in the pericarpum and seedlings of the Lucs variety', *Acta. Agron. Acad. Sci. Hung.*, **16**, 95–100.

Lassanyi, Zs. and Lorincz, K. (1968) 'Test on terpenoids present in parts of *Coriandrum sativum* L. II: Thin-layer chromatographic and histochemical examination of the linalol and the aldehydes', *Acta. Agron. Acad. Sci. Hung*, **17**, 215–22.

Lassanyi, Zs. and Lorincz, G. (1969) 'Characteristics of the essential oil of *Coriandrum sativum* var. Lucs', *Herba. Hung.*, **8**, 57–62 (*Chem. Abs.*, **72**–124983d).

Lassanyi, Zs. and Lorincz, C. (1970) 'Test on terpenoids present in parts of *Coriandrum sativum* L. III: Histology of the developing structures of *Coriandrum sativum* L. var. "Lucs" and properties of the volatile oil canals', *Acta. Agron. Acad. Sci. Hung.*, **19**, 25–32.

Laza, A. and Silva, F. (1970) 'Effect of mineral fertilizers on yield and quality of coriander', *An. Inst. Cerct. Cereale Plante Teh-Funlulea, Acad. Stunte Agr. Silvice*, ser. B, **38**, 407–11 (*Chem. Abs.*, **78**, 158294u).

Lesnov, P.P. and Pekhov, A.V. (1970) 'Qualitative composition of the essential oil from the herb and the ripe fruits of coriander', *Maslob. Zhir. Prom.* 36 (12), 26–7 (*Chem. Abs.*, **74**, 79475t).

Logvinov, V.A., Volodicheva, L.F., Dedukh, A.Y., Logvinova, A.P. and Sunkin, V.M. (1975) 'Changes in the essential oil content and quality of ripening coriander fruits', *Tr. Vses. Nauch. Issled. Inst. Efirnomaslich Kult.*, **8**, 18–24 (*Hort. Abs.*, **47**, 7759).

Lorincz, G. (1966) 'Results of comparative trials with coriander varieties and strains', *Herba. Hung.*, **5** (1), 25–30 (*Hort. Abs.*, **37**, 7527).

Lorincz, K. and Tyihak, E. (1965a) 'Study of the content of terpenes in coriander during the period of vegetative growth', *Herba. Hung.*, **4**, 193–208.

Lorincz, K. and Tyihak, E. (1965b) 'Problems of essential oil determination in selections of coriander', *Wiss. Ztsch. d. K. Marx Univ., Leipzig*, **4**, 439–40.

Lowman, M.S., Gilbert, N.W. and Kelly, J.W. (1949) 'Coriander yield and quality', *Amer. Perfumer and Ess. Oil Review*, Sept., 209–12.

Lukyanov, I.A. (1962) *Agrobiology*, 936. (Cited by Tsvetkov, 1970.)

Lukyanov, I.A. and Berestovaya, M.M. (1971) 'Accumulation and changes in the essential oil of coriander during ontogenesis', *Tr. Vses. Nauch. Issled. Inst. Efirnomaslich Kult.*, **4** (2), 5–12.

Lukyanov, I.A. and Berestovaya, M.M. (1973) 'Changes in coriander during seed storage', *Tr. Vses. Nauch. Issled. Inst. Efirnomaslich Kult.*, **6**, 170–3 (*Chem. Abs.*, **83**, 65318t).

Lukyanov, I.A. and Mukhanova, M.M. (1964) 'Heterogeneous nature of the essential oil in the fruits of coriander', *Maslob. Zhir. Prom.*, **30** (9), 19–22 (*Chem. Abs.*, **62**, 2663).

Lukyanov, I.A. and Mukhanova, M.M. (1968) 'Changes of essential oil composition during germination of coriander fruits', *Tr. Vses. Nauch. Issled. Inst. Efirnomaslich Kult.*, **1**, 121–7 (*Chem. Abs.*, **74**, 72871k).

Lytkin, I.A. (1953) 'An experiment on the cultivation of coriander in Siberia', *Agrobiologiya*, **4**, 151–2 (*Hort. Abs.*, **24**, 2887).

MacLeod, A.J. and Islam, R. (1976) 'Volatile flavour components of coriander leaf', *J. Sci. Food Agric.*, **27**, 721–5.

Mahran, G.H., El-Alfy, T.S. and Saber, H.H. (1967) 'Analysis of the volatile oil of *Coriandrum sativum* cultivated in Egypt', *Bull. Fac. Pharm., Cairo Univ.*, **6**, 57–69.

Marakova, G.M. and Borisynk, Y.G. (1959) 'Coriander essential oil', *Farmatseut. Zh.* (Kiev), **14** (3), 43–6 (*Chem. Abs.*, **58**, 2320e).

Marsh, A.C., Moss, M.K. and Murphy, E.W. (1977) *Composition of Foods, Spices and Herbs. Raw. Processed. Prepared.* Washington DC: USDA Agric. Res. Serv., Agric. Handbook, No. 8–2.

Meerov, Y. and Bykova, S.F. (1971) 'Extraction of coriander essential oil', *Maslob. Zhir. Prom.*, **37** (6), 22–3 (*Chem. Abs.*, **75**, 912360).

Miller, C.E. (1952) 'North Dakota volatile oils, III. Comparative studies of coriander oil', *J. Amer. Pharm. Assoc*, Sci. Ed., **41**, 598.

Nosti Nava, J., Torres, J.C. and Vidal, M.P. (1953) 'The culture of coriander. The effect of ammonia and phosphorus fertilizers', *Farmacognosia*, **13**, 71–80 (*Hort. Abs.*, **27**, 670f).

Obuchow, A.H. and Kondrazki, A.P. (1946) *Technology of the Production of Essential Oils*. Moscow.

Ochse, J.J. and Van Den Brink, R.C.B. (1931) *Vegetables of the Dutch East Indies*, Buitenzorg: Archipel Drukkerij.

Patakova, D. and Chlader, M. (1966) 'A contribution to the evaluation of fruit quality in foreign varieties of coriander', *Bull. Vyzk. Ust. Zelin. Olomonc.*, **10**, 129–36.

Peneva, P. and Krilov, A. (1977) 'Effect of ecological conditions on the productivity of some Soviet varieties of coriander', *Rasteniev ud Nauki*, **14** (1), 67–76 (*Chem. Abs.*, **87**, 164206u).

Penka, M. and Bacikova, A. (1960) 'Water balance and accumulation of essential oil in *Coriandrum sativum*', *Ceskoslov. Farm.*, **9**, 9–15 (*Chem. Abs.*, **54**, 7073h).

Pertsev, M. and Pivnenko, G.P. (1962) 'Chromatography of essential oils used in pharmacy. III', *Farm. Zhurnal*, **17** (2), 35–40 (*Chem. Abs.*, **58**, 7781c).

Pillai, O.R. and Boominathan, H. (1975) 'Effect of N, P, K fertilizers on the yield of coriander', *Arecanut and Spices Bull*, **6** (4), 82–3.

Popescu, H. and Tugui, I. (1976) 'Amino acids in *Coriandrum sativum* fruit', *Farmacia*, **24** (2), 107–11 (*Chem. Abs.*, **85**, 166553n).

Puri, S.C., Vashist, V.N. and Atal, C.K. (1968) 'The essential oil of Kulu coriander', *Indian Oil and Soap J.*, **34**, 70–2.

Rakova, N.V. (1961) 'Changes of the assay of essential oil upon storage of coriander seeds', *Spiritovaya Prom.*, **27** (5), 13–16 (*Chem. Abs.*, **55**, 26375e).

Ramstad, E. (1942) 'Coriander', *Medd. Norsk. Farm. Selsk.*, **4**, 77.

Ranganathan, S. (1935) 'Effect of storage on vitamin C in leafy vegetables, potency of foodstuffs', *Indian J. Med. Res.*, **23**, 755–62.

Rao, B.S., Sudborough, J.J. and Watson, H.E. (1925) 'Notes on some Indian essential oils', *J. Indian Inst. Sci.*, **8A**, 182.

Rasmussen, S., Rasmussen, K.E. and Baerheim Svendsen, A. (1972) 'The occurrence of anethol in the volatile oil of *Coriandrum sativum*', *Medd. Norsh. Farm. Selsk.*, **34**, 33–6.

Razinskaite, D. (1966), 'Coriander in the Lithuanian SSR. I. Comparative study of varieties', *Liet. T.S.R. Mokslu Akad. Darb.*, Ser. C., **2**, 39–56 (*Chem. Abs.*, **66**, 83075q).

Razinskaite, D. (1967) 'Alteration of the essential oils in the mature fruits of caraway and coriander plants', *Nauki Laimejimai Biol. Biochem., Liet. T.S.R. Jannuju, Mosklininku — Biol. Biochem, Moksline Konf*, 35–8 (*Chem. Abs.*, **70**, 94011z).

Razinskaite D. and Slavenus, J. (1966a) '*Coriandrum sativum* in the Lithuanian SSR. III. Effect of mineral fertilizers on the content and quality of essential oil', *Liet T.S.R. Mokslu Akad. Darb.*, Ser. C., **2**, 71–7 (*Chem. Abs.*, **66**, 83077s).

Razinskaite, D. and Slavenus, J. (1966b) '*Coriandrum sativum* in the Lithuanian SSR. II. Changes in the essential oils in *Coriandrum sativum* organs during vegetation', *Liet. T.S.R. Mokslu Akad. Darb.*, Ser. C., **2**, 57–70 (*Chem. Abs.*, **66**, 83076r).

Redgrove, H.S. (1933) *Spices and Condiments*, London: Pitman.

Reisch, J., Schratz, E. and Quadry, S.M.J.S. (1966) 'Die zussamensetzung des aetherischen oeles in den Fruchten und der Lebenden Pflanze von *Coriandrum sativum*. II. Identifiziernung und synthese des Tridecen-2-al-(1)', *Planta Med.*, **14**, 326–36.

Ridley, H.N. (1912) *Spices*, London: Macmillan.

Rosengarten, F. (1969) *The Book of Spices*; Wynnewood: Livingston Publishing Co.

Salzer, U. -J. (1975a) 'Uber de Fettsaurezussamensetzung der Lipoide einiger Gewurze', *Fette, Seifen, Anstrichmittel*, **77**, 446–50.

Salzer, U. -J. (1975b) 'Analytical evaluation of seasoning extracts (oleoresins) and essential oils from seasoning', *Flavours*, **6**, 151−7.

Sankevich, N.K. (1936) 'Contents of ethereal and fatty oils in the kernel and husk of coriander seed', *Maslob. Zhir. Delo*, **12**, 389 (*Chem. Abs.*, **31**, 1646).

Sarkar, B.C. and Chavan, U.P.S. (1963) 'Strontium in some Indian vegetables', *Curr. Sci. (India)*, **32A**, 418−19.

Sastri, B.N. (ed.) (1950) *The Wealth of India: Raw Materials*, Vol. 2, Delhi: Council of Scientific and Industrial Research.

Schimmel and Co. (1895) 'Coriander Oil', *Ber. Schimmel*, Oct., 12.

Schimmel and Co. (1909) 'Coriander Oil', *Ber. Schimmel*, 47.

Schratz, E. and Qadry, S.M.J.S. (1966a) 'Die zussamensetzung des Aetherischen Oeles in den Freuchten und in der Lebenden Pflanze von *Coriandrum sativum* L. I. Untersuchung des Freuchtoeles', *Planta Med.*, **14**, 310−25.

Schratz, E. and Qadry, S.M.J.S. (1966b) 'Die zussamsetzung des Aetherischen Oeles in *Coriandrum sativum* L. III. Oelkomposition in Verlauf der Ontogenese', *Planta Med.*, **14**, 436−42.

Semmler, F.V. (1891) 'Uber olefinische Bestandthiele aetherische Oele', *Chem. Ber.*, **24**, 201−11.

Sergeeva, N.V. (1974) 'Rutin and other polyphenols of *Coriandrum sativum* herb', *Khim. Prir. Soedin*, **10**, 94−5.

Shankaracharya, N.B. and Natarajan, C.P. (1971) 'Coriander − Chemistry, technology and uses', *Indian Spices*, **8** (2), 4−13.

Shellard, E.J. (1963) 'Oil of coriander. Comparison of oils of coriander according to the Polish Pharmacopeia III (1954) and the British Pharmacopeia (1963)', *Acta Pol. Pharm.*, **24**, 183−92.

Shlyapnikova, A.P. and Ponomarev, E.D. (1970) 'Losses of oil in crushing of coriander fruit', *Maslob. Zhir. Prom.* **36**, (7), 30−1 (*Chem. Abs.*, **73**, 101934v).

Shlyapnikova, A.P., Ponomarev, E.D., Kopeikovskii, V.M. and Shlyapnikov, V.A. (1972a) 'Heat stability of coriander fruit', *Izv. Vyssh. Uchebn. Zaved., Pishch. Tekhnol.*, **3**, 17−19 (F.S.T.A., **6**, 7T396).

Shlyapnikova, A.P., Kopeikovskii, V.M., Ponomarev, E.D. and Shlyapnikov, V.A. (1972b) 'Hygroscopic properties of coriander fruit', *Izv. Vyssh. Uchebn. Zaved., Pishch. Tekhnol.*, **4**, 26−9 (F.S.T.A., **5**, 7T340).

Shlyapnikova, A.P., Ponomarev, E.D. and Shylapnikov, V.A. (1974) 'Quantitative and qualitative changes in the essential oil when drying coriander', *Tr. Vses. Nauch. Issled. Inst. Efironomaslich Kultur*, **7**, 151−6 (*Chem. Abs.*, **84**, 15500w).

Shtovkhan, N.P., Koshevoi, E.P., Maslikov, V.A., Kurnosov, A.G. and Troitskaya. N.S. (1977) 'Study of the phase states of the coriander essential oil − fatty oil − liquefied CO_2 system', *Izv. Vyssh. Uchebn. Zaved. Pishch. Takhnol.*, **3**, 123−4 (*Chem. Abs.*, **87**, 157756v).

Smolianov, A. (1964) 'Noveaux elements dens la technologie de production des huiles essentielles', *Proceedings of 3rd Int-Congress of Essential Oils*, held in Plovdiv, Bulgaria in May 1964, 88.

Spiridonova, S.I. (1936) 'Changes of coriander essential oil in relation to plant growth', *J. Gen. Chem. (USSR)*, **6**, 1536−8 (*Chem. Abs.*, **31**, 1949).

Stankeviciene, N., Morkunas, A. and Alinkanite, A. (1973) 'Changes in the quantitative composition of essential oils of *Coriandrum sativum* in relation to fruit ripeness', *Polez. Rast. Priblat. Respub. Beloruss., Mater. Nauch. Konf., 2nd, 1973.* 269−72. (*Chem. Abs.*, **81**, 126673m).

Strauss, D. (1977) 'Der Gehalt an aetherischen Oel bei Gemahlen Gewurzen', *Deut. Lebensmittel-Rundschau*, **73**, 332−4.

Tanasienko, F.S. (1960) 'On the drying of coriander before storage and processing in relation to certain biological characteristics', Krasnodar: Dissertation. (Cited by Lassanyi & Lorincz. 1968.)

Tanasienko, F.S. (1961) 'Content of essential oil in the split fruit of coriander', *Sb. Nauchi-Issled. Rabot po Malichr i Efiromaslich Kultur, Krasnodar*. **2**, 156−62.

Tanasienko, F. and Mezinova, M. (1939) 'Production of coriander oil from the seeds', *Maslob. Zhir. Delo*, **15** (6), 25–6 (*Chem. Abs.*, **34**, 3438).

Tanasienko, F.S. and Sobeleva, E.B. (1961) 'Effect of storage conditions on the linalol content of essential oils', *Maslob. Zhir. Prom.*, **27**, 24–6.

Taskinen, J. and Nykanen, L. (1975) 'Volatile constituents obtained by the extraction with alcohol – water mixture and by steam distillation of coriander fruit', *Acta Chem. Scand.*, **B29**, 425–9.

Topalov, P.G. and Kalichkov, M. (1962) '*Coriandrum sativum* and its essential and glycerol oils', *Nauch Tr. Vissh. Inst. po. Khranitelna i Vkusova Prom. Plovdov.*, **9**, 99–107 (*Chem. Abs.*, **58**, 12365a).

Torricelli, A. (1937) 'Loss of essential oils from drugs kept in ordinary packages', *Mitt. Lebensm. Hyg.*, **28**, 117–20.

Tschogowadse, S.K. and Bachtadse, D.M. (1977) 'Untersuchungen zur Veranderung der aromatischen Stoffe des Korianders durch die Warmer und Sublimations-trocknung', *Lebensmtl-Indust.*, **24**, 513–15.

Tsvetkov, R. (1970) 'Study of the fruit quality of some Umbelliferous essential oil plants', *Planta. Med.*, **18**, 350–3.

Tucakov, Y. (1957) 'Contribution to the study of the fruit and essential oil of Yugoslav coriander', *Perf. Ess. Oil Record*, **48**, 212–16.

Turbina, N.V. (1945) 'Development, yield and oil content of coriander in relation to conditions of mineral nutrition', *Doklady Vsesoyuz Soveshchaniyn Fiziol Rastenii 2; Trudy Inst. Fiziol Rastenii im K.A. Timiryazeva*, **4**, (2) 77–90 (*Chem. Abs.*, **42**, 6033d).

Vaghani, D.D. and Thakor, V.M. (1958) 'Chemical investigations of *Coriandrum sativum*', *Curr. Sci.* (*India*), **27**, 388–9.

Varentzov, V.I. (1927) 'The mutual relation between the size of the seed and the yield of essential oil from coriander', *Trans. Sci. Chem.-Pharm. Inst., Moscow*, **17**, 183–6 (*Chem. Abs.*, **23**, 1722). (See also a letter from Varentzov to the Schimmel Co., printed in *Ber. Schimmel*, 1927, p. 23 and reproduced in Gildemeister and Hoffmann, *loc. cit.*)

Vijayalkshmi, B and Rao, S.V. (1972) 'Fatty acid composition of phospholipids in seed oil containing unusual acids', *Chem. Phys. Lipids*, **9**, 82–6.

Viswanath, B. and Ramaswamy Ayyar, C.V. (1934) 'Report on the examination of samples of Indian and foreign coriander', *Agric. Livestock, India*, **4**, 583–604.

Walbaum, H. and Muller, W. (1909) In '*Festschrift Otto Wallach*', 654, Gottingen: Univ. of Gottingen.

Wellendorf, M. (1963) 'The essential oils in the Pharmacopoea Danica 1948: Gas chromatographic and thin-layer chromatographic examination', *Dansk. Tidsskr. Farm*, **37**, 145–7.

Willkie, H.F., Kolachov, P.J. and Scofield, E.H. (1940) *The Domestic Production of Essential Oils from Aromatic Plants*, National Farm Chemurgic Council Bulletin, August 1940, Columbus: National Farm Chemurgic Council (77pp.).

Winton, A.K. and Winton, K.B. (1939) *The Structure and Composition of Foods*, New York: John Wiley & Sons.

Yankulov, Y. (1963) *Bull. Inst. for Plant Breeding*, **16**, 131. (Cited by Tsvetkov, 1970.)

Yegna Narayan Aiyer, A.K. (1944) *Field Crops of India*, Bangalore: Govt. Press.

Zelenova, K.P. (1973) 'Some results of national variety trails with essential oil crops', *Byulleten Gosudarstvennogo Nikitskogo Botanicheskogo Sada*, **2** (21), 28–30. (*Hort. Abs.*, **45**, 4370).

Zukov, D.G. (1964) 'Essential oil production in the USSR', *Proceedings of 3rd Int. Congress of Essential Oils*, held in Plovdiv, Bulgaria, in May 1964, 127–32.

Glossary of Technical Terms

A glossary of the agricultural and botanical terms used will be found in *Tropical Crops: Monocotyledons*, pp. 547–66, by J.W. Purseglove (1972), published by Longman, where there is also a conversion table on pp. 454–6.

Aroma: The distinctive smell imparted by the volatile constituents present in the plant material, its distilled essential oil (q.v.) and its oleoresin (q.v.) extract.

Cohobation: A technique sometimes used in water distillation and water–steam distillation (q.v.) operations to minimize losses of the more water-soluble constituents of the distilled essential oil, thereby enhancing the quality of the resultant oil. Any increase in the oil yield is of secondary importance and, in most cases, is small. The gain is in oxygenated compounds which are important contributors to the aroma and/or flavour of the oil. A small amount of these compounds in the essential oil emerging from the condenser can dissolve in the water and may be lost if the water accumulating in the collector vessel is allowed to run off. Cohobation involves simultaneously returning the condensed water from the collection vessel back to the still, where it is boiled again and recondensed. The total volume of water is kept and constant, and only a very small quantity of the more soluble constituents of the essential oil is lost.

Essential oil: The aromatic oil obtainable by distillation of the plant material with steam. The distilled essential oil is usually a complex mixture of steam-volatile constituents. It contains all the plant constituents responsible for the characteristic aroma and most, if not all, of the plant constituents responsible for the characteristic flavour. Essential oils do not, however, contain any of the non-volatile flavour contributors or any of the pungent principles (see 'Pungency') present in the plant material. The term 'essential oil' is mainly reserved in this book to describe the steam-distilled product, which may differ somewhat from the natural volatile oil (q.v.) present in the plant owing to the formation of artefacts during the distillation process. (N.B. The term 'essential oil' is derived from 'quintessence' meaning the embodiment of the characteristic aroma and flavour of the plant material.)

Fatty oil: The extractable non-volatile oil of the plant which is com prised of the fat (glyceride) constituents.

Fixed oil: For most spices this term is synonymous with the fatty oil. In some cases, the content of the fixed oil in the plant may slightly exceed that of the fatty oil owing to the occurrence of the some other non-volatile constituents dissolved in the fat.

Flavour: The total sensory response in the mouth to the spice which includes taste and smell. In most spices, the volatile oil constituents are mainly responsible for the characteristic flavour. For convenience, pungency (q.v.) sensations are mentioned separately from other flavour sensations in this book.

Hydro-distillation: see 'Water-distillation'.

Oleoresin: This term is used to describe prepared oleoresins rather than natural oleoresin-exudates from the plant. Prepared oleoresins are the solid or semi-solid residues obtained by solvent extraction of the plant material followed by evaporation of the solvent. A carefully prepared spice oleoresin should possess the full organoleptic (q.v.) character of the natural spice. It would contain the volatile oil and/or the pungent principles present in the spice. Some other extractable constituents of the spice, including the fatty oil, may be present in the oleoresin, depending upon their solubility in the particular solvent employed.

Organoleptic: This term is used to describe the total sensory impressions associated with the spice, i.e., the aroma, flavour, pungency and bitterness sensations, etc., imparted to the nose, mouth and throat.

Pungency: The 'hot' sensation produced on the tongue by certain constituents of some spices, e.g., by the gingerols in ginger, by piperine in pepper, and by the capsaicinoids in *Capsicum* species. These pungent principles are normally not volatile in steam and are, therefore, absent in the distilled essential oils of these spices. However, the pungent principles are present in the prepared oleoresins.

Steam-distillation: The procedure of obtaining an essential oil by passage of 'dry' steam, generated in a separate boiler, through plant material in a still.

Terpeneless oil: This term is used to describe an essential oil from which the hydrocarbon constituents have been removed by fractional distillation. The aliphatic, aromatic, monoterpene and sesquiterpene hydrocarbon components of essential oils normally contribute little to the flavour, being in most cases coarse, rank or merely neutral, and are insoluble in aqueous media. Consequently the terpeneless oil is often prepared for use in the flavouing of food products.

Water-distillation: In this method of distillation, the steam is generated in the base of the still and the plant material is wholly or largely immersed in the boiling water.

Water–steam distillation: This is also done by generating steam at atmospheric pressure ('wet' steam), in a separate boiler, and passing this into the still below a grid which supports the plant material. Some of the steam is condensed in the plant material and accumulates in the base of the still, where it is controlled by boiling from time to time with a closed steam coil.

Volatile oil: The constituents of a plant which are volatile in steam, and which upon distillation provide the essential oil. The term 'volatile oil' is used in this book to distinguish the natural volatile oil present in the plant from the distilled essential oil which may be somewhat different in composition owing to chemical changes occurring during distillation.

Index